The Complete

BOOK
OF THE DOG

The Complete
BOOK
OF THE DOG

CHARTWELL
BOOKS, INC.

A QUINTET BOOK

Published by Chartwell Books
A Division of Book Sales, Inc.
110 Enterprise Avenue
Secaucus, New Jersey 07094

ISBN 1-55521-492-4

This book was designed and produced by
Quintet Publishing Limited
6 Blundell Street
London N7 9BH

Creative Director: Peter Bridgewater
Art Director: Ian Hunt
Designers: Stuart Walden, Sara Nunan
Project Editor: Amanda O'Neill
Editor: Belinda Giles

Typeset in Great Britain by
Central Southern Typesetters, Eastbourne
Manufactured in Hong Kong by
Regent Publishing Services Limited
Printed in Hong Kong by
South Sea Int'l Press Ltd

The material in this publication previously
appeared in *The Dog Care Manual, The Dog, An
Introduction To Dog Care* and *Understanding Your
Dog*

CONTENTS

Chapter One

INTRODUCING THE DOG

Out of all the animals that share our lives, the dog is the one that we call 'man's best friend'. It is unique amongst domesticated animals in its closeness to man, in the wide range of functions it performs for him and even in the extent to which it has been affected, physically and mentally, by domestication.

Throughout history, the dog has fulfilled a variety of roles – guard, herder, hunting companion, draught animal and guide – as well as being valued for the affection and friendship it offers as a pet. It has developed an astonishing variety of forms – from giant to miniature, from squat and compact to tall and rangy, from extremely long-coated to quite naked – as well as a range of specialisms such as speed, scenting powers, protective instincts, etc. Different breeds vary tremendously in appearance and physical characteristics, but all dogs share certain fundamental behavioural traits of obedience, loyalty and adaptability. They are also distinguished by their sensitivity and responsiveness to their 'pack' – canine or human.

These special qualities that make the dog stand out amongst domesticated species derive from its ancestor the wolf, long maligned as the emblem of savagery but in fact the most intelligent and socially organized of predators. Wolves live in family groups with elaborate social structures. Within these groups, there is always an order of dominance, based on strength, gender and age. The domestic dog, although most often kept singly, retains its social instincts; for this reason, it is both easy to train and dependent on its human companions for affection and attention.

The human family has become the dog's pack, for which it has an innate sense of responsibility and a very real predisposition for social interaction and affection. Its natural sense of dominance within a social order prepares it to accept restraint and discipline – pets and working dogs respond to their owners as they would to the dominant member of the pack, provided the owner maintains control and consistency of approach.

Although some individual dogs will themselves be of a naturally dominant character and will push to take up the role of pack leader themselves unless very firmly handled, man has bred dogs selectively over thousands of years to produce a high proportion of followers rather than leaders, ideally suited to fit into and augment the human household as well as to fulfil practical tasks.

In many countries, the keeping of a dog is seen as a way of completing the family. The dog is the most common household pet, and surveys show that it is generally considered to give its owners more enjoyment than any other. Because of its naturally highly social nature, it is a natural participator in family life rather than a mere cohabitee with man.

THE ANCESTRAL WOLF STOCKS

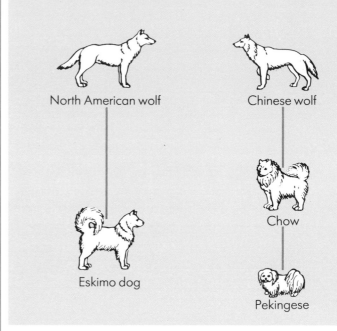

North American wolf

Chinese wolf

Chow

Eskimo dog

Pekingese

ABOVE: *The diversity of modern dog breeds is partly ascribed to their descent from different geographical races of wolf with varying physical characteristics. The likely lines of descent are depicted here as a family tree.*

THE ORIGINS OF THE DOG

The dog is not only 'man's best friend' but probably also his oldest, for archaeological evidence suggests that it was the first animal to be domesticated by man. The earliest remains of domestic dogs, discovered in Denmark, may date back as far as 10,000 BC, preceding the Neolithic period. Domestication also occurred early in the East; evidence indicates that dogs were kept in Jericho by 6500 BC. In Ancient Egypt, dogs were portrayed on various artefacts, and dog mummies have been found alongside those of pharaohs in the Pyramids. Most early European dog remains, found in localities from Ireland south to Spain, date from the Bronze Age (3000 BC) on. Dogs had been introduced to North America by early settlers from Asia in about 5000 BC, long before Europeans set foot on the continent.

Precisely which animal it was that man made the ancestor of the domestic dog has been the subject of much debate. The closest relatives of the dog are the wolf, the coyote and the jackal, and each of these, or a combination, has been proposed by zoologists as the ancestral stock. It has also been suggested that a wild dog, now extinct, may have lived in Europe and Asia in prehistoric times and have been the direct ancestor of the domestic dog.

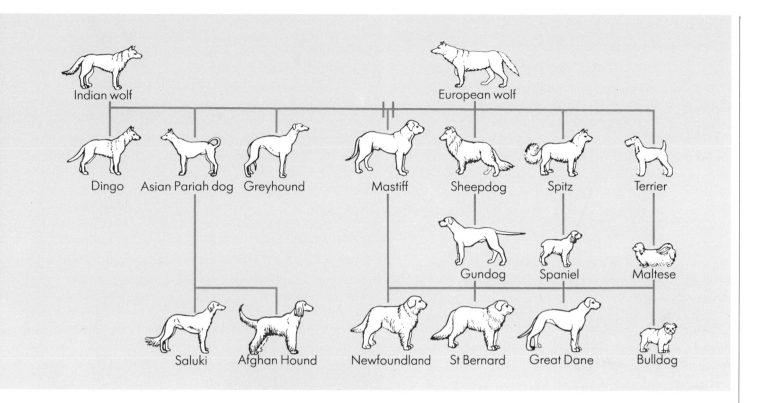

Indian wolf — European wolf

Dingo | Asian Pariah dog | Greyhound | Mastiff | Sheepdog | Spitz | Terrier

Gundog | Spaniel | Maltese

Saluki | Afghan Hound | Newfoundland | St Bernard | Great Dane | Bulldog

RIGHT: *The wolf is now considered to be the principal ancestor of the domestic dog, its highly evolved social behaviour giving rise to the dog's unique ability to participate in the human family's life.*

BELOW: *The jackal may have been involved in the development of the dog, but behavioural and anatomical differences suggest that its contribution, if any, was small.*

It is now generally believed, however, that the dog is almost entirely descended from the wolf, which formerly had a much wider distribution than today. Studies have revealed a close similarity between the skeletal structure of smaller wolves and the early domesticated dogs. Furthermore, detailed comparative behavioural studies have shown very close links between these two groups of canids. Differences occur solely in hunting routines, in which domestic dogs are not normally involved. The vocalization of the dog is also closer to that of the wolf than to the wailing and yelping of jackals or coyotes. It is possible that the two latter species may have interbred with the dog from time to time, but zoologists now consider their contribution to have been minor.

There are nearly forty recognized races of wolf in different parts of the world, varying in size and build. The four principal races – the North American, the Chinese, the Indian and the European – are all considered to have contributed to the ancestry of the domestic dog. Attempts have been made to derive contemporary dog breeds directly from specific geographical races of wolf. By this reckoning the North American wolf is believed to be the ancestor of the Eskimo dog, the Chinese wolf is thought to be the ancestor of Chows, Toy Spaniels and the Pekingese breeds, the Indian wolf the ancestor of a large group that includes Greyhounds and Salukis and the European wolf is thought to have given rise to Sheepdogs, Terriers and related breeds. However, thousands of years of dog breeding have intermingled any original strains and it would be hard to trace any modern breed back to a direct ancestral line.

THE DEVELOPMENT OF SPECIALIST TYPES

The earliest domestic dogs appear to have been quite uniform in appearance and certainly lacked the exaggerated traits associated with various contemporary breeds. Domestication tends to produce animals a little smaller than their wild ancestors and characteristically having a smaller, shorter skull which leads to compaction and displacement of the teeth, so these early dogs would have already begun to diverge from the ancestral wolf type. They were probably not unlike the feral dogs of today, the Dingo of Australia, the New Guinea Singing Dog and the Pariah Dog of India, which, despite their geographical separation, show a remarkably consistent type. These feral dogs are of medium size, with a medium length coat often of a tawny colour, and with pricked ears.

As human civilization developed, however, dogs began to evolve to perform particular functions in the community. Bigger forms were gradually developed to act as draught animals; as settlements became more stable, demands arose for more specialized types of dog, for example, to herd stock or catch vermin.

As early as five or six thousand years ago several quite distinct types of dog had been developed in the Near East and in Egypt. By 2000 BC the Egyptians had mastered the principles of dog breeding, as their frescos, bronzes, carvings and written references demonstrate. In Europe the modification of the basic type was slower, but by Roman times, breeds of a sort had developed. Although they were not distinguished as breeds are today, on grounds of colour, size and other specific features, they had certain characteristics, such as good scenting ability, in common. We know that the Romans had separate descriptive names for house dogs, shepherd dogs, sporting dogs, war dogs, dogs which fought in the arena as a spectacle, dogs which hunted by scent and dogs which hunted by sight, as well as recognizing regional types.

Perhaps the earliest truly distinctive type to be developed was the long-legged, slender, swift sighthound of the Greyhound/Saluki type, which appeared very early in Egypt and Mesopotamia. Greyhounds have changed little in appearance throughout the centuries and dogs of distinct Greyhound type are represented on Egyptian tombs dating back to 2900 BC. The Saluki, sometimes called the Persian Greyhound, is considered to be one of the oldest breeds in the world. Dogs resembling the Saluki were mummified and buried with pharaohs in tombs along the River Nile, and it is claimed that the breed itself may have been domesticated as long ago as 329 BC. These swift sighthounds were developed for hunting in desert conditions.

Giant mastiff type dogs for guarding and fighting purposes also evolved early. Dogs of this type can be found on Egyptian monuments of 3000 BC. They were certainly known in Britain at the time of the Roman invasion. Julius Caesar wrote of their courage, and records show that some were taken to Rome from Britain, where they were pitted against various other animals, and even gladiators.

Dogs which hunted by scent like their ancestor the wolf would have been selectively bred for increasingly powerful scenting skills. Hunting with packs of hounds has been a popular pastime ever since the time of the Ancient Greeks. Specialist types for different quarry gradually evolved, although the history of hound types is not so clearly defined as that of the ancient sighthounds. The giant of the family, the Irish Wolfhound, developed for hunting wolves and elk, is believed to have been in existence as long ago as 391 AD, when dogs apparently of this type were sent to Rome from Ireland.

The wolf's naturally cooperative hunting technique provided the raw material from which man developed the herding breeds of dog, for whom man plays the role of the pack towards which the prey animals are driven. Such herding dogs were developed in different parts of the world. Because they needed to be able to protect the flocks and herds from the attacks of wild predators and from human marauders, these tended to be large dogs which combined herding and guarding qualities.

ABOVE: *Large dogs of Mastiff type were developed and trained as hunting companions and war dogs at least as early as 2000 BC, as shown in this detail taken from the bas-relief of Asshurbanipal where they are depicted being used to hunt wild asses.*

LEFT: *Small pet dogs also appeared on the scene at an early date. This Roman funeral urn shows a little dog of Maltese type as part of a family group.*

In the Far East, the Chinese were developing their own miniature breeds quite separately – records of their small, short-faced dogs date back to the sixth century BC, and these would later give rise to the highly individual Oriental Toy breeds such as the Pug and the Pekingese.

The astonishingly wide range of shapes, colours and sizes developed from the earliest dogs is unique – no other species of animal, wild or domesticated, shows such a high degree of variation. There are giant breeds and miniatures, long-limbed slender breeds and compact stumpy-legged ones. Some breeds have coats which trail along the ground while others are almost naked. There are upright ears and pendulous ears, straight tails, curly tails, stump tails and even no tails at all. Indeed, if such a degree of variation were seen in any wild species, it would almost certainly be concluded that there were in fact several different species, or else that new species were about to develop. However, all breeds of dog from Chihuahua to St Bernard are a single species.

The variation amongst the forms of the domestic dog is also surprising because so many different characteristics are affected, for example, coat colour, coat type, body size, limb length, tail shape, head shape, sense of smell and even temperament. Years of selective breeding by man seem to have broken down the mechanisms that exist in most species to limit the variations within the species. It has been suggested that there may be something special about the dog which has allowed this to happen, because comparable variations have not occurred in other domestic species, such as cattle or cats. However, it has been calculated that perhaps as few as 20 mutations account for the wide diversity which exists in contemporary breeds, and there may have been as many as 4,000 generations of domestic dogs in which these mutations have become evident and have been encouraged by selective breeding.

Surprisingly early, too, man developed very small dogs whose purpose must have been solely as pets. By 2000 BC the Ancient Egyptians had produced a miniature dog, clearly depicted in their art as quite distinct from ordinary puppies, while there is evidence of selective breeding for small pet dogs in Greece from a few hundred years BC, and a little later in Rome. These early 'toy' breeds appear to have been of Maltese type.

ABOVE LEFT: *The modern Neapolitan Mastiff is descended from the old Molossus of Roman times.*

LEFT: *Swift sighthounds like these coursing Greyhounds are the earliest known specialist type of dog to have evolved.*

Some popular traits, such as the flattened face of the Pekingese and the shortened legs of the Dachshund, have been found to occur as occasional mutations in wild dogs – and also in other species. Such characteristics would be a handicap to the individual in the wild and would be unlikely to be perpetuated. However, man has selectively preserved such mutants as they occurred for reasons of his own. The short-legged mutation has been developed separately in Europe, America and North Africa by hunters. In some cases this was because a short-legged dog was easier to follow on foot, as we see with the modern Basset Hound; in other cases the hunter made use of the new shape to develop an animal which could go to ground after small quarry, as with the smaller modern Terriers.

The lop ear found in many breeds today has its origins with the dog's wild ancestors: wolf cubs start out with hanging ears, which only become erect as they mature. In the wild the erect ear is advantageous to give the best possible hearing; in the domesticated dog man has perpetuated the mutation that retains the lop ear of puppyhood. Since pendant ears are particularly associated with breeds with a particularly well-developed sense of smell, such as hounds and spaniels, it may have been considered that the sense of hearing was less important to these breeds; or it may have been the case that man simply found the different ear shape attractive.

Certainly the perpetuation of the foreshortened face was in many cases based on purely aesthetic grounds. In breeds like the Bulldog the short face was bred into the strain to give the appalling vice-like grip for which they are renowned. In breeds like the Pekingese, however, the flat face gives no practical advantage whatsoever and was developed purely for its visual appeal to man, the short jaws and large eyes giving a permanently infantile appearance and so creating a perpetual puppy.

Because the innate characteristics of the dog were such as made it useful to man in a wide range of contexts as well as being socially orientated, mutations have been fostered and encouraged where in a species with a more limited role they would not have been seen as advantageous.

RIGHT: *It has been calculated that a mere twenty mutations from the natural canine form provided the raw material for man to create by selective breeding the hundreds of different dog breeds known today, such as this Great Dane and Yorkshire Terrier. The Great Dane was developed for great size as a guard and hunting dog. In contrast, the extreme miniaturization and long silky coat of the Yorkshire Terrier mark a shift of emphasis from its original function as a ratting dog to the role of ornamental companion.*

ABOVE: *With breeds such as the Dachshund man has selectively bred for achondroplasia, an inherited condition causing stunting of the leg bones. Dachshunds have been bred for this shape to fulfil their specialized function as badger hounds, the small size and short legs enabling them to pursue their quarry underground.*

THE MANY ROLES OF THE DOG TODAY

*Dogs have been trained for all kinds of work. Their keen powers of smell enable them to be employed by the police and armed forces as tracker dogs (**LEFT**), while their hunting instincts have been redirected to produce herding dogs (**CENTRE LEFT**) and retrievers (**BELOW**). Their aggressive instincts are deployed in the training of guard dogs (**RIGHT**), while at the other extreme their responsiveness and natural drive to care for fellow 'pack members' has produced guide dogs for the blind (**BELOW FAR RIGHT**).*

4

THE DOG AND MAN TODAY

The dog developed by our ancestors thousands of years ago was bred to fulfil a wide range of roles from the strictly functional worker to what can only be described as a luxury accessory in the form of the lady's lapdog. Today we live in a mechanized world that has largely seen the departure of such long-established working animals as the plough horse or the house cow. This is also reflected in the role of the modern dog in the increasing tendency for it to be kept purely as a companion, but there are still many areas where the working dog remains irreplaceable.

Hunting dogs will always be with us. Although contemporary man generally hunts for pleasure rather than for need, he still makes use of the superior scenting skills and hunting instincts of the dog. In some areas the hunting dog is a vital controller of predators that attack livestock. We still have our packs of hounds, our specialist gundogs that find and retrieve game for the shooting man, our terriers that pursue the quarry underground, our coursing greyhounds and the master of the multi-purpose hunters, the Lurcher.

Guard dogs too have yet to become obsolete. Even the friendly family pet often retains its guarding instincts so well that many insurance companies offer reduced rates to dog-owning households. Those breeds developed for guard work combine aggressive instincts with a high degree of responsiveness so well that the police and army make increasing use of them today, while private ownership of dogs for security purposes has also increased.

The keen nose of many breeds has been utilized not only for hunting purposes but for more serious work. Over 300 years ago St Bernards were trained to track lost travellers in the snow of the Swiss Alps, and today specially trained mountain rescue dogs continue to save lives by seeking out accident victims, often under considerable depths of snow. Rescue dogs are also employed to seek out survivors of earthquakes or similar catastrophes. Police and army dogs are used not only to track criminals and missing persons but to sniff out drugs, explosives, firearms and even bodies hidden where human senses could never detect them.

Although the use of dogs for carrying loads and pulling carts or sledges is limited by their size, their strength, stamina and endurance of the cold have made Huskies and similar breeds the draught animals par excellence in snowbound areas. For centuries Eskimos depended on the Husky for survival; today mechanized transport designed for icebound conditions has partially superseded the dog in this role while sled dog racing has become an increasingly popular sport today.

Herding dogs continue to aid farmers. In these breeds the cooperative hunting instincts of the wolf have been channelled towards man's needs; instead of driving the prey into the jaws of fellow pack members, the herding dog rounds up and directs its charges where its human master wishes. The drovers' dogs of the past, such as the famous and now extinct Smithfield Collie or surviving but rarely worked Welsh Corgi, have become largely obsolete now that we move cattle by road transport, but highly specialized sheepdogs are still invaluable for controlling flocks of sheep. In these breeds the ingrained herding instinct is so strong that it is seen even in untrained animals.

The intelligence and responsiveness of the dog have made it possible to train guide dogs for the blind, or 'seeing eye dogs' as they are called in the United States. The Guide Dogs for the Blind Association began to train dogs in 1931 and today thousands of blind people benefit from these guides. Such dogs must have an almost limitless sensitivity

5

to their owners' needs, learning to be perpetually conscious of matters outside a dog's ordinary scope – for example, a guide dog must watch out for projections well above its own height which the blind owner must be steered round. Only the larger breeds are suitable for guide dog work, with Labrador and Golden Retrievers or first crosses between the two being favoured, and only those individuals which pass all the rigorous temperament tests proceed to full training.

More recently – in 1976 in the United States and in 1982 in Great Britain – 'hearing ear' dogs have been trained to aid the deaf by alerting their owners to such sounds as the doorbell, a crying baby or a boiling kettle. These dogs may be of any size or shape, many being cross-breds, so long as they are responsive to their owners' needs and have a sense of responsibility towards their duties. 'Support' or 'service dogs' are now also being trained to aid disabled people to lead a more independent life, fetching and carrying or even holding open a door for a wheelchair to pass through.

Dogs play their part, too, in the entertainment world. From the time of the Romans, when large aggressive dogs of mastiff and wolfhound type fought in the arena for the amusement of the bloodthirsty mob, blood sports of a type which are now considered cruel and are no longer permitted were popular. Bull-baiting was a favourite sport in England at least 700 years ago and dogs were bred specially for this purpose, sometimes fighting other animals or dogs or even men. This was banned in England in 1835, and in other countries at around the same time. However, it continued illegally for some years, and other sports, such as rat catching, were introduced. Heavy gambling was involved, and the small sharp terriers which were used in the rat pits built up some remarkable records: one Manchester Terrier killed 100 rats in 6 minutes and 32 seconds.

Sport of this kind has now almost completely disappeared, officially at least, but dogs still play a considerable entertainment role. The most popular sport nowadays is greyhound racing, where the dogs chase a simulated 'hare' around a track, with related sports such as whippet racing and coursing. Sheepdog trials consistently attract large audiences, as do displays by police and army dogs which exhibit such skills as scaling fences and jumping through flaming hoops. Hunting in Great Britain today is often a matter of entertainment rather than of need, and many people enjoy the sport of following hounds after a carefully laid scent rather than after living quarry. The exhibition of pedigree dogs, and obedience and agility competitions, are also popular. Dogs have been trained to 'act' in films and to perform complex tricks for the world of circus and side-show entertainment.

Above all, however, the modern dog is kept as a companion – in a recent survey 88 per cent of dog owners gave companionship as a reason for keeping their pets. In this

BELOW: *The modern dog is above all a companion, and especially valued as such by people living alone.*

century the number of dogs kept as pets has grown dramatically, perhaps because changes in the organization of human society have made urban man more dependent on the friendship and affection a dog offers. Dogs provide the physical contact with another living being which western societies are inhibited about between people; it is often forgotten that, just as babies need close contact with their mothers, adults too benefit from touch behaviour. Dogs are sometimes employed therapeutically in hospitals and clinics to help mentally or emotionally ill people come back into contact with the world of normality.

There are other psychological benefits to be had from a dog's companionship. A person's self-esteem can be boosted by a dog's desire to please, uncompetitiveness and non-judgemental qualities. A dog-owner is more likely to make new acquaintances than someone out for a walk alone or with other people; the dog will not only get its owner out walking in streets and parks where he or she might not otherwise go, but will often initiate a conversation with a stranger, acting as a catalyst in human relationships. A survey made by a group of psychologists found that dog and cat-lovers tended to be more friendly towards their fellows than those people who were indifferent to animals.

For children, the family dog can be companion, protector and playmate, as well as an introduction to responsibilities. For elderly people living alone, the pet dog may be the sole source of comfort and friendship. And for many happy, well-adjusted adults, whose lives already contain interests and human contact, the dog sharing their activities provides an extra element of companionship and enjoyment.

PHYSICAL CHARACTERISTICS

Despite the range of shapes and sizes, all dogs have a basically similar structure. The variations lie principally in the proportions of the bones, and in external features such as tail carriage, ear shape or coat type.

SKELETON AND MUSCULATURE

All dogs have the same number of bones, comprising the flat protective bones that contain the vital organs, and the long cylindrical bones for support, and these are of reasonably uniform shape throughout the species. However, centuries of selective breeding have caused the relative lengths of bones to vary immensely from one breed to another. In the Greyhound, for example, the limb bones are very long indeed and the skull and body skeleton relatively small, whilst in a number of breeds the limb bones are drastically stunted, giving rise to achondroplasia. This is exemplified by the short-legged Dachshund, where the abnormality has become normal.

The overall conformation of a dog is a reflection both of the skeleton and the overlying musculature. Show standards specify the 'type' or appearance that would represent the ideal dog of the particular breed in question. In the case of the Clumber Spaniel, for example, the official KC standard demands 'very powerful and well-developed hindquarters', so the muscle masses are prominent.

The dog's physique is essentially designed for running fast over long distances, as the hunting lifestyle of its ancestor the wolf required. Selective breeding by man has modified this in various ways in the different breeds. In the Greyhound types, the build has been adapted to give maximum speed at the expense of endurance, creating an animal which can run over short distances at as much as 40 miles per hour. The skeleton of these dogs is so flexible that, when running flat out, they can bring the hind feet right forward to land well in front of the spot where the forefeet were a moment earlier.

Other breeds have been selected for a shape which has considerably less speed than the ancestral wolf. Dogs such as Basset Hounds, which have long backs and short legs, can only run slowly in a somewhat cumbersome fashion.

Modern dogs retain the wolf's great stamina, although few pet dogs are called upon to prove this. Of all modern breeds, it is the Husky that retains the limb and body structure closest to that of the wolf, and is the breed called upon to display that species' powers of endurance. A Husky will work eight hours a day pulling twice its own weight at between two and three miles per hour, and one team is recorded as having covered 522 miles in 80 hours.

The fit dog is powerfully muscled, and the muscles of the fore and hindquarters are particularly important as these areas do not have so much skeletal support.

Weight distribution varies from breed to breed. The basic type modelled on the wolf has a very even distribution of weight, but man has created some breeds such as the Bulldog which are markedly front-heavy and which have particularly well-developed forelimbs to compensate for this. The angulation of the hindlimbs is also considerably variable amongst modern breeds; the show type of German Shepherd Dog, for example, has strongly angulated hindquarters, so that its back feet stand well behind the rear of the body.

The physique so well designed for speed and endurance is not made for jumping. When an animal jumps, it flexes the muscles of its hind legs very rapidly. A dog's muscles are attached to its bones in such a way that they cannot be flexed very suddenly. Typically, dogs can jump small obstacles, and the long-limbed sighthounds can be trained to

EXTERNAL ANATOMY

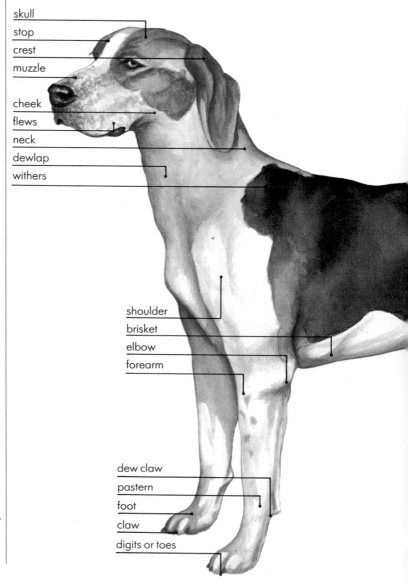

skull
stop
crest
muzzle
cheek
flews
neck
dewlap
withers
shoulder
brisket
elbow
forearm
dew claw
pastern
foot
claw
digits or toes

achieve spectacular leaps using their own weight to build up momentum, but essentially the canine frame is meant for running rather than jumping. Similarly, climbing is not a natural skill for this species. The dog lacks the retractile claws of the cat with which to grip surfaces and cannot twist its legs or feet to assist its grasp.

The Scottish Terrier's unique bone structure shows how selective breeding results in varied physical types.

SKELETON AND MAJOR ORGANS

MUSCLES

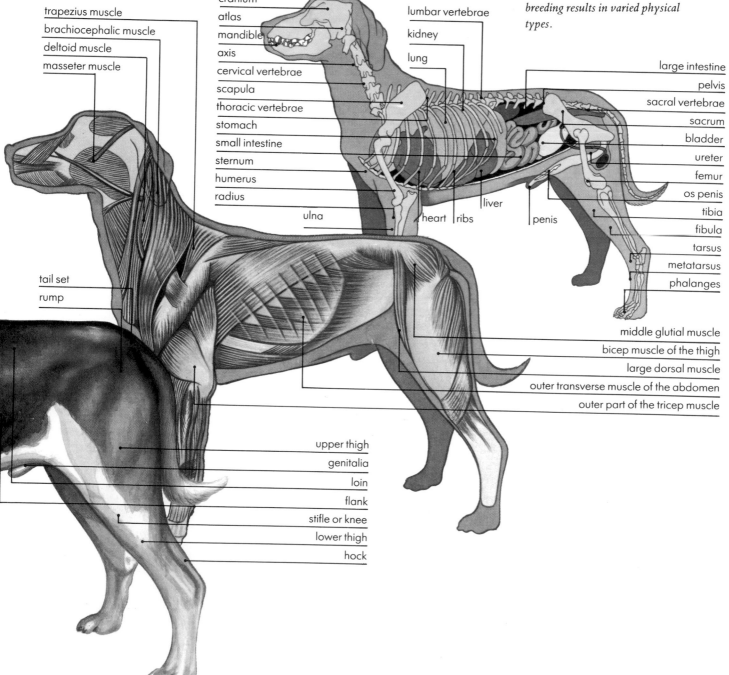

trapezius muscle
brachiocephalic muscle
deltoid muscle
masseter muscle

cranium
atlas
mandible
axis
cervical vertebrae
scapula
thoracic vertebrae
stomach
small intestine
sternum
humerus
radius
ulna

lumbar vertebrae
kidney
lung

heart ribs liver penis

large intestine
pelvis
sacral vertebrae
sacrum
bladder
ureter
femur
os penis
tibia
fibula
tarsus
metatarsus
phalanges

tail set
rump

middle glutial muscle
bicep muscle of the thigh
large dorsal muscle
outer transverse muscle of the abdomen
outer part of the tricep muscle

upper thigh
genitalia
loin
flank
stifle or knee
lower thigh
hock

THE SKULL AND TEETH

SKULL TYPES

dolichocephalic

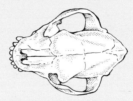

brachycephalic

mesocephalic

The most conspicuous structural variation between different dog breeds is the shape of the skull. At one extreme are breeds such as the Greyhound, Fox Terrier and Rough Collie, which possess a long, narrow head, described as *dolichocephalic,* while at the other end of the scale, the compressed skull of the *brachycephalic* breeds such as the Pug and Bulldog gives a short, snub-nosed, squarish head shape. In the middle are all those dogs such as the Spaniel types which fall between the two extremes with a skull of intermediate length known as *mesocephalic.*

All breeds of dog have the same number and type of teeth. The first, deciduous set is comprised of 28 teeth, and is followed by a permanent dentition of 42 teeth. The incisors at the front of the mouth are small; the adjoining canines are large and pointed, and are used for killing prey

BELOW: *These two skulls show how wide the physical variation between domestic dogs can be. The skull on the left is that of a Golden Retriever; that on the right is a Pekingese.*

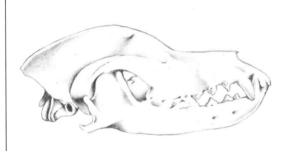

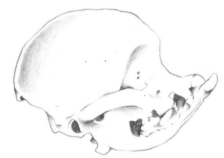

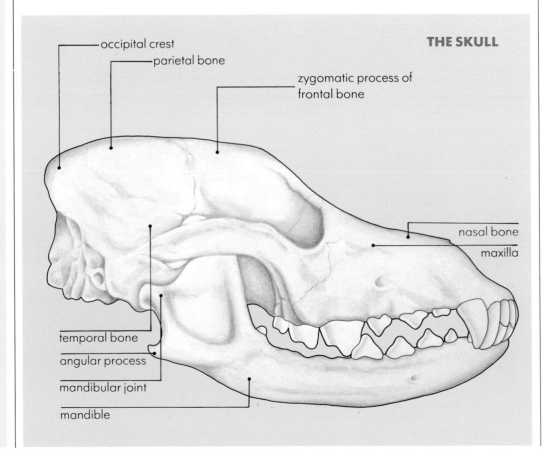

THE SKULL

occipital crest

parietal bone

zygomatic process of frontal bone

nasal bone

maxilla

temporal bone

angular process

mandibular joint

mandible

DENTITION

upper jaw   lower jaw

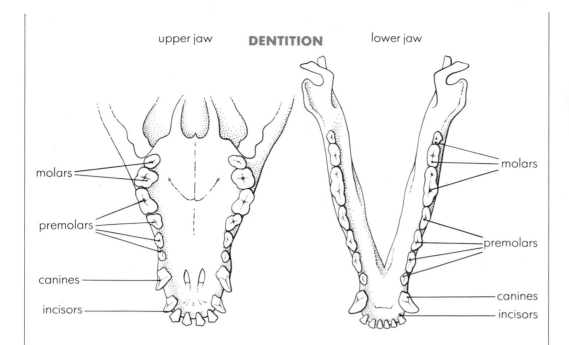

molars

premolars

canines

incisors

molars

premolars

canines

incisors

and ripping flesh. The first molar of the bottom jaw and the fourth premolar of the upper jaw, which are enlarged and known as carnassial teeth, are also used in this way. The other premolars are responsible for crushing food, and the molars for chewing, although dogs generally bolt their meals, rather than masticating food for any great length of time.

Different skull structures affect the effectiveness of the pattern of dentition. The relative lengths of the upper and lower jaws vary. Short-headed dogs are often 'undershot', with the lower jaw protruding beyond the upper. Other dogs may be 'overshot', with the upper jaw longer, or may have a 'level bite' with the teeth meeting or a 'scissor bite' with the top teeth fitting neatly over the lower teeth. In breeds with narrow muzzles, there is a tendency for the incisors to become squashed together, whereas in broad-muzzled dogs like the Bulldog, there may be an undesirable gap between these teeth and some of the teeth may be misplaced or even missing.

Skulls vary considerably in width, and this is largely determined by the shape of the zygomatic arches, the bones below the eyes on the upper jaw. In the Labrador and St Bernard these are strong and arched outwards, producing a big, broad head, while in the German Shepherd Dog and Fox Terrier they are much less prominent.

The skull may be flattish topped or rounded. In some breeds such as the American Cocker Spaniel a high-domed shape is required, while the Pekingese skull must be flat between the ears. Some breeds, including Red Setters and Bloodhounds, have a prominent sagittal crest, the ridge on the top of the skull, allowing for the attachment of extra muscles which are used for biting. It is also excellent protection from a blow to the head.

Selective breeding for looks has tended to emphasize differences in the arrangement of the upper and lower jaws and has resulted in much less effective jaws and teeth in some dogs. The German Shepherd Dog has been bred to ideally have a scissor-like bite (1) and a slightly longer, overshot jaw (2). An undershot jaw in this breed is considered a serious fault, leading to disqualification in the show ring. In the Bulldog, Pekingese and other short-faced breeds, the jaws have become so squashed that there may be no room for some of the teeth and the bite is referred to as undershot (3). In fact, some Bulldogs cannot hunt at all because their bite has become so distorted. The show standard for the Golden Retriever demands a level bite (4). Clearly, any pronounced abnormalities can give rise to difficulty in eating.

KINDS OF BITE

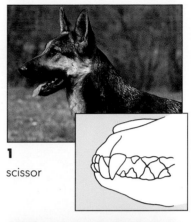

1
scissor

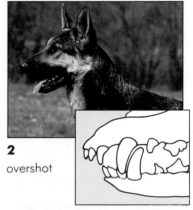

2
overshot

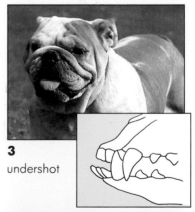

3
undershot

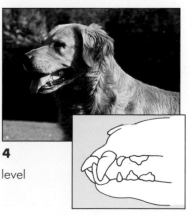

4
level

PANTING

Panting is an important method of temperature control, the evaporation of water from the nasal and oral cavities helping to cool the body.

THE DOG'S PAW

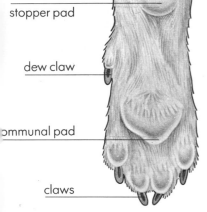

stopper pad

dew claw

ommunal pad

claws

The dog's paw has four functional toes for walking and, usually, a fifth vestigial digit, the dew claw, most commonly found on the forepaws and occasionally also on the hind feet. Dew claws are surgically removed shortly after birth in most breeds, as they serve no useful purpose and may even cause injury if they are snagged or allowed to overgrow. A few breeds have double dew claws which are not removed.

SPECIAL FEATURES OF THE DOG

The internal organs of the dog follow the typical mammalian pattern, with the short gut typical of the carnivore and a large stomach designed to carry quantities of meat, enabling the animal to make maximum use of its prey.

The dog's paws conform to the overall body plan in being made for walking or running long distances. The long, very strong claws are not retractile like a cat's, and dog prints always show the impression of the claws in front of the pads. An important function of the pads is that of temperature control, for this is where the eccrine sweat glands, the only sweat glands used for heat loss on the dog's body, are situated. In hot weather, the dog may leave wet footprints because of these glands. A further function of these glands is to keep the pads moist so that they do not dry out with the continual friction of walking.

The major means of temperature control is by panting, evaporating moisture to cause heat loss. Although most water would appear to be lost from the tongue and oral cavity, in reality, the nasal cavities are more significant. There are lateral nasal glands just inside the nostrils that supply moisture both for heat loss, and to moisten the surface of the nose and improve the sense of smell. As its body temperature rises, the dog will first breathe exclusively through its nose, but if the temperature continues to increase, then it will breathe through the nose and exhale, or pant, through its mouth.

One of the dog's most characteristic features is its tail. The dog's tail performs a different function from that of a cat, which is used largely for balance as well as for communication. The different breeds of dog have tails of all shapes and sizes, but they make a limited contribution to the dog's sense of balance. The swift sighthounds may be seen to make full use of the balancing qualities of the tail when making sharp turns, as when coursing a hare, or as a counterbalance when jumping, and the specialist water dogs tend to use the tail as a rudder when swimming. However, the most important function of the dog's tail is for communication; the dog expresses its feelings by wagging it, letting it droop, and moving it in a variety of ways.

Man has developed breeds with long tails, medium length tails, short tails and even no tails at all. Tails may be set on high or low, carried low between the hocks, level with the back, or curled loosely or tightly over the back. In several breeds tails are further altered by docking to varying lengths; this is sometimes a matter of fashion, and in working dogs is claimed to prevent injury to the tail when going through thick cover. Guard dogs were probably originally docked to make them appear more ferocious; it has been suggested that the aim was to make these breeds more ferocious by preventing the expression via tail language of friendship or submission. Heavily feathered tails such as that of the

RIGHT: *Man has developed considerable variations in the dog's appearance, and tails and ears differ dramatically from the original wolf type in many instances. The German Shepherd Dog (1) features erect, mobile ears and an expressive flowing tail which recall the wolf. The Pembroke Corgi (2) has erect ears but a mere stump of a tail, either naturally so or docked. In the Beagle (3), the tail is of normal length but characteristically carried much higher than a wolf's, while the ears are pendant as in so many scent hounds. The Chow Chow (4) is typical of the Spitz breeds, with small erect ears and a tail carried right over the back.*

EARS AND TAILS

Pekingese, carried over the dog's back like the state umbrella held over court personages, were developed for their ornamental value. One of the oddest tails, covered with tight curls for the first few inches but then becoming abruptly hairless, is sported by the Irish Water Spaniel, whose nickname of 'rat tail' derives from this appendage.

Ears vary as much as tails. The earliest dogs would have had erect ears of medium size, like those of the wolf. These are still found in some modern breeds, especially certain types of Terrier, and are now usually called 'fox ears'. In most breeds the ears are now slightly larger, and are termed 'prick ears'. The largest erect ears, such as those of the French Bulldog, are known as 'bat' or 'tulip ears'. Other breeds have semi-erect ears which fold over slightly at the tip, as in the Rough Collie.

All such breeds retain the wolf's ability to move the ears individually backwards and forwards to act as sound reflectors. However, man has developed breeds with ears which hang down close to the head and which have far less voluntary movement. Such breeds will have slightly less acute sensitivity to sound than the dogs with erect ears. As if in compensation, many pendant-eared dogs have a particularly acute sense of smell. Hounds, other than sighthounds, characteristically have pendulous ears, often so long as to actually obscure the eyes when the dog has its head down following a trail. It has been suggested that the link between long hanging ears and a keen sense of smell may be more positive than a merely reduced importance of sight and hearing; as the ears fall forward they may help to channel the scent towards the olfactory organs.

THE SKIN AND FUR

The dog's skin and fur act as an efficient waterproofing agent, sebaceous glands at the roots of the hairs acting to coat the hairs with sebum for this purpose. They also provide extremely efficient insulation, the hair trapping a layer of air between the skin and the outside to protect the dog against the cold. The dog is essentially designed for cold climates, and Huskies, which live and work in the frozen north, even sleeping outside curled in the snow, demonstrate just how effective this insulation is. However, in hot conditions it makes heat loss difficult.

The earliest wolf-like dogs would have had what is known as a double coat, with a thick short underlayer and a longer outer coat which was straight and lay close and flat. In domestication all sorts of variations have been developed.

At one extreme are the hairless, or almost hairless breeds, like the Mexican Hairless and the Chinese Crested Dog.

At the other extreme, hair growth has been taken to great lengths, as in the Old English Sheepdog or the Afghan Hound. Long hair comes in different types. Breeds such as the Rough Collie have an extremely long outer coat with a dense undercoat. Others, like the Afghan Hound, have a very long but fine and silky outer coat, nearer to human hair in texture. Two Hungarian breeds, the Komondor and the Puli, have very long and dense outer coats that hang in coarse tassels.

Short coats are very common. They may be very short and fine, as in the Boxer and Whippet, or a little longer and denser, as in the Labrador and Corgi. Wire-haired coats too, where the hairs feel stiff and wavy and point in all directions, are found in a number of breeds, including most of the Terriers.

There are numerous variations on these basic types; both short and long coats can be wire-haired; long outer coats can be thin or very heavy; hair can be fluffy like a Poodle, woolly like a Husky, or frizzy like an Irish Water Spaniel.

The skin of the early dogs was tight and well muscled immediately below the surface. In some breeds it has become much looser, and this is especially evident in some short-haired dogs about the face and neck. The extreme example is the Bloodhound which has what is known as a dewlap neck, layers of loose skin under its throat. A breed which takes looseness of skin further than one would think

LEFT: *Breeds such as the Basenji have a short coat.*

RIGHT: *The Rhodesian Ridgeback has a unique pattern of hair growth, with a distinctive ridge of fur running along its back.*

RIGHT: *Long-haired breeds include the Yorkshire Terrier. The 'Yorkie' has fine, silky hair which can grow to astonishing lengths, trailing on the ground.*

LEFT: *The Komondor has an unusual type of long coat whose thick, soft undercoat mats into distinct cords to provide an extreme form of weatherproofing.*

possible is the Shar-Pei, which has been described as wearing a skin several sizes too large for the dog inside.

The colour and markings of the coat have also become increasingly varied through selective breeding. Wolves themselves show considerable colour variation across their range, and this has formed the basis for all the varied coloration seen in breeds of dogs today. Some of the most striking variations include the regular spots of the Dalmatian, the unique and striking shade of grey that gives the Weimaraner its nickname of 'the Grey Ghost' and the brilliant horse-chestnut hue of the Irish Setter.

DIRECTION OF HAIR GROWTH

THE DOG'S SENSES

The dog's senses differ considerably in their emphases from those of man. Its sense of smell is known to be at least 100 times better than man's and has been rated much higher, while its sense of hearing is also considerably more sensitive. Sight, on the other hand, is far less important to the dog than it is to man.

THE SENSE OF SMELL

The dog's olfactory area, the sensory area within the nose which detects smells, is some fourteen times larger than a man's. Within this area the specialized olfactory cells to receive scents are both more numerous and more densely packed than in man.

Under normal circumstances a dog's nose feels wet to the touch. This is generally regarded as a sign of good health. In fact it is another method of boosting the sense of smell: the moisture is a secretion produced by the lateral nasal glands, which dissolves the scent particles in the air to bring them into contact with the olfactory cells.

By breathing with its nostrils flared, a dog can increase the volume of air passing to these cells, and Jacobsen's Organ, a structure not present in humans, located above the roof of the mouth, can also detect particles of scent in the air. In order to accommodate the increased input from the olfactory regions, the area of the brain responsible for processing such information, known as the rhinecephalon, is correspondingly large.

It has been estimated that there are about 40 times as many brain cells connected with smell detection in the dog as in the human. It is also conjectured that the cells in a dog's nose which detect smells may be more sensitive than those of a man, but this has not been proved.

Puppies are, however, born with a very limited sense of smell. It is also possible to affect the scenting ability of a dog. Feeding a dog animal fat will cause this sense to diminish, while a lack of food promotes increased receptivity.

BELOW FAR LEFT: *Gundogs such as this German Short-haired Pointer are bred to have an excellent sense of smell to locate game. Pointing breeds have an inherited instinct to react to the smell of the quarry by freezing on the spot, pointing the nose and the whole body towards the scent and thus marking it out for the human hunter.*

FAR LEFT: *Like all gundogs, the Labrador Retriever has an excellent sense of smell, and this is one of the breeds often used to assist in the detection of illegal drugs and explosives as well as remaining popular with gamekeepers and sportsmen.*

LEFT: *An army 'sniffer dog' is used to locate explosives.*

Aniseed oil obtained from the plant *Pimpinella anisum* is used to lay trails for drag hunting. Tests have shown that hounds have no preference for the strong smell of oil, as is sometimes supposed, but it is easy for them to follow.

Some breeds of dog have been developed for an especially keen sense of smell. The Bloodhound is undoubtedly the best known and the most effective member of the group of hounds that hunt by scent. Dogs possessing this ability can be traced right back to the third century AD, and it is likely that the Bloodhound itself was being bred before the Middle Ages. Working Bloodhounds have been kept for tracking purposes by police forces in many parts of the world. One famous dog, called Nick Carter, succeeded in following a scent that was over four days old, which led to the capture and subsequent conviction of a wanted criminal.

Although not all breeds of dog have such an acute sense of smell, all dogs rely constantly on this sense for information about their surroundings, using their noses to investigate new objects, strange dogs and unknown people, with great interest. The sense of smell is an important part of inter-dog communication, and it is for this reason that dogs always sniff each other when meeting. A great deal of canine behaviour hinges upon smell – the leg-cocking of the male, scratching on the ground to deposit odour from the foot glands, rolling in foul-smelling (to us) deposits and so forth.

Man has made use of the dog's sense of smell in many ways. Hunting dogs – pack hounds and gundogs – use their olfactory powers in much the same way as their ancestor the wolf, and tracking dogs follow much the same procedure. A well-trained tracking dog, like the bloodhound Nick Carter, can follow the scent of a specific in-dividual even when it is several days old and crossed by the trails of many others. Indeed, the dog's ability to follow a trail has even been used to establish that identical twins have the same odour, for it has been found that a dog given the scent of one twin will follow the track of either.

Dogs are also used to find objects. In France 'truffle hounds' are trained to find truffles, elusive delicacies which only grow underground. In recent years, 'sniffer dogs' have been widely used by the police and the army to smell out substances such as explosives and illegal drugs, and have proved much better at finding these things than any machine.

SIGHT

The dog's sense of vision is generally inferior to that of man, although it can see much better than man in poor light conditions. This is because of the arrangement of light-sensitive cells within the eye. There are two types of these cells forming the layer at the back of the eye known as the retina. The first type, known as rods, from their shape, are sensitive to low levels of light, but see only in black and white. The second type, known as cones, are responsible for colour vision, but are most effective in bright light. In the dog there is a much higher proportion of rods to cones than in man, which explains why it sees better in dim light than we do, but not so well in bright light. It was once considered that dogs were colour-blind, but it is now known that the few cones present in the dog's eye enable it to see colour in a rudimentary fashion.

The dog's ability to see at night is further enhanced by the presence at the back of the eye of a special reflective layer, the *tapetum lucidum*. This structure is located behind the retina and acts like a mirror, reflecting light rays back through the retina and increasing their stimulatory effect on the rods and cones. It is the reflection from the tapetum which causes a dog's eyes to shine green when lit by a car's headlights at night. Any light entering the dog's eye passes through the layer of rods, and is then reflected back through them again. This increases the eye's sensitivity to light, but it also causes a loss of detail.

The dog perceives still and moving objects very differently from humans. A man can see both with ease, but a dog only seems to see objects well if they are moving, or if it is moving itself. This means that dogs see static shapes very poorly, but that they are sensitive to movement over very long distances. For example, a shepherd's hand signals can be picked up by his dog at distances of up to a mile.

Dogs are extremely sensitive to anything that makes a sudden or unusual movement, an asset made much use of by retrievers, pointers and hunting dogs. Guide dogs for the blind use this facility all the time as they lead their owners amongst crowds and across busy streets.

Another major difference between a dog's vision and that of a man is caused by the position of the eyes on the head. A man's eyes point forward and the field of view overlaps almost completely between the two eyes, whereas a dog's eyes point to the side to a varying degree, depending on head shape, giving less overlap but a wider field of vision. This means that dogs can detect movement over a much wider field than humans, although they can judge distance less well. As a hunter, the dog needs this wide field of vision to locate prey; binocular vision is also necessary to pinpoint the exact position of prey. The two different images received from both eyes naturally overlap to a certain extent, and are superimposed by the brain to create this facility.

The long-headed (dolichocephalic) breeds have the widest field of vision, with only a small overlap in the area covered by the two eyes. This gives them the widest possible view, but narrows the field of vision immediately in front of them. The short-headed (brachycephalic) breeds, in contrast, have the eyes situated towards the front of the head, giving a narrower overall field but a greater area of overlap.

HEARING

Hearing, with smell, is one of the two senses which are more highly developed in the dog than in man. The appearance of the outer ear varies considerably between breeds and affects sensitivity of hearing to a slight extent, the prick-eared dogs having the advantage over breeds with pendant ears, but all dogs are more sensitive to sound than any humans.

Dogs can detect most sounds from four times the distance that a human can, and can also hear sounds of a frequency so high as to be inaudible to the human ear. It is likely that they can differentiate between frequencies better than man as well, because they can distinguish between a wide range of words used for training them or identify the sound of an individual vehicle.

RIGHT: *Dogs have a greater field of view than humans because their eyes are located on the side of their heads. Whereas a human has a range of 100°, a dog with wide-set eyes can have as much as 270°. A dog with a shorter face giving more forward-pointing eyes, however, will not have such a coverage, as the diagram illustrates. Dogs also have better sight in poor light conditions than do humans. This is partly because of the reflective layer (tapetum lucidum) at the back of the eye, but also because they have relatively more rod receptor cells on their retina, which respond to poor light.*

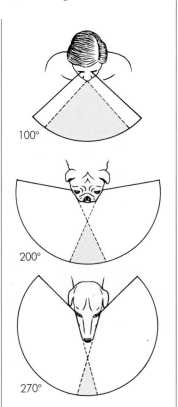

100°

200°

270°

ANATOMY OF A DOG'S EYE

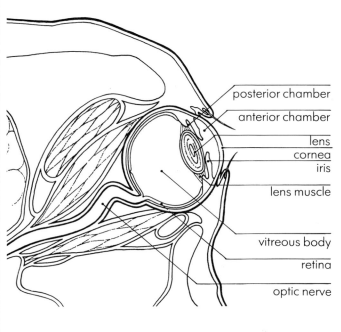

posterior chamber

anterior chamber

lens

cornea

iris

lens muscle

vitreous body

retina

optic nerve

ANATOMY OF A DOG'S EAR

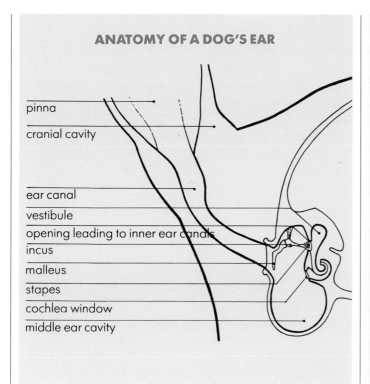

pinna
cranial cavity

ear canal
vestibule
opening leading to inner ear canal
incus
malleus
stapes
cochlea window
middle ear cavity

COMPARATIVE HEARING OF DOG AND MAN

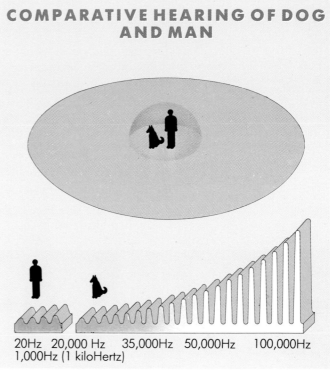

20Hz   20,000 Hz   35,000Hz   50,000Hz   100,000Hz
1,000Hz (1 kiloHertz)

Studies have shown that for low notes, the limits of detection and sensitivity are about the same for dogs and humans. However, as frequencies rise, the dog's ear becomes progressively more sensitive than the human's, and the upper limit at which it can detect notes is much higher than that of people.

Children can detect notes up to frequencies of about 20 kiloHerz (kHz), adults rather less, but dogs are known to be able to hear notes up to 35 kHz, and some authorities suggest that their limit is as high as 100 kHz.

This ultrasonic hearing – the ability to hear notes above the range of humans – enables dogs to detect the calls of small prey animals and is obviously an advantageous adaptation for a hunting animal. Man has made use of this ability in designing the 'silent' dog whistle, which is virtually inaudible to the human ear but can be detected by a dog a long distance away.

The dog is aided by determining the source of a sound by its independently moveable ears, one or both of which can be directed towards the sound, enabling it to be located much more precisely than by the human senses. Again, this is important to an animal which in the wild depends upon accurate location of its prey for its survival.

The superiority of dogs' hearing is perhaps most commonly observed in their ability to detect the sounds of particular cars – normally the owner's – and individuals' footsteps. Dogs are now being trained to act as 'hearing ears' for deaf people, listening for sounds of importance to their owners – a kettle boiling, a telephone ringing, a baby crying – and passing on the information.

HEARING

A dog has much more acute hearing than its owner (ABOVE). Although both have a similar lower limit, dogs can hear sound frequencies up to 35kHz and probably higher, whereas the upper limit for man is about 20kHz. In practical terms this means that dogs can detect sounds of a higher pitch, such as the calls of small prey animals and the note given out by the 'silent' dog whistle, which are inaudible to the human ear. The degree of sensitivity to sound does vary slightly between different dog breeds, those whose ear structure has been modified from the natural erect form losing a little in acuteness of hearing, and ageing dogs tend towards deafness just like ageing humans.

THE SIXTH SENSE

Does the dog have a sixth sense? It has been suggested that it does possess a special extrasensory perception which humans lack. Many pet-owners know that their dog will become aware of the impending return of a member of the family when he is still several streets away. A dog will often recognize sinister intent on the part of a stranger before this is apparent to another human. Many a well-trained dog will obey a command before it is given: shepherds have often reported being able to 'think' an instruction to a collie without needing to speak or signal.

There are many stories of apparently supernormal aware-ness demonstrated by dogs. There are dogs which are re-

BELOW: *The ability of a highly-trained dog working in close association with its owner to understand his or her wishes can be developed to a point where it seems like telepathy, although probably it owes much to the dog's sensory awareness and responsiveness to tiny changes in body posture. An animal such as this guide dog can achieve astonishing feats of understanding.*

ported to have been left behind when their owners moved house and to have found their way to the new home several hundred miles away. There are many well-attested accounts of normally quiet dogs suddenly breaking into a howl at what is subsequently found to be the exact time of the absent owner's death. And of course there are numerous stories of dogs 'seeing ghosts', bristling and snarling at something invisible in haunted houses, or even appearing to greet and welcome a dead master in his empty chair.

The so-called sixth sense is not something which can be identified and quantified. Certainly the dog's awareness of its surroundings and of the people and animals with whom it shares them goes beyond anything our human senses can realize. However, much of what we find astonishing in the

dog's responses can be ascribed to its highly developed senses of smell and hearing.

As we have seen, dogs can detect sounds pitched too high for the human ear; their sense of smell is superior, and it is possible that they can detect warmth through special receptors in their noses. This helps to explain some of their more unusual feats, such as detecting a bugging device from its high pitched emissions and giving early warning of a fire using their sense of smell. It may even explain how dogs have apparently predicted earthquakes by suddenly behaving in an odd way some time before the event: one theory is that dogs can smell gas seeping from the ground, and another is that they detect low frequency warning vibrations.

The dog's ability to obey a command before it is given is almost certainly due to its intense sensitivity to tiny physical signals too slight to register upon the human senses. This has been demonstrated by the so-called 'counting' dogs which have been exhibited to the public from time to time apparently carrying out mental arithmetic. The dog is asked some problem of addition, subtraction or multiplication and barks the answers – one bark for one, two barks for two, and so on.

Close study of such performances revealed that the 'counting' dog is not actually making calculations to produce the answers. Quite inadvertently, the owner gives the dog a cue as to when to stop barking. As the owner waits for each bark, his body signals his expectation, and on the final bark he relaxes slightly – movements so slight as to be unnoticed by the human audience, and even by the owner himself, but picked up by the keen perceptions of the animal.

The dog's heightened sensory awareness and its instinctive responsiveness to body postures enable it to be extremely sensitive to such signals and therefore to amaze us by apparently picking up our thoughts before we express them. Naturally, the closer the relationship between dog and owner the more likely this is to occur.

'Homing' dogs may be partially explained by the known fact that many animals have navigating powers far beyond anything human – as spectacularly demonstrated by migrating birds. However, it remains a mystery how a dog knows which way to go when it pursues a lost master to a place where it has never been before and where it has, apparently, no way of knowing that its master has gone.

The question of the sixth sense will probably remain an unanswered mystery. Whether the dog's extraordinary sensitivity to its environment and to its companions is ascribed to the acuteness of its five known senses or to the possession of an extra-sensory sixth, what is clear is that it perceives the world in a way other than that of humans, and that this finely attuned perception is one of the factors that make it such a rewarding participant in our lives.

Chapter Two

DOG BREEDS OF TODAY

THE EMERGENCE OF BREEDS

Today more than 400 breeds of dog are recognized, each with its distinguishing features of physical appearance and temperament, yet the strict classification of dog breeds as such is to a considerable extent a modern creation. As we have seen, the broad groupings of dogs – sheep-herding dogs, hounds, terriers and pet dogs – arose at an early stage in the development of the domestic dog, simply because dogs were used, and therefore bred, for different purposes. However, the division of these broad groupings into individual breeds with precisely defined characteristics is a relatively new phenomenon. Prior to this, the appearances of different dogs belonging to the same breeds were much more varied than today. For example, a hundred years ago the German Shepherd dog was not a distinct breed, but instead there were German 'sheep-dogs' of varying sizes and colours.

With the increasing complexity of human society, an increasing number of strains of dog were developed for increasingly specialized functions. The precise modern definitions and classifications of individual breeds arose with the introduction of the dog show as, for purposes of competition, breed characteristics had to be agreed and set down in the form of agreed breed standards.

The breeds recognized today include some which have changed very little over thousands of years, some which have been modified considerably from an ancestral type, and some truly modern creations.

Of existing breeds, the Greyhound and the Saluki can be traced back farthest; very similar dogs were depicted in Middle Eastern art several thousand years ago. At the other extreme, one of the most modern breeds is the Australian Terrier. This was developed by breeding between various English terriers, including the Yorkshire, Cairn and Dandie Dinmont, and the Australian Silky Terrier, another recent breed. This process began about 100 years ago, but the characteristics of the breed have been firmly fixed only for about 25 years.

In some instances, disagreement over interpretation of breed standards has led not merely to different types within a breed but even to the creation of two breeds from the original one. In the United States in 1945 the American Cocker Spaniel was given separate breed status from the English Cocker Spaniel. This new breed with its longer, thicker coat and markedly domed head shape had been selectively bred from English stock until it diverged so far from the original standard as to be recognizably a breed in its own right. The Spaniel itself is an old breed; the name was used by Chaucer in 1340, and some authorities believe the breed originated in Spain even earlier than that. At that

BELOW: *Hunting dogs were among the first man-made 'breeds'. This portrayal of the hunt by Dürer shows both sighthounds and scenthounds.*

time, the term Spaniel would have included a fairly mixed-looking group of dogs. It is only in comparatively recent times that today's dozen or so Spaniel breeds have emerged, each with a well defined appearance.

CLASSIFICATION OF BREEDS

Many attempts have been made to classify the different dog breeds into some kind of logical and coherent groupings. This is a near impossible task. Ancestral types have been intermingled over the centuries, sometimes accidentally, since breeding of dogs in the past was not so rigidly controlled, and sometimes deliberately in an attempt to combine the virtues of two or more types. The divisions between the functions of the breeds are not as clear-cut as at first appears, either. Differentiation between herding and guarding dogs, for example, is often blurred since many types were evolved to fulfil both tasks.

The earliest attempts at a classification were based upon function, like the Roman categories of house dog, shepherd dog, etc. Zoologists have sought to class dogs according to their presumed ancestry. The Austrian zoologist Konrad Lorenz, in his early writings about the domestic dog, distinguished between those breeds which he considered to be descended from the wolf (*Canis lupus*) and those which he believed to be descended from the golden jackal (*Canis aureus*). The former, which he designated the 'lupus' type, included the northern Spitz dogs such as the Husky, Chow-Chow and Elkhound; the latter, the 'aureus' type, he considered to comprise the majority of pet dogs.

More recently zoologists, including Lorenz, have come to doubt the significance of the jackal's contribution to the development of the domestic dog, and it is now generally held that the dog is derived almost entirely from wolf stock. However, the different geographical races of wolf show significant variations, and today zoologists group dogs according to the race of wolf from which they are considered to have arisen. For example, the marked differences between European Toy breeds and Oriental Toy breeds are ascribed to descent from the European wolf on the one hand and the Chinese wolf on the other. This classification, however, can only be regarded as a framework and not as definitive, because of the intermingling of dog types and strains over thousands of years.

For show purposes dogs have been fitted (sometimes in distinctly procrustean fashion) into groups based principally upon function. The difficulty of classification is reflected, however, in the fact that there is no international agreement as to how these groups should be constituted.

In the United Kingdom and in Australia there are six groupings for show purposes: working dogs, gundogs, hounds, terriers, utility (non-sporting in Australia), and toys. In the United States there are also six groups, but they are not the same: sporting, non-sporting, working, terriers, hounds and toys. On the continent of Europe, there is some variation between countries , but most frequently seven groupings are used: hounds and greyhounds, gundogs, guard and utility dogs, sheep-herding dogs, terriers, large companion dogs and small companion dogs. Hunting dogs may be subdivided into those which pursue large game and those which follow small game; sometimes gundogs are divided up to separate pointing breeds from the rest or even to distinguish the British breeds from the Continental ones.

The Spitz group of dogs is split up between at least three other groupings for show purposes in the United States and the United Kingdom. In Sweden, however, where this group is especially strong, they are shown together as a single group in their own right.

Even where there is agreement between different countries as to general groupings, some individual breeds are classified differently within the groups. Despite the variations, however, some agreement as to the broad classification of breeds is evident. For the potential dog-owner, this categorization by function provides a useful starting-point for selecting a breed, because, although many modern breeds have diverged considerably from their original roles, the inherited behavioural tendencies and temperament of any breed will derive from the requirements of those roles.

For example, certain types of sheepdog, notably the Border Collie, will show an inherent tendency to try to round up even people, and will try to do this without any special training. A breed like this has the urge to work built into it, and will not usually make a suitable pet unless alternative mental activity, such as obedience work, is provided. Similarly, while any dog can act as a watchdog, because all dogs have a natural tendency to defend their own territory, some breeds are undoubtedly much more effective in this role than others, and this often reflects their historical function. The ancestors of such breeds as the Doberman Pinscher and the Mastiff were developed as guard breeds, and the modern dogs retain a strong guarding instinct.

The sheer number of modern breeds makes a description of each well beyond the scope of this book, but this chapter aims to provide a broad introduction to the main groups and some of their more popular members.

ABOVE: *Pet dogs with no other function beyond companionship were developed in early times and have always remained popular. Here a Victorian child cuddles her pet spaniel.*

HOUNDS

Hunting, using its superior scenting powers, speed and endurance, is the way of life of the ancestral wolf, and it was natural for man to make use of this propensity when the domestic dog entered his world. Dogs were used as hunters and hunting companions from the start, and are still bred for this role after several thousand years. The first hunting dogs were probably very fast runners and would have been used to chase various types of quarry. Their descendants include several different breeds which are generally grouped together as hounds.

The varying types of hounds were evolved in response to the different hunting techniques required for each quarry animal, and today's hounds are often named directly for the animal they were bred to pursue, for example the Foxhound, Deerhound, Otterhound and Irish Wolfhound; the Saluki, the great hunting dog of the desert, is sometimes called the 'Gazelle Hound', and the little Dachshund's name means 'Badger Hound'.

The modern hound breeds may be divided into two groups, the sighthounds, which hunt by speed, and the scenthounds, which are slower and depend upon stamina to wear down their prey.

SIGHTHOUNDS

The sighthounds are characterized by a slender, long-legged build and, as their name implies, by their trait of hunting largely by sight rather than by scent. They were developed many thousands of years ago in the Far East to hunt gazelles and other swift prey, and were selected for the quality of speed, at some expense of stamina. Most of the modern breeds are fairly tall dogs, although the elegance and typically kind disposition of sighthounds led early on to the development of an ornamental miniature, now known as the Italian Greyhound and classified today amongst the toy breeds rather than amongst the hounds.

The **Greyhound** may be considered the archetypal sighthound, which has changed little in appearance throughout the centuries. It has been described as a 'racing machine', and Greyhound racing remains a popular sport today. The mechanical 'line' was devised in 1912 by O. P. Smith in the United States, and Greyhound track racing began in the 1920s. The natural quarry of the Greyhound is hare, but they have been recorded as taking a variety of game. The most famous meet is the Waterloo Cup in Britain, which first took place in 1836, and has been an annual event ever since, apart from 1917 and 1918.

The racing career of a Greyhound is short, and ex-racers are often sold as pets at three or four years old. With training to reduce the urge to pursue anything that moves, they usually adapt well to life as domestic pets. As a breed they are good-natured, affectionate and gentle with people, but the hunting instinct is strong in them and they are best muzzled when off the lead.

The **Saluki,** an ancient breed from the Far East, combines the elegant lines of the Greyhound with a soft, silky coat which gives added glamour. Salukis have been kept by the nomadic tribes of the Middle East for centuries, and are still highly esteemed. They can outrun gazelles, which rank among the fastest of the antelopes, and have also been used successfully against hares, foxes and jackals. These sleek hounds hunt predominantly by sight, although they also possess a keen sense of smell. Formerly, it was not unusual for Salukis to hunt alongside hawks; the birds harassed the quarry so that the dogs could close in on it.

The Saluki makes a faithful companion, though somewhat more aloof than the Greyhound; like that breed it retains its strong instincts to chase any potential quarry and needs to be kept under control.

One of the most glamorous of the sighthounds is the **Afghan Hound,** which adds to the typical elegance of this group of dogs a very long, flowing coat. Developed in Afghanistan by the ruling dynasties, it was bred to take a range of different quarry animals over demanding terrain, and consequently combines speed with stamina and scenting powers with keen eyesight to a degree unusual amongst sighthounds.

The beauty of this breed has attracted much attention, but it is a demanding dog to keep. The long, relatively soft coat needs constant attention to maintain its attractive appearance. The hunting and chasing instincts of the breed live on in contemporary dogs, which can lead to some training difficulties. Afghans also require plenty of space and a great deal more exercise than a Greyhound, as well as requiring a firm hand in training because of their independent natures. However, few breeds can rival them for elegance and individuality.

In the colder regions of the world, sighthounds tended to be larger and rough-coated. The **Irish Wolfhound** is famous today as a giant breed, but although Irish hounds were famous for their size and power from Roman times, the great height of today's Wolfhounds is a fairly recent development. Despite its awesome size, the Wolfhound is a gentle breed which can be a loyal and affectionate housedog – provided you have the space it requires. It is not a breed to acquire lightly. Its size dictates that it must be kept in spacious surroundings, and also means that puppies can be a particular liability until they are trained.

Russia evolved its own rough-haired giant 'Russian Wolfhound', the **Borzoi,** which has the typical elegance of

BELOW: *A typical sighthound, the Pharoah Hound is a recent introduction to Britain.*

all sighthounds and a characteristic gracefully curved back. Borzois have retained the speed which enabled them to outrun wolves, and they are still kept for coursing in some areas. They require a considerable amount of exercise to keep them fit, and must be allowed to run free off the lead. Their coats also need constant care and attention to maintain the truly aristocratic image of the breed.

The sighthound breed best adapted to modern urban life is the 'poor man's racehorse', the **Whippet.** Smaller than its cousins, it was evolved in the industrial cities of northeast England as a racer which could be kept in the house by people who could not afford the expense of maintaining and kennelling a larger dog. Many a 'rag dog' (so called because they were trained to chase a waving rag rather than an electric hare) earned its keep as a rabbiter in the fields outside the towns.

Today the Whippet, true to its origins, retains its speed, its sporting instincts and its suitability as a house dog. Elegant, gentle and affectionate, it is a great comfort-lover which will curl up like a cat in your armchair or even your bed. It does need exercise, and it also needs its hunting instincts borne in mind if you do not wish your neighbour's cat to suffer!

SCENTHOUNDS

Most of the hounds which hunt by scent are pack hunters, designed to run down their quarry by persistence rather than speed – indeed, some breeds have been evolved deliberately with very short legs to make them slow enough for humans to follow the pack on foot. They are more heavily built than the sighthounds, more vocal, and differ considerably in temperament, most of them being unsuited to life as pets because the instinct to pursue a scent outweighs all other considerations with them.

Hunting with packs has been popular for centuries, especially in France, where a great many varieties of specialist hounds have been bred. Today, the archetypal pack hound in Great Britain is the **Foxhound,** probably developed from hounds brought to England by the Normans. Foxhounds today are kept exclusively by foxhunting packs and cannot be bought as pets. Since they have been bred for centuries as pack hounds, they would not adapt to domestic life, requiring the discipline of the pack and far more exercise than a pet owner could provide. Typically of hounds, they have a powerful, unexaggerated build designed for stamina, and the pendant ears so characteristic of scenthounds.

Another ancient pack breed is the **Otterhound,** which was in existence as long ago as the fourteenth century. It is adapted to the pursuit of its quarry through a watery environment by a thick, rough, water-repellent coat and by webbed feet to assist in swimming. In Britain today otter-hunting is now illegal, and the packs have either been disbanded or turned to other quarry such as mink.

A breed in which scenting powers have been developed to the extreme is the **Bloodhound,** which derives its name not from any bloodthirstiness but from its ancient lineage – 'blood' signifying breeding. In fact it is a gentle and affectionate breed which makes a delightful pet – provided your home is large enough.

While the scenting ability and power of the Bloodhound may be advantageous in the field, these qualities can lead to problems when training a dog to become part of a household. They require considerable exercise, and are likely to be sidetracked by an interesting scent, rather than returning when called. Bloodhounds are also very sensitive, a trait that further complicates training. They make great companions despite their drawbacks and prove most affectionate, especially with children. While Bloodhounds are not as common as some breeds in the show ring, separate scenting trials are often organized, ensuring that this talent is not allowed to diminish over successive generations.

The only pack hounds which have acquired any real popularity as house pets today are the Basset and the Beagle. The **Basset Hound** is a very short-legged breed evolved to accompany hunters on foot, rather than riders. The typical hanging ears of the scenthound have become exaggerated in the Basset to fall well below the chin, framing the face like a judge's wig.

The unique and appealing appearance of the Basset, coupled with its friendly and tolerant nature, has attracted many pet-owners seeking a family dog. As a pet, it shares the faults of most pack hounds, being as stubborn as it is amiable, lacking a predisposition to obedience, and retaining its hunting instincts. It is sometimes forgotten that, despite its short legs, it is a working breed which requires plenty of exercise. Like other short-legged dogs, it suffers if allowed to become overweight – in cases of severe obesity, the penis of a male dog may actually suffer direct trauma from the ground.

In spite of these disadvantages, however, the Basset

ABOVE: *An unusual hound, the Basenji is sometimes known as the 'barkless dog'; although it does not bark normally, it produces a characteristic yodelling cry.*

LEFT: *Most famous of all scenthounds, the Bloodhound is famous for its tracking powers and is said to be one of the oldest hound breeds.*

makes a delightful pet in sensible ownership, and is very tolerant with children.

Much the same holds true of the **Beagle,** a small hound derived probably in the sixteenth century for hunting rabbits and hares and today as popular as a domestic pet as in the role of hunter. In common with other hounds, Beagles can prove disobedient having found a scent, and are gluttons for food, yet their friendly, vivacious manner provides more than adequate compensation for such tendencies. The Beagle is an active, even-tempered hound, and makes a good guard dog, possessing a surprisingly loud bark for its size.

A more exotic and very ancient hound breed is the **Basenji,** which bears a striking resemblance to dogs portrayed on Ancient Egyptian artefacts and has certainly been kept for centuries in central Africa, where it was trained to hunt in packs, driving game into waiting nets. A very distinctive breed, it is sometimes called the 'barkless dog'. Its laryngeal structure is modified, which prevents a normal bark, although it has a characteristic yodelling cry of its own.

The Basenji has an intelligent, alert appearance with pricked ears, dark eyes and a broad, wrinkled forehead. The fine, silk-like coat of the Basenji emphasizes its sleek appearance. It is reddish-brown in colour – chestnut-red being the preferred shade – with white markings on the feet, chest and tip of the tail, which curls over to one side

of the back. Basenjis are clean, adaptable and friendly, and lack the typical 'doggy' smell of most breeds. They can be obedient, but have a great deal of mischief in them, particularly when young. The only real drawback of this breed is a tendency for individuals to challenge each other when kept together, as happens naturally in wild packs of dogs. Once such skirmishes are over and an order of dominance is established, serious disputes are rare.

There is one group of scenthounds which has both a very specialized function and a very special place in modern life as a housedog, and that is the **Dachshund.** Dachshunds, unlike other hounds, were bred to follow their quarry underground, hence their small size and characteristic build, with the long body and short legs that earned them their nickname of 'sausage dogs' – hence, too, their courage and tenacity, for their task was to tackle such formidable opponents as foxes and badgers.

Dachshunds are confident, sporting little dogs with a great deal of personality which has won them their popularity as companion dogs rather than as hunters. They are loyal and affectionate, make good watchdogs with a bark which sounds like that of a bigger dog, and make delightful if somewhat self-willed family pets. Like that other short-legged breed the Basset, the Dachshund must not be allowed to become overweight, and the long back can be prone to disc problems, but their non-athletic build will not prevent them from enjoying as much exercise as their owner wishes to give them.

The original smooth-haired form has given rise to two sizes of Dachshund, standard and miniature, and to two further coat types, long-haired and wire-haired, giving rise to six varieties of Dachshund in all. All have the delightful Dachshund character, with slight differences in temperament arising from the fact that the variations on the original smooth-haired standard were achieved by outcrossing to different breeds. The long-haired Dachshund's dash of spaniel ancestry is said to make it a little shyer than the other varieties, while the terrier contribution to the wire-haired form may account for its slightly greater obstinacy.

GUNDOGS

While some dogs have been bred and trained to catch and kill prey, others have been developed to assist with hunting, rather than to do the killing themselves. Their origins can be traced back about 2500 years to a report by the Greek historian, Xenophon. He described dogs that, instead of chasing prey on sight, would stand completely still, looking at the animal or bird, quivering with excitement. This trait was originally exploited by falconers.

The breeding of dogs of this kind was stimulated considerably by the invention of the gun. Mainly using their sense of smell, the dog, or dogs, would search out the game, and indicate its position by standing still and pointing its head in the appropriate direction. On command the dog would then move forward to flush and retrieve the prey.

In Great Britain, and also in the United States, the trend in gundog development was to create specialists, with distinct types of dog for locating and marking game, flushing it, and retrieving. In Europe, the interest was in developing more all-rounder breeds with a single dog performing all the functions, hunting, marking and retrieving. These multi-purpose gundogs, scorned at first by aficionados of the specialist groups, are gaining in popularity today, but the specialist spaniels, pointers, setters and retrievers continue to have their followers.

SPANIELS

Spaniels, as a group, date back to at least 1368. 'Spanyells', as they were known, took their name from *espaignol*, 'Spanish dog', and are believed to have developed from the ancient sporting breeds of Spain. The original spaniels were quite an assortment of types, used for flushing out game for the human hunters. These were subsequently divided into two distinct groups: water spaniels and land spaniels. A further sub-division of the latter group occurred, with the smallest breeds becoming known as 'toys'. The rather bigger, working spaniels were separated into two categories, on the basis of the working styles: the 'starters' or 'springers' flushed out game for purposes of falconry, while 'cockers' were evolved especially to hunt woodcock.

Localized breeding gave rise to different types, and gradually the modern breeds began to emerge. The typical spaniel is a medium-sized dog with a silky coat and characteristic long feathered ears; although they are not unpopular as pets, many spaniel breeds remain essentially working breeds which are not ideally suited to urban life.

In Wales and southwest England the small 'cocker' evolved into the modern **Cocker Spaniel,** which by the 1930s had become the most popular breed in England. The 'merry Cocker' remains outstanding at flushing out game and also makes a good all-purpose gundog. Its affectionate and cheerful temperament also make it a good companion

ABOVE: *The 'Merry Cocker' has long been one of the most popular Spaniel breeds.*

LEFT: *Welsh Springers are versatile workers, well able to adapt to an extensive climate range, and prove good water dogs as well as suitable retrievers on land.*

RIGHT: *Another of the rarer spaniels is the Sussex, named for the county where it was developed. The unusual golden-liver colouring is characteristic of the breed.*

dog and family pet. As often happens with the more attractive working breeds, the exhibition type and the working type have to some extent parted company; indeed, the show-ring's emphasis upon looks has in the United States created a distinct breed in the American Cocker Spaniel, a dome-headed, trailing-coated dog which makes little pretence at being a hunter.

The taller, larger forms of early spaniel were named 'springers' from their function of 'springing' or flushing the quarry from its hiding-place, and these gave rise to the modern **English Springer Spaniel.** The Duke of Norfolk was one of the first to keep a kennel of Springers, and, as a result, these dogs were known as Norfolk Spaniels for a period.

The Springer was only recognized as a distinct breed in 1902. Like the Cocker, it has since diversified into a working and an exhibition type. Those kept for working purposes are smaller and stockier than their show counterparts, and the head is not as fully developed. Springers remain excellent companions in the field; they have a wider range than similar breeds, and prove very good retrievers, ready to enter water if necessary. As a pet, the Springer is intelligent, loyal and friendly, although it requires more exercise than some owners realize.

The **Welsh Springer** is closely related to the English breed, but distinguished by its smaller size, shorter and less heavily feathered ears, and its characteristic rich red and white colouring. It is a versatile working dog with great stamina, probably better suited to the working life than to the less demanding existence of a house pet.

Not unlike the Welsh Springer in appearance is the **Brittany Spaniel,** another versatile worker which, despite a long history in France, was only introduced to Great Britain in recent years.

Other land spaniel breeds tend to be less popular today. These include the **Clumber,** a massive breed with an unusual lemon and white coloration; it is a slow but steady worker with good scenting powers. The **Field Spaniel** derived from black Cockers, but about the turn of the century a vogue developed in this breed for an impractically long-bodied and short-legged type, of little use in the field. Attempts have since been made to breed back to the original type, and the modern Field Spaniel is an excellent worker, although still small in numbers. The **Sussex Spaniel** is another breed that has never gained any great popularity. It is a massive and strongly built dog with a distinctive golden-liver colouring. A slow but steady and tireless worker, it is essentially a working breed rather than a suitable pet.

The chief representative of the water spaniel breeds today is the **Irish Water Spaniel.** It is known that dogs something of this type were being bred in Ireland as long ago as the seventh century AD, but the breed in its present form probably developed more recently from several spaniel breeds.

The Irish Water Spaniel differs from the land spaniels in its curly coat and unusual colouring, a rich dark liver with a purplish bloom. It is an all-rounder gundog, particularly suited for wildfowling, with its cold- and water-resistant coat. It also makes a loyal, intelligent and fun-loving companion dog, provided enough exercise is given.

A not dissimilar breed is the **American Water Spaniel,** but this variety remains scarce outside the United States.

The miniature spaniels evolved as companion rather than working breeds and are classified as Toys.

POINTERS AND SETTERS

ABOVE: *The Pointer today is still clearly a working dog, with puppies showing pointing instincts often by the age of two months. Type has not been separated from working ability in these dogs, and they also do well in the show ring, adopting the frozen stance that is a typical feature of their work in the field.*

The Pointer and Setter breeds were evolved to locate game and mark its position for the human hunter, rather than to pursue it themselves. The sense of smell, and the ancestral wolf's instinct to freeze upon marking prey before proceeding to the hunt, were highly developed through intensive breeding, while actual prey-taking skills were not required.

These breeds were originally evolved to work with a falconer, or in conjunction with Greyhounds, but with the development of the gun they came into their own as an adjunct to the shooting man. They work in front of the guns to locate game and pinpoint its direction.

The **Pointer** takes its name from the fact that it marks the position of game by literally pointing to it with its whole body – 'coming to the point' – in a characteristic rigid position, with the body and tail forming a straight line and one fore-foot typically raised towards the scent.

The earliest Pointers evolved somewhere in the seventeenth century as a breed to locate hares for coursing Greyhounds. By the start of the nineteenth century, Pointers had become valued companions for sportsmen and were trained to find and indicate the position of the game until a gun could be fired. Working in pairs to ensure a close fix

ABOVE: *The elegance and rich mahogany colouring of the Irish Setter have made it a favourite as a family companion, although its high spirits and energy can make it scatty and uncontrollable if deprived of adequate exercise.*

on the location of the quarry, they took over the role of the beaters who had been such a feature of hunting on large country estates.

The modern Pointer is still very much a working dog, a powerful animal with plenty of energy and pointing instincts so strong that baby puppies will point at a bumble bee. Type has not been separated from working ability, and these dogs also do well in the show ring. Although they are responsive and affectionate, the urge to work is very strong in them and they are not well adapted to the life of a household pet.

Setters indicate the presence of game in a different fashion. As long ago as the sixteenth century, there were dogs that located game by means of a combination of scent and sight and then sat, waiting for the next command. These became known as setting (sitting) dogs, and later simply as setters. Some early engravings show considerable similarities between these setters and spaniels, but the types gradually diverged in their specialist directions, and today we have several distinct setter breeds. The English and Irish Setters are often purchased as pets, but the intending buyer should bear in mind their need for more exercise than the average pet is likely to receive.

The **English Setter** is a handsome dog of characteristically flecked or mottled colour known as 'blue belton', 'orange belton' or 'tricolour'. The development of the modern breed can be traced back to 1825. Friendly and quiet by nature, English Setters make good companions, provided that adequate exercise can be given.

The **Irish Setter** is a most glamorous dog whose spirited personality and rich horse-chestnut red colouring have made it the most popular of setter breeds. It first appeared in the nineteenth century, probably developed from spaniels, pointers and other setters. Despite its other name of 'Red Setter', the early dogs were more often red and white than solid red, and today Red-and-White Setters are emerging again as a distinct variety in their own right.

The modern Irish Setter is perhaps more popular as a show dog and pet than as a worker. It is not the easiest gundog breed to train, with an extrovert temperament that can appear as wayward and flighty, but with proper training these dogs can become obedient and trustworthy companions. As pets, they have the assets of beauty and personality, but the disadvantage of the working breeds' need for considerable exercise.

The less well-known **Gordon Setter** is as handsome in its own way, with its heavier build and gleaming black and tan colouring. Setters of this type were first kept during the late eighteenth century by the 4th Duke of Gordon. The early dogs were often tricoloured, despite being known as 'Black and Tan Setters', and were fairly heavily built; crosses with Irish Setters were undertaken to contribute a sleeker outline.

The Gordon Setter is a steady, reliable and tireless worker, and no clear division has arisen between working and show strains. A slow developer, it can be trained to a high standard and is the ideal companion for the solitary sportsman; it is less well suited for pet life.

RETRIEVERS

The retrieving breeds, as their name informs us, were developed to retrieve the game once it was killed by their masters. Speed was not required, but keen scenting powers and a high degree of trainability were essential. These dogs had to learn to sit patiently until the command was given to go and fetch the quarry, and to retrieve promptly to hand rather than holding on to the game; they needed a steady, friendly temperament that would enable them to work for whoever held the gun rather than a single owner, and a soft mouth to enable them to carry the game without damaging it.

Today, retrievers still perform the job they were designed for, but their steadiness and responsiveness have made them popular pets as well as a favoured type for guide dog training, while their highly developed scenting abilities have led to their employment by the police and army as 'sniffer dogs' to locate illegal drugs and explosives. Like the setters, they should only be kept by those with the time and energy to give them adequate exercise.

The ever-popular **Golden Retriever** was supposed to have developed from a troop of performing dogs from a Russian circus, but almost certainly evolved from earlier gundogs including water spaniels and retrievers. The breed rapidly gained favour in England at the end of the nineteenth century. Its continuing popularity is hardly surprising, given its handsome appearance with its lustrous golden coat, its natural intelligence and its loyal, gentle and companionable behaviour. As a family dog this breed is ideal, easily trained and trustworthy with children, although it does require at least two hours' walking a day to do it full justice.

Equally popular is the **Labrador Retriever,** evolved in Newfoundland as a wildfowlers' dog and brought to Britain at the beginning of the nineteenth century. The first

LEFT: *The Flat-coated Retriever was once the most popular gundog breed, but is less fashionable today despite its good working qualities.*

RIGHT: *The Curly-coated Retriever was known as early as 1860 and probably owes its characteristic curls to Water Spaniel blood.*

ABOVE: *The German Wire-haired Pointer resembles its short-haired cousin in all but coat, although it may have a slightly more aggressive temperament.*

Labradors were black, but later yellow became increasingly common, and chocolates are also bred today. Like the Golden, this breed combines outstanding working abilities with the desired qualities of a companion dog. Sensible, gentle and friendly, it makes an ideal companion for children and all-round family dog. Pet Labradors are particularly prone to obesity if under-exercised.

Also originating from Newfoundland is the less fashionable **Flat-coated Retriever,** bred in black or liver. These steady, intelligent dogs perform well both as show dogs and in the field, where they earned their title of 'the gamekeepers' dog', and, like other retrievers, are well suited for the role of family dog, provided their exercise requirements can be met.

Markedly less common is the **Curly-coated Retriever,** whose tightly curled coat probably derives from the old English Water Spaniel, perhaps with contributions from the Irish Water Spaniel and Poodle. This breed has never attracted the same following as the other retrievers; it has a tendency to stubbornness and a reputation for being relatively hard-mouthed when retrieving game. It is a breed which needs to work, and is less well adapted to pet life than some of its cousins.

The **Chesapeake Bay Retriever** is another of the less frequently encountered retrievers. Very much a worker, it takes its name from Chesapeake Bay where it is an invaluable wildfowlers' dog, effectively insulated against freezing waters by its thick undercoat and oily topcoat. Its characteristic brownish colour, varying from darkish brown to dead-grass, becomes paler during the summer. Highly intelligent and steady, this breed has been successfully trained as a guide dog for the blind, but it is too much the worker to be content with a purely pet existence.

MULTI-PURPOSE GUNDOGS

The less specialized gundog breeds evolved on the Continent are today growing in popularity in Great Britain and the United States, where they are known as hunt-point-and-retrieve (HPR) dogs. These all-rounder dogs will perform all the tasks performed by the other gundog breeds and are increasingly favoured by shooting men who wish to work with a single animal.

Probably the best known is the **Weimaraner,** an elegant dog with a particularly striking combination of grey coat and light eyes which have earned it the nickname of the 'grey ghost'. This German breed is of relatively recent origin, first produced during the nineteenth century from a combination of native breeds. Used at first for large quarry such as wolves and wildcats, they developed into a more versatile breed when such game became scarce. They were introduced to Britain during the 1950s.

Weimaraners are now highly valued as hunting dogs which can happily spend the rest of their time in domestic surroundings. Intelligent and responsive, they are also assertive animals which require experienced training. They show stronger guarding instincts than most gundog breeds, which must not be allowed to get out of hand.

The **German Short-haired Pointer** is regarded by some authorities as the most versatile gundog of all, working as both pointer and retriever, on land and in the water. This breed is par excellence a working dog, robust, intelligent and eager. It is an all-weather dog, tough and hardy as well as powerful and tenacious. Given the work to do, it makes an ideal companion for the shooting man; denied work and cooped up in a house, its energy and drive prove unsuitable for a household pet.

ABOVE: *The distinctively coloured 'grey ghost', the Weimaraner, was developed in the nineteenth century in Germany and first introduced to Great Britain in the 1950s. Since then it has become deservedly popular not only as a gundog but as a companion, and also performs well in competitive obedience.*

Hungary has produced another versatile gundog in the **Vizsla,** a handsome and aristocratic breed with a distinctive russet gold coat. Fast, clever and energetic, it is becoming increasingly popular as a worker but is unsuited to a sedentary lifestyle.

Another breed which is developing a following outside its native land is the **Large Munsterlander,** which in appearance falls midway between the setters and the retrievers. It is always black and white in colour. Like other gundogs, it is easily trained, loyal and affectionate; however, it is somewhat too energetic for a purely domestic existence.

TERRIERS

The terriers, the third group of hunting dogs, derive their name from the Latin *terra* ('earth') because they were bred to pursue their quarry under the ground. They are typically small, active and aggressive. Of the many breeds existing today, the majority evolved in Britain, where they have been used for hundreds of years for killing vermin, both unsupported and in conjunction with packs of hounds.

Different regions developed terriers to suit their own terrain and local quarry, and the terrier breeds range from the small, short-legged breeds which are underground specialists and the taller, long-legged breeds which will also hunt well above ground. In addition to these typical terriers there are also two giant breeds, as well as the bull breeds developed for dog fighting.

Terriers have become popular in the show ring, the characteristic fiery temperament lending itself well to showing themselves off in competition. Most have coats which require stripping and/or clipping to present a smart appearance, and for many breeds a great deal of time and skill is required to present a dog in show coat. As with other working dogs, there has been some divergence between working and show strains.

Many of the Terriers are popular as pet dogs, their small size and bold characters suiting them well for this role. The typical terrier is a bright, bustling little dog which will put the same energy into participating in family activities as into its great passion, hunting, and its natural alertness makes it a good watchdog. Most terriers will adapt well to town life provided their abundant vitality is satisfied – not necessarily by the long walks required to keep larger breeds fit; plenty of romping in the garden will augment shorter town walks. More aggressive than the hound and gundog breeds, terriers may be quarrelsome and some are deadly fighters.

Amongst the short-legged, low to the ground breeds evolved to go to earth, the **West Highland White** is one of the most popular among pet owners, an attractive, rough-coated little dog with a bright, whiskery face. It is one of the Scottish breeds originally grouped together as 'Small Highland Working Terriers' and was bred to bolt foxes. The pure white coat requires daily grooming as well as stripping twice a year. A good house dog, the 'Westie' enjoys family life and is responsive to training.

The **Cairn** is another Highland breed which has achieved popularity with pet owners. It takes its name from the cairns or rock piles that its quarry, typically the fox, uses for a hiding place. Its shaggy, weather-resistant coat may be red, sandy, grey, brindled or nearly black and is presented in as 'natural' a fashion as possible, show dogs being smartened up without appearing styled. An intelligent and affectionate little dog, it makes a good family companion.

The **Scottish Terrier** is equally attractive and sporting but has a less outgoing temperament; it is sometimes described as dour, having a great loyalty to its owners but a mistrust of strangers which makes it a good guard dog. A heavily-built thickset dog, it has a distinctively long, square-muzzled head. It is usually black, but brindle and wheaten are also recognized.

The **Dandie Dinmont** is distinguished as the only dog breed to take its name from fiction, being named after a character in Sir Walter Scott's novel *Guy Mannering*. This distinctive breed, not unlike a Dachshund in shape, has an unusual longish coat and silky topknot; the only recognized colours are pepper – ranging from bluish black to silvery grey – and mustard – from reddish brown to pale fawn. Like the Scottie, this breed tends to be a 'one-man' dog.

The **Skye Terrier** is one of the oldest breeds, with an unusually long and glamorous coat for a terrier; the thick undercoat and long, harsh top coat evolved to give protection against dense undergrowth when pursuing quarry. Despite its beautiful appearance this is a real terrier, eager to hunt and something of a fighter, as well as a good house dog which distrusts strangers.

Amongst the longer-legged terrier breeds, the **Smooth and Wire Fox Terriers** are perhaps the best known. The stylish dogs derive from the old English Terriers which were used to hunt fox and badger. Today Fox Terriers still perform their original function but are also elegant show dogs and lively, good-natured companions, differing only in coat.

Regional variations on the long-legged terrier type include the smart black-and-tan **Lakeland Terrier,** evolved in the Lake District to control foxes, and the **Welsh Terrier,** another black-and-tan breed which was used to hunt a variety of game including otters. The **Border Terrier** is the smallest of the working terriers, a breed of abundant

vitality which can keep up with a horse; its characteristic 'otter' head has powerful jaws to tackle fox and badger. Like other terriers, these breeds make good if energetic pets as well as continuing to work as vermin controllers.

The **Irish Terrier** is another handsome breed which has all the terrier virtues plus the typical terrier aggressive nature; if not checked, it can be a real fighter. This is a distinctive looking breed, stylish, wiry and graceful, with a characteristic red, yellow-red or wheaten colouring. It makes a good companion, particularly trustworthy with children as well as being an alert guard and eager ratter. Irish Terriers were employed as messenger dogs in World War I.

Another distinctive breed is the **Bedlington,** a dog which combines the appearance of a woolly lamb with typical terrier fire and courage. The breed was created from the blend of a northern working terrier strain with the Whippet

ABOVE: *The Smooth Fox Terrier's long, lean head was developed for powerful jaws which enabled it to tackle the fox.*

LEFT: *Terrier owners display their animals, a Border on the left and a Lakeland on the right, at a local country show.*

FAR LEFT, TOP: *The Skye Terrier has a long, flowing coat which hangs profusely over the face and ears. Highly popular in the last century, it is now one of the less common terriers.*

FAR LEFT, BELOW: *The Norfolk Terrier, one of the smallest terrier breeds and a drop-eared version of the prick-eared Norwich, is a lively little dog once known as the 'Cambridge Terrier' from its popularity with Cambridge students.*

The Lakeland Terrier is a descendant of the old English Black-and-Tan Terrier. It was developed in the English Lake District, where the high sheep population made fox control vital, especially at lambing time, and these courageous little dogs were kept, along with packs of hounds, for this purpose.

to give speed, and with the Dandie Dinmont to give the thick, linty coat. Like other terriers, the Bedlington makes a good family dog, responsive to training and trustworthy with children, although despite its almost fragile appearance it can be a terrible fighter.

No account of terriers would be complete without mentioning the **Jack Russell,** although this variety is not recognized as a breed by the Kennel Club because of the wide divergence of types. The Jack Russell is a working dog, developed to bolt foxes, which has also become very popular as a pet. Typically white with coloured patches, like the Fox Terrier, it may be long-legged or short-legged, smooth or rough-coated, depending on the demands of the local hunting terrain.

Then there are the two giant terriers, atypical of their group in size, being too big to go to earth, yet retaining all the terrier fire and energy. The largest of the terriers, the **Airedale,** is known as 'King of the Terriers'. This tall handsome dog evolved in Yorkshire, with Otterhound blood probably contributing to its size. Its size and courage make it an ideal guard, and it has been used by the police and army, as well as being kept to hunt big game in North America, parts of Africa and India. The Airedale makes a faithful guard and house dog.

The other giant breed, the **Kerry Blue,** evolved in County Kerry, Ireland, and like the Airedale makes a good companion and alert guard, while it has also been employed as a gundog and even herder. The coat is soft and wavy, tending to grow long and requiring skilful presentation; puppies are born black, gradually lightening to the deep blue shade that characterizes the breed.

ABOVE AND FAR LEFT: *The majority of terrier breeds were developed in Britain. The Jack Russell (***ABOVE***) is a popular English type, while Scotland produced several breeds such as the Dandie Dinmont (***FAR LEFT TOP***) and Irish breeds include the giant Kerry Blue (***FAR LEFT CENTRE***). However, the European Continent has created a few terriers of its own, such as the German Hunting Terrier (Deutscher Jagdterrier) (***FAR LEFT BELOW***), developed in Bavaria during the present century.*

ABOVE: *Despite its origins as a fighting dog, the modern Bull Terrier makes a friendly and jaunty companion, although it may retain its aggression towards other dogs.*

Finally there are the bull breeds. These were created as fighters in the days when dog fighting, badger baiting, and rat killing were popular sports upon which big money depended. The old Bulldog, with its fighting instinct and terrible tenacity, was crossed with terriers to bring in the typical terrier fire and agility, producing the fighting machine known as the Bull-and-Terrier. From this unpromising beginning evolved the modern **Bull Terrier** and **Staffordshire Bull Terrier,** breeds which today retain the impressive power of the old fighters but whose temperament has been ameliorated by selective breeding to create dogs which are suitable for domestic life and for the show ring.

The 'Staffie' more closely resembles its Bull-and-Terrier ancestors in appearance, a burly, powerful animal, while the Bull Terrier is the result of a deliberate programme by a Birmingham dog dealer called James Hinks to refine the fighting dog for the show ring without losing its gladiatorial qualities. His creation had a mixed reception at first, until the success of the new breed was proved by his white bitch Puss, who on one day won a fight against one of the old Bull-and-Terriers and was sufficiently unscathed to win an award at a dog show the very next day.

Both breeds are strongly built and muscular, with massive jaws; the more elegant Bull Terrier is characterized by its distinctive egg-shaped head with a Roman profile. Both make loyal and affectionate companions, trustworthy with people and fearless guards although always needing to be watched with other dogs. The fighting blood still slumbers beneath the surface and if they meet with aggression they are likely to finish the fight.

ABOVE: *The Bedlington Terrier takes its origins back to 1820, when Joseph Ainsley took the old Rothbury Terrier and, by outcrossing to Whippets and Dandie Dinmonts, produced a very distinctive breed whose oddly delicate appearance belies the character of a real working terrier.*

The Border Collie is the supreme sheepdog today all over the world.

WORKING DOGS

The Working Group is made up of dogs developed to work for a man in a non-sporting capacity and comprises the herding, guarding and draught breeds. These dogs were evolved to work in close cooperation with their owners, and in consequence in many cases are characterized by a high degree of intelligence and responsiveness which have made them popular today as companion dogs.

HERDING DOGS

One of the first uses to which man put the dog was the herding, driving and protection of domestic livestock. A single aspect of the natural hunting drive of the ancestral wolf, the instinct to drive groups of prey animals towards other members of the pack, formed the basis for the creation by selective breeding of a variety of specialist herding breeds, which today make up the largest part of the Working Group.

The different kinds of livestock they were required to work, and varying terrains, led to a wide range of regional types. Today there are many breeds across the world whose names reflect their former, and in some cases current, function: the Old English Sheepdog, the German Shepherd Dog, the Australian Cattle Dog, the Yugoslavian Herder and many others. In many areas the herding dog's duties included the defence of livestock against predators such as wolves, and consequently the typical herder is a large animal with a strong guarding instinct; often this trait was utilized to develop dual-purpose herding and guarding breeds.

Amongst livestock, sheep are far from the easiest animals to manage, and some highly specialized sheepdog breeds were evolved. For this work man needed dogs with intelligence and initiative, which were forceful enough to dominate the flock, yet responsive enough to be under the shepherd's absolute control. They had to have immense stamina to work all day, often in adverse weather conditions which required weather-resistant coats.

The success with which man developed the type of dog he needed is reflected in the fact that even in this mechanized age working sheepdogs are still employed all over the world, and are invaluable in countries such as Australia where sheep rearing is a major industry. In addition, competitive obedience work is dominated by sheepdog breeds, notably the Border Collie and German Shepherd Dog.

The supreme sheepdog today is the **Border Collie,** whose intelligence and working capacity have been acknowledged for centuries although the breed has only recently been recognized by the Kennel Club. The natural herding instinct in this dog is coupled with a special characteristic, the hypnotic eye with which it controls sheep by staring directly at them. Unparalleled as a working sheep-

ABOVE: *The characteristics which make a good herding dog also produced an unparalleled companion dog in the German Shepherd Dog, which has become well-known as a faithful and intelligent guard, often used by the police and armed forces.*

RIGHT: *One of the more unusual herding breeds, the Anatolian Karabash is a mastiff type developed centuries ago in Turkey and today becoming increasingly popular in Great Britain and the United States.*

BELOW: *The Bouvier de Flandres was originally developed in northern France and southwest Flanders, where it acted as a cattle dog.*

ABOVE: *The Briard is an old working breed from France, kept initially to guard sheep against wolves and other predators but gradually taking on the role of herder.*

LEFT: *The ancestors of the Hungarian Puli were brought by the Magyars into the country now known as Hungary about a millennium ago. This small black sheepdog has an unusual corded coat.*

dog and in the obedience ring, the Border Collie has too strong a drive to work and too much energy to be contented with a purely pet existence.

More dramatically handsome, its cousin the **Rough Collie** – the 'Lassie' collie – with its fine head, flowing coat and variety of colours is rarely worked today but has been adopted by exhibitors and pet owners. The glorious coat features a heavy mane and dense feathering on legs and tail; the recognized colours are sable and white (the sable ranging from gold to mahogany), tricolour and blue merle.

There is also a less fashionable **Smooth Collie,** as well as a charming miniature version, the **Shetland Sheepdog,** which is highly popular as a pet as well as being increasingly successful today in obedience trials.

Europe has produced a wide range of sheepdogs including the Beauceron, Briard and Belgian Shepherd Dog, but its most famous product is the **German Shepherd Dog (Alsatian).** This breed as we know it today was created deliberately from a variety of German sheepdog types to give a tough working dog of outstanding intelligence, and now ranks among the most popular dogs of the world. Its abilities have been utilized as military and police dog, guide dog for the blind, and one of the top breeds in obedience

work, as well as making it a favourite guard and pet.

A well-bred and properly trained German Shepherd is a wonderful companion, obedient, loyal and capable of considerable initiative. As with all highly popular breeds, it has suffered from over-production, with some breeders churning out money-making puppies without care for temperament and physical soundness, so it is essential to purchase stock only from a responsible breeder. The innate sensitivity and responsiveness of the breed is somewhat over-developed in some strains bred for competitive obedience, which may be better avoided by the pet owner seeking a dog easily lived with.

Two more unusual herding breeds are the **Komondor** and **Puli** from Hungary, in which the weatherproof coat of the typical sheepdog is seen in an extreme form. Both these breeds have corded coats which mat into long woolly tassels. The Puli is the smallest of the Magyar sheep-herding breeds; it is squarely-built and usually black. Despite its eccentric appearance it is intelligent and performs well in obedience trials. The Komondor is a larger breed, always white, which was developed as dual herder and guard dog. Highly intelligent, it requires firm training to keep the guarding instinct under control.

ABOVE: *Strong, courageous and good at tracking, the St Bernard has been credited with the rescue of many people who have been caught out in snow storms. Dogs of this type were kept at the Hospice of St Bernard in the Swiss Alps as long ago as the seventeenth century.*

Herding cattle required a different type of dog. The old drovers' dogs used to drive stock to market, such as the Smithfield Collie, have largely disappeared in these days of mechanized transport, although we have a descendant of them in the **Old English Sheepdog.** Affectionately known as the Bobtail, this breed has an unusual bear-like build and lumbering gait. Today the fashions of the show ring have exaggerated the original shaggy coat into an attractive but hardly practical profusion of hair which is often the downfall of pet specimens as owners find themselves unable or unwilling to provide the hours of care required. For those who are prepared to maintain that coat, this is a dog with delightful temperament which is good with children as well as an effective guard.

In Europe the droving breeds gave rise to the **Rottweiler,** a massive and immensely powerful breed which was also used for boar hunting and is popular today as a guard dog. This is a solidly built dog with a broad, impressive head; it is always black-and-tan. Originally the breed was of somewhat dubious temperament, but this has been largely overcome and the modern Rottweiler makes a devoted and loyal companion.

Australia developed its own cattle-herding breed in the **Australian Cattle Dog,** evolved from a blend of Smithfield Collies, Dingos and Smooth Collies. These are relatively small dogs, mottled in appearance, and possessed of great stamina and courage. They are still kept for working

FAR RIGHT TOP: *The two breeds of Corgi, Pembroke and Cardigan, are named after the old counties of Wales where they were first bred. The Pembroke, shown here, is believed to be the older breed, and may date back as far as the twelfth century; it owes its present popularity to its adoption by the British Royal Family.*

ABOVE: *One of the most instantly recognizable breeds, the Great Dane is elegant and graceful, despite its enormous size.*

purposes and are also valued as guard dogs.

Some smaller breeds were also developed to work cattle, the best-known today being the **Pembroke** and **Cardigan Corgis.** These drove cattle by 'heeling', darting in quickly to nip the legs of recalcitrant animals; records of their use date back to 1000 years ago. Today they have become pets rather than workers but retain the tough, hardy natures of their working ancestors. Both Corgis are short-legged and foxy-headed, the outstanding difference being the tail, short in the Pembroke but a long, fox-like brush in the Cardigan, and the colour, the Cardigan having a much wider range than the Pembroke, which is usually red. The Pembroke is by far the more popular breed, probably because of its adoption by the British Royal Family. Both breeds are intelligent, friendly and naturally responsive to training, and make appealing pets as well as tireless workers and alert watchdogs.

GUARD DOGS

While the larger herding breeds often doubled as guards, man also created specialist guard dogs, large, powerful and often highly aggressive animals in which the natural instinct to defend the pack and the territory was highly developed. Such dogs, often of the Mastiff type, were used from early times as war dogs as well as to guard the home.

The term 'mastiff' applies to a group of dogs, apart from the specific **Mastiff** breed. Dogs of this type were bred thousands of years ago: they are depicted on Egyptian monuments of 3000 BC and were certainly known in Britain at the time of the Roman invasion, where Julius Caesar wrote of their courage. They were employed in Rome to fight in the arena, and in medieval times accompanied their knightly masters into battle. Today these majestic giants are simply too big for the average home, but for owners with adequate space, few dogs prove more faithful and gentle, and they certainly deter unwelcome visitors.

Another ancient guard breed, descended from mastiff stock, is the **Great Dane,** whose ancestry may go right back to the Molossus of Roman times. The modern Dane was developed by German breeders to hunt wild boar. It combines great size with more elegance than the typical mastiff. Like most giant breeds it is too big (and too expensive to feed) for most pet owners; for those with the space this magnificent dog proves an affectionate and kindly companion as well as an effective guard.

One of the most famous breeds to arise from early mastiff stock is the **St Bernard,** the legendary mountain rescue breed whose ancestors probably included the Alpine Mastiff or similar guard dogs. This striking dog with its massive head and bold colouring is one of the heaviest breeds in the world. Its dramatic appearance is coupled with a steady temperament, making it a handsome companion. As with

all giant breeds, however, it requires plenty of space and is expensive to feed; it also requires plenty of correct exercise to prevent unsoundness, particularly in the hindquarters. Another drawback is its persistent drooling, and show dogs often have their chests protected by bibs.

The **Bullmastiff** is a more recent development from the Mastiff, created in the nineteenth century as a gamekeeper's dog. Gamekeeping at that time, policing large country estates, was a dangerous occupation; the punitive game laws of the time meant that poachers were fighting for their lives, and gamekeepers were frequently attacked and even killed. They required a dog which would be an effective deterrent, and so the Mastiff was crossed with bull breeds to combine great size with aggression and powerful jaws. The modern Bullmastiff remains a superb guard but

RIGHT: *The Tosa Fighting Dog was bred from mastiff stock in Japan during the latter half of the last century; scarce outside Japan, it is a big, powerful and aggressive animal.*

RIGHT: *The Spanish Mastiff is a large, powerful guard breed which has also been kept for hunting big game and for fighting.*

is far less ferocious than its ancestors, with a reliable temperament.

The **Boxer** is another nineteenth century creation of mastiff descent, and today is one of the most popular breeds worldwide. Active and lively, Boxers respond well to training and were amongst the first breeds used for police work. Character is still regarded as an important feature, and they are typically loyal, intelligent and courageous. They are not generally aggressive, and prove to be good with children, although they may be too boisterous for a home with young toddlers.

In 1870, a German tax inspector called Louis Doberman set out to produce a new breed of guard dog, and his creation the **Doberman** bears his name today. Rottweilers and German Pinschers formed the foundation of the breed, with the later introduction of German Shepherd Dogs and Black-and-Tan Terriers to add refinement. The result was a smart, stylish and highly functional animal which has been

The Samoyed takes its name from the Samoyed Indians, nomads who herded reindeer in northwestern Siberia. Their dogs both guarded and controlled the movements of the flocks, and were used for transport, working in teams and pulling sleighs.

BELOW: *The sled dogs of the north enabled man to live in the hostile environment of the snow-covered northern regions, serving not only as transport but as hunters and guards.*

used successfully for many years as a guard dog and also as an army and police dog. Properly trained, the Doberman is a superb working dog; however, its physical power is coupled with a dominant temperament, and without proper control it may be a liability.

DRAUGHT DOGS

Although the comparatively small size of dogs limited their use as draught animals, it also made them cheaper for this purpose than horses, and some breeds were used to haul small carts in European countries such as Switzerland and the Netherlands. In the frozen north sled dogs were vital for transport.

The use of dogs to pull carts is now banned in most countries, but a number of draught breeds survive, including the **Bernese Mountain Dog,** which also worked as a drover and guard. An ancient Swiss breed, it is thought to

have been introduced by the Romans. This is a large and handsome breed with striking black, tan and white colouring and a long, silky coat, which makes a well-mannered and beautiful companion for those with adequate space.

The draught breeds par excellence are the sled dogs of the north, which include the Alaskan Malamute, the Eskimo Dog, the Siberian Husky and the Samoyed. They are still used both for work and for competitive racing, as well as appearing today with increasing frequency in the show ring. Apart from the Samoyed, which today has become more of a pet and show dog than a worker, their tremendous power and energy generally require a working rather than a pet existence.

The **Samoyed** was developed by the nomad Samoyed tribe in northwestern Siberia as a dual purpose herd and draught breed. Samoyeds have been used as sled dogs on expeditions to both poles, including Roald Amundsen's successful journey to the South Pole in 1911. It is a glamorous breed, with a dense white coat with a lustre reminiscent of glistening snow; friendly, intelligent and active, it makes a lively pet.

The **Eskimo Dog,** first bred in Greenland, is the oldest breed known in the Arctic region and was named 'Kingmik' by the Innuits, an Eskimo tribe of northern Canada. These dogs were an integral part of the lives of the tribe, pulling sleighs, acting as guard dogs and hunting; puppies were kept as pets around the settlement. Eskimo Dogs were able to survive on meagre rations and, as the early explorers soon discovered, they were the only means of transport in the region. Today they are not often needed for transportation, but are still raced and have become more widely known.

Another breed, the **Malamute,** takes its name from the Alaskan Innuit tribe known as the Mahlemuts. The stamina of the breed is noteworthy; teams of six dogs are capable of pulling a sleigh weighing more than 700lb (355kg) for distances of 50 miles (80km) or more in a day. Malamutes are powerful, deep-chested dogs with a plume-like tail carried over the back and a proud and alert air. They are bred in various colours, usually black and white or wolf-grey, and have distinctive facial markings.

Lighter and faster than the Malamute, the **Siberian Husky** was developed by the Chukchi nomads of northeast Asia. Although the Malamute was already established in Alaska, the Siberian Husky was introduced there shortly after the turn of the century and proved successful both in sled racing and in more serious work – a team of Siberian Huskies took some supplies of diphtheria antitoxin across the frozen wastelands of Alaska in 1925 to save the people in the town of Nome. The breed was recognized by the AKC in 1930; in Britain these dogs are being bred in increasing numbers, and races have been organized. They are striking dogs and bold, lively and friendly by nature.

UTILITY DOGS

The Utility Group is a more amorphous collection of dogs. Essentially, these are non-sporting breeds of less easily classified function than the Working Group; in some countries they are termed as 'Large Companion Dogs' (as distinct from the Toy breeds, the 'Small Companion Dogs'), although not all are especially large.

When the Non-Sporting breeds were divided up into three groups, the distinctions between these were not as clear-cut as between, for example, Hounds and Gundogs, and to some extent the Utility Group classifications have an unavoidably arbitrary quality. It is hard to see, for example, why the lion-like Tibetan breeds should be Utility dogs while the related imperial lion dog of China, the Pekingese, finds its place in the Toy Group. Similarly, the Utility group includes the Schnauzer, a guard breed which one might have included in the Working Group. The classification may also surprise where size variations have created distinct breeds from one type, as with the Standard, Miniature and Toy Poodles; the novice might well expect to find the latter in the Toy Group rather than classified as a Utility dog along with its larger cousins.

Some Utility breeds were created for a function which no longer exists, for example the Bulldog, developed for the long-abolished sport of bull-baiting, and the Dalmatian, once employed as a carriage dog, a fashionable accessory to accompany the horse-drawn vehicle. Others have evolved away from their original role, as with the Poodle, once a working retriever but now a decorative companion. Then there are breeds whose function is hard to define, such as the Chow Chow, an ancient Chinese breed which served as herder and guard but was also farmed for meat and pelts, and the Tibetan breeds, the Lhasa Apso, Shih Tzu, Tibetan Spaniel and Tibetan Terrier, small Oriental dogs whose supposedly lion-like appearance gave them religious significance in Buddhism.

The **Bulldog** is famous as a symbol of British tenacity. Descended from ancient mastiff stock, it was specifically bred for bull-baiting, with unlimited courage and a foreshortened head with the nostrils set well back, enabling the dog to breathe while its powerful jaws were locked in the bull's flesh. As with other fighting breeds, the modern specimens have been bred to retain the breed's unique physical attributes and courage while replacing the original aggressiveness with a truly endearing temperament. Show ring fashions have exaggerated head points to a degree that can cause health problems, but a sound Bulldog is a delightful companion.

A more glamorous breed is the **Chow Chow,** a massive, heavily-boned dog which combines a cuddly teddy-bear appearance with great dignity. It is unique amongst dogs in its blue-black tongue, its strange stilted gait and its tem-

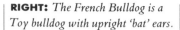

RIGHT: *The French Bulldog is a Toy bulldog with upright 'bat' ears.*

Standard Poodle

Miniature Poodle

Toy Poodle

perament, which is unlike that of any other breed. Devoted to their own family, Chow Chows remain aloof and are highly reserved with strangers; they are strong-willed and are not easily trained.

The origins of the **Dalmatian** have been lost, but the breed's long association with horses dates back to a time when they were common companions of travelling gypsies. During the latter part of the nineteenth century they were commonly kept around stables and became highly fashionable as carriage dogs. With the advent of motorized transport they became a purely companion breed, and being both handsome and of good temperament and intelligence they fit this role well. The characteristic spots may be black or liver, and their size and distribution are important in show specimens.

Most popular of the Utility breeds are the **Poodles,** especially the smaller sizes. There are three breeds of Poodle, differing only in size. Originally the Poodle was a retriever, often working in water; its heavy coat was clipped to assist its swimming ability, as is the case with similar breeds such as the Portuguese Water Dog. The dense, non-shedding coat lends itself to styling, and more elaborate clips were evolved, while the coloured ribbons tied in the top-knot to aid owners in identifying their dogs at a distance also helped lead to the development of the Poodle as a decorative accessory. Fashion played a large part in the growing popularity of the Poodle, but so did the breed's natural intelligence and ability to learn – which have also led to the successful career of the Poodle as a circus dog.

Today the Poodle is one of the most successful and most elaborately presented of show dogs, appearing in the show ring in strictly prescribed clips. For pets, the coat can be much more simply and practically styled, and the intelligence and high spirits of all three breeds makes them delightful members of the family. The largest, the Standard, makes the ideal family guard dog, unaggressive but with a strong sense of territory; the two smaller breeds may lack the impressive size but will also put up a good and noisy defence of their home and owner. As with other highly popular dogs, there has been some indiscriminate breeding of the Miniature and Toy, and it is important to seek out a responsible breeder to be sure of obtaining a puppy which is physically and temperamentally sound.

The **Schnauzers** also exist as three breeds of different sizes, the Schnauzer, Miniature Schnauzer and Giant or Riesenschnauzer. Developed in Germany from terrier stock, they were initially classified as Terriers, then as members of the Working Group, but in Britain are classed as Utility dogs. All three are handsome dogs with all the high spirits of the typical Terrier. The Schnauzer proper has never achieved great popularity, but the Miniature is gaining a well-deserved place as a pet and show dog with its smart appearance and friendly personality. The rarer Giant Schnauzer is a big, powerful dog, originally employed as a guard and drovers' dog, which today has found another role as a police dog.

The four Tibetan breeds are becoming popular today, partly because of their highly attractive appearance and

partly because of the charming and independent personality typical of the Oriental breeds. The early history of the Oriental 'lion dog' breeds goes back thousands of years, although it is difficult to distinguish between separate breeds until the creation of the Tibetan Breed Association in 1934 established clear distinctions.

The **Shih Tzu** and **Lhasa Apso** are short-legged, long-haired breeds with shaggy chrysanthemum faces; the Shih Tzu normally has the frontal hair tied back in a top knot to expose the eyes, while the Lhasa wears an obscuring fringe. Both make delightful pets, although their flowing coats require considerable care. The **Tibetan Terrier** is another shaggy breed, longer in the leg than its cousins and bearing some resemblance to a miniature Old English Sheepdog. Despite the name it is not a terrier in the usual sense, never having been employed to go to ground but having been kept simply as a companion and harbinger of good fortune.

Currently the most popular of the Tibetan breeds is the pretty **Tibetan Spaniel,** not unlike a Pekingese without the exaggeration, being shorter in coat, longer in leg and with a normally proportioned rather than flat face. These dogs were employed in Tibet to work prayer wheels on treadmills, a function intended to push the prayers nearer to their destination.

Other Utility breeds include the two European barge dogs, the **Keeshond** and **Schipperke,** once kept by barge-men as guards and companions. The Keeshond is a very pretty Spitz with a dense and glamorous coat of character-istic wolf-grey colouring, while the Schipperke is a small, bold, active dog of near-Spitz type with a tail which is either naturally absent or docked.

TOP: *Tibetan Spaniels are today the most popular of the Tibetan breeds, being attractive little dogs with great character.*

ABOVE: *The Shih Tzu's leonine appearance (the name means 'lion') had a sacred significance for Buddhists, and these little dogs were kept at the Chinese court.*

RIGHT: *The Giant Schnauzer was originally kept both as a working cattle dog and a guard; when cattle driving declined, the breed found another role as a police dog.*

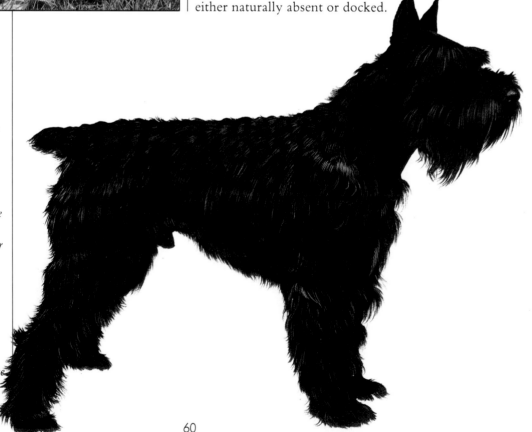

LEFT: *Developed in the Netherlands from Wolf Spitz stock which originated in Germany, the Keeshond has been in existence for over 200 years and takes its name from Dutch patriots Kees de Gyselaer and Kees de Witt.*

BELOW RIGHT: *The Boston Terrier was developed in the United States from Bulldogs and English Terriers and retains characteristics of both breeds.*

BELOW LEFT: *In the nineteenth century the Dalmatian was popular as a carriage dog to accompany horse-drawn vehicles, and today this breed retains its affinity with horses.*

TOY DOGS

Miniature dogs bred purely as ornamental companions have a long history. These were non-functional, luxury animals, selectively bred for small size, beauty and a companionable nature. Attributes which were found desirable in these purely pet dogs included intelligence and entertainment value, a bold, gay personality being an asset. Often reduction in size was accompanied by the development of a permanently juvenile temperament, with puppyish playfulness and the need for a very close relationship with the owner. The typical Toy, indeed, is reminiscent of a human toddler in many of its ways, with the same self-importance, its desire to have its own way, its charming wiles and its need for attention.

The name of the Toy Group is perhaps unfortunate, implying as it does the negative qualities of the over-indulged lapdog and ignoring the personality and spirit that normally characterize these little dogs. The old name of 'comforter' describes their role rather better, as does the classification of 'Small Companion Dogs' employed in some countries.

Many of the Toys were created by the miniaturization of larger breeds. We have a miniature hound in the Italian Greyhound, miniature spaniels such as the Papillon and King Charles Spaniel, and miniature terriers such as the Yorkshire Terrier. The Pomeranian represents the northern Spitz breeds, while there are also Oriental Toys such as the Pekingese and Pug. However, the Toy group excludes the Toy Poodle, which is classified with its larger cousins as a Utility breed.

Toy breeds retain their popularity today, their small size suiting them to the urban lifestyle, and their development as specifically companion animals fitting them well for domestic life. Unlike the larger breeds, they can be kept fit on surprisingly little exercise, and their small size is also reflected in the comparatively small expense of food. One of the charms of the toy breeds is their adaptability; they can be satisfied with a walk round the block, but equally most will enjoy surprisingly long country walks, and many, if given the opportunity, retain keen sporting instincts.

The **Italian Greyhound,** the only Toy hound, has an ancient history. A miniature greyhound-type breed existed more than 2,000 years ago in various parts of the Mediterranean region; by the sixteenth century, these dainty and elegant little dogs were becoming fashionable with royalty all over Europe. Despite their apparent fragility, Italian Greyhounds retain the sporting instinct of their ancestors, and are still raced in Europe.

Miniature spaniels were also popular as court dogs, and King Charles II's delight in his Toy Spaniels is reflected in the two breeds which bear his name. By the 1920s, the **King Charles Spaniel** had diverged from the type favoured by the king to become a short-faced breed; the

Cavalier King Charles was then created in a deliberate attempt to breed back to the original type, and is larger, with a more naturally shaped muzzle and longer tail. Both are gay, affectionate dogs which enjoy exercise. Four colours are recognized, Black and Tan, a rich chestnut red termed Ruby, a tricolour known as the Prince Charles, and a red and white known as the Blenheim from its association with the Duke of Marlborough, who moved to Blenheim Palace in 1702.

Another Toy Spaniel is the **Papillon,** which takes its name (French for 'butterfly') from its large erect ears, thought to resemble butterflies' wings. The original form had more typically spaniel pendant ears; this type is still bred today and is termed 'Phalene' ('moth' – the ears being held to resemble the moth's folded wings). Papillons were popular amongst the ladies of the courts of Europe as long ago as the sixteenth century, and are often portrayed in paintings of the time. They have lost none of their charm as companions today, being sound vigorous dogs which, despite their small size, are not above hunting vermin such as rats. Responsive to training, they have been highly successful in obedience competitions.

Amongst the Toy terriers, the most popular breed is the tiny **Yorkshire Terrier** with its flowing, silky coat. Despite

ABOVE: *A miniature form of the sled dogs of the far north, the Pomeranian is the smallest member of the Spitz group. Its larger ancestors developed in Germany, specifically in the area around Pomerania; the extreme miniaturization of the breed occurred more recently in Great Britain and the United States.*

RIGHT: *The royal dog of China, the Pekingese once represented the Lion of Buddha to devout Buddhists. Today its beauty and personality make it a pet dog of unique charm.*

the name, these little dogs have their origins in Scotland and were probably brought to Yorkshire by Scottish weavers. Today the show and the pet 'Yorkie' diverge considerably in type. The breed can vary greatly in size, and only the smaller specimens are required for the show ring, larger puppies being reserved for breeding or sold for pet homes. The fine, silky coat is easily damaged, and in pets its length is restricted by its tendency to break off, as well as often being clipped for manageability. In show specimens the hair is grown to astonishing lengths, and is protected from damage by paper wrappers termed 'crackers'.

The colour of the breed is as distinctive as the coat, being steel blue and tan, and the breed is spirited as well as ornamental. While Yorkshire Terriers are often highly pampered, the breed retains its terrier instincts and can hunt vermin, if given the opportunity.

The 'Yorkie' was one of the ancestors of a more recent creation, the **Australian Silky Terrier.** This is a less exaggerated breed, larger and with a coat measuring some 5 or 6 inches instead of the flowing locks of the Yorkshire; the coat is blue in colour rather than steel. Although classified as a Toy, this is a real terrier for all its ornamental appearance, and makes a good guard and keen ratter.

A quite different type of terrier is seen in the **English Toy Terrier** and **Miniature Pinscher,** two elegant smooth-coated breeds derived from rat-hunters, the latter representing the Continental terrier type. Both make smart and lively pets, with easy-care coats and alert temperaments.

LEFT: *The Papillon or 'butterfly dog' was once known as the 'Squirrel Spaniel' because of its plumed tail, carried over its back like a squirrel's.*

LEFT: *A Greyhound in miniature, the Italian Greyhound was for centuries a favourite court pet, with its elegance and devotion to its owner.*

Some other toy breeds arising from foreign terriers include the **Griffon Bruxellois** and the **Affenpinscher.** The Griffon is the better known, a square, whiskery little dog of great character. In the early days of the breed, these dogs were frequently found as the companions of Brussels cab drivers. A smooth-coated variety known as the **Brabancon** is also known.

The **Pomeranian** is unusual amongst the toy breeds in that it has entirely replaced the larger breed from which it developed. The original Pomeranians were large dogs, best-known to us today from the paintings of Gainsborough and his contemporaries; they occasionally produced miniatures, and selective breeding perfected these as a tiny breed while the original type disappeared from the scene. The Pomeranian is an enchantingly dainty ball of fluff, cunningly trimmed for exhibition to give a completely rounded shape.

A South American breed is the **Chihuahua,** the smallest breed in the world. It is known that tiny dogs known as the Techichi were kept by the Toltec Indians of Mexico as long ago as the ninth century, and their ancestry may have extended back as far as the Mayan civilization of the fifth century. The breed was introduced to the United States in about 1850, but not until 1934 did it reach Britain, where it only became popular after the Second World War. They have since become greatly valued, both as show dogs and as pets. Part of the charm of the Chihuahua lies in the fact that, despite their small size, they are completely fearless, creating a wonderful impression in the show ring where they are quite unintimidated by the larger breeds, and at home making alert and surprisingly noisy guards. Both longhaired and smoothhaired varieties are found.

The Oriental Toys are distinct from the European breeds, having been developed separately for thousands of years.

LEFT: *The Bichon Frise's pleasing appearance and lively personality have led to its increasing popularity since its recognition by the American Kennel Club in 1972 and the Kennel Club in Britain two years later.*

*The smallest breed in the world, the Chihuahua is bred in both Long-coated (**RIGHT**) and Smooth-coated (**EXTREME FAR RIGHT**) forms.*

They include the Pug and Pekingese, as well as the less commonly seen Japanese Chin.

Although many toy breeds descend from terrier or spaniel stock, the **Pug** is of mastiff origin. Dogs of this type were known in the Orient as long ago as 400 BC. They spread from China and Tibet to Japan and thence to Europe, where they became great favourites in royal circles. William of Orange adopted the breed as the official dog of the House of Orange and introduced the Pug to England when he became king. The term 'pug' probably derives from the popular term for the pet monkeys fashionable in the eighteenth century, the foreshortened face of the Pug giving it a monkey-like expression. Although the popularity of the Pug has declined since the turn of the century, it remains an ideal family pet, with its friendly temperament and easy-care coat. Like other short-nosed breeds, they may snuffle and snort through their compacted noses, and the prominent eyes may be vulnerable.

LEFT: The Maltese may date back to the days of the Roman Empire. It was first introduced to Britain in the early sixteenth century, and quickly became popular.

The **Pekingese** was the royal dog of China, remaining the exclusive property of the Imperial family for centuries. In 1860 British troops sacked the Palace at Peking and four Pekingese were brought back to Britain, where their unique appearance attracted considerable attention. Subsequently further dogs were imported, and the breed became very popular. Today they retain their unique charm, being dogs of considerable personality and wilful independence but capable of great devotion to their owners. Despite their luxurious appearance they are sporting little dogs which enjoy a surprising amount of exercise and can be great hunters if given the chance – individuals have even been trained as gundogs. Some show strains may be too heavily coated for the pet owner's taste, and the short nose and bulging eyes may again be the source of health problems.

A breed which despite its long history is new to both Britain and the United States is the **Bichon Frisé,** rapidly increasing in popularity since its introduction. The Bichon is a small, pure white, curly-coated dog with an appealing and lively character.

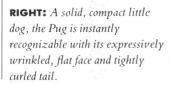

ABOVE: One of the oldest of the toy breeds, the Japanese Chin was, in fact, first bred in China and subsequently some stock was given to the Emperor of Japan.

RIGHT: A solid, compact little dog, the Pug is instantly recognizable with its expressively wrinkled, flat face and tightly curled tail.

DOG SHOWS

There are no short cuts to successful showing for the intending exhibitor. The first step is to become as familiar as possible with the breed requirements, both in terms of the official standard, and show preparation. Special classes are organized for novice exhibitors; it is also important to practise the training routine as much as possible, so that both dog and handler know what is expected when they enter the show ring for the first time. It is also a good idea to attend a few shows to observe the procedures and talk to other exhibitors.

Rules of shows can vary considerably from country to country: puppies, for example, are only shown from the age of six months in Britain, three months later than is allowed under Australian regulations. The routine of showing, however, is broadly similar. A schedule listing the various classes and an entry form must be obtained first from the show secretary. After the form is completed with details of the dog's registration, it should be returned with the entry fee well in advance of the closing date given in the schedule. Prior details of shows are listed in the various dog papers.

The experienced exhibitor plans well in advance for a show. The amount of preparation – such as grooming and clipping – required depends to some extent upon the breed of dog. Good preparation is no substitute for physical qualities, however, but merely serves to emphasize the finest points of the dog.

Larger shows are often 'benched', which means that in between their classes the dogs are on display on 'benches', wooden staging with vertical partitions to create individual cubicles. For security, they are tied up to the bench by a 'benching chain'.

It is advisable to take a blanket, a drinking bowl and a clean container of drinking water to the show. On long trips, a feeding container and food will also be necessary. Grooming equipment, such as brushes, spray and similar items are also important, while a coat and possibly leg protectors may be needed to prevent the dog's appearance being spoiled by bad weather. At the bigger shows, a benching chain will be required; a nylon show lead will be necessary for any show.

Allow plenty of time for the journey, so that the dog is able to settle down on arrival, rather than having to go straight into the show ring. If a dog detects an atmosphere

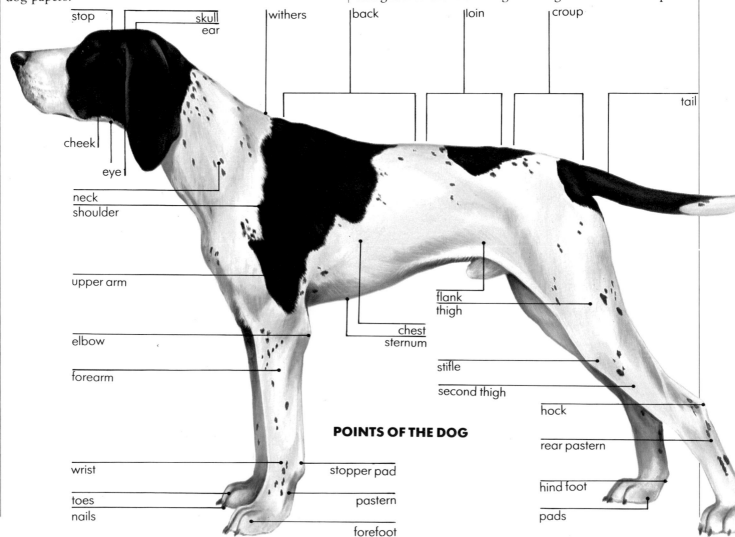

stop
skull
ear
withers
back
loin
croup
tail
cheek
eye
neck
shoulder
upper arm
flank
thigh
chest
sternum
elbow
stifle
forearm
second thigh
hock

POINTS OF THE DOG

rear pastern
wrist
stopper pad
hind foot
toes
pastern
pads
nails
forefoot

of anxiety, it may prove difficult to handle. At the show ground, the first step is to acquire the catalogue, which gives the times of classes and numbers of entries. Judging takes place in rings, with several operating at once at larger events. Locate the bench space allotted to the dog, and its show ring. The benching chain is used to tie the dog to the metal loop on the staging. Once the dog is settled, it can be left safely while you locate the show ring. This is generally close to the benching area for the breed concerned.

The ring number card that identifies each entry must be clearly worn by the exhibitor in the ring. The class will be organized by a steward, who will call the exhibitors into line. The judge then decides how the dogs are to be walked; be sure to follow the judge's wishes.

The dogs will be judged to the official breed standard, devised by the National Kennel Club or council. At American conformation shows, a maximum of five points are awarded for each winner, depending on the number present in the class and other factors. Dogs which score three or more points at a single event have achieved a 'major'. These points are accumulated, and once 15 have been scored, the dog is then awarded the title of Champion. In Britain, the system differs in that Challenge Certificates rather than points are awarded, and when a dog achieves three of these certificates, under different judges, it becomes a Champion. The FCI, to which many kennel clubs are affiliated, awards its own certificates, the CACIB, to outstanding dogs; these, in turn, can compete for the title of International Champion.

Judges are usually willing to advise novice exhibitors after the official judging is over. Their verdict may not always be encouraging; in which case, it may be necessary to retire the dog from the ring.

There are several different types of show. In Great Britain, these range from the large Championship shows at which Challenge Certificates are on offer and which may run over two or three days, down through several smaller types without Challenge Certificates, such as Open shows, open to any intending exhibitor, or Limited shows, where entry is restricted to members of the organizing society. The smallest kind of show is the Exemption, which, as its name suggests, is exempt from many of the Kennel Club regulations. There are usually four classes for pedigree dogs, plus a varying number of 'fun' classes open to both pedigree and mongrel.

In addition to breed shows, where dogs are judged against the breed standards, the governing canine authorities organize other competitive events, such as obedience and working trials, field trials for gundogs and agility competitions. These events test the dog's abilities rather than its appearance, and are judged accordingly.

Showing your dog can be a highly enjoyable hobby for both you and your pet, and it is not necessary to win in

ABOVE AND LEFT: *The most famous dog show in the world, Crufts was inaugurated in 1886 under the patronage of Queen Victoria and taken over by the Kennel Club in 1948. Today, Crufts has grown so popular that dogs are required to qualify for entry by winning elsewhere beforehand, and the exhibition now extends over four days.*

order to have a good day out. Indeed, this is not a hobby for the person who cares only for winning, for even the best dog can have its off days, or come up against a judge who is looking for something slightly different. The right attitude to showing is demonstrated by the man who came away from a show without having won anything, but having thoroughly enjoyed seeing the dogs and talking to the people, remarking, 'I brought a good dog here today, and I'm taking a good dog home.' If you value your dog for what it is, and not for what it might win, dog shows can give you both a great deal of fun.

Chapter Three

CHOOSING A DOG

WHY HAVE A DOG?

Dogs are uniquely rewarding pets, but they also rank amongst the most demanding animals to keep in a domestic environment – a fact that is sadly illustrated by the thousands of dogs abandoned by their owners every year. Before undertaking the responsibility of caring for a dog – a commitment that may last for 15 years or more – it is essential to consider how you will cope with the restrictions and disruptions that it will unavoidably bring into your life.

Because dogs are social animals, a dog needs a great deal of company and attention – almost as much as a child. The dog is not born with an instinctive understanding of your personal routines and lifestyle, but will require time and patience on your part to enable it to fit in. If you cannot provide these, the dog will never be anything but a liability and a nuisance, both to you and to other people, and may well end up as just another statistic in the records of some animal rescue scheme – or worse.

If you go out to work and there is no one at home all day, a pet cat will sleep for much of the time and can let itself in and out through a cat flap, with the opportunity to pursue its own feline pursuits in the outside world. A dog in similar circumstances will suffer unacceptably from boredom and loneliness, and is likely to become destructive and noisy. Not only is this unfair on the animal itself, but it is hardly the way to obtain any advantages from pet-keeping.

All dogs need exercise. It is one thing to envisage pleasant country strolls in the sunshine at weekends, but the dog will also need his walks in unpleasant weather and when you are tired or busy. He will also need considerable training at first to make him into a pleasant walking companion that does not pull on the lead, lunge at other dogs or people, or race uncontrollably off into the distance when off the leash. Many breeds need a great deal more exercise than is commonly realized, and a stroll around the block once a day will leave most dogs still bursting with unused energy.

Once you have acquired a dog, you can no longer go out for the day without planning for the dog's needs, either arranging for someone else to look after him or fitting the day around his requirements. Increasing restrictions on where dogs are permitted to go limit the dog-owner's activities: most shops, nearly all restaurants and many public houses ban dogs from entry, while practically all the places of interest you are likely to visit on holiday will have a No Dogs' rule. You may be able to leave your pet in the car, but in hot weather the car will turn into an oven. Careful planning will still make it possible to take your dog out and about with you, but you do need to consider whether

ABOVE: *It would be unfair to expect an energetic gundog like this Hungarian Vizla to adapt to the restrictions of city life.*

RIGHT: *The dog needs daily exercise. If your inclination for exercise is limited, it would be unfair to acquire a large and energetic animal which may require at least 2 hours' walking every day to remain happy and healthy.*

you will find these restrictions unendurably irritating.

Introducing a dog of any type into the home will inevitably cause some disturbance to the domestic routine, and it is certain to result in extra work. For example, all dogs shed dead hairs and these rapidly accumulate unless they are cleaned up daily. Some damage to the home or furnishings may also result from ownership of a dog, especially a puppy. Puppies take time to learn that destructive behaviour is unacceptable and, without any malice or forethought, can ruin furniture, carpets, books – any of your prized possessions. Even an adult dog, if bored and not monitored, can take to chewing the legs off chairs.

Grooming can be a demanding chore. The attractively long-coated breeds need daily attention if they are not to become smelly and unsightly, and both time and patience will be required to maintain their appearance – and general health.

The cost of keeping a dog can prove a significant burden on finances too. There will be expenditure on food, equipment and routine veterinary care, and certain breeds may require professional grooming. Other incidental costs are boarding kennels and licensing.

Having taken into account the demands that a dog makes upon its owners, if you are prepared and able to meet these, no other animal can share man's life so fully or so rewardingly. Actively seeking the companionship of humans, giving affection openly, the dog can by its very presence make life happier and fuller for its owner.

WHAT KIND OF DOG?

It has been said that choosing a dog is like choosing a marriage partner – since you will be living in a close relationship with it for many years, it is important to choose a dog that suits you as an individual. As we have seen, dogs show greater diversity of size, shape and temperament than any other domestic species. This wide range of choice makes it possible to select an animal that will fit your own temperament and circumstances. All too often we see a frail old lady struggling with a large and boisterous dog, a sedentary man reducing one of the more energetic breeds into an overweight slug of a dog, or a highly sensitive animal suffering as a child's plaything rather than playmate. This can so easily be avoided by planning your choice rather than acquiring the first puppy that attracts your eye.

Think carefully about what you want from your dog. Do you want a devoted one-man animal, or a more social and outgoing pet? Do you want a highly responsive and sensitive type, or a calmer, easy-going companion? Do you want the dog to carry out any practical function such as guarding?

Think about your lifestyle. If you have people coming and going all the time, a dog with a very strong guarding instinct could be a liability. If you spend a lot of time enjoying country walks, a heavily-coated animal which picks up mud and water like blotting paper would not be the first choice. If you like to spend long periods of time sitting down with a book or the television, a high-powered working-type dog is going to go mad with inactivity, and probably drive you round the bend as well.

Think about the composition of your family. If you have young children or frail elderly relatives living with you, this will have some bearing on your choice.

Think about your own temperament, and what sort of canine temperament you will find it most easy to live with. Some dogs are actually too sensitive to their owners' moods and can become neurotic in response, where other breeds, not necessarily less intelligent, will take emotional ups and downs in their stride.

You need also to consider the dog's requirements, in terms of the space available for its use, the time and enthusiasm you have for exercise and grooming, and the amount you can comfortably afford to pay for its upkeep – the large breeds can eat you out of house and home. Many of the working breeds actually need to be worked in some way, and if not provided with some real mental stimulus such as serious obedience training will become bored and destructive: it is not fair to acquire a dog of this type unless you have the time and interest available to employ its intelligence.

DOGS AND CHILDREN

Growing up with a dog can be a delightful and rewarding experience for a child, provided the parents really want, and are prepared to take full responsibility for, the animal. The dog as companion, playmate and protector can help the child to develop a sense of responsibility as he or she is encouraged to help in caring for the pet, feeding it, and taking it for walks. The young child begins to learn about empathy for the feelings of others from a pet, discovering the difference between the cuddly toy that can be mauled and squeezed and kicked, and the living animal that needs gentle handling.

A child's relationship with a dog can help him or her to develop confidence in human relationships. It is significant that recently dogs have been used with great success in certain mental hospitals to encourage withdrawn patients to communicate, first with the animals and gradually, via them, with fellow humans. In a similar way the dog's responsiveness can be of great value in a child's social development.

It has been found that families with children are twice as likely to have a dog as are childless households, which reflects the value we place upon the contribution of the dog to a happy childhood.

The choice of a dog for a home where there are young

children necessitates particular care. A dog of a fairly tolerant breed such as a Whippet or a Labrador Retriever is to be recommended. A highly-strung dog is clearly unsuited to be a child's companion, and some of the working breeds may have over-riding instincts which are not desirable in the family situation. For example, a pup from a working sheepdog strain will have a predominant urge to round up stock, and such a puppy has been known to terrify young children by herding them compulsively into a corner. A large boisterous animal can bowl a small child over quite unintentionally, whilst very little dogs are not always to be encouraged because they themselves may be injured if handled roughly and are more liable to bite as a result.

In any event, always supervise contact between the children and the dog, particularly in the early stages when they are unfamiliar with each other. Children must be taught not to hurt the dog by playing roughly with it, and they should always be encouraged to participate in its care, even if only to offer the dog its food bowl. It is of course vital to follow a strict deworming schedule, as advised by your veterinarian, because of the slight risk of the transmission of parasitic worm eggs from dog to child. This is more likely to occur outdoors, and dog excrement should be removed from the environment on a daily basis to minimize the risk.

LEFT: *A dog can be a wonderful companion for a child, but no child should be expected to take full responsibility for a living creature. Unless the parents are prepared to take an interest and overall supervision in the dog's well-being, it is unkind to acquire a dog purely as a child's pet.*

LEFT: *As companions for elderly people, dogs are often ideal. But the choice of dog needs to be considered carefully – obviously, a large and boisterous puppy would be unsuitable in many cases.*

BELOW: *The elderly owner may benefit physically from the companionship of a dog, which will provide stimulus for regular exercise.*

THE ELDERLY OWNER

As companions for elderly people, dogs can be ideal. Studies being undertaken into the relationship between pets and their owners are confirming the importance of pet owner-ship, particularly for people living alone. An elderly person in our society can easily be cut off from human contact, and a dog not only provides friendship within the home but encourages its owner to go out, often acting as a bridge between the owner and other people. For the very old and frail person, of course, the practicality of dog ownership depends to a great extent upon continuing physical health and on the amount of assistance available from family or neighbours.

The choice of dog needs to be considered carefully – obviously a large, boisterous animal would be unsuitable in most cases, and a long-coated dog needing a great deal of grooming is likely to be less desirable than one with an easy-care coat. Some of the small breeds, such as terriers, may be too energetic and excitable to make suitable com-panions for the elderly.

An adult dog may well be a better choice than a puppy, to avoid the demanding tasks of house-training and teaching basic good manners. It is sometimes possible to obtain an older dog, known to be of reliable temperament, through one of the animal rescue schemes, which not infrequently need to rehouse animals which have lost their owners.

BELOW: *An uncontrollable urge to chew is typical of young puppies as their set of deciduous teeth is shed, and replaced by adult dentition. With a puppy in the house, constant watchfulness is necessary to deflect its attention from furniture and other household items towards its own, approved toys.*

RIGHT: *Adult dogs are often available for rehousing through no fault of their own. However, many such dogs may not have been properly trained by their previous owners, and may have bad habits such as pulling on the lead, which will take time and patience to overcome.*

PUPPY OR ADULT?

Generally speaking, a puppy is more trouble to introduce to your household than an adult dog, but has the advantage that it will grow up as part of your family. It will not have acquired any vices, although it will not yet have learned any manners. It is up to you to shape it. It will take time and patience to teach the puppy civilized behaviour, and at first you will have to endure puddles on the carpet, crying and chewing. On the credit side, a puppy can also be great fun, and you will be able to train it to fit into your lifestyle since it has known no other.

The adult dog will have been shaped, temperamentally, by its previous owner or owners. It may have vices not immediately apparent. Older dogs can prove nervous, especially if they have had several homes previously, and they may not be used to children. They will take longer to settle into the domestic environment and are likely to be relatively unresponsive to training. Difficulties that can arise are, for example, the inability of the dog to respond to a new name and its initial reluctance to remain with its new owner when let off the leash. If it was attached to a previous owner, you will have to earn its affections; the change of ownership may make it feel very insecure, and you will have to work hard to restore its confidence. Even if it is already well-trained, the previous owner may well have had different expectations of behaviour from your own.

Given time and patience, however, such problems can be overcome to a great extent, but the settling-in period for an adult dog can be a difficult time, especially for the novice owner and particularly if the dog's origins are unknown.

For the home with young children, a puppy is generally to be preferred, partly because it will prove more adaptable and partly because it will grow up with the children and they will establish a close relationship.

If you intend to exhibit your dog later, you may want an older individual whose show potential can be assessed more easily than a puppy's. Many breeders prefer to run on puppies to an age where their show points can be evaluated, rather than risk missing a potential winner. However, a dog that has lived most of its life in a kennel is likely to have difficulty adapting to a domestic environment. Studies have shown that there is a so-called socialization period in the life of young dogs between the ages of about six and thirteen weeks during which time they need to be exposed to human company. The more attention they receive during this time the better they will settle in the home. A particular difficulty associated with dogs kept under kennel conditions during the early formative months of their life is that they have never been housetrained, and this can prove difficult to teach at a later stage.

DOG OR BITCH?

The gender of the dog is another factor to take into consideration before choosing an individual. There is a significant difference in temperament between male and female, although this is more marked in some individuals than in others. Either sex can make the right pet for you, and the choice comes down to personal preference, but it as well to be aware of the differences.

Male dogs on the whole possess more dominant natures than bitches and tend to be more independent and less demanding, although this is not always the case. They are interested in the opposite sex all the year round and are more prone to wandering than are females, particularly if there is a bitch in heat in the neighbourhood. They may prove harder to train.

Some very dominant and/or oversexed males may display excessive aggression towards other dogs. Some degree of intermale aggression is natural to dogs; however, in a properly socialized and well trained male this should not cause problems.

Bitches are often more affectionate and more amenable, and it is because they are generally easier to train that they are preferred to males as guide dogs. It depends upon you as an individual which type of temperament appeals more. It has been suggested that people may be best matched with a pet of the opposite sex to themselves, a generalization which quite often holds true.

The major drawback of owning a female dog is the two periods of heat which are likely to occur every year through to old age, and the accompanying risk of unwanted puppies. At these times bitches may themselves wander away to look for a mate and are more highly strung. The accompanying discharge from the vagina can cause problems around the home, and the bitch must be closely supervised to prevent uncontrolled mating. Male dogs will be attracted to the bitch's vicinity by her scent when she is on heat, and are likely to make a nuisance of themselves congregating around your doorstep.

There are certain health problems associated with the female reproductive cycle, too. Unmated bitches not infrequently suffer from false pregnancy, a condition in which the symptoms of pregnancy are reproduced although no litter will be forthcoming. Affected bitches may prove temperamental at these times, possibly even aggressive, and can make a nuisance of themselves adopting puppy substitutes such as an old shoe which will be jealously guarded. Older bitches may suffer from serious uterine infections necessitating surgery to remove the uterus.

In neither sex are the disadvantages insuperable. Training and supervision will serve in the majority of cases, or, if the animal is not required for breeding, neutering may be considered.

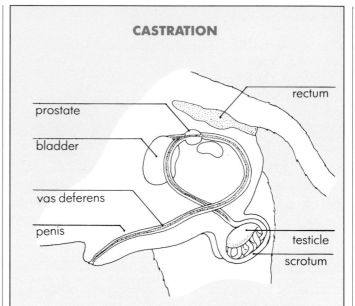

CASTRATION

In castration the testicles are removed by a single incision in the scrotum and the wound is then closed with a few external stitches. Owners may be advised in certain circumstances to have their male dogs neutered as a means of curbing certain behavioural problems, such as excessive aggression and wandering.

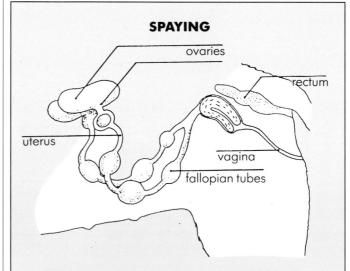

SPAYING

This operation is technically an ovariohysterectomy and entails the removal of both uterus and ovaries. It is ideally performed in the period between heats (anoestrus). The abdominal cavity has to be opened either at the flank or through the midline of the ventral surface. The wound heals quickly and stitches are normally removed about 10 days afterwards. Spaying is recommended for the pet bitch, not only to avoid the inconvenience of 'heat' but to prevent common health problems ranging from false pregnancy to ovarian cysts.

NEUTERING

If a bitch is not to be bred, the problems of heat can be prevented by spaying – the surgical removal of the ovaries and uterus. The inconveniences of oestrus can be tackled to some extent by chemical contraception, but this is more of a one-off measure (for example, to postpone a heat if the bitch is due to come into season when you plan to take her on holiday) than a lifelong practice. Spaying is not a cheap operation, but will permanently prevent the bitch from coming into season and will remove the risk of false pregnancies or disorders of the reproductive system.

The bitch can be spayed at any time once she is physically mature, and it makes no difference to her well-being whether she has had puppies previously or not – the old wives' tale that a bitch should be allowed to have one litter 'for her health's sake' has no basis in fact. Ideally, the operation should be carried out in the anoestrus period, the time between heats, when the uterus is in a dormant state.

Spaying is carried out by a veterinary surgeon, who opens the abdominal cavity via either the flank or the midline of the abdomen on its lower surface. The approach will vary, depending on the bitch concerned. When a flank incision is used, the coat colour immediately surrounding the site of the flank will probably appear paler than the rest of the coat for life, but the small scar will be obscured. The wound heals quickly, and the external stitches (sutures) should be removed by your veterinarian about 10 days after surgery. Keep an eye on the incision, however, in case any sutures break prematurely, revealing internal tissue. Contact your veterinarian as soon as possible in this event.

After the operation, the bitch will need to be kept quiet for a few days, exercised on a lead and prevented from jumping or leaping about. Once the stitches have been removed and the wound has healed, she should suffer no ill effects from the operation, although there is some slight risk of incontinence later in life and also an increased tendency to put on weight if the diet is not sensibly monitored.

Owners may be advised in certain circumstances to have their male dogs neutered as a means of curbing certain behavioural problems, notably wandering.

There are two schools of thought concerning the castration of male dogs, one holding it to be unnecessary and even disadvantageous and the other recommending it for all pets. The extent to which the sex drive dominates a dog's life varies from individual to individual. Many male dogs make good companions, but some are literally over-sexed and will benefit from neutering both to enable them to fit into the domestic environment and to make their own lives more comfortable by removing the constant drive to locate bitches.

The over-sexed male dog will be hard to train. The urge to wander off in search of bitches will outweigh any liking for his owner's company or any predisposition to bitches, he will persist in inappropriate sexual behaviour such as mounting cushions or human legs, or cocking a leg indoors to mark his territory, and he may well show excessive dominant and aggressive behaviour.

Castration, entailing the surgical removal of the testes, is a relatively straightforward operation and will considerably ameliorate behavioural problems associated with masculinity, such as aggressiveness, wandering and inappropriate sexual activity, in most male dogs. It is not an automatic cure-all for such problems, however, and the older dog will also need training to unlearn undesirable behaviour.

In castration the testicles are removed by a single incision in the scrotum and the wound is then closed with a few external stitches. The operation is irreversible and is ideally carried out before the dog is sexually competent, yet sufficiently mature for surgery.

Neutering is not an option if you wish to show your dog, as it renders it ineligible for competition. One possible disadvantage in some breeds is that hormonal changes arising from neutering may cause the growth of an atypically heavy coat which may be undesirable.

It is commonly believed that neutering will make a dog or bitch fat and sluggish. Certainly the neutered animal has a greater disposition to put on weight, but a sensible attitude to diet and exercise on the part of the owner will prevent this from becoming a problem. All guide dogs for the blind are neutered, to prevent the sex drive from distracting them from their vital duties, and they are normally the picture of health and alertness, because their owners have been trained to take proper care of them before taking them on.

An alternative to castration for the male dog not required for breeding is a vasectomy, an operation in which the testicles are not removed but the spermatic cords are cut to prevent the issue of sperm. Vasectomy will have no effect upon the dog other than rendering it sterile: it will retain all its masculine characteristics, including its interest in the opposite sex, and will not acquire any predisposition to put on weight. It is not an especially common operation, since most pet owners who wish to ensure that their dogs are unable to sire a litter also require the loss of interest in bitches produced by castration, but it has been suggested that compulsory vasectomizing of all male dogs not required for breeding would considerably reduce the population of unwanted dogs.

RIGHT: *A first-generation crossbred, in this case the progeny of a Cavalier King Charles Spaniel and a Whippet. In cases of deliberate cross-breeding, both parents will be known, just as with a pedigree dog.*

FAR RIGHT: *With a pedigree dog such as the Basenji (top) or these English Setters (below), the ancestry is known and the characteristics of the puppy are to some extent predictable.*

BELOW: *The mongrel is generally of unknown ancestry and it is impossible to predict the adult appearance and character traits of a mongrel puppy. This puppy was the offspring of a mongrel terrier bitch which was allowed to wander and was mated by an unknown dog, an example of unselective breeding which is less likely to produce a pet with a companionable temperament than careful breeding for desirable qualities.*

PEDIGREE OR MONGREL?

The difference between a pedigree dog and a mongrel is that the former has been carefully bred over generations to conform as closely as possible to the prescribed physical appearance and temperament for its particular breed, while the latter is the product of random matings between dogs of any type, and its ancestry is not usually known. The pedigree puppy will resemble its ancestors in general appearance and in broad temperament, while the mongrel will have ancestors of such assorted physical and mental types that it is impossible to predict how it will turn out.

People who favour pedigree dogs tend to despise mongrels as less attractive or less intelligent, while mongrel-owners often hold that pedigree dogs are less physically and temperamentally sound. Both assumptions are based on generalizations which fail to hold true upon examination.

Whether the possession of a pedigree is advantageous or disadvantageous to a dog depends upon the human breeders responsible for the existence of the individual puppy and its ancestors. The idea behind breeding pedigree stock is simply to produce an animal of established type, and, in the hands of reputable breeders, the pedigree dog is a highly desirable product. You should be able to buy a puppy and know that it will possess certain specified traits to a much higher degree than would a dog bred at random.

But a pedigree is only as good as the breeders who produced it. The ideal is produced by careful and knowledgeable selection of breeding stock. A pedigree puppy may equally well have been bred by a well-meaning but ignorant breeder who has simply mated together two dogs of the same breed without regard for bloodlines, or by a greedy breeder who aims to produce money-making puppies in quantity without regard for quality. Since it is as easy to breed in faults as it is virtues, a carelessly-bred puppy may inherit physical or temperamental faults, again to a higher degree than a randomly-bred mongrel.

If you have decided upon a pedigree puppy, it is important to find out – from books on the breed concerned, or simply by asking your veterinarian – if there are any inherited faults associated with your chosen breed. In the case of some popular breeds, show points have been pursued at the expense of bodily and mental soundness. The fashions of the show ring have sometimes exaggerated existing features of a breed to an extent that is detrimental to the dogs.

The commonest inherited defects associated with particular breeds tend to be hip dysplasia – a malformation of the hip joint causing lameness – and progressive retinal atrophy (PRA) – a condition of the eye causing progressive blindness. Responsible breeders are aware of problems within their breeds, and many breeds have a vetting scheme for breeding stock by which it is hoped to reduce and eventually eradicate these defects.

Although many individuals will never suffer from such difficulties, potential breed weaknesses must be thoroughly considered before a final choice is made. Even relatively minor flaws can be distressing. The noisy, snuffling breathing of the brachycephalic dogs, such as the Pekingese, which is due to their compressed faces and nasal passages, is one such example. Deafness, typically associated with white Bull Terriers, also requires understanding from the owner. It is worth noting, too, that the show ring craze for exaggeratedly long coats has produced some dogs whose coats are a positive liability for the pet owner.

It is important to be aware of these potential problems with pedigree dogs, but nobody should be deterred from ownership of a pedigree animal by this knowledge. There are many responsible breeders whose care is to produce sound, healthy and sweet-natured pups which will be a delight to their owners. What is important is to make sure that your pup is purchased from such a breeder and not from one of those who care little for the future of the breed.

If you decide on a pedigree puppy, you have a right to expect that it will have the general physical appearance, temperament and behavioural traits associated with its particular breed, but remember that there will be considerable variation between individuals of a breed. Some puppies will conform more closely to the physical ideal set out in the show standard than others – a factor which will affect not only the show potential but the price. If you only want a companion and not an exhibition animal, you will be able to buy a puppy which is perhaps not of ideal colour or markings for the show ring, and priced accordingly, which will make just as good a pet as its more conventionally handsome litter mate.

Some puppies will display the typical breed temperament more strongly than others. It is worth noting the breeder's motives for producing the litter. If the breeder's only interest is the show ring, good looks may have been given priority over working qualities or even good temper and intelligence. If the breeder's aim is to produce working dogs, the puppies may have the working instinct so highly developed that they will not be happy unless they are worked. In the case of some breeds which are popular both as show dogs and as workers, different types have emerged with different priorities regarding appearance and temperament – for example, in the English Springer Spaniel there is today a noticeable difference between working and exhibition strains. Those kept for working purposes are smaller and stockier than their show counterparts, and the head is of a different shape.

The price of a pedigree puppy will depend both upon the breed and upon the show and breeding potential of the individual. In many breeds, a puppy bred as a companion dog rather than for the show ring will cost three figures, and for a potential show winner the price will be very high indeed.

Mongrel puppies can often be obtained at little or no cost, since you do not have to pay for time and care that has gone into developing a bloodline. The notion that mongrels are sounder and healthier than pedigree dogs has no basis in fact, although they are less likely to suffer from hereditary defects since they derive from a wider genetic pool. The obvious disadvantage is that the adult appearance and temperament of the mongrel puppy cannot be predicted. Some indication of the adult size of the puppy can be obtained from the size of its feet, however: relatively large feet compared with body size suggest that the puppy will develop into a big dog. By the age of four months, any dog, including a mongrel, should be about two-thirds of its final adult size.

It is important to visit the litter if at all possible: although the pups will not necessarily inherit their dam's temperament, you can at least tell if she has any obvious temperamental faults that she might have passed on.

Mongrels can make just as good companions as pedigree dogs, but, just as with the latter, it pays to consider the amount of care the breeder has given to the litter. One disadvantage that should be borne in mind is that many mongrels are the result of unplanned matings. A bitch whose owners allowed her to roam free when in season may not have been sufficiently well cared for during pregnancy and after the birth to give the puppies the best start in life. It is also probable that the pups will have been sired by the most aggressive and highly sexed of the local free-roaming male dog population. Since heredity plays a considerable part in temperament, you may be acquiring a pup which takes after its father and is not really suited for domestic life. Although it is said that there are no bad dogs, only bad owners, there certainly are dogs which are less well adapted to the companion role than are others, and it makes sense to try to avoid these.

As much care should be taken when choosing a mongrel, therefore, as when selecting a pup with a pedigree. The ideal choice would be the offspring of a much-loved pet whose owners deliberately chose to perpetuate her line and selected her mate. However, many a delightful mongrel has been acquired which was of unknown parentage.

It should be appreciated that not all non-pedigree dogs are, strictly speaking, mongrels. The true mongrel is the product of generations of mongrels and cannot lay claim to descent from any particular breed. The first cross between two different breeds is not strictly a mongrel but a cross-bred, and such a dog will usually partake recognizably of some characteristics of each parent.

First crosses are not uncommonly made deliberately, to obtain the virtues of two breeds in a single animal. What often results is a mixed litter, some pups taking more after the dam and some after the sire, perhaps some blending undesirable characteristics from both sides, and, with luck, one or two which are exactly what the breeder was aiming at. First crosses are highly regarded by some breeders of working or companion dogs, and it is worth noting that first-cross Labrador/Golden Retrievers are being bred specifically for guide dog training. Provided that one bears in mind that the puppies will not automatically inherit the desired qualities, a first cross can be a very good buy if you are not interested in exhibition, and often has the advantage over the real mongrel of having been bred deliberately rather than by accident, and therefore probably raised with greater care than the offspring of a chance mating.

LEFT: *Traditionally, the Lurcher is a cross between a sighthound and another breed. Size, coat type and general appearance will depend upon the constituent breeds, as will temperamental qualities; generally speaking, the Lurcher breeder aims to retain the speed of the sighthound ancestor with the responsiveness to training of the other breed.*

LEFT: *Dogs of working sheepdog type need an outlet for their intelligence and working drive. The same factor which makes them unsuitable for a purely pet existence makes them highly successful performers in competitive obedience.*

ABOVE: *This mongrel terrier is a good example of a dog of mixed parentage. If a dog is being bought as a pet, the quality of parentage in show terms is of little consequence, because it is only on the showbench, and not in the personality, that such parentage will be reflected.*

There are also some kinds of dogs which fall in between the strict classifications of pedigree and non-pedigree. These are dogs which do not belong to an officially recognized breed and which in general are not as distinctly fixed in type as the pedigree types, but which nonetheless have been bred with a view to perpetuating certain desired characteristics. These are sometimes called 'typed dogs', and where the type becomes truly fixed it may eventually gain official recognition as a breed, as has happened recently in the case of the Border Collie in the United Kingdom and the United States.

Probably the best known of the 'typed dogs' is the Jack Russell Terrier. These small spirited hunting terriers are a common variety in many countries, as well as in Britain, but to date no agreement has been reached on the exact type, with different breeders favouring short-legged or long-legged, rough-coated or smooth-coated stock, and while such variation exists the Jack Russell cannot be considered a true breed.

Then there is the Lurcher – or rather, there are the Lurchers, for there are many types. In essence, the Lurcher is a cross between a sighthound and another breed, generally chosen for greater intelligence or tractability. The classic Lurcher is the first- or second-cross Collie-Greyhound, but many other crosses are used, from the smaller Whippet crosses to the showy Saluki crosses. The aim is to produce a hunting dog of great speed and unparalleled canniness, the ultimate 'poacher's dog'. Today, Lurchers are coming into fashion as pets and some are being bred with more attention to looks than to working qualities, the rough-coated deerhoundy type being favoured in this area, but this is not a town dog and keeping a Lurcher as a fashion accessory is rather like keeping a racing car for local shopping.

First and second crosses between two different breeds of sighthounds are termed 'long dogs' and are bred for coursing.

Another 'typed dog' not uncommonly met with is the working sheepdog, which is just what its name says. They are generally of near-Border Collie type and today are seen in the obedience ring as well as at their traditional work, sharing with the Border Collie the intelligence and responsiveness needed for competitive obedience.

RIGHT: *The Golden Retriever is deservedly popular as a family pet. Its working heritage has produced a gentle, amenable and intelligent dog which is trustworthy with children.*

BELOW: *Small breeds such as the Japanese Spitz are small enough to fit into a limited space and require less exercise than the larger breeds, while thoroughly enjoying long walks if these are on offer.*

RIGHT: *The Afghan Hound is one of the most fashionable breeds to acquire, but people do tend to overlook the fact that it is also one of the breeds that demand most attention.*

FAR RIGHT: *Small terriers such as the Norfolk, can be accommodated in the restricted space of the urban home, and are adaptable to a variety of lifestyles, although their abundant energy needs to be given an outlet.*

CHOOSING A BREED

The choice of breed involves consideration of a number of factors, ranging from issues of personal taste to more practical questions. In general, dogs with long coats or hair which requires constant trimming will need more care than the short-haired breeds, and may create more mess around the home during periods of moulting. Larger dogs need more space, more food and usually more exercise; dogs that have been bred for their working characteristics, whatever their size, are less easy to manage in a domestic environment. Some working breeds, such as working sheepdogs, should never be kept as pets. Certain breeds are naturally quieter than others, which can be an important consideration if there are neighbours close by.

The amount of exercise needed by a dog does not depend solely upon size: some of the larger breeds are comparatively sedentary, while many of the little dogs seem to have boundless energy which will take a great deal of walking off.

Temperament varies widely from breed to breed. Some breeds are naturally placid, some excitable. Some are much more easily trained than others. The independence and wilfulness of the Pekingese, for example, makes it an enchanting companion but incorporates no innate predisposition towards obedience – it has been said that nine out of ten Pekes are disobedient, and the tenth is really deaf! A naturally trainable breed such as the German Shepherd Dog or the Border Collie, however, will actually require obedience training to occupy its mind and keep it content.

Guard dogs such as the Rottweiler are often highly suspicious of strangers but generally tolerant of those they know well. Perhaps the least satisfactory group of dogs in terms of temperament for use as family pets are those breeds which for one reason or another were bred to have an aggressive temperament. Several of the terriers have a naturally fiery disposition that fits them better for their original role of attacking such formidable adversaries as foxes or badgers than for sharing the family home. Those dogs originally bred for fighting, such as the Staffordshire Bull Terrier, may be better avoided as family dogs, too. Although modern breeders have made strenuous efforts to purge aggressive traits from contemporary bloodlines, the fighting strain takes a lot of breeding out.

Function also affects the amount of exercise a dog requires. A gundog bred to range the grouse moors, probably covering in excess of forty miles in a day, is not going to fulfil its exercise needs in a stroll through the streets. A dainty lapdog designed to ornament a lady's boudoir, on the other hand, while it will almost certainly enjoy normal family life a great deal more than the over-luxurious environment for which it was created, will nonetheless not be the first choice for someone with an extremely active lifestyle.

It is worth visiting dog shows to see the variety of breeds available and to talk to breeders about the advantages and disadvantages of the types that appeal to you. The variations to be found amongst dogs make it possible to choose an animal that will please your eye as well as fit into your lifestyle, but never pick a breed on looks alone if you want a successful partnership.

The degree of sensitivity to human moods varies from breed to breed, too, and you need to consider this quality before obtaining a dog. An over-sensitive dog matched with a moody or irritable human makes a poor combination, where a more phlegmatic animal which copes better with human ups and downs can have a calming and comforting effect upon the owner. If you have children, too, it is particularly important to obtain a sensible and not too excitable breed.

Bearing in mind the original function for which a breed was developed will be helpful when you are choosing a breed. Gundogs such as a Retriever are relatively responsive to training compared with others such as the so-called sighthounds like the Afghan Hound, which have been developed for chasing game over a considerable distance.

HEREDITARY DEFECTS

DISORDER	OBSERVATIONS	BREEDS TYPICALLY AFFECTED
Clefts of lip and palate	May be hereditary in origin, but other factors, such as a nutritional deficiency in the bitch, may also be responsible.	American Cocker Spaniel, Beagle, Bernese Mountain Dog, Boston Terrier, Bulldog, Dachshund, German Shepherd Dog, Shih Tzu
Deafness	Dog often appears unresponsive, even stupid, until this disorder is recognized.	American Foxhound, Bull Terrier, Collie, Dachshund, English Foxhound, Great Dane, Scottish Terrier
Distichiasis	A double row of eyelashes; most common on upper lids. Causes severe irritation and excessive tear production. Surgery is the only effective treatment in the long term.	American Cocker Spaniel, Bedlington Terrier, Boston Terrier, Boxer, Griffon Bruxellois, Kerry Blue Terrier, Lakeland Terrier, Yorkshire Terrier
Ectropion	Eyelids directed outwards. Causes inflammation of the conjunctiva and cornea, with increased tear production. Needs to be corrected by surgery.	American Cocker Spaniel, Basset Hound, Bloodhound, Bulldog, Clumber Spaniel, St Bernard
Hip dysplasia	Deformed hip joints. Signs extremely variable: lameness in severe cases, yet may pass unnoticed in a mild case. Detected by radiography. Inherited, hence the need to check potential breeding stock for this weakness.	American Cocker Spaniel, English Setter, German Shepherd Dog, Giant Schnauzer, Shetland Sheepdog
Invertebral disc abnormalities	Symptoms influenced by locality of abnormality, as is the prognosis for treatment. Total, confined rest is essential for recovery, irrespective of other therapy. Surgery can be of assistance in some cases.	American Cocker Spaniel, Beagle, Boxer, Dachshund, Dandie Dinmont Terrier, Pekingese
Luxating patella	Results in lameness, typically about five months of age. Caused by movement of 'knee bone' or patella. Degree of weakness variable. Surgical correction is the only treatment.	Boston Terrier, Bichon Frise, Chihuahua, Pomeranian, Yorkshire Terrier
Progressive retinal atrophy (PRA)	The first sign may be that the dog appears to be having difficulty seeing at night. As its name suggests, this disease is progressive, and ultimately blindness will result. The time span may extend from months to years. It appears to be an inherited condition; different forms of PRA are believed to be inherited in different ways, so it can be either a dominant or recessive trait.	Border Collie, English Cocker Spaniel, English Springer Spaniel, Golden Retriever, Gordon Setter, Labrador Retriever, Pekingese, Pomeranian, Poodle, Samoyed, Shetland Sheepdog, Welsh Corgi
Umbilical hernia	Distinct, noticeable swelling around the umbilicus or 'belly-button', resulting from a partial protrusion of the abdominal contents. Can be corrected by surgery if necessary.	Basenji, Bull Terrier, Collie, Pekingese, Pointer, Weimaraner

Responsible breeders will have their dogs checked for potential inherited defects, of which the most significant tend to be hip dysplasia and progressive retinal atrophy (PRA). There are a large number of inherited and congenital problems however, often linked with particular breeds.

WHERE TO OBTAIN YOUR DOG

Puppies are available from a variety of sources but not all are suitable. Certain pet shops stock mongrel and even pedigree puppies and there are also large suppliers, who advertise a range of breeds in newspapers. Since in neither case are the puppies likely to have been bred on the premises, such sources are usually best avoided. The puppies will almost certainly be stressed, after having been moved from a breeding unit and mixed with other dogs in an environment which may not be ideal. Stress has been shown to be a major predisposing factor to parvovirus infection.

Many people prefer to acquire mongrels from animal welfare organizations. Addresses of these societies can be found in telephone directories, or obtained from a veterinarian. Litters of mongrel puppies are frequently given to these organizations, and make delightful pets. If new homes are not found for these puppies, they often have to be destroyed.

Obtaining an adult dog from this source is riskier, however, especially if the temperament and background of the dog are unknown. No organization will knowingly try to find a home for a vicious dog, but an individual may prove relatively withdrawn and nervous after maltreatment by previous owners. Due allowance must be made for such behaviour, especially at first, but, despite being warned beforehand, people still take on such dogs, only to return them a few days later. Ill-treated dogs require considerable patience and may never completely regain their trust in

humans. Those closest to them will probably be accepted eventually. Homes with small children are not ideal environments for dogs of this type, because any teasing, particularly with food, can have serious consequences.

Increasing numbers of pedigree dogs are also passing into the care of welfare organizations, often because their owners can no longer afford to keep them as pets. Before allowing pedigree dogs to go to new homes, many societies will want to be assured that the dog will not be used for breeding, and will often retain the dog's pedigree for this

TOP: *Selecting a puppy from a private home means that you can meet the mother, note how the puppies behave among their littermates, and pick one out at your leisure. Puppies from a private home are usually well balanced, due to the benefits of good personal care and early contact with people.*

RIGHT: *Dogs which have been kept in kennels may take time to adapt to the domestic environment. They may need to learn basic matters such as house training and respect for the owner's possessions, just like a young puppy.*

RIGHT: *Puppies from a breeding establishment need plenty of human attention before they are ready to go to their new homes. A reputable breeder will ensure that his or her puppies are properly socialized so that they are friendly and outgoing towards humans.*

LEFT: *Puppies which have been reared with children under sensible adult supervision will have had a good introduction to family life. Supervision of children with dogs is always essential to ensure that play does not become too rough, on either side. While most dogs are patient and tolerant – puppies more so than adult dogs – it is important that children are taught not to handle a dog roughly or provoke it by teasing.*

reason when a new home is found. Some insist on neutering, and the new owners will probably be interviewed to establish whether they will provide a good permanent home for the dog. Enquiries of this type and even home visits are not unusual, and should not be taken as a personal slight. The society is just trying to ensure that the dog has a stable future.

Animal welfare organizations are invariably self-financed and rarely wealthy. Do not forget to give a donation to help their work continue. Hopefully, the public can be educated eventually to adopt a more responsible attitude.

Greyhounds which have been retired from the racing track, certainly by the age of five years and often younger, are sometimes offered as pets. Since these dogs have been kept in kennels, it may not be easy to adapt them to a domestic environment: they need house-training, and de-conditioning so that they learn to control the urge to chase everything that moves. However, there are specialist greyhound homing societies which undertake such training before seeking to place the dogs in pet homes, and such animals can make ideal family dogs.

Breeders occasionally wish to place retired show or breeding animals in pet homes, and again such dogs should

be regarded with caution. A caring breeder will genuinely be looking for a home where a valued animal can enjoy well-earned individual attention, but some breeders will simply be attempting to pass on kennel animals which have never been properly socialized.

The ideal source from which to obtain a pet will always be direct from the breeder. In this way you can inspect the puppy's environment and at least one of its parents, you can obtain detailed information about the breed's requirements and usually a helpful after-care service, and the puppy itself is not exposed to the additional stress and risk of infection from changing home more than once. The majority of breeders are genuine enthusiasts who, although they cannot keep all the dogs they breed, have an interest in ensuring their subsequent welfare.

There are various means of discovering the addresses of such people. Local newspapers often carry advertisements from breeders in the immediate vicinity, but for more unusual breeds, travelling further afield will probably be necessary. Directories listing breeders under breed headings are published in many countries, and revised annually. These may be available in libraries. Specialist papers and periodicals will also provide details of breeders and reports of

shows, revealing which bloodlines are winning consistently. Visiting shows is also recommended for those seeking a potential show dog. Veterinarians may also be prepared to pass on addresses of breeders known to them. If you have problems in locating puppies of a particular breed, the dog press will enable you to contact the secretary of the breed club with an enquiry.

Ensure that you make your requirements clear to the breeder, whether you want a pup as a pet, for working, or for exhibition. A poorly coloured or mismarked puppy may be available to a pet home at a substantially lower price than one with exhibition potential. Bargains of this nature must be approached with slight scepticism, however, if the dog has a real deformity, since this could prove a costly source of trouble later. It is well worth enquiring about any examination which the breeding stock may have undergone, for hip dysplasia for example, with a view to minimizing the risk of hereditary or congenital diseases in the puppies. Most breeders will readily volunteer such information.

CHOOSING AN INDIVIDUAL

Choosing a puppy or adult dog is almost certainly the most important decision regarding his pet that an owner ever makes, for the animal chosen will be his companion for many years to come. Obviously, it makes sense to select a healthy individual, but it is also important to consider the puppy's temperament and behavioural traits.

The temperament of a dog is crucial and depends on many factors. One of these is certainly its parentage, so at least the mother, and if possible the father, should be seen and their temperament assessed. Environment is also an important factor. The actual phase of social development in puppies is concentrated largely in the 4- to 12-week period after birth. Individuals are at their most impressionable at this time and start to relate to their littermates and other creatures, including humans. If the litter has not been handled frequently by the breeder, and accustomed to some of the bustle of a normal human household, a vital stage in socialization will have been missed out.

Puppies will not be fully independent and able to go to a new home until they are seven or eight weeks old, and many breeders prefer to wait a little longer, especially if they are breeding for exhibition and want to be able to assess show potential. However, a puppy left with its littermates for too long will become more strongly socialized towards other dogs than to humans. Research has revealed that if puppies have not experienced human attention by the age of three months, they are likely to be withdrawn, and subsequently prove unresponsive to training. Individuals isolated too soon from other puppies show the reverse effect, being disadvantaged in later life when meeting other dogs, and bitches may even refuse to mate for this reason.

Breeders are generally happy for litters to be seen before they are ready to go to new homes, often around five weeks after birth, and this provides an opportunity to decide whether the litter, the parents and the environment come up to your standards.

The environment where the puppies are being kept is significant. Their surroundings should be relatively clean, and any motions in the pen must be firm, not loose or runny in consistency, which indicates a digestive disturbance. A litter which has been reared close to people, rather than being kept isolated in a kennel, is likely to prove more amenable to human company, and the puppies will settle more quickly in a new home.

It is important to be able to recognize whether a puppy is healthy or not. A youngster which appears thin, with its ribs in evidence, is likely to have been undernourished and if it also has a pot belly, it probably has worms. In any case, a closer examination of a puppy should always be carried out, with the owner's permission. The coat is an important indicator of good health and should be shiny

and full, unless it is wiry. Signs of fleas, or lice (more common in puppies than adult dogs), indicate a general lack of care.

The skin of a puppy is quite pliable, and should be loose to the touch. It is worth feeling the skin underneath the puppy, in the midline, to see if there is a swelling under the skin, which could indicate an umbilical hernia. This is not usually a serious complaint, although it may require surgical correction later. Herniation elsewhere on the abdomen is less common. The eyes must be clear and bright, while the ears should not show any signs of discharge or smell unpleasant. There should be no hint of lameness when the puppy walks.

Puppies vary in temperament, even within the same litter. Bearing in mind the fact that young puppies sleep for a great deal of the time, it is worth visiting at feeding time, when they will be alert and demonstrating their individual personalities. Take time to play with the litter and study how each individual responds to you. Which puppy out of a litter most appeals to you comes down to personal preference. There is unlikely to be one best dog in any litter, because differences in human personality mean that different dogs appeal to, and suit, different people. For example, a bold assertive dog would not suit a quiet, elderly person living alone; similarly a gentle, submissive bitch might not suit an outgoing person with a forceful personality.

It is best to try and judge the potential character and degree of dominance of a young puppy, and then relate this to the character of the future owner. It is obviously difficult to make judgements of this kind for either party, but is certainly worthwhile studying a group of puppies for a time and attempting to assess something of their character in terms of timidity, friendliness, alertness, activity and dominance.

It can be a mistake to pick the most outgoing pup of a litter, the one that flings itself joyfully upon you and worries your shoelaces: this one is likely to be the most dominant puppy, and may require much more training to fit into the household. Equally, the puppy that is reluctant to investigate a visitor will be the most submissive one, and will need a great deal of gentleness and encouragement if it is to grow up into a confident adult. For a companion dog in the typical human family, puppies that fall between these two extremes are likely to be the best choice.

You may well find that a conscientious breeder is as eager to vet your suitability for one of his or her puppies as you are to investigate the suitability of the puppy for your own home. A breeder who cares about where the puppies are going is likely to have given the litter the best possible start in life, so do not be offended if you find yourself being grilled about your lifestyle and your expectations of a dog!

CHOOSING AN ADULT DOG

When choosing an adult dog, it is just as important to check its physical condition and take note of its behaviour. Physical health should be apparent in a clean, shiny coat, free of parasites; in bright alert eyes, and in clean nose and ears. Watch the animal walk to be sure that there is no lameness or lack of coordination.

Find out as much as you can about the animal. Has it had any training at all? Is it house-trained and leash-trained, at least? Has it any known vices? A country dog which has developed the deadly fault of chasing livestock may be thought to be suitable for a home in the town where it will be well away from farm animals; but, before taking it on, consider that this vice can easily be transmuted to urban cat-catching, and may make you extremely unpopular with cat-loving neighbours. A confirmed escaper may simply have suffered from unendurable boredom at the hands of busy owners, and may be broken of this habit by a new master who can keep it occupied; but on the other hand the vice may be too well-established to be cured and you may be taking on more than your garden fence can contain. An aggressive dog which has never learned to acknowledge human mastery is best avoided by all but the most experienced dog-trainers.

In the case of dogs obtained from a rescue home, there may be little information available about their propensities. Something can be learned from seeing how such a dog reacts to its present handler, and of course how it reacts to you. A wagging tail is easy to interpret, but an adult dog in need of rehousing may well be uncertain simply because of the circumstances rather than through any defect of temperament. A cold or unfriendly immediate reception may indicate a dog that will not make a good pet, or it may simply be a response to insecurity, even fear, in which case

sitting and talking to the animal for a while may encourage it to come out of its shell and demonstrate a willingness to make friends.

Ask if you may take the dog out on a collar and lead before committing yourself. You may find that it has never been leash trained and pulls like a maniac, which will take time and patience to remedy, or that it is aggressive with other dogs or even human passers-by. It may be wildly excited at the prospect of going out, and you need to establish whether it will quieten down or whether it is a neurotic individual which will drive you mad with perpetual leaping and barking. It may be confident enough in its kennel, but once outside demonstrate a fear of the outside world from lack of exposure to noise and traffic, which again will take hard work to cure.

If you have children, introduce them to the dog before you completely make your mind up, and find out how it reacts to them. It is essential to pick a dog which is reliable with children. If it simply does not like children, neither they, the dog nor you will have an easy time.

One simple test of temperament which may be carried out is to see how the dog behaves when presented with its food bowl. It may eat placidly without minding your presence, but it may growl and demonstrate pronounced possessiveness towards its dinner, in which case it is predisposed towards dominance and will not be easy to train.

It is always worthwhile, when obtaining a dog as an adult, to check if arrangements can be made to return it if after a few days if it proves impossible to fit into your household. While many adult dogs can and do change homes successfully, it is not always possible to find out all about the dog on immediate acquaintance and there may be a personality clash. Some individuals, regrettably, simply do not respond well to re-housing, and you may need to acknowledge this fact.

RIGHT: *A litter of puppies enjoying the fresh air. This breeder has gone to the trouble to ensure that the puppies are well housed and reared in a healthy environment to give them the best possible start in life.*

*Puppies are very appealing, whichever breed they are, but they do not remain puppies for long and it is important to take into account the eventual size and temperament. The Staffordshire Bull Terrier puppy (**RIGHT**) will grow up to be a medium-sized but powerful dog, a delightful companion and good with children but with a tendency to aggression with other dogs. The Jack Russell puppy (**FAR RIGHT**) will make a smaller, more excitable adult, a lively companion which may have a strong hunting drive.*

LEFT: *An adult dog will be the product of its previous upbringing. It may have the advantage of having been taught good house manners before you acquire it; it may also have developed some bad habits which are not immediately apparent, such as possessiveness over bones, which will require patience on the part of the new owner to eradicate.*

Chapter Four

THE NEW DOG

EQUIPMENT

Prepare for your new pet's arrival by acquiring the basic equipment needed before you fetch the dog or puppy home. A vast range of pet equipment is now available, but only certain items will be essential at the outset. What must be provided comprises: somewhere for the animal to sleep; bowls for food and water; a collar and lead; and something to play with. For the young puppy, the equipment that you buy will be for short-term use – like a child, it will outgrow these and need a different type of gear as it grows up. For the older dog, initial purchases should be made with care as they will last much longer.

EQUIPMENT FOR THE PUPPY

The young puppy spends a high proportion of its time sleeping. Its bed is therefore a very important part of the puppy's world and the puppy must be taught to recognize its bed as its own particular territory. In the beginning, there is no point in providing an expensive or elaborate bed. For one thing, the puppy has a long way to go before it attains adult size, so a much smaller sleeping area is required at this stage. For another, puppies are inevitably destructive, especially during the teething period, and the bed is going to be chewed – apart from the mess, the pup runs the risk of swallowing fragments.

At this stage, therefore, the most satisfactory bed will be a clean cardboard box, with the front cut away for easy access. The bottom of the box should be lined with newspaper, and a blanket provided on top. The box can easily be replaced if it is soiled or chewed, and as the puppy grows, it is simple to provide another box of a larger size. Once the deciduous teeth are lost, and the accompanying chewing stage is passed, it will be time enough to think about a permanent sleeping basket.

It is quite a good idea to construct a playpen around the puppy's box, where it can be confined when necessary. This will be useful to prevent the puppy from slipping out into the street when the door is open, to keep it out of the way when you are engaged in some household task that would not benefit from the puppy's assistance, and also to protect the puppy itself from excessive attention from young children. It is possible to buy wire mesh panels for this purpose from a pet shop. The panels clip together as required and will store flat when not in use; some types can be fitted into the back of the car to make a travelling cage. However, it is quite easy to construct a home-made pen, and, since it is for short-term use, you may prefer to save the expense of a manufactured one.

There is a growing fashion for indoor kennels, which combine the function of bed and playpen: the door can be

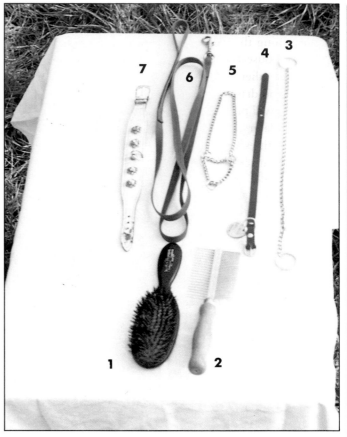

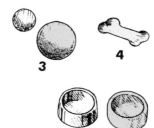

LEFT: *Essential equipment for a new dog includes: a cardboard box (1) or dog basket (2) for sleeping purposes; toys such as rubber balls (3) or a hide chew (4); feeding dishes (5); and drinking dishes (6).*

ABOVE: *Collars and leads and grooming equipment will also be required. This selection for a poodle puppy comprises: bristle brush (1) and stainless steel comb (2), with wide teeth on one side and narrower on the other; a check chain (3) for training purposes; buckle collar with identity medallion (4); double-action check chain (5) as an alternative to (3); lightweight nylon lead (6); and a traditional jewelled poodle collar (7) for special occasions.*

left open so that the pup can use its bed or not as it chooses, or shut to confine the animal. This is useful both in terms of accustoming the animal to accept restraint, and also for facilitating house-training, for the pup will be reluctant to foul the area where it sleeps.

Feeding and drinking bowls are obviously necessary, although you will probably have to think in terms of buying a larger set later on when the pup has grown and needs greater quantities of food and drink. Various types of pet bowl are manufactured, and are stocked by most pet shops. Plastic generally is not to be recommended, since most bowls made of this material are easily chewed or scratched, and prove difficult to clean thoroughly as a result. A puppy of one of the larger breeds, with powerful jaws, may even be able to chew a plastic bowl up and swallow the pieces, with detrimental results. Stainless steel containers are relatively expensive, but are much more hygienic, although they can be tipped over quite easily and, because they are so light, a playful pup may be tempted to pick them up and carry them around the house, spreading the contents with gay abandon. The traditional glazed earthenware bowl is easy to clean and stable, and may be the best buy at this stage.

Although your puppy will not be able to go out for walks until it has completed its course of vaccinations to protect it from infection, it is recommended that you obtain a lightweight collar and lead so that the pup grows accustomed to them around the home. Collars may be made of leather, nylon or plastic. It is a good idea to buy a collar specifically made for puppy wear, which will be soft, both for comfort and to avoid wearing away the baby fur, and will also be fully adjustable to allow for growth. Check that the collar fits properly: remember that the puppy's neck grows with the rest of the body, and never fasten the collar too tightly. The leash at this stage is intended for accustoming the pup to the idea of one rather than for control, and should also be lightweight.

When the puppy is old enough to go outdoors, it will need an identity disc attached to the collar. This is not only sensible, ensuring that if the puppy escapes accidentally it will carry your address and/or telephone number so that it can be returned home without difficulty: it is also a legal requirement in various countries, including Britain and the United States. It makes sense to attach such a medallion to the puppy collar from the start, not only just in case the puppy somehow slips out and is lost, but to accustom it to the feel and jingling sound.

Various types of identity disc are available, the commonest being a metal medallion on which the information is etched, or a plastic capsule, containing a piece of paper on which the information is written in indelible ink. It is also possible to have an identity number tattooed directly on to the dog, either on the inside of the ear or on the inner

ABOVE: *A playpen where the puppy can be confined for short periods is useful initially. The area should include a bed, as well as food and water pots. The puppy will soon come to recognize this as its own territory, and, having been out playing, will return to sleep here.*

thigh where the hair is thinner, but this is not yet a usual method of identification.

Puppies will play with anything they can take in their jaws, and if you provide approved toys from the start it will be easier to deflect their attentions from articles which are not permissible such as your shoes. Toys should be chosen with care, as many of those for sale in pet shops are unsuitable, and could be chewed into sharp fragments or inadvertently swallowed. Small balls are included in the latter category, and may even prove lethal, so ensure that any ball is too large to fit into the puppy's mouth.

Rubber rings are useful for training purposes because they can be thrown for the dog to retrieve. These are unlikely to be harmful, but chewing should not be allowed. The young dog's desire to chew is quite natural and needs to be encouraged properly otherwise expensive shoes and furniture may be damaged irreparably by a puppy's teeth. Give the puppy a pair of old rubber slippers for the purpose, or buy one of the special chew toys that can be obtained from a pet shop.

A young puppy may enjoy a soft toy such as an old teddy-bear as a comforting substitute for its littermates. If you provide anything along these lines, never underestimate the power of the pup's teeth and ensure that the toy is well constructed.

EQUIPMENT FOR THE OLDER DOG

The older dog can be provided with a permanent bed, but make sure that this is easy to clean and remember that even an adult dog may while away an hour chewing thoughtfully on its bed. Choose a bed large enough to accommodate the fully-grown dog in comfort. The traditional wicker basket is not as easy to keep clean as some types of bed, and is particularly vulnerable to chewing. Plastic or fibreglass dog beds are widely available, and can be washed down; lined with a blanket, which should also be washed regularly, they can be very comfortable as well as durable.

Some dogs show a marked preference for a raised bed. The most successful dog bed of this type of the writer's experience was a home-made half-size camp-bed, but many dogs will opt for a comfortable armchair, and an old chair can be made over for the dog's use. Of course, given a chance, the average dog would choose to share its owner's bed!

During recent years, bean bags manufactured for dogs have gained greatly in popularity. These are available in various sizes and are usually filled with polystyrene granules. They should have two coverings; the outer one should be removable and washable. A beanbag can also be a play area, but be sure that the covering is strong and cannot be ripped open accidentally. It is also safer to opt for one of the more expensive types with fire-retardant properties. Beanbags appear more comfortable than the traditional bed and are probably of value for dogs suffering from arthritic problems, because the dog is not restricted to a single position when resting on a beanbag as it is in a dog bed.

An appropriate collar and leash will be required. A confusing array of collars is available, but these can be considered as fitting into two basic categories, those which buckle around the neck, and 'choke' or 'check' collars which slip loosely over the dog's head and are tightened or slackened by control of the lead. You will almost certainly require one of each.

Buckle collars may be made of leather, nylon or plastic; they may be flat, either broad or narrow, or rolled. The different shapes are designed for different breeds. Dogs with a hard, short coat can wear the broad collars, which would damage the fur of long- or soft-coated breeds; for the latter the rolled collar is recommended. It is worth finding out which sort of collar your breed traditionally wears, both for practical and aesthetic reasons. Hound collars as worn by the sighthounds are usually wide and may be plain or ornamented; the powerful and thick-necked bull breeds traditionally wear strong, heavy collars, often decorated with studs. Poodle collars as worn by the pet poodle are usually wide and jewelled, but it should be borne in mind that these are only suited to the short pet trims as they will break the fur.

Check collars may be made of chain or nylon. They are useful training aids, properly used, but it is important to choose the right size and weight. Too short, and the collar will be hard to put on and uncomfortable for the dog; too

LEFT: *A variety of collars and leads is available. Essentially you will require a buckle collar to carry an identity medallion, which should always be worn by the dog when it is off the lead, and some form of training collar.*

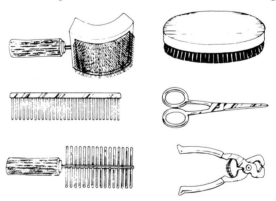

ABOVE: *The necessary grooming implements vary according to the kind of coat your dog has. For the puppy a soft brush to accustom it to regular grooming will be adequate at first; later you will need a brush appropriate to the type of fur, plus a comb for longer-coated breeds.*

LEFT: *A dog guard restricts your dog to the back of the car so that it cannot distract the driver. Try to accustom your dog to travelling from an early age.*

long, and it will be too easily slipped; too heavy, and it will damage the fur and also fail to hang correctly. As a general rule, the larger linked chains are less damaging to the coat.

It is recommended that you acquire one of each type of collar. The check collar is by far the easier type on which to train your dog. However, it should not be left on when the dog is off the leash or tied up, because it can easily snag on something and choke the animal; it can also be slipped off. The buckle collar should be worn when the dog is tied or running free, and this will carry the identity medallion.

An alternative to the collar is a harness. This is not a good training aid, because it is easy for the dog to pull against it, but in the case of breeds such as the Dachshund, which may be prone to neck problems, it will ease the tension in this sensitive area. An elderly person may find a harness helpful in picking a dog up because it can support the dog's weight.

Food and water bowls need to be substantial and easily cleaned. It is surprising what large bowls a big dog will require, and, once the dog has outgrown the destructive age, a breed the size of a German Shepherd could well be provided with a washing-up bowl for the food and a bucket for water.

Grooming equipment is mandatory for an older dog, and can be useful for a puppy to accustom it to this procedure from an early age. The tools required will depend to some extent on the coat of the dog concerned. Metal combs are available in various sizes, and some have handles which makes grooming a long-haired dog, in particular, easier. Plastic combs tend to break and are thus not advisable. While combs will remove some dead hair and help to prevent the coat from becoming matted, a stripping brush is recommended for the breeds that do not shed in the conventional sense. There are other brushes that can also be used for removing dead hair; they are made from either rubber or horsehair and are known as hound or grooming gloves because they fit over the hand. These are also used to polish the coat and give it an attractive lustre. Another type of brush which fits over the hand by means of a strap is the dandy pad. It is often used on terriers and is thus sometimes called a terrier palm pad. In fact, the brush derived its name from the Dandie Dinmont Terrier.

You will need to consider if any equipment is needed in connection with transporting the dog from one place to another. A carrier is always a useful acquisition for the smaller breeds, enabling them to be taken in comfort to the veterinary surgery or on holiday, and it can double up as sleeping quarters. These are available in various sizes, and made of wicker, fibreglass or wire-coated mesh. It is worth remembering that a dog in such a carrier travels free on a train, whereas if it is not in a container you will have to pay half fare.

When taking your dog out in the car, it is a good idea to restrain him behind a dog guard. Certainly until it is perfectly trained no dog should be allowed to ride loose in the car, as it could cause a fatal accident by distracting the driver's attention. Dog guards come in various types: always choose a design with square or rectangular mesh rather than a series of bars. This is especially important for fine-nosed breeds such as the Whippet as they may get trapped in a barrier with bars. Dog guards do not necessarily have to be fitted to the structure of the vehicle. Simply attach them to the floor and roof by means of adjustable screw feet. If in doubt, consult your garage. With smaller dogs, it is possible to use an all-mesh carrying cage as an alternative to fitting a dog guard. These are more convenient and enable you to transport several dogs safely in a relatively confined space. Many exhibitors take several dogs by this means in the back of an estate car, with the rear seats down, when travelling to and from shows.

Other essential equipment for the dog owner is a towel that can be used for drying the dog after a bath or when it has been raining. It is surprising how often you will come back from a walk with a soaked dog, and a brisk rub down with a towel will not only save the dog from developing a chill or even rheumatism, but will considerably extend the lives of your carpets and furniture.

Dog coats should be considered for thin-coated breeds such as the Italian Greyhound, which can suffer from the cold, although a dog with normally dense fur will actually be warmer without a coat, as the insulating qualities of the fur are reduced when it is squashed down under fabric. Dogs will often do their best to remove coats, and a strong fastening on a coat of the appropriate size is essential. Some designs incorporate luminous material; this can be particularly useful in country areas because it alerts approaching car drivers to the presence of the dog and its owner on roads where there are no pavements.

The adult dog as much as the puppy will enjoy carefully selected toys, and the same rules apply of picking playthings which cannot be chewed up or swallowed.

BELOW: *For the first week or two, the puppy's diet should be the same as was provided by its breeder, to reduce the risk of digestive upsets.*

SETTLING IN

Helping your new pet to settle in well begins when you make your arrangements to collect it from the breeder. Remember that this will be the first time the puppy has been moved: it will not be accustomed to the noise and bustle of the outside world and may be frightened, nor will it be used to the unfamiliar sensation of travelling by road, which may well upset it and it may even be sick. If you are driving, try to persuade a friend to accompany you so that the puppy can travel on a passenger's lap, which should be protected with an old towel or blanket. Otherwise, take a secure container to put the puppy in, and make sure that it really is secure. A frightened puppy could escape from a cardboard box, and this could distract the driver.

If you plan to use public transport (pets are usually permitted on trains and buses, but find out in advance), remember that you may have to pay for the puppy and that it should be contained securely, preferably in a purpose-made carrier or basket. It is not uncommon for a puppy to urinate while in transit, and a cardboard box may well disintegrate when wet. A thick layer of paper and a blanket should be placed on the floor of the carrier, to absorb urine and to make the puppy more comfortable. It is not recommended that you simply carry the puppy in your arms, because it is likely to wriggle frantically, and in any case, this would expose it to infections against which it as yet has no immunity.

It is always better to collect the puppy during the morning if possible, so that it will have time to settle in its new surroundings before nightfall. Allow yourself time to talk to the breeder, and obtain as much information as possible about the pup's requirements. The breeder should provide you with a diet sheet, to show what the puppy has been eating and the frequency of feeding. For the first week, it is sensible to follow this closely, to minimize the risk of digestive disturbances. Changes in feeding should only be introduced gradually, over a period of time.

After the journey, the puppy will want to relieve itself, and should be encouraged, right from the start, to do this outside, supervised so that it cannot run away. If the weather is bad, the puppy should be taught to urinate or defecate on a sheet of newspaper, preferably placed close to the door where it would normally go out to perform its functions.

The house should have been prepared for the pup's arrival before you collect it. Decide where you want your puppy to sleep and place its bed in this position. The site shold be relatively warm and draught-free, and it should be easy to clean up after any accidents, bearing in mind that the puppy will not be house-broken. It is also important that the puppy should not be isolated, but integrated as far as possible into the family. Many people decide to use the

ABOVE: *At first, the new puppy will miss the comfort of its mother or its siblings. Loving reassurance will help it to redirect its affections towards its new, human family.*

kitchen for this purpose, provided it is large enough. The kitchen usually has a floor which is easily wiped down, and is usually near an outside door, which will help with house training.

The puppy will take time to adjust to its new environment and may not eat heartily at first. When food is offered, the puppy should be left alone with its bowl for about a quarter of an hour. Any food remaining after this period should be removed, but a fresh supply of water must always be available. After a brief period of play, the young dog can be placed in its bed and will probably go to sleep.

At first, the puppy needs to investigate its new surroundings and new family. Do not push yourself upon the youngster if he is shy at first, but allow him to build up his confidence. Remember that young puppies need a great deal of rest, and do not allow any members of the family, particularly children, to disturb the pup when it is resting.

Always handle the puppy gently and carefully. When picking it up, be sure to provide adequate support from beneath so that the hindquarters do not hang down. You can carry a puppy resting in the crook of your arm with its hind legs being supported from beneath and its forelegs restrained by your other hand. It is useful to pick up a puppy regularly so that it will not be frightened when handled in this way later in life. Although a bitch may carry her pups when young by the scruff of the neck, do not follow this method as it can lead to injury in an older

puppy and is uncomfortable. Methods of handling an older, larger dog will vary depending on its size.

The first night in strange surroundings can be an upsetting experience for a young puppy. Do not be surprised if it howls for long periods at this time. Try to get it to settle down in its bed. It will miss the warmth and comfort of its littermates, and may settle down more easily if you provide a hot water bottle under its blanket – but make sure that this is securely protected from sharp puppy teeth, or you may come downstairs in the morning to find water everywhere and a very disconsolate puppy. A soft toy such as a teddy-bear may provide a substitute for littermates, and some breeders recommend an old alarm clock wrapped in a blanket, whose ticking simulates the heart-beat of a companion.

If all else fails, you may want to place the puppy in a pen in your bedroom. Protect your rug as far as possible with a layer of plastic sheeting covered with a thick layer of newspapers on top. The major problem with allowing the puppy to sleep in the bedroom is that it may refuse to sleep elsewhere in the house without considerable persuasion after it settles into its surroundings. When introducing strange dogs to each other, it is probably best to keep them apart at night at first, in case both decide to sleep in the same place and disagree accordingly.

The typical puppy will cry when left alone at night, and it may keep this up for some time. Never get angry with a young dog at this stage, even if it howls incessantly. This will simply upset it more than ever. Dogs are very sensitive animals and respond to the tone of your voice; it is much better to attempt to comfort the puppy by speaking in a soft, reassuring manner.

On the other hand, never capitulate to the pup's demand to be allowed to have its own way, or you will be building up trouble for the future. Once you have decided where it is to sleep, try putting up with the noise for a night or two in the hope that it will realize that this does not achieve anything. If you find it necessary to tell the pup to be quiet, speak to it firmly through the closed door (or from the comfort of your bed if it is in a pen in the bedroom), but do not make the mistake of going to the animal. If you do so, even if this is only to reprimand the pup, it will redouble its efforts to attract your attention next time.

Try to establish a routine with set mealtimes for your puppy right from the start as this will be very reassuring. Follow the feeding directions provided by the previous owner as closely as possible at first. Decide upon the name for your pet and always use the name at every opportunity so that the puppy associates itself with this sound. If the whole family can be involved in the puppy's care from the start, so much the better because this overcomes any tendency for the young dog to develop into a 'single person animal'.

INTRODUCTION TO THE HOUSEHOLD

When you bring your new puppy home, it has to learn to live with your existing household, and they too have to learn to live with the pup. If you live alone, you have basically only your own preferences and habits to take into account, although you will have to think in terms of the puppy's interaction with the other people in your life, from friends and visitors to the milkman and postman, and even the strangers you encounter in the street or in the park.

If there are other adults in the household, you should have talked about your attitudes towards and expectations of the puppy before you acquired it. If one of you wants the pup and the other does not, allowances will have to be made on both sides. If your expectations of the puppy differ and you treat it differently, it will become confused and will be difficult to train.

If you have children, you will need to explain to them how the puppy should be treated and encourage them to take a responsible and caring attitude. Particular care must be taken if the children are too young to understand, or somebody may get hurt. You may already have other pets in the household, and in that case introductions need to be carefully planned and the ensuing relationships monitored to avoid mishaps and even fatalities!

CHILDREN

A child has no instinctive understanding of an animal's needs, and has to learn how to handle the puppy, as well as to respect the pup's need to be left in peace some of the time. If a child handles a puppy roughly, the new pet may be hurt or even killed. Equally, it may retaliate and bite the child. The puppy, too, has to learn to restrain its natural rumbustiousness in play, and at first it is likely to use its teeth too much, tearing clothes and nipping fingers. Smaller children may be knocked over by a puppy as small as a Miniature Poodle, while the larger breeds are quite capable of bowling over even an adult as they leap joyously around.

Constant supervision is the only rule for safety, at least until the child is of an age to be truly sensible and the dog has lived with you long enough for you to have complete confidence in both child and animal. No baby or toddler should ever be left alone even for a moment with any dog.

If you have a very young child, however, shutting it away from the dog all the time is no way to teach the dog that this is a member of the family. Introduce them to each other under restraint, holding the child and keeping the pup on a leash so that it cannot startle the baby with a sudden lunge or be grabbed by a small hand. A very young child can be repeatedly encouraged to be gentle, with an adult holding its hand and demonstrating that the puppy should be stroked rather than bashed or tweaked. The combination of a baby human and a baby puppy can be very demanding of adult time and you may prefer to delay the acquisition of a dog until the child is older; however, if you are prepared for the extra work involved, the two will grow up together and often seem to develop a close and understanding relationship, having much in common as the two least civilized members of the household.

Jealousy can be a problem, for the dog's growing love for his owners may be very possessive and it may resent attention given to the children; similarly, a young child may be jealous of the time spent on the dog. It is important to ensure that both parties understand that each is a member of the family and entitled to attention. If the dog demonstrates too much jealousy, it may be advisable to think about re-homing it, as this problem often grows worse and the child may be bitten.

On the whole, animals seem to show an understanding of the difference between adults and children, and many dogs will allow a child to get away with behaviour they would not accept from adults, but it is not fair on the dog to allow roughness on the part of the child to go unchecked. Children must learn to respect the dog's sleeping area and food bowls. Some dogs which are otherwise reliable will snarl and even bite if a toddler crawls up to their food, and you should be on the alert for warning signals.

The older child should be encouraged to join in looking

LEFT: *With patience, a dog can be taught to accept other pets as part of the family. This Pekingese has learned to regard the Dwarf Lop rabbit as a companion rather than as a potential prey animal.*

after the dog, and can be a great help in teaching your pet its manners. Many dog training clubs have special classes for child handlers, and this can be very rewarding for both child and dog.

OTHER PETS

You may already have a dog, and wish to introduce a puppy into the household. If you take care over the introduction, the older dog may appreciate the company of a younger companion, although if the established dog is already of an advanced age it is not really fair to expect it to put up with the disturbance created by a new puppy.

The risk is that the established dog may resent the newcomer, and it is up to you to minimize the likelihood of conflict. Remember that the new arrival is invading the territory of the resident dog, and therefore particular reassurance needs to be given to the older dog so that it does not feel that its position as the dominant individual is being usurped by the newcomer. Hierarchy is important to dogs and invokes strong instinctive feelings that are derived

LEFT: *The bond between a child and a dog can become very strong.*

RIGHT: *A dog that is past middle age may find the introduction of a lively puppy to the household too demanding.*

from their ancestors – packs of wolves.

The introduction of a new adult dog means that a rank order has to be established. It may be a good idea to introduce the two animals first on neutral territory outside the confines of the home – in a nearby park, for example. Bitches as a rule tend to be less aggressive than male dogs, and they are more likely to live alongside each other in harmony than are two male dogs. Continued supervision will be needed at first to prevent the dogs fighting to decide the order of dominance. Feeding times are always especially likely to lead to disagreements, and the dogs should be fed separately, well out of reach of each other, and preferably in separate rooms.

The most important contribution to harmony that the owner can make is to ensure that the established dog's dominant position is confirmed by giving it slight but definite precedence over the newcomer, reducing the likelihood of a challenge.

There is less likelihood of conflict if the newcomer is a puppy, for its youth clearly marks it out as of lower ranking. Nonetheless, the established dog should still receive equal, and preferably more attention than the puppy to confirm its ranking.

With other pets, like cats, a similar method of introduction should prevent difficulties arising, although the cat may resent the puppy for a few days and disappear for longer periods than usual. It will take several weeks for dog and cat to accept each other fully but they may then become devoted companions.

Remember that cats and dogs do not speak quite the same language. The puppy demonstrates its willingness to be friends by bouncing joyfully at its new furry friend, who may well take this as an unjustified assault and retaliate with claws out, so make sure that you are on hand to supervise early meetings, encouraging polite behaviour on the one hand and giving reassurance on the other. Avoid forcing the animals upon each other but allow them time to grow used to each other's ways. The dog is naturally a protective animal, and will accept the cat as a member of its family to be looked after and guarded. The cat, in contrast, is a more reserved and solitary creature, but it will gradually come to tolerate and, at times, even positively welcome a dog into its home territory.

Even if you do not yourself own a cat, dogs should be introduced to the species and taught that it is not permissible to chase them. Quite apart from the fact that your neighbours will not welcome having their cats hounded by your pet, the cornered cat is a deadly opponent, and very few dogs can safely take on an enraged feline. To avoid the risk of serious injury to your dog at some stage, it should

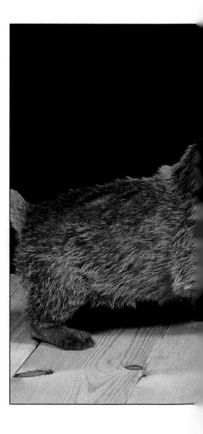

be accustomed to cats at an early age.

Because the dog is a social animal, it can develop a warm and friendly relationship with other species. Small pets, such as rabbits and guinea-pigs, will at first be perceived as playthings or prey, but with gentle training the dog can be taught that these too are members of its household, to be treated with respect and even affection. As always, the introduction should be gradual and well supervised, but it is much better to have a dog that can be trusted with smaller pets than one which is perpetually yearning to dismantle your child's favourite guinea-pig.

While on the subject of other animals, it is worthwhile introducing your dog to farm stock at an early age if at all possible. The dog is a hunter, and its instinctive reaction to a field of sheep or cows is to chase them. This will not do the animals any good at all, and any farmer is at liberty to shoot a dog he sees chasing his stock. Even if you live in a town you may want to spend the occasional day in the country, and the earlier the better for teaching your dog that chasing livestock is absolutely forbidden.

LEFT: *Puppies are naturally inquisitive and will naturally be interested in other animals. A strong bond can develop between a puppy and kitten as they grow up together. This Norfolk Terrier puppy and tabby kitten are both babies with no negative experience to overcome, and will readily make playmates.*

ABOVE: *An older dog may well appreciate the company of a young individual, although care must be taken in the early stages to ensure that the established dog does not feel challenged by the newcomer.*

CARE OF THE NEW PUPPY

The new puppy requires some special care in terms of feeding, exercise supervision, worming and protection against disease. The breeder from whom you obtain your puppy should provide information to help you care for your new acquisition, but certain general rules apply.

PUPPY FEEDING

As with all creatures, the nutritional requirements of the dog vary during its life, the very young and the very old needing special care. Puppies need a high input of food, to support their fast rate of growth. Their digestion cannot cope with the single large meal a day which suits most adult dogs, and they need several smaller meals during the course of the day.

At first, it is a good idea to allow the pup to settle into its new home with as few changes as possible, so obtain a diet sheet from the breeder when you collect your puppy and stick to the same diet for at least the first week. Once it has settled in, you can gradually change the diet to the type that you prefer.

At first, the puppy will not be able to digest an adult diet. Manufacturers of pet foods now produce a range of tinned foods and biscuits specially designed for puppies, which provide a convenient way of ensuring that their nutritional needs are fully met. The breeder may recommend that you provide at least one milky meal a day at first, to ensure that the pup obtains the calcium needed to grow strong bones, but some puppies do not digest cow's milk well.

EXERCISE

It is a common mistake to over-exercise young puppies. Initially, the puppy will obtain all the exercise it needs by racing around in play. Walks should be introduced gradually and should not be too long. This is particularly important in the case of giant breeds, such as Wolfhounds, since too much exercise before they are skeletally mature can damage the joints. Discourage the young puppy from jumping off chairs and running up and downstairs, as it is all too easy to deform the elbow and shoulder joints while they are still soft, resulting in a dog which is 'out at elbow' with the joint misaligned.

WORMING

Puppies are often infected by parasitic internal worms before they are born, most commonly roundworms. Although the breeder will normally worm the bitch before the puppies arrive, this does not destroy larvae dormant in her tissues. The development of these worms is triggered by the bitch's pregnancy, and they then migrate, crossing the placental barrier to settle in the developing puppies' lungs and livers. A week after the puppies are born, the larvae move to the intestines and mature into adult worms.

Puppies may not show any outward sign of worm infestation, although obvious symptoms may include pot bellies, diarrhoea and vomiting. Occasionally a puppy will vomit adult worms or pass them in its stools. The eggs are shed in the stools, but they are so small that they are not visible to the naked eye; your puppy may well have roundworms without your knowing.

A puppy which builds up a heavy infestation of worms will not thrive, and some damage to its system may accrue. In addition, the worms can be passed on to humans, and children are particularly at risk. It is therefore essential to treat all puppies for worms automatically, and this treatment should have begun before you acquire the puppy from its breeder and continue once it is in your hands.

The responsible breeder will have carried out at least one worming treatment before the pups are weaned, and should tell you when the next is due. At one time, puppies were wormed by a variety of drastic home methods such as forcing a wad of chewing tobacco down their throats to make them vomit up the worms, techniques which reduced but could not eradicate the internal worm population and tended to make the puppy rather ill. Today worming is simpler, safer and much more effective. Worming tablets may be purchased at pet shops, but it is always preferable to obtain them from your veterinarian, as the most effective types are only available on prescription.

Your veterinarian will also be able to advise you how frequently to treat the pup in future. Dogs will need to be treated at regular intervals throughout their lives to reduce the risk of infection to humans, and if you have children it is advisable to take special care over this. Considerable media attention has been focused on the slight but nevertheless real risk to human health posed by the canine roundworm known as *Toxocara canis*. The eggs of this worm, when present in the faeces, are not immediately infectious but must remain outside the body for some time before the larval stage can develop. Once primed, however, and ingested accidentally by the child, for example, the eggs will hatch in the gut and the larvae will migrate through the body, a process known as *'visceral larval migrans'*. If the larvae develop in the eye, blindness can result. They may also invade the brain, with serious consequences. Worming your puppy, and continuing treatments at regular intervals throughout its life, will eliminate the danger posed to human health.

VACCINATION

At one time, so many puppies died from the infectious disease distemper that intending purchasers were advised to buy only those which had caught the disease and survived, establishing future immunity. Today, it is possible to vaccinate your puppy against the commonest serious infectious diseases, and you should not neglect to do so. The vaccinations most often given in Britain are for *leptospirosis, distemper, infectious hepatitis, kennel cough* and *parvovirus*. These are all serious diseases, and the protection afforded by inoculation is highly recommended.

Many vaccines now available offer protection against a number of these diseases in a single injection. In the case of puppies, it is usual to give two injections at the ages of eight and twelve weeks followed by annual 'boosters' to maintain immunity. This system follows the protection provided to puppies early in life by their mother's milk, specifically the portion known as *colostrum* which is produced for a short period immediately after the birth of the puppies. In the human child, protective antibodies against infections early in life are passed via the placental connection before birth. But this route is of very little significance in the dog, and antibodies are passed via the colostrum. These specific proteins are not digested but absorbed into the young dog's body.

As the puppy's own immune system starts to function to protect it from infection, so the level of the antibodies from the colostrum declines. In some cases, depending on the quantity of colostrum consumed by the individual puppies, the maternal antibodies may have disappeared before eight weeks of age, but this is generally the shortest time they will be effective. The protection afforded by the colostrum will have been lost in all cases by twelve weeks, but in certain specific instances, notably *parvovirus* in the Rottweiler, it can persist longer.

It is difficult to know precisely when the maternal antibodies have disappeared, and so, in the case of puppies which have contact with other dogs, as in a kennel, the first inoculation is given at eight weeks. This will then afford protection if there are no maternal antibodies left. Since antibodies will interfere with the action and efficacy of the vaccine, however, it is usual to reinoculate at twelve weeks, by which time the antibodies from the colostrum will have disappeared from the puppy's body. The vaccine can then stimulate the development of antibodies by the puppy's own immune system.

There are variations in this basic outline in the case of rabies inoculations, although these are not presently administered in Britain. If you are going abroad, however, or the puppy is being exported, then refer to your veterinarian for advice. A single injection given at eight weeks of age is not likely to offer full protection for the reasons given above, so be sure not to overlook the second set of inoculations. There are usually no side effects, and your puppy can be taken out shortly afterwards.

No reputable boarding kennel or dog training club will accept a dog without proof that it has been vaccinated against infections. An unvaccinated dog could be incubating a disease whose symptoms are not yet apparent, and would therefore endanger all other dogs with which it comes into contact.

Vaccination will not only protect your dog from common serious diseases, but prevent it from endangering other dogs.

PUPPY TRAINING

Just as the human toddler is not yet ready for school, the baby puppy is too young for high-level obedience training. However, the toddler is given a great deal of guidance long before he or she is ready for formal lessons, and similarly the puppy can learn much about what its human 'pack' requires of it from the moment you carry it through the door. You will make life easier, more pleasurable and more interesting for both the puppy and yourself if you remember that it is learning all the time, from what it is encouraged to do, what it is left alone to get on with and what it is stopped from doing.

The early days are crucial for the puppy's social development. Long formal lessons would certainly ask too much of its infant powers of comprehension and concentration, but by being consistent from the start you can lay the foundations for the future, encouraging suitable behaviour and discouraging undesirable habits. If you allow the pup to rampage about uncontrolled, you are failing to establish the social ranking order by which you are his pack leader, and when you realize that things have gone too far and decide to start training, the pup will have no conditioning towards obeying you. In the natural social hierarchy of the wolf pack, youngsters are encouraged and chastized by their superiors until they learn their places. If you fail to do this for your puppy, it will be much harder for it to learn proper attitudes when it is older.

What the puppy most needs is your time. A puppy is an active bundle of curiosity which is driven to investigate everything which takes its attention, and investigation is liable to lead to destruction. Left to its own devices, the pup will, without any evil intent, move anything movable, chew anything chewable and generally create chaos, and if you are not there to prevent this chaos, the youngster has no way of knowing that this behaviour is unacceptable. By giving the pup as much of your time as possible, you will not only be creating and strengthening the bond between yourself and your pet, but you will be in a position to deflect its attentions from your possessions towards its own toys.

ENCOURAGING GOOD BEHAVIOUR

The puppy needs to start learning sensible and civilized behaviour from the moment it enters your home, and probably the first lesson to teach is house-training.

Dogs are naturally clean animals and do not soil their quarters as a general rule. They tend to relieve themselves in specific areas delineated by scent. This can lead to conflict in the domestic environment, however, because a puppy, having soiled a rug once, will then be attracted by its scent and return. It is therefore vital that an area that has been dirtied be left completely free of scent as well as being cleaned up thoroughly. Various preparations for this purpose are sold in pet shops. White vinegar is also useful, as is bleach on a suitable floor (being diluted as required). Accidents can be prevented by watching the puppy for the tell-tale signs, which are often apparent after a meal or when the young dog awakes. It will search for a suitable spot, sniffing the floor beforehand.

At regular intervals, and always when you spot the signals that indicate the need, take the puppy to the designated place, outside when the weather permits and otherwise to the sheet of newspaper or dirt tray provided. The puppy will almost certainly want to urinate and defecate when it first wakes up, and immediately after meals, so make a point of attending to its needs at these times.

Best results are likely if the puppy is monitored during this activity, rather than being allowed to wander off, or follow its owner back to the door. Once it has performed, it should be praised. Good training relies on repetition of words or action. Repeated use of a phrase such as 'Clean dog' will help to ensure that the pup learns to associate this sound with the desired response, which will be useful later on when you need to train it to use the gutter rather than foul the pavement.

It will take about three months to train a puppy to ask to go out when it needs to and slightly longer before it performs on demand. In unfamiliar surroundings, such as a veterinarian's surgery when a urine sample is required, the latter command may be ignored, particularly by bitches. Whereas a puppy might relieve itself as much as six times during the course of a day, an adult dog will defecate once or twice and has much better control of its bladder. Letting the dog out last thing at night and early in the morning should ensure that there is no soiling indoors. When the dog is asleep, urine production falls naturally in any case.

Like young children, puppies vary in the length of time it takes for them to become clean at night, and you may need to provide a newspaper for urination at night for some time after the dog is reliable during the day.

In the case of male puppies, when they first start cocking a leg to urinate instead of squatting they may forget their manners indoors and need to be reminded that this is not permissible behaviour.

Another very important lesson that the puppy needs to learn in the early days is to respond to its name. A short simple name is easiest for the puppy to learn, so even if the name on his pedigree is ten syllables long choose a plain and easily recognizable call name for everyday use. Dogs respond best to a monosyllabic name, ideally beginning with a distinct consonant, which is why old favourites like 'Ben' or 'Dan' crop up so often – they are easy for the

HOUSE TRAINING

The pup will prefer to urinate on newspaper, not the floor. (1)

The paper is moved progressively closer to the door. (2)

The paper is finally placed outside, then dispensed with altogether. (3)

After a meal, the puppy will show signs of wanting to relieve itself. (4)

It should be gently lifted up and taken outside. (5)

owner to call and for the dog to recognize.

You will want the puppy to learn to come when its name is called, so ensure that it associates this with coming to you for fuss and affection. If you use its name every time you need to scold it, it will connect the sound with trouble and be less eager to respond.

You can make use of the three or four feeds a day to start inculcating good manners. Encourage the puppy to sit quietly while food is being prepared. It may not understand at first, but it is no more trouble to take the time to keep showing the pup, gently, what you want than it is to put up with leaping and yelping. Instead of placing the bowl immediately before the puppy, pause to tuck it into a sitting position, telling it to 'Sit', and hold it there for a moment before releasing it to feed. As well as making mealtimes easier for you, you will be laying the foundations for later training as the pup learns that quiet behaviour is rewarded and that certain sounds are associated with certain required responses.

A further step towards good manners can be taken by making use of the puppy's association of its bed with comfort. Every now and then pop it into its bed, using the word 'Bed', and hold it there for a moment. As you release it use some word such as 'Okay' or 'All right' to indicate that the command has been carried out and that it is now leaving the bed because you are permitting this and not because it is getting away with ignoring the command. You can reinforce the association of the command with the desired practice by saying 'Bed! Good boy,' when you see the pup climb into its bed spontaneously. Almost without realizing it, it will be learning to retire to its bed when told and stay there until it is released, a useful practice when you have visitors who dislike dogs, for example, and also a good foundation for more advanced work when you want to teach the pup to 'Stay' later on.

Related to 'Bed' training is the first use of the command 'Wait'. From time to time you will want the puppy to stay more or less where it is put. This is not the full-scale 'Stay' exercise of the obedience ring, in which the animal must remain in the position in which it is left until released, but you may for example wish the pup to stay in the sitting room while you answer the front door, or to remain downstairs while you go upstairs. At first it will have no idea what you mean, and you will have to reinforce the command by shutting the sitting-room door on it, or repeatedly carrying it downstairs, but if you consistently repeat the command over and over each time it will gradually realize that you do not wish, and will not allow, it to follow you when this command is given.

Perhaps the most important training opportunity is that afforded by play. Puppies, like children, need to play, and indeed this is part of their appeal. Handling and playing with your puppy in the early days is a valuable stage in proper socialization and, again like children, puppies can learn a great deal about what is expected from them in the course of a pleasant game. While playing with your puppy you can make it clear that approved behaviour includes playing with permitted objects but not with forbidden ones; mock biting but not real use of teeth; a certain level of noise but not hysterical shrieking.

You can also demonstrate through play your relative positions in the pup's new social hierarchy. Your dominance is confirmed when you and not the pup make the rules of play. You can hold the puppy on its back for a moment during a rough and tumble, just as its canine social

RIGHT: *The puppy should be provided with its own toys, such as this leather bone, to give it an outlet for its playful and destructive instincts. Constant watchfulness will be needed at first to deflect its interest from potential playthings such as shoes towards its own, approved toys.*

superior would. You should be the one who decides when play finishes, with a calm 'That's enough,' rather than allowing the puppy to play until it is tired of the game. Establishing, kindly and sensibly, that you are the pup's pack leader is not a matter of brutally dominating the little creature: it is the way to give it a sense of security.

All puppies love to chase a toy that is thrown for them; some will have a natural predisposition to bring the toy back to you, while others will prefer to stay at the far end of the room and chew it. You can encourage the beginnings of retrieving while you play. As you throw the toy, give the command 'Fetch' and if the puppy does return it, praise it lavishly. It will probably be reluctant to actually hand over its toy. If you can take it easily, do so with the word 'Give', but never make the mistake of fighting the pup for it or chasing it. The puppy will think this is a splendid game, and be even more prone to hold on to the toy in future to provoke this reaction. If it is reluctant to give up the toy, simply stop the game and walk away, only agreeing to play again when it puts the toy down and allows you to take it. It will soon learn that relinquishing the toy to you means a continuation of the fun, while refusing to give it up means being ignored.

Another lesson puppies need to learn in the early days is acceptance of a collar and a leash. Slipping a soft puppy collar on to the pup while it is at home, long before it is ready to go out for walks on the lead, will accustom it to the sensation. When it completely ignores the collar, it is time to add the lead, allowing the pup to wander around the house while you hold the end of the lead, but do not, as yet, attempt to control the puppy by it.

When the puppy is confident and relaxed with collar and lead, it is time to start teaching it what these are for. If you delay lead training until the puppy is old enough to go out, it will have to cope with the two strange experiences of constraint and of the noisy outside world at the same time. You can make the process easier for both of you if you start lead training in the quiet of your own home and garden.

You will want the dog eventually to walk calmly beside you on a slack lead, without pulling. You can lay the foundations for this with the young puppy by walking it up and down the garden along a fence or similar barrier which will prevent it from pulling away from you and encourage it to walk in a straight line. By the time the puppy is taken out for the first time it should have learned to walk beside you without lunging all over the place or tripping you up.

Never overdo this early training. Lessons of five minutes, or ten at most, will be more effective than if you persist beyond the puppy's attention span. Remember that training sessions should be fun for the puppy: when it does as you want, praise should be lavish, but if it fails to respond immediately scolding will achieve nothing but to teach the puppy to dislike the lessons.

DISCOURAGING BAD BEHAVIOUR

A certain amount of antisocial behaviour is natural to puppies. They will make a lot of noise when you want them to be quiet, nip fingers with their sharp teeth, jump up at people and ladder stockings or leave muddy pawprints on clothes, snatch food from plates and chew up carpets and shoes. They will persist in going into rooms which you have decided should not be permitted to dogs, run off with your gloves when you are trying to get ready to go out, knock over ornaments, wreck the garden, welcome burglars and attempt to assassinate the milkman.

At first, the puppy has no way of knowing that you are not going to approve of such activities. It is your task to teach what is not allowed, without either cowing the pup or watching your home disintegrate before the lesson is learned.

Your first action to minimize the chaos is to remember that prevention is better than cure. Before the puppy arrives, take a good look at your home and assess what is most vulnerable, what can be most easily protected or removed, and, in particular, which things are actually going to be dangerous – such as unprotected electrical wires or an open fire.

Fragile objects should be removed from vulnerable positions, so that they cannot be knocked down and broken.

The puppy will happily chew any exposed electric cables or flexes, so make sure that there are none within its reach or you could have a badly burned or dead puppy or even a house on fire. You may wish to put some some temporary fencing around parts of the garden you hope to protect, until such time as the pup is able to understand your views on the subject. In the kitchen, remember that vegetable racks and pedal bins are apt to be viewed by the puppy as toy boxes provided for its delight, and find some way of securing them against its attentions.

You will have to prepare yourself as well as your home, training yourself to shut doors, put food out of reach, and wear old clothes for playing with the puppy. Puppies will investigate anything left lying around, and any item which can be taken into the mouth is likely to be chewed or swallowed, so you will have to teach yourself never to leave your possessions lying around. Sewing implements are a common cause of accidents, with puppies attempting to swallow a needle and thread and ending up with the needle lodged in the throat.

Providing a play-pen in which you can shut the puppy at hazardous moments, such as when you are lifting a joint out of the oven, will make life easier and safer in the early days. It is also helpful to collect a supply of approved playthings with which to distract the puppy from forbidden items. These need not be expensive purpose-made toys

RIGHT: *Dogs enjoy their comfort and will quickly find the most comfortable chair. If you will not welcome wet or muddy paws on your furniture when the dog is adult, it should be trained from puppyhood not to climb on to chairs.*

from the pet shop – indeed, since the first toys are going to receive very rough treatment, it is as well to have a store of improvised playthings that cost nothing. An old sock knotted into a ball, the cardboard inner tube from a toilet roll, even an empty washing-up liquid container well washed out and with the top removed, will all make safe and suitable playthings which are easily replaced when destroyed.

The puppy will learn fastest if you remain calm when it does something dreadful. Quiet firmness and complete consistency will teach it what is permitted and what is not much more effectively than screaming and throwing things! Try to be positive in your approach, encouraging your pet as far as possible, rather than scolding it if it fails to respond or disobeys. Dogs are usually keen to please their owners, and this trait should be uppermost in the trainer's mind. If a puppy starts jumping on you, place it firmly on the ground and say 'no'. After a short period, it will realize that such behaviour is not permitted, and stop doing it.

Plan ahead, to prevent bad habits developing as early as possible. The baby puppy jumping up at your legs in excited welcome can be rather endearing, for example, but when it is fully grown you will not want a large, heavy and probably muddy dog flinging itself at you, so discouraging this behaviour from the start will save trouble later. If you teach the puppy not to jump and sleep on chairs, you will not have to prevent it from clambering on the furniture when it has grown up.

Humans have a wide vocabulary with which to say 'Stop doing that', but the puppy will learn fastest if you react to all unsuitable behaviour with the same word – 'No'. Once the puppy has learnt that magic word, you should be able to stop it in its tracks with this, whatever it is doing.

For a sensitive puppy, the word 'No' will soon be enough. A tougher puppy will need some form of physical reproof. Smacking the puppy tends ultimately to have a negative result, making it less responsive. If instead you act as its mother would have done, shaking it by the scruff of the neck, this is a rebuke it will understand. A really dominant puppy will wriggle under your hand and attempt to bite, but never allow it to get away with this. If the puppy is allowed to beat you, as an adult it will consider that it has every right to take the dominant role.

An uncontrollable urge to chew is typical of young puppies, especially during the teething phase, up to about seven months. The upper incisors are pushed out at about 14 weeks of age, as the permanent teeth erupt. The lower incisors are changed several weeks later, and the canines also at about 18 weeks. By about seven months the full set of adult teeth should be through, but in the meantime you have to protect your belongings. When you see the puppy chewing your shoe or a chair leg, first stop it with a repri-

mand but then divert it to an approved object from its collection of playthings. Just stopping it from chewing the first object is not enough, since the need to chew will still be there.

Play-biting is also natural behaviour in the young puppy. Biting its littermates was part of the play activity it learned before leaving its mother, and it simply does not know that the human hand is more tender than a fur-covered fellow puppy. This innocent but painful nipping must be discouraged from the start by stopping play at the touch of teeth, with a firm 'No'.

When you start taking your puppy out on the lead for walks, undesirable behaviour to be discouraged includes nervousness, over-friendliness and aggression. The more you can take him out in the early days, the better foundations you are laying for good lead behaviour – little and often should be the rule. It may well at first be frightened by the noise of the outside world, so plenty of exposure to rushing traffic, road works with pneumatic drills and the like should be accompanied with plenty of encouragement to demonstrate that none of this will harm him. It is a good idea to take it down to the railway station and buy a platform ticket so that it is exposed to the potentially terrifying uproar of trains and hurrying crowds; your reassurance and control will teach it that all this noise can be safely ignored.

Most puppies love everybody, and at first your pup will want to bounce at all passers-by and other dogs. It needs to be gently but firmly taught that this is not appropriate behaviour. Its early meetings with other dogs need to be carefully monitored. If you know the other dog to be friendly, it is a good idea to allow your pup to greet it, introducing some 'off duty' command such as 'Say hello then' to mark the difference between being expected to walk to heel and being allowed to investigate. If you snatch your puppy up every time you see another dog to protect him, you are teaching it that other dogs are to be feared and dreaded and laying the foundations for future aggression towards them.

Puppies tend to be highly vocal, and it pays to discourage noisy behaviour while they are young. You will probably find that your puppy will respond better to a whispered 'No' or 'Shh' than to a louder command. After all, it does not speak English. If you react to its noise by making more noise, it is natural to it to take this for encouragement and make even more!

The innate desire to please means that your puppy can be discouraged from unsuitable behaviour at an early age, and you can prevent bad habits from developing. Neglect of its behaviour at the beginning will mean much harder work for both of you later on.

Chapter Five

DAILY CARE

HOUSING

Most pet dogs live in the house with their owners. For the average pet, this is really the best arrangement, enabling the social animal to integrate as fully as possible into the human family and giving the owner the fullest opportunity for conditioning the dog towards acceptable behaviour. The more time a dog spends with its family, the more fit it becomes to do so, and outdoor kennels are not conducive to creating a close relationship between an owner and a dog.

Some owners prefer to restrict the dog to certain agreed areas of the house, for example, downstairs only, and with absolute consistency and firmness in the early days it does not take long to teach a dog which rooms are out of bounds.

However, in some circumstances an owner may find it desirable to provide an outdoor kennel or pen for the dog to use at night, or for part of the day when it cannot be supervised. Provided that the dog has adequate company, exercise and stimulation during the rest of the day this can be perfectly acceptable. Many working dogs, for example the average shooting man's companion, are kept in kennels rather than the house for much of the day, the time spent kennelled being counterbalanced by the time spent outside in training or working. However, if your dog is to spend some of its time penned up or kennelled, it is important that the reduced quantity of time spent with you should be compensated for by concentration on the quality of that time.

If you visit a dog breeding establishment, you will probably find some or most of the dogs living in kennels, but it is common practice for breeding stock to take turns living in the house to maintain the close relationship with their owner without which they will cease to be pets and become merely livestock kept for breeding purposes.

Many owners wish the family pet to double as a guard dog. It is a common misconception that the best guard dog is the dog chained to a kennel with minimal human contact. In fact, the closer the relationship the dog has with its family the more highly motivated it is to carry out its guarding responsibilities towards them. A pet that is to act as a guard should be integrated into the home as far as possible.

If you have decided that you wish to provide outdoor accommodation for your pet, it is important to make sure that the kennel is well situated and completely weatherproof. It should be located in a sheltered spot out of direct sunlight, and within easy reach of fresh water.

You can purchase a ready-made kennel or make one yourself. It must be large enough for your dog's comfort – the animal should be able to curl up well away from the entrance. In the case of a wooden kennel, check that the wood has not been treated with any toxic chemicals in case your dog starts to chew the structure. For the same reason, if the kennel is to be painted avoid lead-based paints, which are poisonous.

Set the structure on a base of bricks and a damp-proof material such as a thick plastic sheet. Make sure that it is sited in such a way that rain will not drive in through the door. Damp conditions will be far worse for your dog's health than any degree of cold. Wood provides a snug environment but has a limited lifespan. A more permanent structure can be built using cement blocks; these provide more insulation than bricks but may be subject to planning controls. If the interior is plastered, it will be easier to clean. Structures of this type are expensive, however, and clearly not portable.

The inside of the kennel should be made warm and comfortable with straw or a blanket, but remember that all bedding should be changed regularly.

Rather than a simple kennel, you may choose to provide a run to give your dog more freedom of movement while being securely penned up. The larger the run the better. As with kennels, ready-made runs incorporating a kennel for shelter can be purchased, or you can construct your own. Wire mesh on a wooden framework will usually be adequate. If there is any chance that the dog will try to jump or scrabble up the wire, a roof will be needed for security. For reasons of hygiene, a solidy, easy to clean floor – tarmac, concrete or paving stones – which can be hosed down is desirable, and a little forethought in giving this a gentle slope away from the kennel and towards an outside drain will greatly facilitate cleaning.

An alternative to the run, giving the dog a certain amount of exercise space while keeping it under restraint, is the running chain. The dog can be tethered on a long chain attached to a stake fixed firmly in the ground. To avoid the risk of the animal tangling the chain around itself or on an obstacle, it is more usual to run a long wire down the length of the garden, well above the dog's reach, and attach the chain to the wire. This greatly extends the limits of the chain as well as reducing the risk of accidents and enables the dog to cover quite a large area without actually being free. Shelter must be available from the sun and the elements, and water must be within easy reach. Dogs do seem to resent being tethered for any length of time, however, and may try to escape. Tethering can also encourage aggressive tendencies.

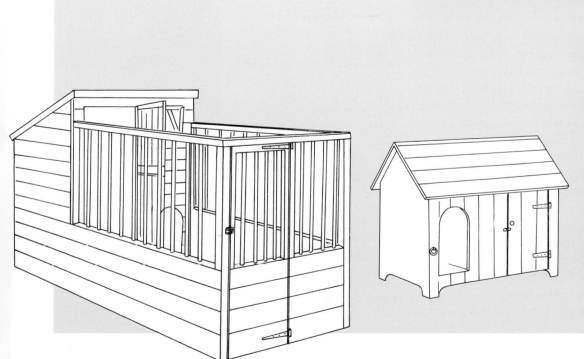

ABOVE: *An outdoor kennel can be a useful investment for dogs that will be spending much of their time outside.*

FAR LEFT: *Blankets make suitable bedding material within the kennel, but will need regular washing to keep them clean and comfortable.*

LEFT: *Various designs of outdoor kennels are commercially available, ranging from the doghouse alone to a more elaborate structure with attached run.*

FEEDING

Dogs are essentially carnivorous in their feeding habits, yet they are not obligate carnivores like cats. They show a preference for meat, but will also eat a wide variety of other foods.

Dogs have certainly been reported to eat, and apparently enjoy, a huge range of foods, some of which seem rather bizarre. The partially omnivorous nature of the dog's diet is probably why the dog needs less protein in its diet than does the cat. Like all other animals the dog requires a mixture of carbohydrates, fats and proteins. These all supply energy, and protein is also required for body building. Certain important minerals, such as calcium for bones and salt for body fluids, are also required. Other minerals and vitamins are necessary for specialized functions within the body; for example, the red blood cells depend on iron.

Wild dogs obtain all these substances from their naturally varied diet. In the wild, the dog's food intake would consist largely of proteins and fats from the muscles and viscera of its prey. Carbohydrates such as starch and sugar are not present in any significant amounts in body tissues. Typically of hunting animals, dogs can consume large amounts of food in a short space of time, because of their dentition and relatively big stomachs. Their omnivorous habits make pet dogs easier to feed correctly than cats, but also more prone to suffer from obesity.

Proteins, composed of amino acid residues, are necessary both for growth and for healing damaged tissue, and can also be converted to energy if necessary. Fats protect vital organs such as the kidneys and provide a concentrated course of energy. Both fats and proteins are vital to cells, forming an integral part of cell membranes, as well as being necessary for many cellular functions.

Carbohydrates in the diet are used essentially to meet the body's energy requirement, and are frequently provided in the form of biscuit meal, rice or bread. These ingredients of the diet are relatively cheap and are often used to bulk up a ration. Excess carbohydrate, surplus to the body's immediate energy needs, can only be converted to fat. A relatively small amount is stored, mainly as glycogen in the liver, to be used as a quick source of energy if required.

Maintaining the correct balance of proteins, fats and carbohydrates is of considerable importance in keeping a dog healthy and well nourished.

Vitamins, minerals and trace elements, although only required in minute amounts, are vital to the well-being of your dog. Vitamin D for example, is especially important, since it controls the calcium stores of the body and is ultimately responsible for sound bone development; the minerals calcium and phosphorus are also significant in this respect. Vitamin A is one of the fat-soluble group of vitamins that are stored in the liver. It helps to ensure good eyesight and prevent infections. Vitamin C, important for preventing infections, is less vital in a dog's diet, since most can manufacture this vitamin in their bodies. About one dog in every 1,000 is unable to carry out this process, however, and will require dietary supplementation: 100mg of ascorbic acid for every 55lb (25kg) of body weight. Vitamin C is a relatively unstable compound, and can deteriorate quite rapidly: it should not be stored for long periods before use.

A small amount of roughage, such as bran, is also beneficial. Although indigestible, and thus not of nutritional value, it provides bulk and assists the movement of food through the intestinal tract. To provide themselves with roughage might be why dogs consume grass. Grass may also act as an emetic; young puppies suffering from roundworms often eat grass and then vomit both grass and worms in an apparent attempt to purge themselves. In view of such behaviour, it is unwise to treat areas of rough grass with chemicals: these areas, rather than lawns, are favoured for this purpose.

TYPES OF FOOD

Various options now exist for feeding dogs. Essentially, the choice is between fresh foods and manufactured pet foods, the latter being available in canned, dry or semimoist forms. Your dog can be kept fit and healthy on whichever type of diet you choose, so long as you keep the basic canine nutritional requirements in mind.

■ **FRESH FOODS** Variety is important if you elect to feed your dog on fresh foods, to make sure that the diet is adequately balanced.

RIGHT: *The storage of dog food will vary according to its ingredients. Fresh items need to be kept refrigerated, and if deep-frozen for any reason, they must be allowed to thaw completely and warm up before being fed. Canned items, once opened, must also be kept refrigerated. Foil packaging maintains a product's freshness: items packaged like this should be used up as soon as possible once the foil has been opened. Dried foods, with a very low water content, can be kept for a considerable period of time, although the vitamin content will decline. Once water or other fluid is added to a dried ration, it should then be treated as fresh food, and disposed of within a day, if not eaten.*

It is not adequate to feed just meat on its own, since this is deficient in various vitamins such as A, D and E, as well as minerals such as iodine. In addition, the ratio between calcium and phosphorus, which should be of the order of 1.2 to 1, is seriously imbalanced in meat, with the tissues containing excessive amounts of phosphorus. This will cause skeletal abnormalities, particularly in young dogs. In severe cases, bones may fracture easily, and the dog will be reluctant to walk.

The high protein level of a strict meat diet would also be a waste of money, since the protein would be broken down to provide energy when there are much cheaper alternative sources, such as potatoes, available. It could also prove harmful in a dog that was already infected with kidney failure.

Various meats sold cheaply by butchers for pet food includes lungs and spleens, as well as tripe. All are valuable sources of protein, but the latter, being the stomach of ruminants, smells highly unpleasant unless 'dressed'. Ground meat invariably has a high fat content, especially if sold specifically for pets. In order to provide a balanced diet, the meat component should be mixed with a suitable biscuit meal or dog biscuits. Check that the brand you use is supplemented with the vitamins and minerals likely to be low in the meat content of the diet. It may be necessary, particularly for dogs with sensitive teeth, to soak the biscuits for a few minutes before feeding in order to make them more palatable.

Approximately equal quantities of fresh food and biscuit should provide an adequate balance. Some dogs are allergic to gluten, which is a component of protein present in flour,

and cannot be fed biscuits or meal. Potatoes which have been well boiled, or boiled rice, can be given as alternatives, with a vitamin and mineral supplement.

While there is certainly no truth in the story that raw meat makes dogs aggressive, various parasites and infections can be transmitted by this means; to kill these, it is always advisable to cook meat before feeding it to the dog. The meat should be cooked for about 20 minutes; any longer and excessive loss of vitamins will occur. Allow the meat to cool to prevent burning the dog's mouth, but slightly warm food is more palatable than cold, and may tempt a dog with a poor appetite to start eating again. It is often easier to cook a relatively large quantity of fresh food at one time – perhaps a week's supply – and then freeze some for later use. All frozen food must be completely thawed before feeding to the dog to prevent digestive disturbances.

Suitable table scraps, such as left-over meat or vegetables, may be used to augment the dog's diet, although it is advisable not to offer these from the table while you are eating. Otherwise, dogs soon learn to expect food when other members of the family are eating and can become a real nuisance at mealtimes, as well as running the risk of obesity over a period of time.

Although vegetables are not an essential addition to the dog's diet, a certain amount included with its food will be beneficial. Green vegetables, together with the water in which they were cooked, may be added to meat and biscuits, although an excess of greens may cause flatulence. Many dogs will enjoy a little fruit from time to time, particularly apples, and it is not uncommon for a dog to learn to help

RIGHT: *In general, a healthy dog has a healthy appetite and will eat its food rapidly. Certain individuals do prove fussy eaters, however, and may need encouragement to eat adequately.*

RIGHT: *There is no convincing evidence to confirm that dogs become bored with the same kind of food every day, and indeed, sticking to the same diet on a regular basis reduces the risk of digestive upsets.*

itself to blackberries or similar fruits from the bush.

The vegetarian owner sometimes wishes to maintain his or her dog on a vegetarian diet. This is a possibility, but will require extra work, and your efforts may not be appreciaed by the dog, especially if it has been used to a meat-based diet. It may be possible to wean a puppy on to it successfully, but it will certainly be harder with an adult dog. Since plant protein is not as balanced in terms of its amino acid content as meat, opt for soya protein, which is the best form available. Unfortunately, amounts above 1 ounce per 12 pounds of the dog's weight tend to cause diarrhoea. The carbohydrate content of the diet is easy to provide, but fat can be more of a problem. Eggs and high-fat cheese will be necessary, along with corn oil to act as a source of linoleic acid. Vitamins and minerals can be provided by way of a suitable preparation sprinkled over the food, and specific food items, such as carrots, can be used as additional sources on a regular basis. Apart from being more time-consuming, a vegetarian diet may also prove more expensive, and although it may appeal to the owner, it is probably not in the dog's best interests.

■ **PREPARED FOODS** Commercially prepared dog foods are carefully manufactured to fulfil dogs' nutritional requirements and also to be palatable to the dogs and convenient to their owners. It is not only easier, but also safer to use a prepared diet to reduce the risk of nutritional deficiencies.

The canned diets are still the most widespread and palatable of all the commercial dog foods, and most of these offer a complete, balanced diet. The label should always be checked nonetheless – a few brands contain only meat, with no added vitamins or minerals. Generally, the canned foods contain a mixture of muscle meat, stomach, heart, liver, lung, barley, corn, vitamins and minerals. Some canned foods have a higher level of carbohydrate than others, usually the cheaper brands. Those with a low carbohydrate content should be supplemented with cereal flakes, cooked rice or corn meal.

Manufacturers often suggest supplementing canned food with a biscuit meal, especially if the brand contains a relatively high proportion of meat. This helps to reduce the overall cost, as the biscuit is used to provide the energy content of the diet, while the meat contributes protein. It is important to feed the biscuit meal according to the instructions on the pack, since an excessive intake will lead to obesity, particularly in a dog that is not working.

Manufacturers have recently started to produce more specialized foods. Many ranges now include canned foods designed for puppies, which contain a relatively high level of protein to assist growth. Small cans are also marked for fussy eaters or delicate dogs, notably some toy breeds. Canned cat food can be fed to dogs (but not vice versa, since cats require the amino acid taurine in their food) and is generally higher in protein, which may tempt fastidious eaters.

All canned foods can be kept, unopened, for over a year. Once opened, however, even if stored in a refrigerator as recommended, they will not stay fresh for more than a few days.

Canned foods contain a high level of water, sometimes more than 80 per cent. If water content is high, the dog will need to eat more to satisfy its nutritional requirements.

Recently, the market for semi-moist dog foods has been expanding. Although designed to resemble succulent chunks of meat, these foods often contain relatively high levels of soya and have a lower water content, about 25 per cent, compared with their canned rivals. They are usually sold in foil-wrapped sachets packed in boxes, and they may feature other ingredients, such as sucrose, which serve to preserve the food and improve palatability.

These products are sold in sealed foil packets and, unlike canned foods, do not need to be refrigerated, but must be used within three months or so.

Dried dog foods are marketed in various forms, such as pellets, flakes, meal and expanded chunks. Heat is used in the manufacturing process, and serves to make the starch component more digestible, but also destroys certain vitamins, particularly Vitamin A and members of the Vitamin B group. To compensate for this loss, vitamins are added in proportionately larger amounts at the start of the process, or included in the fat that is sprayed on to the foodstuff after the water has been removed to improve its palatability. Dried dog foods do contain some water, normally about 10 per cent, and can be stored without refrigeration. They can also be kept for long periods without losing their vitamin content, but most manufacturers specify an expiry date on the packaging.

There are certain advantages in feeding dry food. Relatively little in terms of weight is required, and dry food is also supposed to reduce the risk of accumulations of tartar on the teeth. Manufacturers usually recommend soaking dry food when first introducing it to the diet, and there is no reason for not continuing this preparation, apart from the fact that any remaining uneaten at the end of the day must be discarded, or it will turn mouldy, particularly in damp weather. If dried food is not soaked, the dog will need to drink more water to compensate.

Various meat products are also available, sold in blocks or tubes in many pet shops. Most need to be kept refrigerated, especially once opened, and contain no additional vitamins or minerals, or even cereal in some cases. These foods do not provide a balanced diet on their own and must be mixed with biscuit meal to ensure that vital nutrients will not be deficient.

ABOVE: *If table scraps are to be fed, they should be placed in the dog's bowl after the human meal is over. Feeding the dog from the table encourages it to pester its owner for food, and also makes it hard to assess its intake.*

RECOMMENDED NUTRIENT CONTENT OF DOG FOODS			
NUTRIENT	**CANNED %**	**SEMI-MOIST**	**DRY %**
Dry matter	25.00	75.00	90.0
Water	75.00	25.00	10.0
Protein	12.00	19.95	24.0
Fat	9.725	6.75	8.0
Linoleic Acid	0.275	0.825	1.0
Fibre	1.00	3.00	3.6

HOW MUCH AND HOW OFTEN?

Dogs in the wild will gorge enormously at a meal, since the next meal is never guaranteed, and their stomachs are adapted to this system. Although the pet dog will be supplied with food at regular intervals, its natural instinct is still to make the most of every meal opportunity, and so it is up to the owner to regulate his or her pet's intake to avoid the risk of obesity. Conversely, domestication has produced some very finicky eaters, particularly in certain breeds, which need encouraging to eat up to their requirements. It is therefore rarely practical to feed to appetite, and quantities need to be carefully worked out.

When convenience diets are fed, suggested quantities are normally provided by the manufacturer. Dried foods are given in smaller quantities because they contain less water. As a general guideline, only 28 grams (1 ounce) of dry food is required for every kilo (2.2 pounds) of the dog's weight whereas 100 grams (3.5 ounces) of a complete canned food will be necessary for the same dog. Smaller dogs tend to eat relatively more than their large counterparts because food requirement is a reflection of surface area, not body weight.

There are various other factors involved in assessing the dog's nutritional requirement. The level of activity of the individual will have a bearing on its feeding needs: a working dog needs more food than a pet dog. Age is also significant; older dogs tend to need less food. In the latter stages of pregnancy, a bitch's appetite will increase considerably. Puppies, not surprisingly, also have a relatively high feed requirement to support their rate of growth.

It is hardest to estimate the amount of home-cooked meat and biscuit that should be provided. Mix the biscuit on an equal weight basis with the cooked meat and feed about 28 grams (1 ounce) per kilo of body weight for a dog of average size.

The obvious indication as to whether you are providing correct quantities of food is the dog's condition. If the dog is overweight or underweight, this can be seen clearly just by standing back and looking at the animal. If the dog's coat is too thick for you to judge its condition by eye, you can assess it by placing your hands on the sides of your pet and feeling for the ribs. In general, if the ribs stand out like pencils the dog is too thin, while if you cannot feel each rib individually, without exerting undue pressure, it is probably too fat. Remember that particular breeds are built differently, however, and that a Greyhound in perfect condition, for example, will feel much ribbier than a Pug.

The growing puppy needs more frequent feeding than an adult dog, and you should follow the breeder's directions. By the age of about nine months, most dogs are receiving either one large meal, usually in the early evening, or two smaller meals given morning and evening. This latter regimen is most applicable to smaller dogs. The main point, however, is to develop a system that suits you, as well as the dog. Feeding the dog immediately before the family meal will make it less likely to be a nuisance at the table. It is best not to feed your pet late at night, since food in the stomach stimulates intestinal movement and it will probably need to relieve itself afterwards.

Dogs are essentially creatures of habit, so they will be best suited to fixed mealtimes every day as far as possible. Try to avoid changing the time significantly as this will upset your pet.

Dogs normally bolt their food down within minutes of its being provided. When the dog has finished, its bowl should be washed thoroughly, separately from the utensils used for humans. Any left-overs should be discarded, unless you are using dry foods, as fresh or canned food left out will tend to sour, attracting flies, while bacteria will also develop rapidly under these conditions, especially during the warmer months of the year.

The dry foods can be left down without spoiling, and in the United States, it is fairly common practice to leave the dog with food throughout the day so that it can help itself. Studies have revealed that dogs transferred to this system may eat more than usual at first, but the vast majority then tend to regulate their food intake in accordance with their energy expenditure. This method of feeding is not recommended for young dogs, however.

DIETARY SUPPLEMENTS

Pet food manufacturers today produce a bewildering array of vitamin and mineral supplements for dogs. Generally speaking, if your dog has a balanced diet it is unlikely that supplementation will be necessary, although under certain circumstances, it may be recommended. A dog with kidney failure, for example, may need a Vitamin B supplement because excessive levels of this group of vitamins may be lost from its body. Perhaps one in a thousand dogs is incapable of making its own Vitamin C, and specific supplementation to prevent scurvy from developing will be essential. This can be achieved by adding a tablet to its food. Allow 1 gram for a dog weighing 55 pounds. This vitamin deteriorates rapidly; do not purchase a large quantity and always keep it stored in the dark.

A shortage of Vitamin D is unlikely because this vitamin is made by the action of sunlight falling on the dog's coat. It is stored in the liver along with the other so-called fat-soluble vitamins, A, E and K. There are specific instances when a Vitamin K deficiency could occur, notably as a result of certain types of poisoning or excessive antibiotic therapy.

A calcium supplement is often required by pregnant bitches and growing puppies, but it is advisable to administer this under your veterinarian's directions to avoid the

FEEDING GUIDE FOR ADULT DOGS					
	TOY BREEDS less than 4.5 kilos (10lb) for example Yorkshire Terrier, Toy Poodle, Chihuahua	**SMALL BREEDS** 4.5–9 kilos (10–20lb) for example Terrier, Beagle, Cavalier King Charles Spanel	**MED. BREEDS** 9–22 kilos (20–50lb) for example Basset Hound, English Springer Spaniel	**LARGE BREEDS** 22–34 kilos (50–75lb) for example German Shepherd Dog, Labrador, Irish/English Setter	**GIANT BREEDS** 34–63 kilos (74–140lb) for example Great Dane, Irish Wolfhound, Newfoundland
Approximate daily calorie needs	2,000–4,000	4,000–7,000	7,000–14,000	19,000–30,000	
Canned dog food (14 ounce cans) with mixer biscuit, fed in proportions of 2–1 by volume	¼–½ can	½–1 can	1–1½ cans	1½–2½ cans	2½–3½ cans
Semi-moist dog food	113–127 grams (4–4½ ounces)	127–226 grams (4½–8 ounces)	226–245 grams (8–15 ounces)	425–595 grams (15–21 ounces)	595–935 grams (21–33 ounces)
Dry dog food	56–99 grams (2–3½ ounces)	99–184 grams (3½–6½ ounces)	184–382 grams (6½–13½ ounces)	382–524 grams (13½–18½ ounces)	524–822 grams (18½–29 ounces)

The feeding chart above, is simply a guide since food intake varies according to the level of activity and physiological state of individual dogs.

risk of over-dosage. Oil supplements are beneficial for dogs with a tendency to dry, scurfy skin, and cod-liver oil is also a good source of Vitamins A and D, although here it is vital to avoid over-dosing and only very small quantities should be given.

If the basic diet is adequate, and there are no special circumstances such as pregnancy or illness, your dog is more likely to be at risk from an overdose of vitamins and minerals than to suffer a deficiency. It is certainly not true of dietary supplements that if a little is good, a lot must be better. Always follow the directions given on the package.

The young, growing dog is most at risk from excessive supplementation, and large breeds are the most susceptible since they normally develop more slowly than small breeds. Various abnormalities in the growth of their skeletal system and possibly other symptoms such as lameness will result.

A wide range of herbal supplements is available which some breeders swear by, seaweed powder being one which is very popular as a conditioner. The advantage of such herbal compounds is that generally there is no risk from over-dosing.

*Highly active dogs like this racing greyhound (**ABOVE**) or these terriers (**RIGHT**) engaged in racing after a dummy prey, will require a higher food intake than more sedentary pets.*

LIQUID INTAKE

Always make sure that your dog has a clean bowl of drinking water available; change the contents every day. There is no fixed amount that a dog will drink during a day. The quantity consumed will vary, depending on such factors as its diet, the temperature and the amount of exercise it receives. Typically, dogs fed on a dry diet will drink more to compensate for the relatively low amount of fluid in their food. More water will be drunk during warm weather and after a period of exercise.

Various medical conditions can give rise to an abnormal thirst; if a disorder of this type is suspected, the amount of water drunk each day should be recorded to help the veterinarian make a diagnosis.

Never withhold water from your dog even if it is incontinent. This could be fatal because the dog needs to make up the excessive water loss from its body. The only circumstance in which it may be best to prevent your dog drinking water freely is when it is vomiting, as drinking water can precipitate further vomiting and further loss of vital body salts. Provide only a small quantity after vomiting appears to have ceased and seek veterinary advice. Conversely, there may be occasions when you need to encourage your dog to drink. This is usually when it has an infection of the urinary tract, or has deposits such as bladder stones in the tract.

Many dogs prefer to drink from puddles rather than a bowl and this should be discouraged because of the danger of disease. They must also be prevented from drinking from toilet bowls, not only for reasons of hygiene, but also because of the risk of ingesting harmful substances such as bleach. This behaviour can be avoided by ensuring that the lid of the toilet is always kept down.

Your dog's water intake may be reduced if you are providing milk for it to drink. Remember that milk is not essential and is indigestible for many dogs, including greyhounds, which lack the enzyme, lactase, necessary to break down the sugar present. The sugar is then converted by bacteria in the gut into lactic acid, which causes diarrhoea. Other beverages are not recommended, although some individuals get a taste for tea, but this is probably because of its milk content and any sugar that may be present. Do not encourage your dog to drink any form of alcohol; this is potentially harmful, and dogs, like humans, can become addicted to alcohol, with similar consequences. If you are going to the beach for the day in the summer, take a supply of fresh water and a bowl for your dog. Otherwise, in hot weather especially, a dog may resort to drinking sea water, and this can prove fatal in any quantity because of salt-poisoning.

TITBITS

A wide variety of doggy titbits are manufactured and may be purchased at pet-stores, chocolate drops made especially for dogs being highly popular. Regard such treats as you would regard sweets for children. They will be enjoyed by the dog and will do no harm when eaten occasionally and in limited quantities, but large quantities will spoil the dog's appetite for nutritionally valuable food, and will probably lead to tooth decay, obesity and possibly diabetes.

Some dogs respond well to the use of titbits as a reward during training, and manufactured treats can be used for this, within reason. However, there are other, healthier titbits that can be used as rewards during training and at other times. Raw carrots cut into small pieces appeal to many dogs to the extent in some cases that they may attempt to dig up carrots growing in a garden once they acquire a taste for them. Yeast tablets are also very palatable to dogs and provide a source of Vitamin B. Always restrict the amounts of such items that you give, so the dog does not come to view them as an extension to meals rather than a reward for good behaviour. A dog that comes to regard titbits as a right will become a nuisance.

ABOVE: *Begging for food can be very appealing, but can lead to continual pestering of the family and guests at mealtimes, which can prove very troublesome.*

BONES

From a strictly nutritional viewpoint, there is probably no need to provide bones, provided your dog is being fed correctly. Yet dogs certainly appreciate being able to gnaw on a bone. This may also lessen the risk of furniture and carpeting being chewed and helps to prevent a build-up of tartar on the teeth. Great care must be taken, however, not to give bones that can splinter, or be swallowed and become lodged in the mouth or throat. Big marrow bones, obtainable from butchers, are most suitable, providing the cut ends show no signs of flaking. Bones from poultry and rabbits are among the most dangerous, and should never be given; make sure none are left lying around where dogs could steal them.

Some dogs become very possessive about bones, so make sure that you train your pet right from the beginning that it must relinquish its bone on command. Aggressive behaviour over a bone must never be tolerated.

*Feeding titbits between meals can spoil the dog's appetite for more nutritious food. Human treats such as ice-cream (**LEFT**) are better avoided: natural treats such as apples or carrots can be substituted.*

FAR RIGHT: *Dogs should not be allowed to eat from dishes used for human food because of the risk of transmitting disease. Scavenging should also be discouraged, since it can lead to a variety of problems such as digestive disturbances, loss of appetite and obesity.*

BELOW: *Obesity is more likely to affect middle-aged dogs, and the risk of obesity increases with age, as the level of activity declines and food intake remains constant. The side effects are especially noticeable in warm weather, with the dog panting excessively, like this Labrador Retriever – a breed which is particularly prone to overweight when kept in a domestic environment. Interestingly, studies have shown that the majority of obese dogs also have overweight owners.*

THE FAT DOG

Obesity can kill, and the overweight dog will certainly not enjoy life as much as the dog in sound physical condition. Amongst pet dogs, obesity is a regrettably common condition – most estimates suggest that some 30 per cent of dogs in the United States and in the United Kingdom are overweight.

Certain breeds are more likely to become overweight than others – Beagles, Labrador Retrievers and Cocker Spaniels are commonly affected, while others, like the Irish Setter and many of the Terriers, are less susceptible. The problem also affects small breeds such as the Dachshund, perhaps in this case because of the owner's attitude to his or her pet, all too often seen as a love object to be plied with food and under-exercised. Obesity more often affects bitches than male dogs, and neutered dogs are most at risk. Overweight often becomes a problem in middle age, when a dog's level of activity declines.

It is interesting to speculate why dogs should show such a high susceptibility to obesity. Palatability of food may be one factor – certainly a dog is likely to eat more than usual if he is given an especially tasty meal. However, in the long term most dogs cease to react in this way and regulate their intake as before. Another factor is the social aspect of eating. Studies have revealed that puppies eat more if they feed in a group than if they are fed alone. This may still apply to adult dogs with the owner's mere presence encouraging a dog to eat more.

However, the majority of cases of obesity are almost certainly due to the dog's own weight control mechanism rather than to these external factors. For one thing, all breeds would show the same tendency to obesity if external

factors were wholly to blame. Interestingly, it has been shown that the majority of obese dogs also have over-weight owners, which indicates where much of the blame belongs.

Most obese dogs are overweight because they are being given too much food, and too little exercise. Surplus carbohydrates are not being used on energy expenditure and are thus converted to fat. It will be necessary to reduce the intake of food – special obesity diets can be obtained from a veterinarian, or the overall amount of food can be reduced by about 40 per cent. It is vital to cut out all snacks while the dog is on a slimming diet, and to make sure that no food is being scavenged or begged from neighbours. On a diet, part of the body's fat reserves are burned to meet the dog's energy demands and so the fat is gradually reduced with a corresponding loss of weight.

Keep a check on the dog's weight on a weekly basis. Weight loss in the smaller breeds should work out to about 100 grams (quarter of a pound) weekly and will be about treble this figure in the case of big dogs.

A gradual increase in exercise will be beneficial – to dog and owner! – but be sensible about this and do not expect a fat, out-of-condition dog to cope with a sudden dramatically increased exercise regime.

Once you have succeeded in slimming your dog down to a better weight, try to ensure that it does not become fat again. Increase the amount of food offered by about 20 per cent so it is receiving just 80 per cent of its previous food intake. Obesity does not always result from excessive feeding, but hormonal changes with a similar effect are quite rare in dogs. In severe cases of obesity, a veterinarian may recommend hospitalization so the dog can be placed on a crash diet with only water being provided.

THE THIN DOG

Some dogs can be very finicky eaters and seem to eat only enough to keep themselves alive, never putting on enough weight for good physical condition. The persistently thin dog may need veterinary attention, since this could be a symptom of illness. However, if the dog is just fussy about its food, there are two courses of action that may help. One is to make sure that the animal has built up a proper appetite for its meal by avoiding all titbits and extras between feeding times; the other is to make the food as attractive as possible. Try different types of food to see if the animal has a marked preference. If a dog is genuinely fastidious about food, it is possible to improve palatability by smearing margarine or some other type of fat over the surface. Canned or fresh foods are generally more acceptable than dried diets.

Some breeds, such as the Pekingese, have a tendency to become very thin in old age, and, provided that a veterinary check-up reveals no medical problem, such dogs can remain in good condition and full of life despite looking gaunt.

An entire male dog may lose his appetite if there is a bitch in season nearby. If the situation is recurrent and unavoidable, it may be necessary to consider castration to stop him fretting and keep him in healthy condition.

BAD DIETARY HABITS

The dog's natural habits were not designed for human convenience, and certain dietary tendencies need to be discouraged if the dog is to fit in with our ways.

Scavenging is one such problem. Unfortunately, all dogs, to a greater or lesser extent, are scavengers by nature and will steal food if a suitable item presents itself. This is an undesirable practice as far as humans are concerned, because nobody wants to spend all their time guarding every remotely edible item from the family pet. The confirmed scavenger will not only steal what we recognize as food, but will regard the kitchen pedal-bin or even its owner's handbag as larders to be raided. It is also undesirable from the dog's point of view, as eating unsuitable items is likely to cause digestive troubles such as vomiting or diarrhoea; it may also pick up dangerous items such as splintery bones from a chicken carcass, and even if it has the digestion of an ostrich there remains the likelihood of obesity.

Prevention is better than cure, so try to prevent a dog scavenging by placing food out of reach, and keep a close watch when you are out walking in case the dog finds the discarded remains of a picnic such as a chicken carcass. No amount of watchfulness will be as effective as training, so ideally the dog should be taught right from the beginning only to eat what it is given.

A habit which most owners find unacceptable is copro-phagy, or the eating of faeces, which is not uncommon. Various reasons have been suggested for such behaviour in dogs. It could be that the dog is suffering from a digestive problem, notably a deficiency of certain B vitamins or Vitamin K which are normally manufactured in the gut by bacteria. By consuming its faeces, it obtains these essential elements, which otherwise would be lost in large quantities from the body. It may be worth supplementing these vitamins to see if this overcomes the problem. Yet such behaviour appears to be addictive and is often seen in dogs that have been kennelled under fairly unsanitary conditions for part of their life. A bitch will frequently eat the stools of her puppies, and they may consume hers early in life. It may be that this helps to establish the beneficial vitamin-producing bacteria in their intestinal tracts.

If a dog is suffering from a malabsorption disease, part of the food will pass through the digestive tract unaltered, and re-emerge in the faeces. These are attractive to dogs because of the undigested foodstuff present in them. A condition of this type requires veterinary attention; the behaviour can be corrected by appropriate therapy for the original problem.

Nevertheless, in many cases there is no clear-cut explanation for the habit. To the dog, anything that possibly can be eaten counts as edible, and it has no natural distaste for its own faeces. From the human point of view, it is not a habit to be encouraged, both on aesthetic grounds and because of the risk of the dog re-ingesting worms which may have been passsed with the stools. Always try to clear up the faeces as soon as possible after they are expelled from the body so the dog has no opportunity to eat them.

As with scavenging, training the dog to accept human control over what it does and does not eat is the best solution. In severe cases, veterinary advice may be sought: your veterinarian may prescribe the use of a drug to make the faeces taste unpleasant to the animal or even to cause vomiting if it eats them.

A few dogs develop abnormal appetites for potentially harmful items such as pebbles. Supervision and firm training are needed to stop this tendency. While the canine digestive tract is fairly tolerant of foreign bodies, pebbles can become stuck, causing serious consequences. It is not uncommon for veterinarians to have to operate to remove pebbles, fragments of toys or even such objects as purses from a dog's stomach.

Bad feeding manners, such as pestering the owner for titbits, demanding a share from the human dinner-table, leaping around and barking while food is being prepared, or aggressiveness over the food bowl should never be tolerated. Teach your dog right from the start to wait quietly while his food is prepared: even a baby puppy can be encouraged to sit for its dinner. Make a point of teaching your pet that you have the right to move its food bowl if

you wish. It is tempting to offer scraps from your plate, but avoid this while you are actually eating. It may not be easy to stop your children from doing this, however, but you must try. Otherwise, dogs soon learn to expect food from the dinner table and become a nuisance at human meal-times.

ABOVE: *Chewing bones is an enjoyable activity for dogs and may help to keep teeth clean, but from a dietary point of view, bones are not strictly necessary.*

127

EXERCISE

Exercise requirements vary considerably from breed to breed. Toy breeds are often quite content with a walk of about half a mile (1 km) every day, but larger dogs, especially those with a working ancestry, need up to 8 miles (13km). Size can be deceptive, however, when assessing a dog's exercise requirements.

Generally speaking, most pet dogs are under-exercised. The sedentary lifestyle of urban man means that all too often people envisage an hour's stroll around the streets as a long walk, forgetting that a working breed such as a sheepdog was developed to keep fit on a full day of hard running. Even less obviously active breeds will benefit from more exercise than they are often given. The writer's Pekingese in his prime demanded a five-mile walk every day, and revelled in a ten-mile run through the countryside!

In certain cases, exercise must be restricted. Young puppies of giant breeds, such as Wolfhounds, must not be exercised excessively before they are skeletally mature, since this can cause problems later with their joints. Old dogs, especially those with heart complaints, and pregnant bitches will also need less exercise. Dogs should not be taken out during the hottest part of the day in summer; during warm weather, Pekingese, Boxers and similar flat-faced breeds may become distressed and start to breathe very noisily.

Regular daily exercise is important, rather than marathon sessions at the weekend. Remember that it is not the length of time spent in exercise that gives it its value, but the type of exercise taken. A steady walk on the lead is one form of exercise; running free is quite another. The dog off its lead will probably cover several times as much ground as its owner as it races to and fro. If you teach the dog to retrieve a ball or toy, it will gain valuable exercise chasing after this in a comparatively restricted area. Both road walking and free running are valuable in building up the dog's muscles and keeping it fit.

The best guide as to whether your dog has had enough exercise is its response when you get home. If it soon settles down to sleep, then its walk will have been long enough. If the dog shows no sign of fatigue, then it is likely that additional exercise could be recommended.

If walking is to be enjoyable for both you and the dog, training is essential. On lead, the dog should walk at your pace without pulling. Off lead, it must be trained to come back when called and not to make a nuisance of itself to other people.

Under no circumstances should dogs be allowed to run free close to livestock, especially sheep. Dogs can inflict hideous injuries on sheep, especially at lambing time, and farmers are legally entitled to shoot to protect their flocks or their herds. For the dog's own safety, running free off the lead should also be curtailed in urban areas. In some cities, this is banned by law, in any case.

Many dogs enjoy swimming, and this is another valuable form of exercise. Make sure that your dog is only encouraged to swim where it is safe, with no risk of drowning either because of a strong current or because he cannot climb out of the water. Furthermore, the water should be clean, with no obvious oil or other contaminants on the surface. Swimming should only be encouraged where the dog is not likely to disturb wildlife, such as nesting ducks.

After emerging from the water, the dog should always be dried with a towel. This will not only prevent him from drenching the inside of your car or your home, but will prevent him from catching a chill or developing stiffness in the joints. Most dogs will thoroughly enjoy a brisk rub down and, like regular grooming, it helps to confirm the bond between pet and owner.

Exercise is vital to keep your dog fit and healthy. An active working breed requires the opportunity for plenty of free galloping as well as walks on the lead, but even toy breeds will benefit from more exercise than is commonly expected of them.

ABOVE: *Swimming is a useful form of exercise which many dogs enjoy. Some breeds tend to be more aquatic than others, for example, retrievers which were evolved to retrieve waterfowl.*

LEFT: *Once a dog is sufficiently well trained to be let off the lead, it can enjoy free exercise. However, dogs should always be closely supervised when off the lead, particularly when in the vicinity of livestock.*

Chihuahua
Average daily walk: ½ mile (0.8km)

West Highland White Terrier
Average daily walk: 1 mile (4.8km)

Greyhound
Average daily walk: 3 miles (4.8km)

Labrador Retriever
Average daily walk: 8 miles (12.9km)

Irish Wolfhound
Average daily walk: 9 miles (14.5km)

Great Dane
Average daily walk: 6 miles (9.6km)

Exercise requirements do vary considerably, even between breeds of similar size. A 'Westie', for example, enjoys a good walk, whereas a Chihuahua is more than happy with a short stroll each day. Surprisingly, the Greyhound does not require nearly as long a walk as the Labrador, a working dog which needs good, solid exercise every day. The bigger dogs should have a substantial daily outing, although puppies must avoid lengthy walks as these can affect bone and muscle development. Remember that the mileage required by each of these dogs does not mean that the owner has to walk this distance, as a dog off the lead will usually run to and fro, covering at least twice as much ground.

GROOMING

Wild dogs care for their own coats, scrubbing off dirt and teasing out mats with their teeth, attempting to control the numbers of skin parasites such as fleas, and keeping the fur in good condition to maximize its insulating and water-proofing qualities. Pack members will also groom each other, both to help with inaccessible areas and to reinforce the social bond.

The domestic dog requires grooming from its owner, partly to satisfy human standards of hygiene which differ from those of the canine world, and partly to care for coats which in many cases have been developed by man to suit our ideas of beauty rather than for easy maintenance. The amount and type of grooming your dog will need will depend on the kind of coat it carries, but regular grooming should be part of every dog-owner's routine.

The aims of grooming your dog are to keep its skin and fur in a healthy and attractive condition, to control parasites, to remove burrs, grass seeds and splinters before they cause injury, to reduce the natural doggy smell which can otherwise permeate your house and clothing, to enable you to detect certain ailments at an early stage, and to reinforce the bond between dog and owner. A brisk (but not harsh) brushing will stimulate the skin and help to keep it healthy, and also serves as a massage to tone up the muscles. Grooming a dog for exhibition is a specialized technique, an intensive beauty care routine which goes beyond this maintenance work in the same way that the beauty routine of a top fashion model goes beyond that of the housewife.

Grooming should be a pleasurable experience for both dog and owner, and so make sure that you choose a dog with a coat you can enjoy caring for, and accustom your pet to being groomed from an early age.

As noted in Chapter 4, a wide range of grooming equipment is available, but essentially you should think in terms of a brush, plus a comb for longer hair. Different types of coat need different types of brush, and if you have a pedigree dog you should ask the breeder for guidance. If your dog is a mongrel you will have to assess its coat type yourself and decide on the most suitable tools.

For most types of coat, a brush of natural bristle is recommended; nylon brushes create static electricity and may damage the hair. Wire brushes are suitable to remove dead hair from some densely-coated breeds during the moult, or from breeds which do not moult in the conventional sense, such as Poodles, but can be harmful if used excessively. For a smooth-coated dog, a rubber brush with a strap which fits over the hand, or a studded hound glove, will help to give the coat a good lustre, and a silk cloth or chamois leather is a useful accessory to give the coat a final polish after brushing. Soft brushes are best for puppies.

For the long-coated breeds, a comb is essential to re-

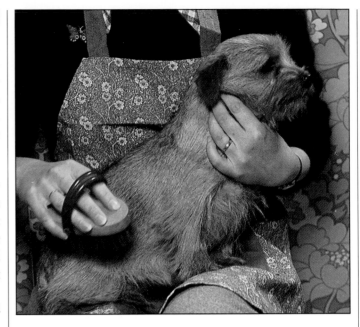

ABOVE: *Small breeds can be groomed sitting on your lap if you prefer. Both large and small dogs need to be taught to remain still while being groomed. Here a dandy brush is being used on this Norfolk Terrier to disentangle matted fur.*

move tangles. Plastic combs can be used on very fine coats, but steel combs, with rounded teeth to prevent damage to the skin, are best since the teeth will not break off easily. For general purposes a wide-toothed comb is preferable. A fine-toothed comb, on a dense coat, will tend to slide over the surface without penetrating to the layer of fur underneath, although it can be used on the head and for finishing touches.

For certain coat types, specialist equipment may be recommended, and advice may be obtained from breeders, but if in doubt you will not go far wrong with the bristle brush and wide-toothed metal comb.

Teach your dog to accept a grooming routine, and to stand or lie still while being groomed. It is important that the animal be placed on a firm surface where it will feel secure, at a comfortable height for the groomer. Many people like to groom their dogs on a table for this reason. With the larger breeds, the task will probably have to be carried out with the dog standing on the floor. The small breeds can be groomed on a table or on your lap, as you prefer. Heavily-coated dogs such as Poodles or Pekingese should be taught to lie on their sides to enable you to tackle the long fur on legs and bellies easily.

With all coat types, start grooming at the head and work backwards towards the tail, following the direction of the fur, and make sure to groom the whole body.

Grooming the short-haired dog is an easy task. Use a bristle brush or a hound glove over the whole body. During the spring and autumn moults, you will have to spend a little longer on the task to remove shed hairs. If you wish, when the coat has been brushed over, you can finish off with a silk cloth or a chamois leather to bring up a shine on the coat.

Some relatively short-haired breeds have longer hair in certain areas, typically feathering on the tail, the ears and the backs of the legs, which will need combing through to prevent tangles. These dogs may have rather denser hair in areas which are prone to soiling, such as the chest, which easily picks up food traces, around the penile sheath, and under the tail, all of which will require extra attention. Wire-haired breeds will require regular combing through to keep the coat tidy and free of mats, as well as needing clipping or stripping from time to time (see page 137).

The long-haired breeds need the most time and attention of all. It is regrettably common for people to buy a long-haired dog for its glamorous appearance without realizing that up to an hour's work a day may be needed to maintain that glamour. Fashionable breeds such as Afghan Hounds and Old English Sheepdogs have suffered greatly from such owners. A few days' neglect can cause such dogs real discomfort, while a few months can reduce a heavy coat to a matted mass which will need to be completely removed

ABOVE: *Show dogs in many breeds require specialist grooming techniques. The exhibition Yorkshire Terrier's long, silky coat is easily tangled or broken, so after each daily grooming session it is protected by paper wrappers ('crackers').*

ABOVE: *Grooming can be facilitated by training your dog to stand on a table so you can reach all parts easily.*

by clipping down to the skin, in severe cases under general anaesthetic.

If you are attracted by a long-coated breed, do think very carefully beforehand about the implications of that coat in terms of time and care.

There are different kinds of long hair found in dogs, some of which require more work than others. Breeds such as the Rough Collie, the Newfoundland, or the Old English Sheepdog combine a long top coat with a very dense undercoat, and need a great deal of attention, particularly during the moult. Others such as the Afghan Hound and Pekingese have a coat which is long but fine and silky. Although such coats very quickly show the effects of neglect, the daily grooming sessions can be less time-consuming than those of the harsher-coated breeds, provided a longer session once a week is scheduled as well.

Then there are the so-called non-shedding breeds, such as the Bedlington Terrier, which appear not to moult because the shed hairs are retained in the coat. These dogs depend upon regular clipping to keep their coats under control, but also need careful daily brushing to prevent those shed hairs from building up into mats. An unusual type of long coat occurs in the corded breeds, such as the Hungarian Puli and Komondor, where a controlled type of matting is permitted to form the coat into separate cords.

When grooming a long-coated dog, it pays to seek guidance from an experienced breeder concerning the most appropriate tools and techniques. Common to all types is the need to take your grooming right down to the skin; it is all too easy to brush over the surface of the coat, so that the dog looks well brushed to the eye, and to neglect the undercoat, allowing tangles to build up underneath. In most breeds it will be best to work right through the coat with a brush, going against the natural lie of the hair, and then follow through with a wide-toothed comb to make sure there are no mats. Ear fringes and tail feathering will require combing through.

If you make grooming a daily routine, you will find it possible to maintain the coat with quite short daily sessions supplemented by a thorough going-over at weekends.

The long-haired dog's coat, like long hair in humans, will be prone to the odd knots and tangles. If you groom every day, you should pick these up before they consolidate into mats and become difficult to deal with. Any knots you find should be tackled before you go on to deal with the rest of the coat. Particular problem areas are behind the ears and in the armpits and groin, places where the hair of two parts of the body meets and rubs together, and also where the casual glance fails to spot incipient tangles.

If possible, tease the knot out gently with dampened fingers, taking care not to pull away from the skin, which will hurt the dog and make it less co-operative. More awkward knots can sometimes be eased apart gently with the end of a tail comb. If the knot has been missed for a day or two and felted up into a solid mass, you will probably have to sacrifice some of the hair and cut into it. Simply cutting the whole knot out will leave an unsightly patch amongst the fur. It is better to hold the knot flat between your fingers and cut straight down the centre, then tease apart as much as you can; repeat the process as necessary before cutting out what cannot be saved.

Most breeds have their traditional finishing touches, which you may or may not like to adopt. Some breeds are given a centre parting down the back. Dogs with long hair on the face which obscures the eyes are treated in various ways. The hair may be left hanging forward, as in the Old English Sheepdog, or tied up in a topknot, as in the Shih Tzu and some Poodles, or trimmed back, as in other Poodle trims; Maltese often have this hair neatly plaited.

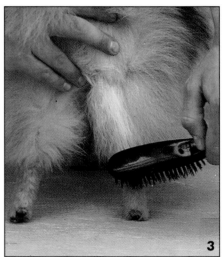

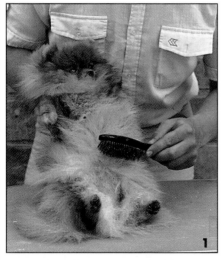

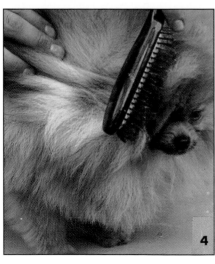

LEFT: *This Pekingese puppy is an appealing ball of fluff which as yet requires little grooming. However, this is the time to accustom it to a regular grooming routine, so that by the time the coat has grown to its full length the dog will look forward to the necessary session.*

BELOW: *The adult Pekingese has a long dense coat with flowing fringes, which requires loving care to keep it healthy and attractive. Knots will form easily if the coat is neglected, and those long ear fringes will need careful combing. Daily grooming will include ensuring that the wrinkle above the foreshortened nose is dry and clean and that the large, vulnerable eyes have not suffered any scratches.*

LEFT: GROOMING YOUR DOG

(1) Begin with the stomach, brushing upwards from the hair roots with firm short strokes. (2) Groom the rest of the body, working from the tail towards the head. (3) Groom the 'trousers' on fore and hindlimbs, holding the tail to one side while you brush each leg down. Brush the tail thoroughly, working from the root to the tip. (4) Brush the neck and ears, holding each ear while grooming beneath it and teasing out any tangles with your fingers, keeping the brush and comb away from the dog's face. (5) Groom beneath the head and under the chin, holding the head up. (6) Grooming completed.

GROOMING AS A HEALTH CHECK

During grooming, the opportunity should be taken to check the skin for parasites, and to inspect ears, eyes, teeth, anal glands and paws.

Occasionally, a flea may be spotted moving in the dog's fur, or the presence of fleas may be detected from their tiny gritty black-red droppings in the coat. Other parasites which may be noticed include mites, ticks and lice. All these need prompt attention as, although apparently minor irritations in themselves, they can give rise to worse problems. Close inspection of your dog's coat during grooming sessions will enable you to detect parasites at an early stage, which will make control much easier (see pp 209-215).

The ears should be inspected for any signs of infection such as the accumulation of dark brown wax, often accompanied by a detectable acrid smell, which indicates the presence of ear mites. Dogs with long, heavy pendant ears, such as Spaniels, are most at risk from ear infections, as the ears form a closed, warm environment in which bacteria will thrive. Some breeds, such as Poodles, have a heavy growth of hair within the ears which needs plucking out, both to prevent conditions conducive to infection and to improve the dog's hearing: your veterinarian or local dog trimming parlour will show you how to manage this as painlessly as possible.

It does not take a moment to check that the eyes are clear and bright. Eyes which are dull and sunken, or sore and watering or discharging, indicate illness. Some breeds are prone to watering eyes, particularly the short-faced breeds whose compressed muzzles lead to distortion of the tear ducts. These may show tear-stains on the fur below the eyes, which should be gently bathed with cottonwool soaked in warm water. Dogs with wrinkled faces will need the wrinkles carefully drying to prevent soreness. Inflamed or discharging eyes may indicate the presence of a foreign body such as a grass seed in the eye: if you can see the object, try to wash it out with cool water, but you may need veterinary assistance to remove it.

The dog's teeth should be inspected as a matter of course and cleaned once or twice a week. Puppies need to be trained to permit this attention from an early age, for neglect of the teeth can lead to problems just as in humans. Chewing on bones or hard dog biscuits will help to keep the teeth clean, but the best way to prevent a build-up of tartar deposits is to incorporate regular tooth cleaning into your grooming routine. Special dog toothpastes are available to facilitate tooth care and may be applied with damp cotton wool or a soft toothbrush.

Paws should be checked daily. The toe nails should be examined to be sure that they are wearing down evenly and do not need cutting; if the dog has dew claws, these will certainly need to be trimmed regularly. The pads are vulnerable to injury when the dog is walking, and a small cut or splinter, if not detected at an early stage, can develop into a nasty injury as the dog keeps using the paw. Unpleasant substances such as chewing gum or tar can easily be picked up on the pads and need removing immediately. Even mud can become impacted hard between the pads, causing soreness, so paws should always be washed down in warm water after a muddy walk.

The space between the toes should be examined daily for foreign bodies such as grit or grass seeds, which can quickly work their way into the flesh and cause abscesses which are hard to cure. Some dogs are prone to infections between the toes in any case. The cause of interdigital cysts is not known, but these painful, matter-filled swellings are not uncommon, particularly in certain breeds, including Labrador Retrievers and Boxers. If they occur the foot should be bathed in warm salt water to bring the swelling to a head and ease the discomfort.

GROOMING THE HEAD

(1) To open the mouth of an obstinate dog hold the lower jaw firmly with one hand and at the same time block the nostrils; inspect the teeth with special attention to the molars.

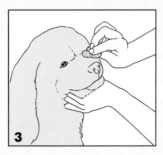

(2) Using a toothbrush may hurt the dog's gums if they are sensitive and so it is preferable to use a damp cottonwool ball to remove superficial debris. Special dog toothpastes are available.

(3) Any tear-staining, loose hairs or eyelashes can be cleaned away gently using a moistened cottonwool ball; use a fresh one for each eye.

(4) The ears should also be groomed thoroughly and inspected for any signs of infection. Dogs with long, heavy ears that hang down such as Spaniels, are most at risk. Any grooming around the head should be done gently and every few days.

LOOKING AFTER THE PAWS

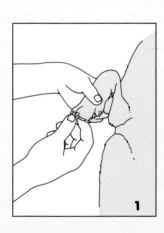

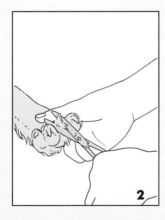

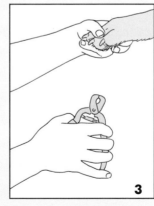

FAR LEFT: Toe-nail clipping is another attention your dog needs to learn to accept from an early age, although most healthy dogs will wear their nails down naturally with normal exercise.

1. The space between the toes should be examined carefully for grit and small stones. If there is a grass seed in the dog's foot, it can be removed using a pair of tweezers but it is probably preferable to seek veterinary advice. Inspect the undersides of the foot pad and remove any embedded mud with moist cottonwool.

2. Excess fur between the toes can be carefully trimmed away with round-tipped scissors, so as to minimize the risk of any infection.

3. Overgrown nails should be clipped with a stout pair of clippers, specially designed for the purpose. It is safest to simply trim off the sharpest points – never cut too short or near the quick.

BELOW: *It is essential that the dog be thoroughly dried after its bath to prevent the risk of chilling. A hairdrier is a useful aid, but be gentle, as the noise and unfamiliar sensation of warm air may initially frighten the dog if it has not been accustomed to the process from an early age. It is also important to take care not to burn the dog by holding the drier too close.*

BATHING

Regular brushing and combing will serve to keep your dog's coat healthy and clean; bathing is an occasional extra, needed at intervals to prevent 'doggy' smell or in special circumstances, as when the dog is being prepared for exhibition, or when it has rolled in something foul. If a dog is simply muddy after a walk in the rain, you can simply rinse off its legs and undercarriage in a washing off bowl, using lukewarm water and no soap and drying the animal carefully with a towel afterwards. Excessive bathing will remove too much of the natural grease and leave the fur dull and unattractive.

Try to accustom your dog to bathing from an early age so that it will accept this treatment. If introduced to bathing at a late stage, it may resent it. Bathing a dog can be a messy process, and if the weather permits it is a good idea to perform this task out of doors, using a suitable tub of metal or plastic. A dog's claws are sharp, and can puncture inflatable pools or scratch the enamel of a bathtub. If the dog is not accustomed to being bathed, it will be useful to have a helper on hand to hold the animal in the bath while you wash it.

The choice of shampoo depends upon the dog's coat. Shampoos intended for human use, apart from baby shampoos, are not suitable as they will remove too much natural grease from the coat. A wide variety of canine shampoos is manufactured; these range from all-purpose shampoos suitable for all breeds to specialist ones, perhaps to highlight particular colours or to suit puppies or dogs with delicate skins. Medicated shampoos should be used only under veterinary guidance; any insecticidal preparations must be mixed and used strictly in accordance with the manufacturer's instructions.

A long-coated dog should be brushed thoroughly before bathing, as any mats and tangles are likely to felt up when wet and will then need to be cut out. Protect your clothing with a plastic apron or similar waterproofing, and half-fill the bath with lukewarm water. Place the dog gently in the water, and then, with a clean bottle or jug, pour the water gently over it, starting at the hindquarters and progressing forwards. Apply the shampoo and work it into a lather. Be sure to shampoo between the toes where the eccrine sweat glands are.

The head should be washed last, taking care not to drip shampoo into the eyes. Once the head is wet, the dog will probably shake itself, spraying water everywhere. Rinse the coat with clean water; certain medicated shampoos, however, may have to be left on the coat for a period before rinsing.

Lift the dog out of the bath and set about drying it. It is important to dry the dog thoroughly. An old towel can be used to rub off as much of the moisture as possible, and then a hair-dryer of some type can be used for the final stage, taking care not to scorch the dog's hair and skin. Separating the wet fur with a brush will also help it to dry more quickly; again, with a long-haired breed it is important to brush as you dry to prevent tangles. Some breeds will benefit from the use of a canine hair conditioner after the shampoo and before drying to settle the coat.

After the dog has been bathed, its natural instinct will be to run off and roll in something strong-smelling to compensate for the body scent which has been removed by washing, so shut it indoors to prevent this behaviour.

Dry shampoos can be used as an alternative to bathing, and will not strip the coat's natural oils in the same way; they are often used for show dogs, and in cases where bathing is inadvisable, for example, with an elderly dog. The powder is rubbed into the coat, left for a little while, then brushed out again. Dry shampoos will not clean a very dirty coat, and traces will show up on dark fur. Considerable brushing may be needed to remove them from the fur, which may cause a build-up of static electricity and prevent the coat from settling down properly. Powders can also irritate the eyes and cause sneezing if applied carelessly around the head.

Various commercial preparations are also available to improve the appearance of the coat, including quick-drying liquids or aerosols sprayed on to the fur to give body or shine. The value of such products is chiefly for giving finishing touches to exhibition dogs before a show.

CLIPPING AND STRIPPING

Most breeds moult naturally and do not require clipping. However, non-shedding breeds such as Poodles need their coats clipping at intervals of about six weeks, while many of the wire-haired breeds require stripping – the removal of dead hairs from the coat. A number of breeds have the coat tidied up by clipping of long fringes; spaniels benefit from having some of the long hair on the ears removed to reduce the likelihood of ear infections. Owners of dogs with long heavy coats such as Old English Sheep-dogs may choose to have their pets clipped for ease of care or for the dog's greater comfort in hot weather; and elderly dogs will often benefit from trimming of the hair to prevent soiling.

WASHING YOUR DOG

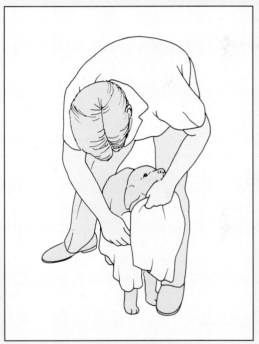

Outdoors is the best place to wash your dog, to avoid water all over the house! Having placed the dog in the water, begin shampooing at the hindquarters and gently massage your dog. Ensure that all the shampoo is thoroughly rinsed before drying the dog with an old towel. Wearing a protective overall is recommended, as the dog will shake itself vigorously to remove excess water from its coat.

Many owners prefer to have their dogs trimmed at a grooming parlour; some of these will visit the dog's home for this purpose. Alternatively, one can learn to do one's own clipping; there are courses where such skills can be learned, or the breeder for whom you obtained your dog may be willing to teach you.

Show dogs require specialist clipping or stripping, and the novice will require guidance from established breeders to present a dog for exhibition. With pet dogs practicality rather than beauty is usually the guideline, although there is no reason why both should not be combined.

Breeds such as Poodles whose coat grows continuously are clipped to prevent them disappearing under a mound of uncontrolled hair. Electric clippers are used, and it is important to accustom the dog to the sensation at an early age. Various styles of clip have been developed. Show dogs must be exhibited in an elaborate trim with a heavy mane which requires loving maintenance, the actual style specified differing in different countries; the tradition is supposed to have developed from a working trim in which the dog's hindquarters were clipped to prevent waterlogging when retrieving game from rivers, while the forequarters were left heavily coated to prevent chilling. The elaboration of the show trims should not deter the owner who wants a companion dog, for pet poodles are usually trimmed in a much simpler style for easy care.

Wire-coated breeds generally need to be stripped twice a year, in the spring and autumn. For show dogs, this stripping out of dead hair is carried out by hand, which takes considerable time and skill. As a result, the showing of such breeds as the Airedale Terrier requires considerable dedication. Pet dogs which do not need to meet exhibition requirements still need stripping to prevent the coat from matting up with dead hair, but are usually stripped with mechanical clippers and thinning scissors.

POODLE STYLES

ABOVE: *Three popular poodle trims. The Lamb Clip is a popular short clip, with ears left long and a pompom on the tail, for the pet poodle. The Continental and English Lion Clips are required presentation for the show ring.*

LEFT: *This pet puppy is serviceably clipped to a manageable 1½ inches all over, with the feet trimmed close for reasons of hygiene and the face also close-clipped to avoid fur in the eyes. Moustache and beard have been left on in this case but could have been trimmed off for easy care. A poodle in this trim would not be eligible for exhibition.*

ABOVE: *Wire-haired breeds such as this Schnauzer require professional trimming for the show ring. Most of the coat is trimmed short to give a smart appearance, with longer hair left on the legs and face carefully shaped.*

TRAVEL AND HOLIDAYS

At some point, the dog will have to be transported by car and will probably adapt fairly quickly to the experience. During the journey, the dog must be properly restrained so that it will not distract the driver, or damage the upholstery. If a dog is allowed to travel free in the car, it should be accompanied by a passenger who can restrain it if necessary in the back seat. Travelling cages which fit into the back of an estate car or station wagon are one solution but another option is to install a dog guard. These can be acquired from motor accessory stores and, depending on the model of car, either may need to be fitted to the body shell or may be held in place by suction pads attaching to the roof or floor. With fine-nosed breeds such as Greyhounds, square or rectangular meshes are essential, as it is possible for the dog to push its head through horizontal bars and get stuck.

A dog must never be allowed to ride with its head out of a window. Apart from the obvious and fatal risk of colliding with another object at speed, the velocity of the air is likely to lead to conjunctivitis, and small particles of gravel may

Dogs should not be allowed to travel with their heads out of the car window because of the risk of injury to their eyes, either from the wind setting up irritation or foreign bodies being blown into them. A dog that is trained to sit quietly, away from the windows, is both safer and less likely to distract the driver. Most breeders transport their dogs in special carrying pens or behind fitted dog guards for added security.

also enter the eyes. In warm weather the interior of a car heats up very quickly and, without ventilation, a dog can be killed in a frighteningly short space of time. Always ensure that windows are left partially open if the dog has to be left in a car for any length of time.

All dogs should be kept on a lead when you are travelling on public transport. Small dogs can be held on the lap; large dogs should be kept under close control, well out of the way of other passengers. If the dog has to be transported by air, special shippers can be contacted to organize both the necessary paperwork and the crating. Various health tests will also be required for dogs being sent abroad.

When you plan a holiday, you will need to decide what arrangements to make for your dog. You may be able to take the dog with you, and a well-trained dog will enjoy this. However, if you are travelling abroad, quarantine regulations will prevent you from taking your dog, and even within this country you may find that there are restrictions. Not all hotels will accept dogs, and if you plan to go sightseeing you may not want your holiday to revolve around the problem of what to do with your pet every time you encounter a 'No Dogs Allowed' sign.

Remember, if your dog does come with you, it will be in a strange environment. It is vital that you can control it adequately so that it does not run off and disappear. To be on the safe side, ensure that the dog wears its collar with identity medallion all the time – and do check that your address is still legible on the disk. When travelling, remember to take food and water bowls, a supply of clean drinking water for the journey, your dog's usual food (and a can-opener if necessary), and your dog's bed or a familiar blanket to encourage it to settle down at night.

If you cannot take your dog with you, you will have to arrange for its care during your absence. It may be possible to leave the animal with friends; it is not advisable to leave it alone at home with someone popping in to feed and exercise it. Under these circumstances it is likely to be lonely and bored, and behavioural difficulties may well develop. In most cases the most satisfactory solution will be a boarding kennel. If kennelling is necessary, then the arrangements should be made as far as possible before the date of departure. Satisfied clients will take their dogs to the same kennels every year, and it is often difficult to find a vacancy at peak holiday times, especially in a well-run establishment. A kennel should be chosen on recommendation, either from a breeder or veterinarian; if not, then a visit to the kennels under consideration should be arranged, as this will afford an opportunity to inspect the premises. Much can be gathered from simply seeing the surroundings and meeting the people who care for the dogs. The kennels and outside runs ought to be clean, with no signs of overcrowding. The occupants should look alert and well. The interiors of the kennels should be dry and snug, and the

ABOVE: *While farm dogs ride happily in the back of open vehicles, this type of transport cannot be recommended for most dogs, which are liable to be distracted by a scent or another animal and might easily attempt to jump out, risking serious injury.*

water bowls should be filled and clean.

In most countries, reputable kennels ask for certificates of vaccination against leptospirosis, canine infectious hepatitis, distemper and also parvovirus. For additional protection, vaccination against *Bordetella bronchoseptica,* a bacterium which is partly responsible for the kennel cough syndrome, is now available. This disease is normally relatively minor, but spreads rapidly among dogs in kennels at holiday time. It is important to inform the kennel staff of any significant medical condition, such as a heart complaint, and to supply the correct treatment, together with the name, address and number of the dog's veterinarian. A vet may be prepared to take a chronically sick dog, such as a diabetic, for a holiday period.

Ask the kennel what, if anything, it would like you to provide when you take your dog in. Although many kennels look rather like prisons with wire to prevent escapes, the vast majority of dogs, unlike cats, settle very readily after a few days. Nevertheless, a favourite blanket or toy is likely to be appreciated and may assist in the settling-in phase. Generally, older dogs prove the least adaptable and may pine if they are not used to kennel life. If you are going away for any length of time, make sure that the kennel staff are aware if you have a bitch that may come into heat during this period. Again, some kennels will not take bitches at such times because of the disturbance they cause in the community as a whole. There are ways of preventing a heat, provided that arrangements are made beforehand. If possible, leave your telephone number.

Chapter Six

UNDERSTANDING YOUR DOG

THE CANINE ETHIC

'Dogs,' we say fondly, 'are almost human,' but of course they are not. Because their nature enables them, on the whole, to interact so well with man and to adapt to his ways successfully, we tend to forget that dogs' perception of the world and innate responses to it are quite different from our own. Most dogs are surprisingly good at adapting to human lifestyles and expectations; the owner who, by attempting to understand canine nature, creates a two-way communication will be rewarded by an increase in mutual understanding and enjoyment.

The key to the dog's mentality lies in the fact that it is a pack animal. Because it has evolved towards a communal and cooperative lifestyle, it is predisposed towards social interaction with its fellows, whether dogs or humans. Its social nature has called for a high degree of responsiveness to its family; it tends to be demonstratively affectionate towards them, protective of them, highly aware of their moods and requirements, and communicative. The factors which enable it to lead a successful life as a pack animal in the wild also enable it to become the ideal companion to humans.

BELOW: *Poodles, despite their undeserved lapdog reputation, are generally acknowledged to be one of the most intelligent breeds of dog. Their ability to learn complicated routines has made them successful in a range of roles from circus performers to working gundogs.*

Other innate characteristics arising from the dog's natural lifestyle include the hunting instinct and the aggressive instinct. Both these can either be turned to man's advantage or become positively disadvantageous depending on the requirements of the individual human and the strength of these drives in the individual dog. As we have seen, the different breeds have been developed with differing emphases upon these natural instincts, and it makes sense to bear this in mind when choosing a dog. For example, a town-dweller wanting a loyal companion dog which will act as a guard would be ill-advised to choose a hound, which will have highly developed hunting instincts which cannot be satisfied in the urban context, but be low in aggression.

All dogs have a degree of playfulness, even in adult life, which is linked partly with the social instincts, serving to establish and confirm social bonds, and also with the hunting and aggressive instincts, as the dog acts out in play the patterns associated with chasing and killing prey and with fighting. Again, different breeds have developed differing emphases upon play. The toy breeds generally retain a high degree of infantile behaviour in adult life and will be especially playful. The owner who goes to the trouble of considering what underlies the pattern of play with his or her pet will benefit by reinforcing their relationship, increasing mutual communication and being able to utilize 'fun' play sessions to direct the dog's behaviour in a socially desirable way.

We expect our dogs to make the effort to understand us. The owner who reciprocates and tries to understand the dog will both put more into the relationship and derive much more benefit from it.

INTELLIGENCE

Dog owners generally agree that one of the attributes that make dogs such valued companions is their intelligence. However, a dog's intelligence is not quite the same thing as human intelligence. An obvious difference is brain size; with a dog of comparable weight to a human, such as a St Bernard, the brain weighs only 15 per cent of that of a man. Not only is the brain smaller, but proportionally more of it is given over to decoding messages received by the senses – for example, the area of brain connected with the sense of smell has 40 times as many cells as the same area in the human brain – and less of it to the association of ideas. The dog's mental capacity is therefore clearly less than man's.

Intelligence in animals is hard to define as well as hard to measure. Often when we talk about dogs' intelligence, we are really talking about their responsiveness to training. Dogs have been taught to carry out highly complicated tasks, as when guide dogs for the blind are taught not only to steer their owners but to watch out for obstacles which do not affect the dog directly, such as a branch jutting out at human eye level. Yet the identification of intelligence with the capacity to respond to training fails to take into account such factors as breed characteristics, individual environment and even the skill of the human trainer.

The different breeds have been developed for specific abilities. Some breeds have been selectively bred for a very high receptiveness to training. In competitive obedience trials, a very high percentage of the dogs entered are Border Collies and German Shepherd Dogs, and this reflects the innate trainability of these breeds – not necessarily their higher intelligence.

Dogs can be trained to very high standards in areas for which they have been bred to have a special aptitude. A retriever puppy will learn to carry out an impeccable retrieve much more easily than a Pekingese puppy. The retriever is the end product of generations of selective breeding for a strong retrieving instinct, as well as for keen sensory abilities to enable it to locate the item to be retrieved, while the Pekingese has never been bred for any particular predilection towards obedience but rather for an appealing independence, even wilfulness, and its sense of smell is less keen than that of most hunting breeds. The breeding, or genetic background, of a dog is a major factor in its capacity to accept training.

The admirer of the retriever will take the ease with which it is trained and the perfection with which it subsequently carries out its task as signs of true intelligence. The admirer of the Pekingese will see the same qualities as mere submissiveness to the trainer, and will claim that the Peke is 'too intelligent to obey'. Similarly, people who have tried to train Salukis for obedience work regard them as a breed of low intelligence, while people who choose them as companions often describe them as highly intelligent. Our view of canine intelligence in terms of trainability therefore depends upon our individual expectations of a dog.

Selective breeding for particular traits is one factor in a dog's responsiveness and apparent intelligence, but upbringing also has a major influence on a dog's behaviour. A dog kept in kennels for the first four months of its life, with minimal socialization and stimulation, will probably never be fully trainable, certainly not to the extent of a puppy brought into a family at the age of six weeks. Some individuals are innately shy and timid, harking back to the 'wild' temperament of their ancestors, and they too will be harder to train than a bold type. This does not mean that there is any difference in the intelligence of the undersocialized or the shy dog, just that their backgrounds give them a different capacity to interact with humans and to accept training.

Certainly, some dogs perform extraordinary feats,

which apparently require great intelligence. There are dogs which collect the morning newspaper from the newsagent; others can get out of a room by undoing the latch; many dogs learn strange tricks such as riding along with two or three legs on a skateboard. Acts of this kind appear to reflect intelligence, but they must be looked at in the context of the selectively developed qualities of the breeds in question, and also the behaviour of dogs in general. For the retrieving breeds, the collection of a newspaper is an elaboration of a process which comes to them very easily. A dog who opens a door with the latch is likely to have found the solution by chance, perhaps by nuzzling the latch in an attempt to push the door open, rather than by thinking the problem through. Dogs' abilities to learn tricks may depend at least as much on the intelligence of the trainer as on the animal's capacity to respond.

It is clear then that a highly trained dog is not necessarily exceptionally intelligent. Those who seek to measure a dog's level of intelligence must bear several factors in mind, such as the breed and size of dog, its ancestry, and upbringing, whether it has had special training, whether it is a stressed or frightened individual which might otherwise behave more sensibly, and whether it has developed skills by chance or developed them by practice. Only if all these factors can be evaluated can a proper assessment of intelligence be made.

A rather better definition of intelligence is in terms of reasoning power. A human tackles a problem by reasoning. The Greek philosopher Aristotle concluded that, although animals could learn and remember things, only humans were capable of reason, and many students of animal behaviour have held to this distinction. However, tests have shown that many of the higher animals do approach problem-solving in a way that implies the use of some degree of reasoning powers.

Certainly a dog is not capable of abstract reasoning; it cannot think about the nature of the universe. However, dogs have been known to tackle practical problems by what is difficult to regard as anything other than reasoning. An example which has been recorded by a number of people who own more than one dog occurs when the first dog is in possession of an item which the second dog wants. After unsuccessful attempts to take the item directly, the second dog may dash out of the room barking as if someone were at the front door. When the first dog responds by following, the second dog nips back to take the desired object. It has solved the problem by carrying out an indirect course of action to distract its companion – a quite sophisticated routine which implies the ability to put together cause and effect, 'reasoning' that if the first dog can be distracted it will leave the disputed item.

Such a capacity for reasoning is difficult enough to test for humans, and almost impossible for dogs and other animals. Clearly, any test of intelligence must be tailored

RIGHT: *Dogs are generally viewed as intelligent because they have a highly developed social awareness that enables them to form close and responsive relationships with their owners.*

FAR RIGHT: *Receptiveness to training varies from breed to breed. The Border Collie is highly popular with competitive obedience enthusiasts because it is quick to learn and highly responsive.*

to suit a particular species; it is impossible to make more than the broadest of comparisons between species. However, even within the dog species problems arise because there are so many different breeds. To take an extreme example, a Chihuahua and a Great Dane can hardly be given a test which involves jumping up to retrieve an object. Most of the breeds have special aptitudes, and this makes it almost impossible to devise a general test of dog intelligence.

Certainly dogs are able to associate ideas – the famous example is the Russian scientist Pavlov's discovery that his dogs associated the sound of a bell ringing with meal times, and would salivate in response to the bell even if food were not forthcoming. This process of association can be used by the dog trainer to help condition a dog to perform a particular action from its normal repertoire at a specific moment. Dogs also have a good memory and can retain what has been learned, sometimes for a surprising length of time.

However, when we refer to a dog's intelligence perhaps what matters most to us, and what is undeniably a characteristic of the species, is its ability to communicate with us. All animals communicate with each other in some way – vocally, by visual signs, by the sense of smell or by some other method – but the level of communication possible with the human languages is thought by many experts to be in a class of its own. Sentence structure, vocabulary and subtleties of intonation can be used to communicate complex and original thoughts in a way that no animal achieves. Yet anyone who lives or works with a dog will know that the dog's lack of command of language is no barrier to communication. The great appeal of the dog to dog-owners is its desire and capacity to understand our moods and wishes to a very high degree.

This understanding is not a matter of language in the human sense. A dog can learn to recognize and respond to a number of commands, such as Sit, Come, Wait, Heel, and these can be quite complex, but it cannot understand sentences in the way that humans do. Doting dog-owners often boast, 'He understands every word I say,' but in fact that is not what the dog does at all. However, dogs, as social animals, have an innate predisposition towards communication. Within the pack they express their own moods, needs, social status and so forth, and understand each other's signals. Within the human family they seek to do the same.

A dog has senses far more highly attuned than a man's to pick up tiny signals of voice tone, body posture, and so forth: it can learn to pick out a large number of individual human words and associate these with specific meanings. A dog with a close relationship with its owner watches and listens for signals from him or her. It does not understand the spoken sentence as such, but by picking out the significant words and linking them with information received by

its senses of sight, hearing and even smell it achieves a degree of communication with its owner that can be astonishing.

At a simple level, this can be seen in the dog which notes which shoes its owner puts on and knows from this whether the owner is about to take it for a walk or intending to go out without it. People who run dog training classes place particular emphasis on correct use of tone of voice, knowing that a dog can distinguish between the firm tone that indicates an intention to see that the command is carried out, and the less confident voice that suggests that the dog can probably get away with disobedience.

At a more complex level, the dog's ability to respond to its owner's signals is illustrated by such remarkable performing animals as the 'counting dogs' which appear to bark the answers to arithmetic problems, picking up the cues for when to start and when to stop barking from bodily movements on the part of the owner so slight as to be all but imperceptible to a human observer.

Similarly, the owner learns to interpret the dog's signals so that communication is two-way. Everybody recognizes the meaning of the wagging tail or the bared teeth; if the owner and dog are close, the human learns to respond to the subtler signals of body posture and facial expression as well as a range of vocal sounds.

The dog's naturally strong social orientation predisposes it not only to recognize a range of signals from its owner but to respond to these. This innate tendency, which we usually refer to as intelligence, is what makes possible the uniquely close and interactive relationship between a dog and its owner. Pet dogs vary widely in their capacity for understanding and communicating with their owners, and this will depend upon inherited disposition, environmental advantages and disadvantages, and the amount of time and commitment the owner is prepared to give.

SOCIAL INSTINCTS

The dog in its natural state is a pack animal, living and hunting in highly organized social groups. Within these groups a natural dominance hierarchy prevails, based on physical strength, gender, age and temperament, some individuals being naturally more dominant than others. This hierarchy is established and confirmed by aggressive encounters ranging from serious fights to ritualized threat contests. From time to time positions will be challenged; a dominant individual may be weakened by age or injury, or a subordinate youngster may with increasing maturity seek to push its way up the hierarchy, and the rank order will be reaffirmed or altered as a result of such confrontations. The coherence of the pack depends upon every animal knowing its place in the rank order and behaving accordingly.

The pack leader, by virtue of his dominant position, has high status and greater rights over food, desirable sleeping places and potential mates than his followers. He will repeatedly require pack members to demonstrate submissive behaviour confirming their relationship. Subordinate animals have to wait their turn or even miss out altogether when food or other resources are limited; by accepting their lower status and displaying submission to their superior or superiors, they benefit from membership of the group in terms of its protection, its combined hunting powers and the physical and emotional comforts of group interaction.

Within the pack, wild dogs such as wolves display considerable capacity for affection for their group members, as well as a sense of responsibility for their subordinates, particularly puppies. The pack leader is responsible for the defence of his family and their territory. Mature individuals capable of hunting are responsible for providing food for youngsters not able to accompany the hunt, and adult wolves, not necessarily themselves the parents, will carry food for miles to the puppies of their pack.

The domestic dog regards its human family as its pack and in normal circumstances the human owner takes the role of the pack leader, to whom the dog is subordinate. The dog's social instincts give it an innate propensity to interact with its owner rather than merely to co-exist with him. The natural submissiveness and obedience to the pack leader is transferred to the owner. The natural responsiveness to communication of moods and needs by pack members becomes a sensitivity to human expression. Group hunting techniques, not merely attacking prey animals at random but following other pack members' cues to work co-operatively in the pursuit of prey, form the basis for the working relationship between a man and his dog, as demonstrated in the close partnership between a shepherd and his collie, or a shooting man and his retriever.

Ever since man domesticated the dog, he has bred dogs selectively to increase the occurrence and intensity of desired traits and to reduce those of undesired traits, and this applies to the dog's social instincts as well as to more obvious characteristics such as scenting abilities. In general, man has selected over the centuries for tameness and tractability, which in effect has meant breeding more of the submissive dogs and fewer of the natural pack leaders. Of course, strongly dominant pups still occur amongst modern dogs, but the majority of dogs today are predisposed to accept the owner as pack leader – provided that he bears his responsibilities in mind and plays his role adequately – and there are relatively few of the born leaders which find it hard to submit to a master.

Selective breeding enabled man to produce various types of dog for different purposes, and the degree of submissiveness or dominance required would depend upon the function of the breed. A highly submissive guard dog would not be of much use, and so these breeds were developed in general to be naturally high-ranking animals whose innate tendency was to accept a single master but to show dominant aggression towards others. Pet dogs were bred to have a more submissive nature, and breeds developed along this line tend not to be one-man dogs but to accept human dominance in general. The toy breeds in particular are often characterized by retaining infantile behaviour patterns in adult life, demonstrating the highly

LEFT: *Social relationships between dogs are worked out through ritualized displays of aggression to establish dominance wherever possible, rather than by serious fighting. Here a potentially aggressive encounter between two Border Collies is settled by the show of threat through gesture and facial expression.*

RIGHT: *Amongst the many breeds of hounds, the pack instinct is extremely highly developed and hounds will normally enjoy a communal existence without the frequent scraps that would take place amongst, for example, a pack of terriers. There Ibizan Hounds are typically non-aggressive and enjoy each other's company.*

submissive reactions with which puppies appeal to adult dogs.

Puppies only a few weeks old display already their innate predisposition to a place in the social ranking order. While they are still unweaned, it is possible to identify the bold, aggressive pup which is naturally dominant, the timid, passive pup which is naturally highly submissive, and the middle-of-the-road puppies which are confident and outgoing without being especially aggressive. The potential purchaser of a puppy can take advantage of this to select a dog whose innate character will best suit his or her own. For the first time dog-owner, the puppies at both extremes of the dominance scale are better avoided, for the very dominant pup and the over-submissive pup will both require very careful training.

However, environment has as much importance as heredity in establishing a dog's eventual social position. Any puppy which is kennelled for too long and misses out on the essential early socialization process will lack social orientation and confidence in the outside world. Again, the owner will have a considerable effect upon the puppy's social development. The submissive pup in the right hands may acquire confidence; without care and understanding it may become even more shy and difficult to handle. The outgoing puppy which should become a confident, well-balanced adult needs a sensible upbringing to achieve its potential; an over-dominant owner may reduce it to a nervous, submissive animal, while a too indulgent owner may fail to establish leadership and end up with an aggressive, domineering brute.

Because the social instincts of the domestic dog are geared towards a need for a clear hierarchy of dominance, an owner who fails to play his proper role as pack leader by maintaining control and consistency of approach pushes the dog into the position of needing to challenge him or her for the leadership. This can cause all sorts of difficulties in the human/dog relationship. The dog which views itself as dominant will refuse to obey orders, be uncontrollable on walks, 'defend' its owners against visitors and aggressively reserve its right to occupy the best armchair.

In some cases the dog may seek to dominate the whole family; in other instances, it may accept one individual as leader but regard itself as dominant over other members of the household. It is not uncommon for a dog to obey its owner but to display aggressive behaviour towards the owner's spouse, whom it regards as holding a subordinate position.

Children are particularly likely to be regarded by the dog as holding a lower position than itself in the social structure, but this is less of a problem since most animals recognize immaturity in other species as in their own, and the normally well-adjusted dog will regard its position in relation to the children of the family as one of responsibility rather than aggressiveness.

The dog which considers itself dominant over its owner is not generally a happy dog. Where a subordinate animal obtains a sense of security from its 'pack leader', the dominant animal has no such moral support but instead the more stressful position of acting as leader itself. Furthermore, humans do not enjoy being subordinate to a dog, so it is important to establish dominance over one's pet from the beginning and to retain it in all situations. The dog must learn that all the human members of its 'pack' are its social superiors.

The easiest time to tackle the problem is when the dog first tries to assert its dominance, probably when it is quite a young puppy. Seizing it by the scruff of the neck and holding it down in a submissive posture, as another dog would, will establish its lower position in the hierarchy. Puppies are born with the instinct to submit to their

BELOW: *Much of a puppy's socialization occurs between five and fourteen weeks old. During this period, dogs learn their social response towards dogs, humans and any other animals with which they have contact. If deprived of proper socialization during this period, they will have difficulty acquiring balanced responses later.*

mother, who will reinforce this tendency with repeated loving yet firm lessons, and the human owner can simply take up the maternal role.

With an adult dog the problem is harder. Human dominance needs to be reasserted by proving to the dog that it is not master. The fact that the human controls the issue of food and also of affection can be utilized, good behaviour on the part of the dog being rewarded and dominant behaviour punished by the withholding of attention, but adjusting the social balance is a great deal more difficult than establishing it correctly in the first place.

Between domestic dogs, the same social structure applies as in the wild, and when two dogs meet they need to establish their relative positions in the dominance scale. Usually a wary approach, followed by closer investigation, will lead to one dog assuming a submissive posture, after

which the two dogs are able to relax in each other's presence. If neither dog is prepared to back down, a threat display or real battle ensues to establish rank order.

In selectively breeding for desired traits in different types of dog, man has developed varying levels of inter-canine social tolerance in the different breeds. Pack hounds such as Beagles which are expected to live together in large numbers and hunt co-operatively show a high degree of orientation towards other dogs. In contrast, guarding breeds are more highly focused on their owners and less socially oriented towards other dogs, while another group of hunting dogs, the terriers, have been bred for a highly aggressive and competitive nature which makes them characteristically intolerant of other dogs. To try to keep these less social breeds in the communal system that works well with pack hounds would lead to a great deal of fighting to establish a distinct hierarchy.

Where more than one dog is kept in a household they will develop a dominance relationship between themselves which may or may not be readily apparent to the owner. If there is a stable dominance relationship, the dogs will live peaceably together. However, any change in this relationship will result in conflict, which may be settled in a single brief encounter or may lead to a long power struggle with frequent fighting.

It is important for the owner to appreciate the relationship between the two dogs and to play the part of pack leader in confirming it by showing the higher ranking dog precedence over its subordinate. The owner who favours the underdog in the presence of the top dog will put the latter in the position of needing to re-establish their relative status according to the canine code by threatening or even attacking its companion. If the owner then scolds the dominant dog or seeks to protect the underdog, this will intensify the reaction and the relationship between the dogs may break down irrevocably. The owner who reinforces the established hierarchy by paying more attention to the dominant dog establishes a situation which both dogs can readily understand and accept. The underdog will be content to accept its place and will not be subjected to continual pressure to establish ranking order.

Despite their relationship with man, dogs retain a strong social leaning towards their own kind, and you will increase your dog's pleasure in life, and also the quality of his social behaviour, if you make sure that from puppyhood he has the opportunity to mix with others of his own kind and establish friendly relationships with them. The young puppy needs to learn the canine social code so that in adult life he will interact correctly with other dogs. The puppy which has been denied this opportunity will grow up into one of those brutes which cannot be let off the lead in case they attack other dogs, and whose ugly snarling behaviour must be a constant embarrassment to the owner.

FAR RIGHT: *Barking may indicate alertness, a warning or defence of territory; a lonely dog will often bark persistently, probably in the hope of attracting company.*

LEFT: *The threatening growl of a frightened dog clearly conveys its intentions.*

BELOW: *Dominance and submission: the small dog rolls over to expose its belly to the larger one, demonstrating the submissive posture.*

COMMUNICATION

Dogs may not be able to talk as we understand it, but their naturally socially oriented way of life has given them both the need and the ability to communicate at a very high level. Unlike man, who uses spoken language as the primary means of communication, most animals' communicative skills place more emphasis upon bodily posture and facial expression. This is true of dogs, but they have also developed vocal communication to a higher degree than more solitary species such as the cat.

Dogs are highly sensitive to sound, so it is not surprising that they use this method of communication. Most dogs are very vocal creatures, using a range of sounds including whining, barking, howling and growling.

Communication by sound begins as soon as the puppy is born, when it can express distress from cold or hunger by whining or whimpering. A more intense stimulus, such as when the mother accidentally sits on a puppy, will elicit a louder yelping cry.

The infantile whining distress cry will also be used by adults in an attention-seeking mood. Dogs do this much more frequently than adult wolves, probably because generations of domestication have increased the dog's tendency to infantile behaviour. It is significant that adult dogs rarely whine at each other, but reserve the sound to elicit sympathy from the owner – sometimes also to express sympathy with the owner.

Barking is the adult dog's most frequent sound. Puppies usually learn to bark when they are around three weeks old, although some start later and some individuals never bark at all. Adult wolves rarely bark; when they do, it is usually to raise an alarm, issue a threat or indicate excitement during a chase.

Dogs bark in all these situations, and in others as well. That they bark so often is almost certainly due to their being encouraged to do so during their early days of domestication. A dog barking in a prehistoric settlement would arouse people to a potential threat or visitor, just as it serves this protective role in homes today. This barking on their home territory may also spread to other dogs in the neighbourhood, often with two or more dogs taking it in turn to bark. It is not clear what the barking communicates from one dog to another, except perhaps a state of alertness or excitement. Most pet dogs have a natural propensity to bark more than their owners would wish, and have to be taught to moderate the practice. A dog which is left alone for long periods may bark out of loneliness and boredom. Many dogs will bark at apparent intruders such as milkmen and postmen, and have to be taught to cut down this territorial defence reaction for the sake of the peace of the neighbourhood.

Different breeds of dog vary in the extent to which they use their voices. Some dogs such as Greyhounds rarely bark while others, like the Chihuahua, can be extremely noisy. The Basenji, famous as the 'barkless dog', cannot bark normally because of the formation of its larynx, but utters a characteristic yodelling cry instead.

Pack hounds have been selectively bred to give voice when they hunt. This characteristic baying of hounds may serve to keep the members of a pack in contact with each other if they become split up, but the principal reason for its development is to enable the human hunters to follow the 'hound music'.

The howl is the best-known call of the wolf, and this is also heard from the domestic dog, particularly from certain breeds, such as the Alaskan Malamute and the Siberian Husky. Analysis of howling by wolves has shown that it is a very complicated sound, and that all individuals produce a slightly different noise. The function of howling amongst wolves is not altogether clear, but it appears to serve as a social ritual to affirm the relationship between group members. Domestic dogs may howl to indicate loneliness or distress, and another dog in earshot will answer this to howl in unison.

The sound made by dogs with the most obvious meaning both to other dogs and to people is the threatening growl. This is a clear warning of aggressive intent, accompanied by easily read facial and bodily signals. Dogs, particularly puppies, may growl in play, but the accompanying signals of body posture and facial expression make it clear that this is non-aggressive. Of these sounds, developed for communication within the species, many are easily understood by man to give at least an indication of the dog's needs or moods, and most dog-owners learn to interpret a great deal of their pets' 'talk'. In response, a dog with a close relationship with its human family may become more vocal as it learns to make its needs known.

However, it is through visual signals that dogs communicate most, at least at close range. Body posture, gesture and facial expression have evolved into a body language that is both complex and easily read by other dogs. Some of these signals have an obvious meaning to humans; others may be misinterpreted because they do not mean to people what they do to a dog. By body language the dog signals social status and relationships as well as emotions such as aggression, fear, or the wish for attention.

A great deal of body language is founded upon the signals of dominance and submission, for in interaction between dogs the relative status of the individuals is all-important to establish how they will respond to each other. Non-aggressive dominance is expressed by a bold stance, with the head high and the ears and tail in an alert but not tense position. Submission is demonstrated by the dog making itself as small as possible, lowering the body to the ground, flattening the ears and carrying the tail low. The lips are retracted horizontally from the teeth and the mouth held slightly open in the submissive grin, while the eyes are lowered to avoid direct eye contact. In the most extreme exhibition of submission the dog rolls on to its back, raising one hind leg to expose the inguinal area – this is the same gesture that a puppy makes to its mother. This may be accompanied by submissive urination, again an infantile reaction.

Owners often interpret the submissive posture as the dog cowering in expectation of punishment after committing some offence. There may be some truth in this, but what the animal is really doing is displaying submission to the angry look of the dominant owner rather than expressing the equivalent of 'I know I've done wrong and I'm sorry'.

A dog which greets its owner with the full submissive display is not signalling that it is frightened of him or her, as its posture may suggest. It is merely acknowledging their relative ranking in its social hierarchy.

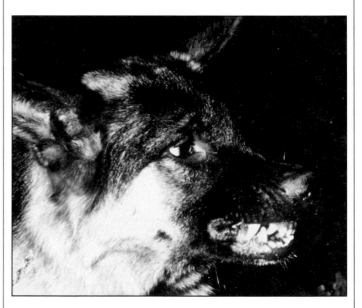

TOP LEFT: *These threatening features indicate aggression: staring eyes, ears erect and teeth bared.*

CENTRE LEFT: *The fearful dog: ears are flattened and teeth bared.*

BOTTOM LEFT: *The dog communicates with its owner in the same way as with other dogs. The friendly wagging of the tail is easily understood, and most owners soon learn to recognize other gestures and expressions.*

LEFT: *In some cases, man deprives the dog of the capacity for 'tail language', either by breeding for taillessness or, as in the case of this Boxer, by docking the tail.*

LEFT: *Artificially cropped ears prevent the dog from using its ears to express its mood. The cropping of ears is illegal in some countries, including the United Kingdom.*

In contrast to the shrinking appearance of the submissive display, dominant aggression is the cue for the dog to make himself look as big as possible. He will stand tall and stiff-legged, with ears pricked and tail held high, increasing his apparent size by raising the hairs on his shoulders and rump, known as the hackles indicating either fear or aggression, he presents himself to his potential opponent looking as big as possible. The teeth will be displayed by a vertical retraction of the lips.

Fear is displayed by a similar posture, but several signals differentiate fearful aggression from dominant aggression. The frightened dog stands erect, but leans backwards slightly on his legs, as if braced for flight. The ears are laid back and the tail is carried low or even between the legs. If fear is the predominant emotion, the lips are retracted horizontally as in the submissive grin, but if the dog's fear is likely to drive it to attack it may combine the signals of aggression and submission to bare the teeth fully with lips retracted simultaneously horizontally and vertically.

The greeting ritual of dogs comprises a clearly delineated series of gestures used to express intention. A non-aggressive meeting between two strange dogs uncertain of each others' intentions begins with the expression of neutrality, mutual submission being shown by lowered tails and ears, and by the avoidance of direct eye contact, while the two sniff each other nose to nose. A similar initial routine is followed when greeting a human, although the dog will sniff the human leg rather than the face, which is usually beyond its reach. If the greeting routine occurs between two dogs which are already friends, it will be accompanied by vigorous tail-wagging from the start.

After the nose to nose introductions, dogs move on to sniff each other's inguinal regions; the display of this area is another sign of mutual submission, similar in meaning to a dog rolling on its side. The investigation of each other's scents is the equivalent of the greeting handshake between humans. This type of contact is not normally made by a human, but a gentle caress in this area mimicking the greeting contact betwen dogs can reassure a nervous animal, and is sometimes used by handlers in the show ring to encourage their dogs to stand well and confidently.

Two more dominant dogs may withhold the signals of mutual submission on meeting and carry their heads and tails high. If there is any show of aggression at this introductory stage, this may proceed to conflict. Often following through a series of ritualized threat gestures enables the dogs to establish which of them is dominant and to negotiate a potentially harmful encounter without actual violence, the subordinate animal turning tail.

Stylized gestures are also used in other contexts, for example the 'play-bow' with which one dog invites another (or its owner) to play. The instigator crouches low on its forelegs, with its hindquarters raised and tail held high, legs standing. He may then move his front paws up and down in a patting motion, and leap up and bound about, wag its tail and sometimes bark to give further encouragement.

As has been seen, tail language is a highly expressive part

SCENT MARKING

When a dog scratches the ground with its hind legs, it leaves scent traces from the sweat glands in its toes and foot pads.(1)

Dogs have a tendency to roll in foul-smelling substances, to augment their own body smell.(2)

An adult male will mark out its territory by urinating on trees and lamp posts, causing other dogs to mark and claim the same areas.(3)

of bodily communication. A relaxed tail carriage clearly shows a relaxed frame of mind, a tail carried high and swaggering indicates a dominant attitude, and a tail clamped down between the hind legs shows submission. Wagging of the tail is a familiar signal showing pleasure, often in greeting or an invitation to play. It can also reflect excitement, and a dog in a very aggressive mood may wave its tail because of this, the difference being clear through the other signals of body posture and facial expression.

Facial expression is an important part of body language, the face acting as a mirror of the dog's moods and intentions. The highly expressive eyes play a significant part in this. The direct stare of one dog at another, or of a man at a dog, is one of the most potent forms of communication. The stare is a threat signal to other dogs, and is ordinarily only given by a dominant dog to a submissive one, or else as a prelude to an attack. If a person stares at a dog, the dog will generally look away and become submissive, although occasionally, a stare can provoke a retaliatory attack from a dominant dog.

This does not mean that a dog will never meet its owner's eyes except by way of a challenge. The eyes can also be used to communicate trust and friendship, when they hold a softer expression and the gaze is not held in the fixed stare of challenge.

The ears too convey clear messages. In the case of breeds with a 'natural' shape of ear, they are highly mobile and can be held erect or flattened against the head. Even dogs with pendant ears such as spaniels can achieve some expression by moving the ears forward or back. In general, ears that are held well back against the head indicate either submission or fear, depending on other aspects of the dog's facial expression. Ears that are held erect indicate alertness. This again must be seen in conjunction with the rest of the dog's facial expression; it can mean either that the dog is friendly and perhaps willing to play, or that he is in an aggressive mood.

A range of feelings is conveyed by mouth and lips, including submission, play soliciting and alertness; again this must be interpreted in the context of other body signals. We have already noted the difference between the horizontal retraction of the lips in the submissive grin, and the vertical lip retraction that bares the canine teeth in an aggressive display.

Some dogs appear to mimic the human smile with a facial expression shown only towards people, never towards other dogs. This canine smile resembles the aggressive threat face with its vertical retraction of the lips but is accompanied by tail-wagging and flattened ears and is clearly a friendly greeting, which some dogs appear to be able to learn in imitation of their owners' expression. Oddly enough, the capacity to learn this quasi-human greeting smile appears to be inherited rather than learned.

ABOVE: *The humans greet each other by shaking hands, while the dogs, whose predominant sense is that of smell, perform their introduction by checking each other's odour.*

Man has interfered with some of the dog's means of communication by selective breeding to perpetuate types of ear or tail which do not lend themselves to the usual usage. Breeds with long hair falling over the eyes cannot communicate with eye expression. Breeds with long floppy ears, such as spaniels, are restricted in the range of signals they can give through ear carriage, and convey a permanent flag of submission to other dogs, as far as the ears are concerned. Breeds with the tail curled tightly over the back or with another non-standard tail carriage, as well as breeds with short or absent tails, are unable to carry out

BELOW: *To invite play, the dog will adopt what is known as the 'play bow' posture: hindquarters and tail held high, the front part of the body crouching. This is one of the classic examples of the dog's body language.*

normal tail signals. The importance of tail language is shown by tailless dogs, which may wag their whole hindquarters in the absence of the appendage.

Man has also altered dogs' appearance by surgery. The cropping of ears to give a permanently alert expression, banned today in Great Britain but still practised in the United States and in Europe, denies the use of the ears to signal. The docking of tails is also practised with a number of breeds.

How much a dog's ability to communicate with his fellows is affected by such matters is uncertain. Certainly one initial aim of ear cropping and tail docking in guard breeds such as the Doberman was to give a more aggressive appearance, and perhaps to increase aggression by removing the means of signalling submission.

In addition to body language, smell is a major means of communication amongst dogs. It is hard for humans, who live in a world dominated by sight and sound, to imagine

BELOW FAR RIGHT: *A sign of subordination is displayed by the Boston Terrier, rolling on its back, while playing with a Dalmatian. This kind of behaviour can also be seen in a domestic situation when a dog has been scolded.*

BELOW (INSET): *The sense of smell is vital to dogs and they recognize each other on the basis of scent. The greeting ritual begins with sniffing, nose to nose, and then inspecting the inguinal area.*

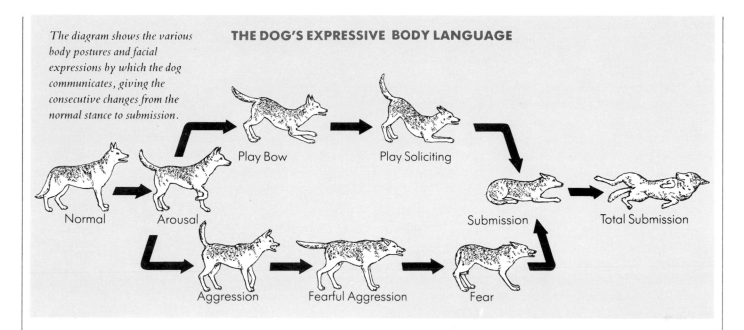

The diagram shows the various body postures and facial expressions by which the dog communicates, giving the consecutive changes from the normal stance to submission.

THE DOG'S EXPRESSIVE BODY LANGUAGE

Normal → Arousal

Play Bow → Play Soliciting

Submission → Total Submission

Aggression → Fearful Aggression → Fear

how a dog perceives its surroundings and its fellow dogs, obtaining information about these primarily through its predominant sense, that of smell. It is by this sense that a dog identifies familiar acquaintances and discovers new ones.

Smell is used for communication both directly and indirectly. When two dogs meet, they go through the rituals of smelling each other first, just as humans shake hands or exchange verbal greetings. First, the dogs sniff noses, then switch to the inguinal region between the hind legs, thus exchanging body smells. Only after this ritual is satisfied do they go on to establish friendly or aggressive relations.

Smell is used indirectly to leave and to receive messages, most commonly by urine markings. The significance of scent markers, known as *pheromones*, has been increasingly appreciated during recent years. These chemicals are present in the urine, and male dogs especially urinate very frequently when out for a walk to leave traces of their scent for other dogs passing on the same route. Male dogs urinate by lifting one of the hind legs; this enables them to direct urine to a particular spot such as a lamp post to which other dogs will also be attracted. This behaviour is not seen in young male puppies however, which squat like bitches when urinating. There may be a hormonal cause for this behaviour since dogs only start to urinate by this means after puberty. The actual administration of the male hormone *testosterone*, however, does not appear to have a direct influence other than increasing the actual frequency of urination once the puppies are independent of their mothers.

A bitch in season will advertise her condition to males by passing urine with increased frequency to leave as many scent markers as possible.

Faeces also may convey a characteristic scent to a dog, and wild dogs certainly use their excrement as territorial markers. The anal sacs or glands produce a secretion which under normal circumstances is transferred to the faeces. A dog rubbing its rear end along the ground is more likely to be suffering from impacted anal glands than leaving a scent trail. The scratching on the ground sometimes seen after urination or defecation may however be a deliberate means of leaving an auxiliary scent. Between the toes of its feet, the dog possesses sweat glands that could leave a scent and the characteristic scratch marks would serve to attract other dogs to the spot.

HUNTING INSTINCTS

The dog's ancestors hunted to live, and the thousands of years of domestication through which the dog's food has been provided by man have not dulled his hunting instincts. It is natural to the dog to chase and try to catch potential prey. This was advantageous to early man when he benefited from the dog's hunting skills; modern man continues to do so in certain contexts, but many dogs today are kept for purposes other than hunting, and their hunting instincts need to be controlled or redirected.

The strength of these instincts will vary from breed to breed according to the function for which they were developed. Obviously the breeds developed specifically for hunting, the hounds, gundogs and terriers, will have very strong hunting urges – indeed, some of these breeds are unsuited to domestic life because the innate need to hunt will always outweigh attachment to family and home. As noted in Chapter 2, man has developed specific aspects of the innate hunting drive to create specialist breeds to fulfil particular hunting tasks. However, the commonalty of the basic instinct is demonstrated by the fact that dogs of traditionally non-sporting breeds have been successfully trained to carry out such roles – Collies, for example, can make superb all-round gundogs. Even the toy breeds, kept for generations as house pets, still have the instinct to pursue prey and if given the opportunity will demonstrate the hunting urge. Pekingese, perhaps the breed most apparently unsuited to a practical existence, have a positive passion for hunting and have been known to take up retrieving with enthusiasm, if sometimes to the detriment of the retrieved game!

The dog's ancestors hunted in packs. Zoologists studying the predatory behaviour of modern wolves are not clear to what extent pack members cooperate in the hunt, whether they work as a close team under the direction of a leader as was once believed or whether individuals respond separately to the observed behaviour of their fellow hunters. Hunting, for the wolf pack, comprises a series of activities – seeking prey, by ranging the country or by scent-tracking, finding, stalking, attacking and either losing or winning the next meal. Because many hunts are unsuccessful, because of the evasive or defensive qualities of the quarry, a great deal of time and energy is spent in this occupation.

The inborn drives connected with hunting do not end with the successful conclusion to the hunt but include an instinct to make the best possible use of the hard-won meat. What is surplus to requirements may be cached away, to be revisited later. There are also social responsibilities connected with the food obtained; food will be carried back, either in the stomach for later regurgitation or, if lightweight, in the jaws, to pack members not present at the hunt, such as young pups and the 'baby-sitter' guarding them.

Most pet dogs are denied the opportunity to fulfil directly their urge to seek out prey, to stalk, bite, shake and kill. Chasing games satisfy some of this need, and the ever-popular business of fetching a ball similarly appeals to the basic hunting instinct. Given a suitable toy, a dog will often carry out all the actions of killing small prey, shaking it violently with apparent satisfaction; most dogs enjoy 'killing' the towel with which they have been dried. In the case of many pet dogs, the hunting instinct is satisfied adequately through play, and if that play is shared with the owner or with another dog it can give the social satisfaction provided by the communal hunt.

The life of the average domestic dog lacks the stimulus provided by such natural instincts as hunting, which is one reason why proper training makes for a contented dog, giving added interest to its life. Some forms of training make use of a positive redirection of the hunting instinct. Retrieving, even in the most basic form of playing with a ball which is brought back to be thrown again, hinges upon the urge to chase a moving object. In higher level obedience work, scent discrimination exercises and tracking utilize the natural behaviour patterns of seeking out prey – and of course the same factor makes it possible to train dogs for such tasks as mountain rescue work or even sniffing out illegal substances.

However, a dog whose hunting instinct is not suitably redirected, or one with a strong hunting drive, may seek satisfaction through undesirable practices such as chasing cats or even cars or bicycles. Dogs which are allowed to wander will tend to form into loose-knit packs roaming the streets, and the hunting instinct is intensified in the pack situation. An animal whose owners regard it as completely trustworthy at home may in these circumstances be impelled to join with its temporary pack members in frenzied chasing of anything moving, and such uncontrolled groups can become positively dangerous. Dogs should be prevented from roaming for this reason as well as for their own safety.

Chasing cats is a natural reaction in dogs, for the cat is small and quick-moving and often arouses the dog's predatory instincts by running away. Usually it will make its escape easily, and it is noticeable that urban cats soon learn to recognize individual dogs within their territory and often seem to enter into the spirit of the chase, showing no signs of fear and even turning round after a while to chase the dog in turn. Dogs will differentiate between their own family's cat and others, regarding the former as one of the household but continuing to chase outside cats. Despite the fact that cat chasing is in most cases harmless, it is best to discourage it from the outset. For one thing, your neighbours are unlikely to welcome the persecution of their pets; and for another, sooner or later your dog may meet up with an aggressive tom which will turn and fight instead of running, and very few dogs can handle an enraged cat without suffering serious injury, often including damage to the eyes.

Quite apart from your responsibility to your neighbours and to your own pet, teaching your dog not to chase after cats when it feels the urge to do so is part of basic training to fit in with the human lifestyle. You will want to be able to let it off the lead in the confidence that it will not suddenly dismiss your control over it and go haring off in pursuit of quarry.

If your dog lives in, or visits, the country, ensuring that it does not chase livestock is another matter. Dogs will not differentiate between 'approved' quarry, such as rabbits, and that which is forbidden, such as farmstock, until they have been taught to do so. Country dogs should be taught this from the outset, and the town dog which has not had the opportunity to learn stock manners must be kept on the lead in the countryside to prevent such crimes as sheep-chasing.

Sheep are particularly vulnerable to dogs; they respond to the chasing dog by panic-stricken flight which encourages pursuit. The dog is excited by this response and very likely to follow up with actual attack, maiming and killing animals. Even if the dog only wants to play and does not attack directly, he can cause considerable damage as the frightened animals may pile up on each other and suffocate the ones underneath, and pregnant ewes will easily miscarry after being chased. Understandably, a farmer who sees a dog chasing his livestock is within his

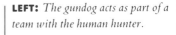

LEFT: *The gundog acts as part of a team with the human hunter.*

LEFT: *Digging to bury surplus food or bones is part of the dog's natural repertoire.*

legal rights if he shoots it, so apart from respecting his needs you should bear in mind that a sheep-chasing dog is liable to capital punishment. In sheep country, always keep your dog on the lead to avoid risks. Even if the animal is well trained and you feel you can trust him, it is only courtesy to local farmers to demonstrate unmistakably that your dog is under control.

As we have seen, in an apparent contradiction, the instincts of the herding breeds are directly derived from the hunting instinct, translating the hunting technique of the wolf into actions which serve the needs of the human master. The closeness of the herding instinct to the more primitive hunting urge is sometimes demonstrated when a working sheepdog takes to sheep-killing, as regrettably sometimes happens. Such a dog may work the flocks perfectly under the shepherd's supervision, only to sneak out at night to fulfil the hunting drive by killing.

Another practice which derives from the ancestral hunting instincts is the dog's tendency to cache surplus food. In the wild, this is a way of ensuring that the meat obtained by a strenuous hunt does not go to waste if there is more than can be eaten at one time but can be recovered at a later date when it is needed. The most common example of this behaviour amongst domestic dogs is the burying of the bone, but any food which is surplus to immediate requirements may be hidden where the dog can easily find it again. Unlike cats, most dogs seem prepared to eat meat that is high almost to the point of rotting.

LEFT AND ABOVE: *The hunting instinct can be deployed by man for various tasks. Police and army dog trainers utilize the dog's ability to follow a trail.*

PLAY

Dogs are playful creatures, and this is one of the canine attributes that appeals to humans looking for a companion animal.

Play may be defined as any activity which serves no practical function – mock fighting without real aggression, running and leaping neither to nor from any object but apparently just for the sake of it, pawing or tossing about an object such as a stick which is of no value for food, etc. Play occurs in most species of mammal, especially in infancy; playfulness continuing into adult life is perhaps particularly characteristic of predators, and dogs show this quality throughout their lives.

Although our definition of play excluded an overt practical function, it is generally agreed that it does serve certain purposes not immediately apparent. Certainly play serves as a learning vehicle for young animals as for children. Even in adults, play seems to have a practical value in providing practice for the more serious exercises, keeping muscles and reflexes honed for the vital business of capturing prey. The dog hurtling after a ball or shaking a stuffed toy goes through the actions it would use functionally when chasing and killing its quarry, just as dogs play-fighting utilize in fun the moves that would be needed in serious aggressive encounters. The repetition of actions in play helps to bring them to perfection for the time when they will be needed.

Amongst animals which naturally live in groups, play also serves an important social function, establishing and maintaining relationships between group members. Immature animals establish their ranking order of social dominance through play as one youngster's greater boldness or aggressiveness enables it to dominate another shyer or weaker animal. Amongst adults, play confirms social roles already established.

Zoologists have always been reluctant to ascribe human-type feelings to animals when seeking to understand their behaviour, and have sought to categorize play as a basically functional activity in terms of its practice and social elements. However, it would seem to be an over-scrupulous avoidance of anthropomorphism to deny the element in play of sheer fun, the expenditure of surplus energy by an animal which is well-fed, at ease and comfortable in its world.

PUPPY PLAY

Play amongst puppies is very much the means by which they learn about themselves, their world and the companions with which they share it. Puppies start playing with objects and with each other before they leave the nest. At first, they simply jump on their fellows and mother, but gradually they evolve a more sophisticated routine in

ABOVE: *The 'play bow' may be directed at other species, including the dog's owner. Here, a playful dog invites a cat to join in a romp: the cat may not recognize the invitation.*

TOP: *Beware of the playful inclination of all puppies to chew any available object!*

which they act out hunting, fighting and sexual behaviour. In the wild, wolf pups are encouraged and supervised in their play not only by their mother but also by other adults of the pack. The puppies of domestic dogs will rarely have a canine pack to direct their play, but as well as their mother they also have a human family, and few humans will be able to resist playing with young puppies.

This infantile play certainly enables the puppies to learn actions and reactions they will need in adult life. Some of the actions used in play are innate, including prey-killing behaviour, seizing, biting and shaking a toy, and immature sexual behaviour, clasping with the forelegs and mounting. Other actions are learned by experience, by watching the mother, and by interaction with each other and with the rest of the pack.

Play helps to expose the puppy to the pleasures and hazards of its environment, and it learns through experience, or trial and error. If it accidentally performs an action which proves rewarding it will probably repeat the action in the expectation that the reward will be repeated. If its play leads it into a situation which is painful or otherwise unpleasant, that too is a useful learning experience. A puppy encountering its first hedgehog will probably bounce playfully at it and find out about hedgehogs the hard way; the next time it meets one it will be a great deal more cautious.

Similarly the puppy learns to ignore things which are not dangerous. Falling leaves or shadows may frighten it at first, but it quickly becomes habituated to these and realizes that they can be safely disregarded or incorporated into its play. Puppies which are kept in a closed environment sheltered from the outside world will be handicapped in adult life through lack of this sort of experience: the ex-ploratory and investigative nature of puppy play is a vital part of preparation for later life, and the puppy gains confidence through this experience.

Perhaps the most vital part of puppy play, however, is laying the foundations of socialization. Studies which have been made of puppies reared amongst their own kind and those reared in isolation have established that it is through their early play that the youngsters learn the basic social vocabulary of their own kind. Through playful exploration the puppy gradually learns canine social customs. It learns to control the use of its teeth as it finds out that its playmates can retaliate if hurt. It learns to respect adult dogs, who will punish it for jumping on them at the wrong moment, for disobeying an order or for failing to exhibit properly submissive behaviour. It learns the art of communication, recognizing the many possible expressions of its family of fellow dogs and humans, together with the appropriate responses.

Through play-fighting the litter of pups establishes dominance and submission, and by about four months of age a social ranking order will have emerged. In some of the more aggressive breeds even young puppies may lack the instinct to inhibit aggressive behaviour in play, and the result may be bloodshed rather than the establishment of a stable hierarchy. It goes without saying that such animals

LEFT: *Play is often a method of emphasizing an order of dominance between individuals: the show of aggression establishes rank order without the need for actual fighting.*

PLAY POSTURES

RIGHT: *The dog may assume different poses during the course of the game, from the classic 'play bow' to solicit play to others indicating submission.*

RIGHT: *Tugging the other dog's tail to elicit a playful response.*

FAR RIGHT: *Tempting behaviour: the opponent is offered the ball.*

RIGHT: *To initiate play with a smaller dog, the naturally dominant larger one will often roll on its back, assuming the submissive posture.*

will be poor at forming relationships with humans as well as with their own kind.

A puppy needs the opportunity to socialize with humans as well as its littermates from an early age, and caring breeders will handle and play with the litter. Once the puppy is ready to leave its mother it should be separated from her and from the rest of the litter and oriented towards humans. If kept with its littermates too long, the pup will have become conditioned to canine society to an extent that will make it harder to adapt to human society. When it is transferred to its new home, the learning element of play is focused upon adapting to the human world.

The owner of a puppy will probably want to play with it simply because this is fun. It is important to remember that for the puppy such play serves the same purposes as play with its own kind, and that this is a valuable opportunity to teach the youngster its social position in the human family. During play it should learn that the human owner is the pack leader to be obeyed. For example, the puppy playing with its own kind will use its teeth, and will be chastised if it bites too hard until it learns to inhibit its play-bites. When the owner plays with a new puppy, it is the human's responsibility to teach the youngster that it is not acceptable to bite hard. If discipline is not introduced into play from the beginning the puppy will never learn control and the result will be a hard-mouthed and unresponsive animal which lacks proper respect for its owner.

The puppy will assume at first that everything movable is a potential toy, including books, soft furnishings and all sorts of items that the owner would prefer to preserve undamaged. Rather than quelling the play instinct the owner should think in terms of deflecting play towards appropriate objects. By removing the forbidden object with a simple rebuke and substituting a suitable toy, the owner enables the puppy to learn through play what is permissible and what is not. Similarly, play sessions can be used to familiarize the pup with potentially frightening objects and situations, encouraging confidence in its owner and in its environment.

ADULT PLAY

Adult animals spend less time in play than youngsters. In many species, play virtually ceases with maturity, although for some animals, including the dog, play continues to have a role in adult life. The social organization of dogs and wolves, in which cooperative hunting is a major element, gives play an importance in social relationships.

Dogs which have established their ranking order will enjoy playing together, one animal inviting the other to play with the characteristic 'play bow' attitude (see p 155). The commonest forms of play are derived from the activities of hunting and fighting. Such games include challenging others for the possession of an object such as a stick, chasing and wrestling. During play the dominance hierarchy continues to be confirmed, although the dominant animal may act out submissive attitudes in play.

Just as play is a tool by which the puppy learns about social relationships, it forms a valuable tool for the dog owner to use in training his animal, whether puppy or adult. Dogs can be taught highly complicated exercises simply by being dominated by the owner and made to do as he wishes, or by taking advantage of the submissive desire to please the owner, but the surest way to teach a dog what you want is by making this fun. When training becomes a game, the dog can often learn more easily. Natural instincts can be utilized, as when the dog's playful urge to chase after a thrown ball can be steered towards a serious retrieving exercise.

AGGRESSIVE INSTINCTS

Aggression is part of the dog's natural behavioural pattern and, indeed, one of the attributes that led man to domesticate this species, as he was able to utilize the dog's aggressive instincts to provide himself with an alert and effective guard.

All animals display aggressive behaviour, ranging from intimidation to outright attack, in appropriate circumstances – self-defence, protection of family, territory or food, establishing social position or sexual rivalry. We tend to be more conscious of this aspect of behaviour in the dog than in, for example, that other popular companion animal the cat. While cats display considerable aggression towards members of their own species, they will only direct this towards humans under special circumstances, when they feel themselves to be under direct threat. The aggressive instincts of the dog are much more obvious because it is a social species which treats us as part of its society and its

LEFT: *A stick is a favourite toy which can provide hours of fun, for the dog alone or with its human playmates.*

aggressive instincts may be employed on our behalf or against us – and also because it is conspicuously well equipped to back up a show of threat with its armoury of powerful jaws and well-developed teeth.

Aggression in the dog is linked to the establishment and maintenance of social hierarchy, and to the defence of the social group and of territory.

TERRITORIAL AGGRESSION

Dogs tend to defend their territory from humans and from other dogs. If their territory is invaded by other animals, such as a horse or some other mammal, they are usually indifferent. This is probably because a dog is reared both with other dogs and with humans, so it regards each of these as its own kind and therefore a potential threat to its territory.

ABOVE: *Dogs and children are natural playfellows.*

In a pack, the dominant dog, likely to be male and large, will take responsibility for the defence of territory. If it is alone on its own territory, even the smallest female is likely to exhibit territorial aggression, irrespective of the size or sex of the intruder. Usually, such a defence is successful by threat alone. The intruder retreats before a fight is initiated.

If a dog has been accustomed by its owners to human visitors, it is unlikely to be territorially aggressive towards these guests. This is especially true where the dog is clearly dominated by its owner. To the pet dog, the family is likely to be regarded as the 'pack', and the dominant member must therefore assume responsibility for defence of territory. If the owner is seen not to show aggression towards a visitor, the subordinate dog may see no need to, either. This often leads people to think their pets are useless as guard dogs. However, in the absence of the owner, some of these dogs may behave in a quite different fashion, keenly taking the responsibility for territorial defence.

There is another, quite different, reason why a dog may be reluctant to chase a human intruder. It may simply be confused because the intruder fails to run away. If the dog's efforts consistently go unrewarded, it may gradually lose its natural territorial aggression. If, on the other hand, the visitor departs as quickly as he arrives, the territorial defence appears to have been most effective and the dog feels greatly encouraged by its success. This may explain why dogs tend to favour postmen, milkmen and sales representatives as objects of territorial aggression.

THE GUARDING INSTINCT

The instinct to defend pack members has been deployed by man in the development of guard dogs. Breeds evolved specifically for guarding duties, such as the Doberman, have this instinct developed to such a high degree that careful training is needed to keep it under control, whereas other breeds such as the gundogs may have minimal guarding tendencies. However, even the gentlest and friendliest of dogs is likely to be ready to defend his owner at need, for the guarding instinct is dormant rather than absent.

The guarding instinct is utilized by the police and army, who work with dogs which have been trained to attack humans. However, these animals will attack only on command; their aggression is aimed at a specific person; generally they will seize their quarry's hand, rather than making a thoroughgoing major assault on more vulnerable areas; and they will let go when their handler orders them to do so.

This complicated routine can be carried out only after extensive training. Though the end result is sophisticated, the methods of training employed follow the same principles as those used in the teaching of domestic dogs to 'sit' or 'stay'.

Training for 'man work' is not recommended for companion dogs because it requires a very experienced trainer to keep the guarding instincts under control once they have been fully awakened. All too often attempts to teach a dog this kind of work result in an animal which is a positive danger to the public. The average pet dog will react adequately if his owner is threatened without the need for specialist training.

Sadly, the dog's guarding instincts are often abused by people who imagine that a dog chained to a kennel or left in a yard, bored and lonely and often encouraged to display aggressive behaviour, is the ideal guard.

Such a dog is merely an antisocial menace: the best guard dog is the animal which enjoys his owner's time and attention and is able to develop bonds of affection which serve, not to make him 'soft', but to motivate his innate guarding instincts.

ABOVE LEFT: *The dog's aggressive instinct to guard its own environment is utilized in the training of guard dogs.*

ABOVE RIGHT: *Serious aggressive encounters between dogs are rare, since the subordinate individual usually backs down, although both will make threatening gestures, including snarling, up to this point. These Eskimo Dogs preserve a distinct hierarchy, reminiscent of the pack behaviour of their wolf ancestors.*

Statistics from hospital casualty departments have revealed that dog bites may account for as much as three per cent of total attendances. However, in only a small minority of cases – less than ten per cent – is the wound anything more than superficial. A study in New York has shown that over half of reported dog bites are incurred by people under 20. Another statistic indicated that only in a minority of cases, less than ten per cent, did a dog bite its owner or a relative of its owner. These results imply a relatively high incidence of dog bites, many of which are received by young people, usually outside the home, but the bites are almost always minor in nature.

Many of these bites are almost certainly caused by territorial aggression. A child who approaches a dog on its own territory is always at a slight risk of provoking a defensive response, which, because the child may not recognize it as such, could end in a bite or minor attack.

However, when children or strangers are bitten, it is most likely that the dog reacts out of fear. Children are especially vulnerable in this respect. If a dog has been brought up in the sole company of adults, he may be afraid of children because they act in quite a different manner.

A child is likely to rush up to a dog with outstretched hands, possibly shouting at it, and this will appear frightening to a dog that is not used to it. If it cannot run away, or before it runs away, the dog may growl, threaten or bite the child, although in normal circumstances it shows no aggression. Couples who have no children are well advised to expose a new puppy to children as it grows up.

All dogs are probably capable of fear-induced aggression, but whether or not they express it is highly dependent on their environment and upbringing. In contrast, pain-induced aggression is more of an innate reflex, likely to be shown by any dog given a sufficiently painful stimulus. This type of aggression is rarely seen, but is occasionally encountered by veterinary surgeons giving injections, or by someone who injures a dog accidentally. It may also be provoked by someone handling an injured dog.

The pain threshold, above which a dog will display this type of aggression, may be altered by particular circumstances. For example, when two dogs are fighting and separate, one may react aggressively to a painful blow from a human intervening, when normally it would not do so.

Another time when a dog may be dangerous is when a bitch is guarding her young ones.

Maternal aggression is seen in most species of wild animals, even in those that normally show no other type of aggression. It is thought to be dependent on the hormonal state of the female after she has given birth, as well as on the presence of her young.

While the other types of aggression are usually preceded by some type of threat, a mother may attack without warning if she fears any kind of interference with her young. However, this type of aggression has rarely been reported as causing a problem. Most people recognize that a good mother will try to protect her babies, and so leave her alone as much as possible.

ABOVE: *Aggression can be a serious problem with powerful guard breeds like the Rottweiler, so it is essential that a puppy of such a breed be trained responsibly from the start. In sensible hands, these dogs can be trustworthy family companions, but owners should be aware that any lapse of control is potentially dangerous. Children must always be supervised with these dogs, no matter how well-behaved, to avoid the risk of accidents.*

AGGRESSION BETWEEN DOGS

The social ranking order between dogs is established by aggression: dominance is proven by the capacity to intimidate the other animal, whether by a show of threatening behaviour or by actual fighting.

Dogs on the whole are more aggressive towards members of their own species. Like other characteristics, aggressiveness has been selectively bred for, either to increase the tendency, as in the breeds developed for dog-fighting, or to reduce it, characteristically in breeds designed for a pet role. Generally speaking, male dogs have a stronger drive towards inter-species aggression than do females: they have an innate tendency to threaten or fight other males. Fighting of this kind is not practised by females, nor do males display this type of aggression towards females.

Very often aggression between dogs will be ritualized into a mere display of threatening behaviour on the one part and submission on the other. There is considerable ritual involved in most animal aggression. It would not be in the interests of the survival of the species if creatures equipped to kill made a habit of using their equipment on their own kind, and so most predators have evolved a high degree of aggressive display in preference to action.

It is important to bear in mind that the different forms of aggression are not mutually exclusive; often more than one factor may be at work in inducing aggressive behaviour. For example, if two male dogs meet on what is a regular walking route for both of them, they may threaten or fight each other partly for territorial reasons and partly to vent their intermale rivalry. However, male dogs may also fight on neutral territory, such as a park or common, thereby displaying pure intermale aggression.

The dependence of this type of aggression on the male sex hormone has been demonstrated by studies of male dogs before and after castration. One study found that about half the dogs tested displayed considerably less inter-male aggression after castration; fear-induced and territorial aggression were unaffected.

The dogs affected by castration were mainly those that showed definite behavioural problems, such as always threatening or attacking other male dogs when meeting them on walks. However, few male dogs display intermale aggression to a level which causes problems. This is because as puppies they are sufficiently socialized towards other dogs, and because they are trained at an early age not to show aggression. Socialization and training of this kind are very important for show dogs, because intermale or fear-induced aggression is not tolerated in the ring, and any dog displaying it will be marked down or disqualified.

Uncontrolled aggression towards other dogs is a regrettably common behavioural problem amongst pet dogs.

LEFT: *Two dogs in the same household need to work out their ranking order. Fighting is particularly likely to break out over food, and until the dogs have established their hierarchical relationship, they should be fed in separate rooms, out of each other's way.*

ABOVE: *Dogs readily detect a bitch in heat and will congregate around her, even if she is not in the receptive phase of her oestral cycle.*

Very often the foundations for this behaviour are laid in puppyhood by inadequate socialization. The owner of a puppy should ensure that it mixes with other dogs so that it learns proper social relationships. It is important to avoid aggressive dogs at this stage, so that the puppy is not negatively influenced, but all too many owners inadvertently teach their puppies to be wary of strange dogs by being too quick to snatch them up protectively at the sight of another dog. Right from the beginning the puppy should be praised for behaving well with other dogs and rebuked for growling.

A dog held on a lead or chained up is predisposed to be more aggressive than one which is running free, because it is not in a position to advance or retreat freely and therefore cannot go through the full display pattern that establishes dominance and submission.

Aggression towards other dogs is not the easiest of problems to tackle, because it arises from a misdirection of a very strong natural instinct. The owner who establishes a clearly dominant position over his or her dog may be able to counter incorrect early conditioning by enforcing calm behaviour amongst strange dogs: a dog that has been trained always to obey basic commands such as 'Sit' should do so rather than lunging out wildly in attack. With a highly aggressive dog, it may prove impossible to counter-condition the animal. In many cases, castration coupled with intensive training will reduce the drive. A persistently

and uncontrollably aggressive dog is a liability: it is no pleasure to own an animal which has to be kept on the lead all the time to prevent it from attacking the pets of innocent passers-by, and the unavoidable restriction limits the enjoyment of the dog itself. If advice from dog trainers and veterinary surgeons proves unavailing, such a dog is probably better being painlessly destroyed.

SEXUAL BEHAVIOUR

Young puppies will display precocious sexual behaviour in their play, going through the instinctive motions of clasping with the forepaws and mounting each other, and this immature sex play helps them to develop normal sexual responses in adult life. Young animals raised in isolation and deprived of social interaction with their own kind may never become correctly sexually oriented towards their own species but tend to make their advances towards their human keepers.

The full gamut of sexual behaviour has to be learned by the young dog, and the inexperienced stud dog will often demonstrate this by attempting to mount the bitch's head or flanks. Adolescent males will often mount inappropriate objects such as a cushion or a human leg and need to be taught that this is not acceptable behaviour.

Once they are more mature, male dogs are in a continuous state of readiness for courtship and mating. It is a characteristic of domesticated species to be more strongly impelled by the reproductive drive than their wild ancestors, and some male dogs, the more dominant individuals, are positively over-sexed to the extent that their over-riding interest in sexual opportunities makes them unsuitable pets. Castration may be recommended to enable such individuals to adapt better to a domestic way of life, and it is notable that guide dogs for the blind are always neutered to prevent them from being distracted from their work.

In female dogs, on the other hand, readiness for sexual activity is cyclical, meaning that the bitch is only sexually active periodically when she is 'on heat', 'in season' or in scientific terms 'in oestrus'. On average a bitch comes on heat twice a year, although the time between heats can be highly variable.

The behaviour of the male is largely determined by the sexual status and behaviour of the bitch. She goes through a period of four distinct phases during her reproductive cycle, described in more detail in Chapter 9. For most of the cycle she is sexually inactive, and a male is unlikely to make any approach to her.

The resting phase is broken when the bitch starts to attract male dogs by a chemical compound in her urine, which will lure males from some distance to congregate in her vicinity. This may inconvenience her owner, but little can be done to mask the smell. Products designed to do so can be purchased, but the dog's sense of smell is very keen, and in any case experienced males will learn to associate the smell of the disguising product with the condition it is designed to conceal. At this stage the bitch may show changes in her behaviour such as excitability, restlessness, loss of appetite and an increase in the frequency of urination. She may show interest in male dogs, but at this stage will not be receptive to mating, walking away from a male's advances or even repelling him with an aggressive display.

Some individuals fail to show the typical signs of the beginning of oestrus. This is known as a 'quiet' season. Although in such cases the signs are not easily or even at all apparent to humans, male dogs will not be misled, and such bitches need to be carefully supervised to ensure that unwanted matings do not take place.

This pre-heat phase of the bitch's cycle can vary in length from two to fifteen days and serves the function of attracting as many males as possible. The gathered males will utilize this period to stake their claims to the bitch, and there will be considerable fighting to establish dominance. Courtship and mating behaviour in all species of animals have developed to ensure that the strongest and fittest specimens have the best opportunity to reproduce their kind, and this period when the bitch attracts the males before she is ready to mate ensures that, by the time she is sexually receptive, the dominant dog will have established his claim.

The next stage of the cycle is the period of heat, when the bitch will accept the male and fertilization can take place. There is usually a dramatic change in the behaviour of the bitch when heat begins. Whereas before she rejected the advances of males quite forcefully, she will become more relaxed and playful, even skittish. She will now go through the normal greeting sequence of actions with the male, beginning with mutual sniffing at the nose and proceeding to the inguinal region, although their interest in each other will be much more intense than on a casual meeting, especially on the part of the male. This frequently leads to a period of play. As a final display before mating, the male will often stand alertly beside the bitch, facing in the same direction with his head and tail erect.

Assuming that she is willing, the bitch will then adopt the receptive posture known as 'standing', where she stands with her vulval region presented to the male and her tail skewed to one side, and the dog will be permitted to mount.

Copulation is protracted by the 'genital lock' or 'tie': once penetration has taken place, the muscles of the bitch's vagina contract around the penis, holding it tightly in place, so that withdrawal is not possible. The dogs remain joined together for a period typically of about twenty minutes, although it may be shorter or last up to an hour. Typically the dog will dismount and swivel round to stand back to back with the bitch while the tie lasts. A maiden bitch may attempt to break free, and this can result in injury to one or both partners; human attempts to separate the pair are also likely to cause damage.

The tie does not occur in every case and is not essential for fertilization – and indeed, Chows in particular often fail to tie when mating – but most dog breeders feel more confident of success when there is a tie.

After successful fertilization the bitch may continue to be receptive to further matings for a period of up to a week or more afterwards. It is even possible for a bitch to bear puppies by different sires in the same litter if matings occur closely together – a process termed 'superfecundation'.

Once her period of heat is over, the bitch ceases to be sexually attractive to the male, and at the same time reverts to refusing any sexual advances that may be made. This behaviour change is usually rapid, but she may refuse a male one day and accept him the next. If successful mating has not taken place she will return to the sexually quiescent phase for some months.

The courtship sequence does not always go smoothly. Experience certainly plays an important part; inexperienced males may find mounting difficult and may initially try from the front or the side, and the build-up to mating will generally be much longer when one of the partners is a novice. Dog breeders try to avoid mating two inexperienced animals together, as if things go wrong one or both dogs may be permanently discouraged. The inexperienced female in particular may show considerable aggression towards the male and may even savage him quite seriously.

Individual preference can also have an effect. While dogs do not form permanent pair bonds, studies have shown that females certainly have a predisposition to hold sexual preferences, and males also, though to a lesser extent. The degree of socialization of the dogs towards their own kind and towards people also plays a part, and of course any kind of disturbance in the vicinity can upset things.

ABOVE: *The receptive bitch adopts the posture known as 'standing', with her tail to one side, to permit the dog to mount.*

Chapter Seven

TRAINING YOUR DOG

THE IMPORTANCE OF TRAINING

Training your dog is neither unkind nor unnatural, but a way of ensuring that both dog and owner obtain maximum enjoyment from their relationship. The untrained dog is no pleasure to live with and may exhibit a variety of behavioural problems, ranging from destructive or aggressive tendencies, to jealousy between pet dogs and attempts to dominate its owner; lacking a clear social position in the family, it will be insecure and less happy than the trained animal. On the other hand, the well-behaved dog becomes a full family member which can participate in all the family's activities, instead of being a liability which has to be excluded.

In the wild, the dog would be 'trained' in puppyhood to proper standards of canine behaviour by older animals, and this would be reinforced throughout its adult life by dominant members of the pack. Appropriate behaviour would be rewarded by pleasurable reactions from other dogs, and inappropriate behaviour punished in varying degrees from threat to biting and shaking. Such social conditioning is vital if pack members are to live peaceably together.

In just the same way, the domestic dog needs to learn appropriate behaviour to enable it to fit into the human world. Proper training serves not only to teach it what is acceptable and what is not, but also to establish dominance on the part of the owner so that the dog has the security of knowing his place in the social order.

Training is simply a matter of conditioning a dog to respond in a particular way to various stimuli. If you neglect to train your pet, you are in effect conditioning it to believe that it can do whatever it wants, when it wants. The dog which is allowed to run riot is learning negative lessons, including lack of respect for its owner – or for anyone else.

Dogs can be trained to various levels of achievement, from simple toilet training through the basic commands such as 'heel', 'sit', 'wait', 'come', 'down' and 'stay', to the complex training of dogs who compete in championship obedience classes. The family pet needs what we might term 'convenience training', to differentiate it from the more rigid structure of competitive obedience training. This will entail learning how to behave in the house, how to interact with people and with other dogs, and how to respond to its owner when out on walks; the basic requirements for what the dog needs to learn will be much the same from owner to owner, but how it carries out these requirements will depend on the individual owner's taste.

Formal obedience training, on the other hand, is geared to winning obedience trials, and the dog is required to react to commands in a precisely specified way. The difference can be easily illustrated with reference to lead training. For obedience work the dog must be taught to walk close to the owner and level with the left knee. The pet owner is usually content with an animal which walks quietly beside him or her on a slack lead without pulling; the exact position of the dog in relation to its owner is unimportant.

Young dogs are most responsive to training, and taking care to condition the puppy correctly from the moment it enters its new home will pay dividends. However, a dog is capable of learning good manners at any age, and the basic techniques will be the same. Some breeds tend to be more responsive to advanced training than others, and it is noticeable that the majority of dogs which compete in obedience championships are Border Collies, Working Sheepdogs and German Shepherd Dogs, but all breeds are capable of learning if taught correctly. Nevertheless, there is a tiny minority of individuals with genuine mental or behavioural problems due to their genetic background or severe distress early in life.

THE PAVLOVIAN DOG

Experiments early this century by the Russian scientist Pavlov led to theories of conditioning that were to form the basis of modern training methods and theories. The essential principles used in training are similar whatever level of response is required, and it is these which owners should try to understand.

The process of training a dog is essentially that of conditioning it to perform a particular action from its normal repertoire at a specific moment. In order to train a dog successfully, it is helpful to understand how conditioning works in the dog's mind.

Two kinds of conditioning are recognized by scientists. Classical conditioning was discovered by Pavlov when his now famous discoveries showed that his dogs always salivated when they smelt their food on its way. Their meal time was always signalled by a bell, and Pavlov then found that, after a time, his dogs would salivate in response to the bell alone, even when no food was offered. It can be seen that this type of conditioning works through a process of association in the dog's mind.

Pavlovian conditioning is useful for house training. Whenever a puppy shows signs of wanting to relieve itself, probably on awakening or after a large meal, it should be gently lifted up and taken outside. If it is taken outside sufficiently often in this way, it will quickly come to associate the place with the act in very much the same way as Pavlov's dogs made a connection between food and a bell. Puppies generally prefer to relieve themselves out of doors anyway, which facilitates this training, but the same principle of conditioning can be applied to the newspaper method of house training.

EARLY LESSONS

Training your dog early in life will eliminate many behavioural difficulties later on. First, teach your puppy to walk to heel on a lightweight lead. It is useful to practise where there is a fence or hedge so that the puppy can be sandwiched between you and the barrier.

The next stage is to teach your puppy to 'sit and stay' in one spot. Put him in the sit position and give the 'stay' command, then raise the lead and walk around the pup slowly in a circle. The pup will probably try and get up or turn around: if this happens, jerk the lead, return it to the sit position and start again.

When the puppy has learned to stay, it is time to practise the recall. Put it in the 'sit stay' position, walk away and then call it to you, using the lead to steer it in if necessary. Praise the pup lavishly for coming.

REWARD AND PUNISHMENT

The second type of conditioning is easier to understand because it is based on rewarding the dog when it has done something that pleases the owner. The principle of this type of conditioning is simply that when a dog is rewarded for behaving well, this increases the likelihood that it will behave in the same way again. As a corollary, if a dog is scolded or punished for doing something, this ought to make it less likely that it will do it on future occasions.

Most dog owners will be able to think of several occasions when these techniques have apparently been unsuccessful. A common reason for this is that a dog can be confused by what appears as a lack of consistency in the owner's behaviour. A dog can only relate a reward or reprimand to its most recent behaviour. Although a human sees that a puppy is scolded because it wet the carpet while the owner was out, it is quite unreasonable to expect the puppy to associate the two actions unless one follows immediately after the other. A delayed scolding only causes confusion in the dog's mind, because it will be behaving in a quite unrelated manner when the owner discovers the misdeed.

Such misunderstandings can arise all too easily. The dog may have ransacked its owner's handbag while she was out, and when she comes home it will come rushing delightedly to meet her with a chewed purse in its mouth. The owner's natural response is to scold the dog and make a grab for the purse. To the dog, however, it will appear that the scolding is for welcoming its owner. It will not associate the rebuke with its undesirable behaviour in taking the purse, and all that will be achieved is the probability that it will be hesitant to approach its owner next time. A more appropriate response from the owner would be to respond to the dog's welcome but take the opportunity to remove the purse from its mouth, gently but firmly, with a 'No' clearly addressed to the action of holding the purse.

Although there is a place for both reward and punishment in the upbringing of a dog, as a general rule reward is always the best policy. A reward for a dog can take many forms. A titbit of food is used by many trainers to encourage or reward correct behaviour; the alternative reward is affection, and most dogs will respond well to praise and a fuss being made of them. Because dogs do not understand language in the way that we do, it is not sufficient simply to remark 'good dog' or words to that effect; the owner must make use of tone of voice and gesture to make his meaning, that he is pleased with the dog, unmistakable.

Whether titbits or praise prove the most effective stimulus to the dog will depend largely upon your own dog's mentality. Some individuals will learn much more readily with the bait of food, while others will work harder to earn a display of affection.

Punishment is normally used to stop a dog doing something, or as a reprimand for a misdemeanour, but it only works if the dog is caught in the act. For example, if a dog has chewed up a pair of shoes while its owner is away and on his or her return the owner punishes the dog as they enter the room where the shoes are, the dog will see this as a reprimand for going into that room. It may then be hesitant to enter the room, but it will not have learned that it is chewing up shoes which is forbidden.

When a dog is actually caught in the act, some consideration should be given as to just how the punishment should be administered. Physical reprimand should never be too

LEFT: *Jumping up, especially if young children are nearby, is undesirable behaviour and should be strongly discouraged. This dog is being scolded by voice and gesture and accepts the rebuke with submissive carriage of ears and tail.*

RIGHT: *The check chain collar is a useful training aid which utilizes the principle of reward and punishment. If the dog walks correctly to heel without pulling, the collar slackens automatically for comfort, but if the dog pulls on the lead, the collar tightens, causing discomfort. To be effective, this type of collar requires the owner to ensure that it is correctly fitted and that the dog is not allowed to keep pulling.*

severe, and a slap on the rump or a shaking by the scruff of the neck is quite sufficient. As with reward training, it is important to accompany punishment with a verbal rebuke such as 'bad dog' or 'shame', so that gradually the dog will learn to respond to the command alone. Often simply ignoring the dog when it misbehaves may be punishment enough. This is one of the simplest ways to eradicate an undesirable habit, such as jumping up; if every time the dog jumps up, the owner walks away and ignores the animal, this should discourage the habit.

Individual dogs vary in their sensitivity, and you need to know your own dog. A highly sensitive dog will be adequately punished by a verbal scolding, and will simply lose confidence in its owner if smacked or shaken. A tougher individual may need a good hard shake to make it quite clear that the owner is in control.

Punishment can have both beneficial and detrimental effects on the general behaviour of a dog. A certain amount of punishment reminds the dog that the owner is the boss, and thereby reduces the likelihood of the dog asserting itself too strongly. On the other hand, too much reliance on punishment can detract from the ideal dog-to-owner relationship of loving obedience. A dog which is frequently punished can become very confused by the unpleasant treatment given to it by its owner, who is also the source

of what love and care it receives.

It must also be remembered that punishment may not always be received by the dog in the way it is intended by the owner. To some dogs, the physical contact involved in most forms of punishment also acts as a positive stimulus. While a slap may hurt momentarily, the fact that the owner is interacting with it physically may be seen by the dog as part of a game; and a dog that craves attention may prefer a smack and a scolding to being ignored. The dog quickly learns that certain behaviour produces a response from the owner – for example, a dog which howls when shut in the kitchen at night may discover that howling gains the desired attention, whereas 'good' behaviour results in being left alone. If a dog sees punishment as partly rewarding, its effectiveness is obviously greatly reduced.

That there are these problems associated with punishment has led some people to advocate and make electric shock collars, which administer a very small but punishing shock by remote control. While these remove the problem of the owner being directly associated with the punishment and make it easier to catch the dog in the act, they have caused a number of problems in practice. For example, if a dog is given a shock during a fight with another dog in the hope of stopping it from fighting, it is likely to round on its opponent more furiously than ever because of the pain it has received. Another disadvantage is that although the equipment may effectively discourage the dog from undesirable behaviour, the animal is merely being conditioned to refrain from actions which it has found to have unpleasant consequences rather than to respond directly to its owner. Since conventional training methods are perfectly satisfactory as well as serving to strengthen the bond between dog and owner, and since electric shocks are as unpleasant to dogs as they are to humans, there seem no grounds whatsoever for the use of these shock punishments.

THE LEAD

ABOVE: *The lead needs to be long enough for distance control, although for much of the training it will be looped up in your hands to prevent dangling slack when the dog is close to you.*

TRAINING EQUIPMENT

The only essential equipment is a collar and lead. Generally speaking, some form of check (or choke) chain is recommended as a training collar since it gives more control than a buckle collar. It is better not to use a check chain on a young puppy under five months, however, and it may not be advisable in the case of some of the short-faced, popeyed breeds such as Pekingese because pressure around the neck can be dangerous in these cases.

A standard check chain consists simply of a length of chain with a metal ring at each end. The chain is slipped through one of the rings to form a noose which will go over the dog's head, and the collar is attached to the other ring. Such collars are available in different sizes of link and in different lengths; it is important to have the right size. You will need a collar long enough to fit round the dog's neck plus three inches extra; if the collar is too long the dog will slip out of it with ease, and if it is too short it will be uncomfortable. A collar with large, broad links is less likely to cut into the dog's neck than a finer chain; alternatively, nylon versions are available.

It is essential that the check chain be put on the dog the right way round, as illustrated. Put on correctly, the noose hangs slackly around the dog's neck unless the lead is pulled tight; if it is put on upside down, it will not slacken and remains tight around the dog's neck, choking it.

A check chain is an invaluable training aid if used correctly but can be an instrument of torture if misused. The two names commonly used, check chain and choke chain, indicate the right and the wrong approach. If the collar is put on correctly and allowed to hang loosely unless a reprimand is intended, it is comfortable for the dog to wear while it is walking correctly but can be used to check the animal when it misbehaves. If, however, the collar is put on upside down, or if the dog is allowed to pull steadily against it, it merely serves to choke the animal.

A variation which is less liable to misuse is the half-check or double-action collar, which consists of two interlinked rings of chain. The larger ring is the correct size to fit comfortably around the dog's neck, while the shorter ring extends it so that it can be slipped over the dog's head. When pulled tight, the shorter ring closes up so that the collar is closed on the dog's neck, but, unlike the standard single-action check chain, it cannot be tightened beyond that point.

The advantages of this type of collar are that it cannot be put on incorrectly and cannot be drawn too tight, although like the single-action version it can be used to check the dog when necessary and slackened for comfort when all is going well.

Leads are available in many lengths, but for training purposes a lead of about four feet will be most useful.

All too often the collar and lead are seen as a method of attaching an otherwise uncontrollable dog to one's person. Think of them instead as a means of communicating your wishes to the dog in the same way as reins are used with a horse. Once you and the dog understand what you are doing, the collar should be loose and the lead slack, a light touch serving as a reminder when necessary.

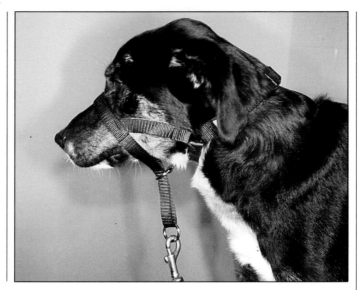

RIGHT: *A recent alternative to check chain is the 'Halti', which fits snugly around the dog's face to restrict movement of the head, thus controlling the body. This device is suitable for large or small dogs, and avoids the risk of injury to the animal that occurs with an incorrectly used check chain.*

FITTING A CHECK CHAIN

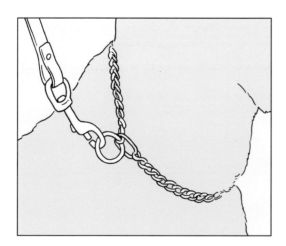

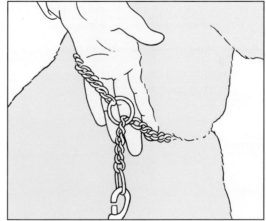

ABOVE: *Check chain fitted correctly, with leash end of chain at top. Like this, the chain will slacken automatically when pressure is relaxed, and tighten only when the dog pulls against it. Remember to remove the dog's everyday buckle collar before putting on the check chain, or the chain may catch on it, preventing proper tightening and slackening.*

ABOVE: *Check chain fitted incorrectly, with leash end of chain underneath. Like this, the chain will remain tight, whether the dog pulls or not, causing discomfort or even injury. Note that the diagrams depict the dog to the left of the owner: if you prefer the dog on your right, the collar should be reversed.*

RIGHT: *A dog which sits on command is demonstrably under control, and this is one of the most useful lessons to teach your pet.*

FAR RIGHT: *The dog should be taught to sit at kerbs. Here a well-trained Golden Retriever patiently observing the rules of the road, as are the children with it.*

TRAINING CLASSES

Dog training classes are held in most areas, under the guidance of experienced handlers, and are highly recommended. Most dog training clubs run separate classes for the beginner and for the more advanced trainer. These classes aim, not to train the dog, but to teach the owner how to do so. The actual quality of the help given to the novice varies widely from class to class, but many are very good, and attending even a poorly run class provides the opportunity both for socializing your dog and for teaching it to attend to you despite the distractions of other dogs.

Details of such courses can be obtained from a veterinarian or a local library or information bureau; the cost is usually nominal.

It is also possible, at much greater cost, to send your dog to a professional trainer. The outcome is less likely to be satisfactory because, although the dog will be trained, the owner will not have been taught how to handle his or her animal and may still lack the understanding to control it effectively. Personal involvement is a prerequisite for successful training.

TRAINING YOUR DOG

The way the basic commands are taught is based upon the methods of conditioning, reward and punishment already described. 'Little and often' is a good rule for the dog's lessons; ten minutes every day will be a great deal more valuable than a marathon session every now and then. Like children, puppies have a short attention span and will quickly become tired or bored; five minutes at a time will be best for the youngster, and the time can be increased as it matures.

Although formal lessons must be short to be effective, the whole of the day can be used for informal conditioning to help the dog fit into your lifestyle. The more time you spend with your dog, the more opportunity you have to reinforce the type of behaviour you want. A reprimand for undesirable behaviour will be reinforced by praise for stopping what it was doing and a distraction in the direction of something more appropriate. If you notice the dog chewing a shoe, for example, distract its attention with a toy, praise it for giving up the shoe and encourage it to play with its own toy. Talking to the dog encourages it to listen to you and to be alert for the words it needs to learn.

The second rule is to make the lessons enjoyable. Like a child, the dog will also learn a great deal faster if lessons are fun. If the owner's voice and actions demonstrate enthusiasm, the dog will look forward to training sessions and be eager to participate. The more the dog enjoys the training, the more eager it will be to please you by learning more; enthusiasm is infectious. Many novice trainers hamper themselves and their dogs by using a flat tone of voice; you will get a great deal more out of your dog if you learn to use voice and gesture like a ham actor, ladling on the praise when it performs correctly and filling your voice with shock and horror when it disobeys.

The third rule is to be consistent. Decide before you start which words you wish the dog to associate with particular actions, and stick to them. It is all too easy to confuse the animal. For example, if you have chosen the word 'down' to mean 'lie down', you will have to take care not to muddle your dog by using the same word to mean 'get off that sofa' or 'stop jumping up'.

Consistency means never giving a command unless you are in a position to reinforce it. If you say 'Sit', then insist that the dog sits, and that it does not get up until you give a release command such as 'okay'. If the dog is still unsteady on this command, avoid telling it to sit when it is on the other side of the room and can run off instead, but make a point of practising when it is on the lead and you can reach down and push it into a sit if it fails to obey. Every time you give a command that is not obeyed, this is negative training, teaching the dog that it can get away with disobedience.

Consistency also entails planning ahead, to avoid establishing patterns of behaviour which may be undesirable in the future. It may be appealing when the small fluffy puppy jumps up at you to express its adoration, but you are unlikely to welcome the same attention from a grown dog weighing several stone, with wet and muddy paws.

If you discourage this behaviour in the puppy, you will avoid the problem when it is adult.

It is helpful if, initially at least, a single member of the family takes responsibility for the dog's training to ensure that consistency of approach is maintained. If the dog is taught in two slightly different ways, learning will take longer.

LEAD TRAINING

All dogs need to learn to walk with their owners on a slack lead. The untrained dog which tows its owner along, lags behind, lunges at passers-by or other dogs, or jerks away without warning to investigate some intriguing smell is no pleasant companion to take for a walk, so this is important.

Lead training can be easy and painless if you start from the beginning with a young puppy. The puppy should have been accustomed early on, to the feel of a soft puppy collar around its neck and to walking on the lead in the garden. By the time it has its introduction to the outside world, it should already have the idea that it walks with its owner rather than disputing the route or pace. Although at first there will be all manner of distractions, from frightening traffic noises to passers-by who will be welcomed like long-lost friends, and the pup is likely to forget its early lessons, the early conditioning forms a foundation upon which correct lead training can be built up.

It is customary for the dog to be taught to walk on the owner's left-hand side, although unless you wish to take up competitive obedience the right side is just as acceptable if you prefer this, in which case reverse the sides in the following instructions.

Taking the end of the lead in your right hand, position the dog on your left and take up most of the slack in your left hand. Before setting off, give the dog the command you intend to use, 'heel' or 'close' being those most commonly used. Walk off at a brisk pace, aiming to keep the short stretch of lead between the dog's collar and your left hand slack. Every time the dog pulls away, tightening the lead, give a short sharp jerk on the lead to bring the animal back into position, simultaneously repeating the verbal command. The jerk will tighten the check collar around the dog's neck, causing momentary discomfort.

Slacken the lead instantaneously so that as soon as the dog is in the correct position the discomfort ceases, and praise it for walking properly. Never pull steadily on the lead. A dog's neck is tough, and the dog will continue to pull against you. Every time it pulls away, jerk and rebuke, and immediately let go and praise. You may have to repeat the pattern a number of times, but the dog will soon learn that it is more comfortable to walk in the correct way, and it will also associate the command with the action. When it

LEAD TRAINING

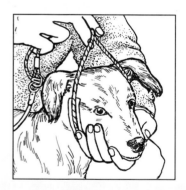

Be careful not to frighten the pup when putting on the lead. The dog may be playful or nervous during the first lessons. Hold the lead in the right hand, reassure or admonish with the left. The lead should be slack, with the pup walking at the owner's pace.

has learned the lesson properly, it should continue to obey the command even when it is off the lead, but do not rush this stage, and be sure to introduce it in a quiet open space where there are no distractions.

Heel training comes more easily to some breeds than to others. For competitive obedience the dog must walk precisely as commanded, but if you have no ambitions in this direction you may find that your particular dog is happier doing this exercise in its own style, perhaps slightly in front of you rather than close beside, and so long as you are both comfortable this is just as acceptable. Small dogs, which are more at risk of a bump from the owner's foot, often prefer to walk slightly further away from your feet, and this also reduces the risk of tripping over them.

'SIT' AND 'DOWN'

Sitting and lying down on command are more than parlour tricks. A dog which sits on command is demonstrably under control. You can take such an animal anywhere in the confidence that it will not embarrass you. You can tie it outside a shop and tell it to sit, and it will remain there looking smart and well-behaved rather than lunging about barking; the animal itself will feel more secure knowing what is expected of it. If you have non-doggy visitors, the dog that can be ordered to sit will not jump at them or sniff around their legs. It is well worthwhile teaching a family dog to sit quietly when it is about to be fed, instead of pestering the person preparing its meal, or worse still a group of people sitting around a dinner table. It is also particularly useful to teach a dog to sit at kerbs when you are waiting to cross the road, to prevent the risk of it stepping out into the traffic.

The 'sit' is taught by putting the dog into the correct position, pushing its hindquarters down, while giving the command. The dog will not realize at first what is required, but this is a natural position for a dog and one of the easiest exercises to teach; repetition, with plenty of praise when the correct attitude is achieved, will quickly get the message across. Hold the dog in position for a moment, then give a release command such as 'okay' to indicate that the exercise is over and allow it to stand up. Do not attempt to hold the sit for too long at first.

Some dogs will react initially by lying right down or even rolling over, and it will help to teach the 'sit' holding the dog's lead so that you can prevent this by keeping the head up. You can reinforce the lesson by watching out for times when the dog takes up the sit position of its own accord and then telling it, 'Sit, that's right, good dog'.

After being shown what is wanted sufficient times the dog will associate the command with the action and will sit when told without having to be put into position. Remember that it is important to insist that the 'sit' is held until the release command is given and that the dog does not just get

TEACHING THE 'SIT'

Sitting is a natural posture for the dog and most do not need much encouragement to sit on command. The command 'Sit' should be given first and then gentle pressure applied to the dog's hindquarters When it has adopted the required posture, it should be praised warmly. Repetition will teach it to respond to the vocal command alone, without the need to be helped into position.

up when it feels like it. Do not force the dog to hold the position for too long; a short sit, correctly performed, achieves far more than a long one ending with a bored dog standing up before he is released.

The 'down' is an extension of the 'sit', but asks more of the dog, because this is a submissive posture. More dominant individuals may be reluctant at first to obey this command, while highly submissive animals may take the pose to its submissive extreme and roll right over on their backs. Apart from being a useful command, it is valuable to teach the 'down' because it asserts the owner's dominance, ultimately adding to the dog's emotional security by confirming its place in the social hierarchy.

'Down' is taught in a similar way to 'sit', with the dog being helped into position. The easiest method is to put the dog into the 'sit' and then ease the forelegs down.

THE STAY

Teaching a dog to stay where it is put is a useful and practical exercise. The traditional method is to start with repeated exercises on the lead. The lead must be long, extended with a cord if necessary, to allow for an increasing distance between the dog and owner. The dog is put into a 'sit' or 'down' and the command 'stay' given in a firm tone, then the owner moves a single pace away. If the dog moves the owner puts it back into position with a rebuke and starts again. Quite soon it will be possible to move a pace away and wait a moment before returning to the dog and praising it. Gradually the owner can extend the distance and the length of time before returning to the dog.

Returning to the dog rather than calling it to the owner reinforces the lesson that it must stay until the exercise is over.

THE RECALL

All too many pet dogs acquire the vice of not coming back when called, which is at best an annoying habit and at worst a social liability and even a hazard. It is essential for the owner to be able to call the dog to him or her in certain circumstances, such as when it is loose with other dogs in a park, or is about to rush away across a road.

The recall can be taught as a follow-up to the 'stay'. With the dog on the lead, tell it to 'stay' and walk to the end of the lead, then call it to 'come'. This command should be an eager invitation; crouching down to receive the dog is a welcoming posture. Use the lead to guide the dog to you if it hesitates. and then give plenty of praise for coming. Gradually the distance can be extended, and then the exercise practised off lead. You will need to introduce the recall in a quiet place with minimal distractions before the dog is ready to undertake it in a crowded park full of enticing smells and other dogs.

OTHER LESSONS

The basic commands that a dog needs to learn in order to become a civilized and responsive member of the household can be augmented by many more, ranging from useful tasks such as retrieving to 'fun' tricks such as shaking hands. The trained dog will take pleasure in extending its range of accomplishments, just as much as will its proud owner, and this can only strengthen their relationship.

Retrieving comes naturally to certain breeds – notably, of course, retrievers, which from puppyhood will delight in fetching objects both desirable and undesirable to their owners. Some breeds, and some individuals, have little natural retrieving instinct, and it will be much harder to teach these than those dogs in which the drive is naturally present. The dog which brings you its ball to throw is already halfway there.

RIGHT: *The dog that walks correctly to heel should sit when its owner halts.*

STAY AND RECALL

The lesson begins with the dog sitting at the end of a long lead. The owner moves slowly away, repeating the word 'stay', perhaps reinforced by a hand signal.

Once the dog has learned to stay, it is taught to come when called. The owner calls 'come' invitingly, with a gentle tug on the lead if necessary. Correct performance should always be rewarded.

187

Retrieving should be fun, so make a great game out of displaying the object you want retrieved before throwing it. The natural retriever will chase after it and come back to you. You will probably have to teach the dog that it must give up the object to you after fetching it, and at first many dogs will think it part of the game to run off with it, inviting you to chase after it for possession. If you do so, you will have changed the game from 'retrieve' to 'chase'! Never chase after the dog, but call it to you invitingly, perhaps displaying a titbit or alternative toy as an attraction. You must make it clear that if the dog does not cooperate, the game is over. When it comes to you, reach for the object in its mouth with the word 'Give', and take it firmly, with much praise when the object is relinquished, and start again. The dog will soon learn that returning the object means the continuation of the game, while retaining it means being ignored.

If the dog runs after the object but loses interest and drops it before returning to you, you may be able to re-arouse interest by picking it up yourself and making a great show of playing with it before trying again. As soon as the dog picks it up, praise its action lavishly and attempt to arouse its enthusiasm.

A dog that enjoys retrieving can go on to scent discrimination, finding a selected article which has been hidden, and this can become a really useful exercise if you drop a glove or similar item when out on a walk. This is taught by hiding an article which carries your scent, and then encouraging the dog to accompany you in the search, showing excitement and pleasure when you 'find' it, and even greater delight if the dog comes across it first.

Many dogs enjoy learning tricks which are purely for fun. 'Shaking hands' is something that many owners enjoy teaching their dogs, and has the advantage that proffering a paw is a natural sign of submission. Teaching a dog to bark on command can be useful in certain circumstances, for example, when you are alone in the house and hear a sinister sound which might be a burglar who could be deterred by evidence of a dog's presence. It has the added benefit that the dog which barks on command is the more easily taught to stop barking on command! Some dogs take to this exercise more easily than others: the simplest approach is to wait until the dog barks spontaneously and then give the command 'Speak', followed by praise, before giving the order to be quiet. Repetition will enable the dog to associate the action with the command.

Dogs can be trained to an astonishingly high level of achievement, as is demonstrated by a wide range of working dogs from those used by the police force to those which entertain the public in the circus. With patience, persistence and consistency, the family dog can be taught a range of accomplishments which will enable both dog and owner to get the most out of their relationship.

*The world of circus and side-show entertainment makes full use of the dog's ability to learn complex tricks. (**TOP**) A typical act with a troupe of Poodles trained to walk on their hind legs.*
(**ABOVE:**) *'Johnny Watson's Canine Wonders'.*

FAR RIGHT: *Retrieving comes naturally to puppies of certain breeds. You can encourage this instinct by always praising the puppy for bringing an object to you, even if it is something it should not have had in the first place.*

COMMON BEHAVIOURAL PROBLEMS

When puppies are teething they are likely to chew anything within reach to relieve the irritation. This is a natural tendency, the effects of which can be minimized by providing 'approved' chews and by ensuring that shoes and similar items are not left where the puppy can reach them. Constant watchfulness may be tiring but is the only way to teach the puppy what may be chewed and what must not. Every time the puppy seizes upon an illicit item it should be gently but firmly rebuked, the object retrieved and a suitable toy given instead. Never chase a puppy which is running off with something, as it will only enjoy the game and will not learn anything; instead take advantage of its abundant curiosity by distracting it.

In older dogs, destructive chewing often occurs when the owner is out for long periods. It may indicate a lack of security or inadequate exercise. The remedy lies essentially with the owner, who must compensate for the deficiency and give the dog more attention. Since the destructive dog has evidently not yet learned about property rights, it also needs the same conditioning as the puppy, with firm but patient teaching that it may chew and play with its own toys but not with its owner's possessions.

Destructiveness may also occur in the case of a pregnant bitch, or one suffering from a false pregnancy, who may chew or scratch in an attempt to make a nest. This is normal breeding behaviour which will pass, although treatment of the pseudo-pregnancy may be required.

Jumping up at people is an annoying habit, and stems from inadequate training. It is often seen as appealing behaviour in the excited puppy welcoming its owner, but should be discouraged from the beginning, before trouble starts with laddered stockings, muddied clothes and people actually knocked over by the dog's exuberance. The dog should be pushed off balance – a firm but not violent knee in the chest will achieve this – and reprimanded. However, we do not wish to discourage the dog from greeting its owner, only from jumping up, so when it has all four feet on the ground the owner should bend or kneel down and make a fuss of his or her pet. The dog will soon learn to welcome its owner without leaping up.

Dogs often bark at the approach of strangers or at sudden, unexpected noises, but prolonged periods of barking must be discouraged, if only for the neighbours' sakes. Such behaviour again stems from excitement and may be more

LEFT: *Puppies should not be allowed to develop the habit of jumping up, as this behaviour is undesirable in a fully-grown dog.*

of a problem with smaller breeds. The well-behaved dog must learn to stop barking on command, and many owners find teaching this difficult. There are various ways of getting the message across. If a dog barks continually at callers it can be put on the lead and the command 'No' be accompanied by a sharp jerk on the check chain. A persistent offender may respond to having its muzzle held firmly shut so that it is physically unable to bark, the action again being accompanied by a vocal order. Squirting the barking dog with a water pistol, taking care to avoid its eyes, is often an effective short sharp shock treatment.

Barking can be unintentionally encouraged by an owner; for example, if a dog barks when it wants to come inside and the door is opened at once, the animal will associate barking with the door being opened, and carry on until its wishes are obeyed. The owner who responds in this fashion, or who reacts to the dog barking at mealtimes by slipping it a morsel of food 'to shut it up', is making a rod for his or her own back.

Leaving a dog alone may also cause it to bark, and this requires careful deconditioning.

Wandering is more common in some breeds than others; Beagles, for example, are particularly bad in this respect. Prevention is the easiest solution. Ensure that all gates are kept closed and fences around the property are well maintained. An urge to wander can result from lack of exercise or from sexual instincts, especially in the case of male dogs when there is a bitch in heat nearby. Neutering has been shown to prevent most males from wandering. If a dog does escape and causes a road accident, its owner may be sued for damages. Insurance against this eventuality is strongly recommended, and is available at a very moderate cost, often as part of a health insurance scheme (see p 198).

TRAINING FOR COMPETITION

Training for competitive obedience and working trials follows similar lines to training the family dog, but the dog must be taught to carry out commands in a precisely specified fashion. Any dog, pedigree or mongrel, is eligible, although certain breeds predominate in practice – notably the Border Collie and German Shepherd Dog – because they are predisposed towards this kind of work. However, obedience competitions have this much in common with the breed shows for pedigrees only, that they should be fun for both dog and owner. If winning matters to you more than enjoying the ups and downs of training and a day out at the show, your relationship with the dog will suffer and the dog will perform less well than another, perhaps less competent, which is having a thoroughly good time.

For competitive obedience you will find it extremely useful to join a local dog training club where experienced trainers will teach you exactly how the different tests have

RIGHT: *Successful training depends on patience and repetition. The winter weather does not prevent this owner and her Border Collie from enjoying their regular training sessions.*

to be carried out. There are different levels of classes in which dogs compete, from those for beginners to championship level; as with breed showing, a successful dog can achieve the title of Champion. At the simplest level, the dog is required to demonstrate the ability to walk to heel on and off lead, to return when called (the recall), and to sit and lie down on command, remaining in position for a set period until released. The classes increase in difficulty, with the introduction of further tests including the 'Send Away', in which the dog is sent away from its owner until told to stop and lie down, retrieving, a ten-minute 'Down Stay' with the owner out of sight, and scent discrimination.

Whilst many owners will aim to bring their dog's training to the point of perfection, just as many are happy to achieve the lower levels, enjoying the social aspects of the hobby as well as the benefit of a well-behaved dog.

Working Trials are also held, in which tests are designed to display skills of a working nature. In these trials, a dog can qualify for titles ranging from Companion Dog, demonstrating basic obedience, agility (scaling a high obstacle as well as jumping), retrieving and nosework, to Police Dog, a highly demanding series of tests appropriate to large working breeds. Other titles include Utility Dog, Working Dog and Tracking Dog.

BELOW: *For working trials, the dog is required to scale a high barrier.*

ABOVE: *The show puppy needs to learn to stand correctly, so that the pose becomes comfortable and natural. It is vital that the show dog is relaxed and happy to display its good points in the ring.*

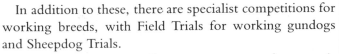

In addition to these, there are specialist competitions for working breeds, with Field Trials for working gundogs and Sheepdog Trials.

A more recent type of test to appear on the scene is Agility Trials, in which dogs compete to complete an obstacle course of considerable ingenuity. These are designed as 'fun' competitions and are open to dogs of any kind over the age of 12 months. As with obedience work, intending competitors will find it most useful to contact their local dog training clubs to teach their dogs such complicated techniques as weaving in and out of upright poles or running through a collapsible tunnel.

SHOW TRAINING

If you want to exhibit your dog, it needs to be taught how to show itself to best advantage. Show dogs are judged on their appearance, but a good-looking specimen which will not stand still to be examined by the judge, or which will not walk or run properly on the lead to demonstrate its gait, gives the judge no opportunity to appreciate its virtues. Furthermore, if it is not happy and confident in the show ring it will not look good.

In most areas it is possible to attend ringcraft classes at which puppies have the opportunity to learn the proper behaviour for the show ring, and these classes are invaluable to give youngsters – and their owners – confidence.

Confidence will be built up by taking the dog out and about as much as possible to accustom it to different environments and socialize it with people and other dogs.

The show dog needs daily training sessions from an early age to learn to stand well. Most small dogs are judged standing on a table, and it will be necessary to practise at home to accustom them to heights. Larger breeds are judged standing on the ground. When you are teaching the dog to stand for examination, set it up in the correct position with the command 'stand' and practise this daily until it is quite confident. A tendency to sit down can be discouraged by gently stroking the belly. Eventually you want the dog to stand in an alert posture with its head up and the tail carriage appropriate to its breed. The actual pose in which the dog is 'set up' will depend on the breed: some are required to stand squarely, while others take a hind leg back to demonstrate the angulation.

You will learn a great deal about how to set your dog up by watching experienced exhibitors in the show ring. Some breeds are shown on a loose lead, the owner standing well back, and others 'strung up' on a tight lead to pull the head up, while yet others are traditionally 'stacked', with the owner kneeling beside the animal and holding up head and tail.

Accustom the dog to being handled while it stands, running your hands gently over it and opening the mouth to examine its teeth. When it is quite happy with this process, ask your friends to do the same to teach the dog to accept examination by other people.

Lead training is vital; the dog will be asked to show off its paces for the judge, and will only appear to advantage if it moves smoothly on the lead without leaping about or trailing behind. The judge may ask you to walk away from him or her in a straight line and then back, or to walk a triangle to demonstrate the side view as well, and after individual judging, all dogs in a class will be asked to walk around together in a circle, so practise triangles and circles and ensure that your dog is used to walking with other dogs.

LEFT: *The breed show is a beauty competition; dogs need to be trained to show themselves off to best advantage, as well as being impeccably groomed.*

RIGHT: *Showing well on a slack lead. Some breeds are traditionally held in the show pose by the handler, but a dog that will show itself on a slack lead like this always looks good.*

ABOVE: *The show dog must accept the judge's close physical examination calmly, allowing him or her to open its mouth and run a hand over its body. Friends can be enlisted in training sessions to accustom the dog to being handled by different people.*

ABOVE: *Small breeds are transported to shows in cages, so show training will include familiarizing them with ths routine.*

ABOVE: *This five-month old Tibetan Spaniel has been trained from babyhood to adopt the correct show stance on a table, so that when he is old enough to be shown he will pose happily and confidently for the judge.*

Chapter Eight

HEALTH CARE

YOU AND YOUR VET

After acquiring a new dog or puppy, it is sensible to choose a veterinarian as soon as possible. While a personal recommendation from a breeder or friend may be followed up, all veterinarians have undergone several years of rigorous training and will prove reliable. In rural areas, veterinarians may concentrate more on farm animals than pets, but they will nevertheless be quite competent to treat dogs. Most 'small animal' practices are based in towns; occasionally, cases requiring specialist equipment may be referred from country practices.

Initially, you will want to visit your vet to arrange for the vaccination, worming and a general check-up of your new pet. Thereafter, you can expect to make at least an annual visit for vaccination boosters, when your vet will probably also carry out a general examination to establish the dog's overall health.

At some stage during the dog's life additional visits will probably have to be made on account of illness or injury. If the dog at any time shows any distressing or unusual symptoms you should arrange an appointment with the vet at once – early treatment of any illness will increase the chances of a full recovery, reducing the period of discomfort for the dog and the size of the vet's bill for you.

It is possible to take out insurance against veterinary fees, and most veterinary surgeons can provide information on different schemes. While such policies do not cover the cost of vaccinations or neutering operations, they can help defray the cost of unforeseen accidents or injuries. Orthopaedic surgery, for example, after an accident, can be very expensive. Since there are a number of different policies on the market, it is important to compare what each offers, paying particular attention to the exclusion clauses, which often concern congenital defects. The minimum amount which the owner must meet in the event of a claim should also be noted, and whether certain benefits, such as costs of advertising, are available if the dog disappears. Combined health and third-party liability policies are available, or both can be taken out separately.

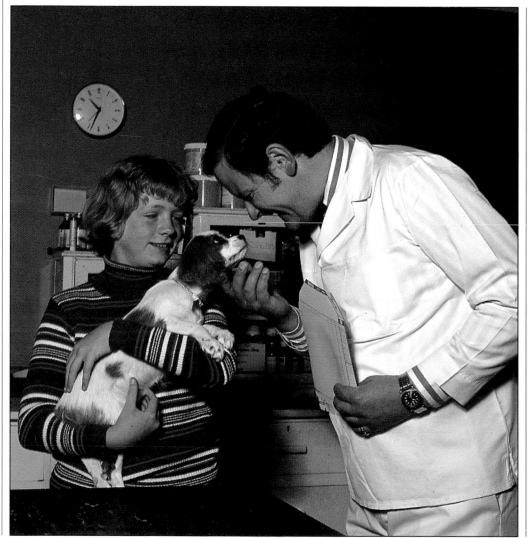

LEFT: *Choosing a veterinarian will be essential shortly after you have acquired your puppy, for preventative medicine is very important for dogs. The puppy will need a course of inoculations to protect it against the major infectious diseases. It will probably also require worming, and your veterinarian will be able to advise you on any particular concerns about your puppy's health care.*

LEFT: *The eyes, nose, mouth and ears are all good indicators of the overall state of health of your dog. The eyes should be clear and bright and the nose free of any discharge or redness; a mucous discharge may be an early sign of upper respiratory disease or even distemper. The mouth and gums should be pink; bad breath may be a sign of tooth decay or gum disease, and a dog with dental problems will also be prone to dribble. Healthy ears should be clean, free from discharge or unpleasant odour. A waxy discharge or an apparent irritation indicates an ear infection.*

BELOW: *Veterinary practices now have a wide range of sophisticated equipment available to assist with the diagnosis and treatment of canine complaints.*

SIGNS OF ILL HEALTH

Regular grooming sessions provide the opportunity to notice many of the early warning signals of ill health. Dull, weeping or discharging eyes, discharge from the nose, bad breath or dribbling, a dull staring coat or bald patches are all unmistakable signs that something is wrong. It is usually accepted that a cold, wet nose is a sign of good health, and generally speaking this is a useful indicator. However, a healthy dog may sometimes have a temporarily dry nose through dehydration or even through sitting in a warm place; in addition, a dog which has recovered from distemper may be left with a nose which is permanently dry.

Many of the symptoms of ill health, such as coughing, sneezing, vomiting or diarrhoea, are easily recognizable and, as with humans, may indicate slight or serious problems depending upon their severity. Remember, though, that a dog showing what in a human would be the symptoms of the common cold may be suffering from something much more dangerous; the runny nose, shivering and coughing may be indications of distemper.

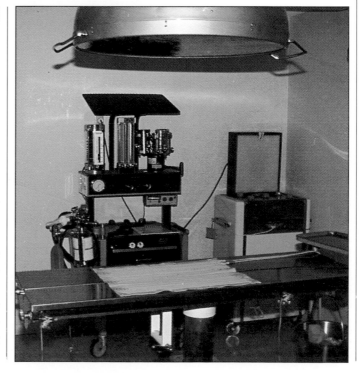

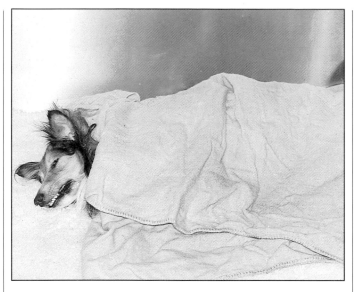

Persistent abnormal bowel movements or repeated vomiting are another indication of trouble. An isolated bout of diarrhoea or vomiting is not likely to signify anything more than some unwise eating, but if this continues, or if blood or worms are seen in the faeces or vomit, visit the veterinarian. Highly malodorous faeces may indicate an intestinal infection. If the dog has difficulty in urinating, urinates with increasing frequency, or passes blood in the urine, again veterinary attention is called for.

Dogs are creatures of habit, and you will soon become familiar with the normal behaviour patterns of your own pet. Any sudden change may be an early indication that trouble is brewing. The key indicators are likely to be the dog's appetite and drinking habits, as well as its general alertness and desire for exercise. It is not uncommon for a dog to lose its appetite occasionally, but if this persists for longer than 24 hours it indicates cause for concern as does any sudden marked increase in appetite, or in thirst.

It will help to write down a list of the symptoms that are worrying you and the length of time they have lasted before visiting the veterinarian, so that you can be sure of giving him or her a clear picture. Other information your vet may require will include whether the dog has been vaccinated, and how long you have owned it; in the case of a bitch, it may be useful to add the date of her last heat, or alternatively to state that she has been neutered. If you have visited the surgery before the dog's case history should be on file, but it is useful to have relevant information to hand. Your vet will probably ask you questions before carrying out an examination of the dog; be prepared to be as precise as possible. If your dog has been drinking more water, specify the amount by saying that it now consumes X litres over the course of a day. It is difficult for a vet to gain a clear impression if you say that the dog empties two bowls without knowing the volume of the bowls concerned.

Dogs are as prone to accidental injury as any other creature, whether household accidents or injury from such hazards as traffic. If your dog is injured, you can do a great deal to help it before the vet arrives, and some basic knowledge of first aid may mean the difference between life and death to your pet.

ROAD ACCIDENTS

Road accidents are sadly not uncommon, especially when dogs are allowed to run loose in urban areas. If a dog has been hit by a vehicle and is lying unconscious, move it with great care to avoid exacerbating any injuries; there may be internal bleeding not immediately apparent, although if this is the case the mucous membranes such as the gums will appear abnormally pale and the colour will not return readily if the area is touched with a finger.

A blanket makes an ideal stretcher; slide one hand under the chest and one under the rump and ease the dog on to the blanket, without twisting the body. Make sure that the airway is clear by clearing any vomit or blood from the mouth and pulling the tongue well forward. Avoid raising the forequarters of the dog above the rest of the body in case the diaphragm has been ruptured, when such an action may force the organs from the chest cavity into the abdomen.

It can be difficult to distinguish between unconsciousness and death. If the dog has been killed outright, breathing will have ceased, the heartbeat will have stopped, the pupils of the eyes will be widely dilated and fixed and the animal will not blink if the surface of the eye is lightly touched. You may be able to feel a heartbeat by flexing the elbow joint on the left side of the body to its maximum extent and placing the hand on the chest in the region that lies below the elbow, or you may be able to see the movement of body hairs in this region if the heart is still beating. However, it can be difficult for an inexperienced person to detect. If you are still in doubt, it is always best to have the dog examined by a veterinarian to confirm death.

FAR LEFT: *An accidental injury may give rise to shock, and the response should be geared to the particular problem. Keep the dog in a warm environment and seek professional advice.*

RIGHT: *An unconscious dog needs immediate first aid treatment and the assistance of a veterinarian as soon as possible. Ensure that the tongue is pulled forward to prevent choking and keep the dog war*

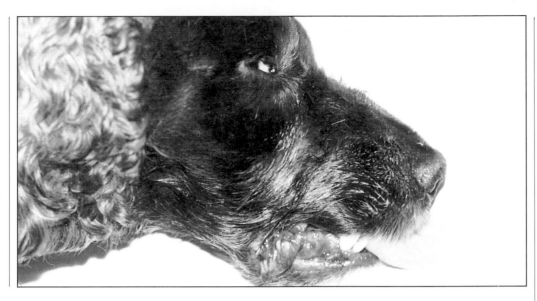

If the dog is conscious, remember that pain and fright may cause the gentlest animal to bite. Always try to catch the dog with minimum disturbance, avoiding passing traffic yourself. Talk quietly to the animal and reassure it as far as possible. To reduce the risk of being bitten, avoid direct handling if possible; use a lead or even a belt or tie to make a noose to slip over the dog's head, then tighten it, keeping your hands out of reach of the dog's jaws. If the dog is very aggressive, a temporary muzzle can be made using a belt or tie looped over the jaws, pulled tight and knotted behind the ears. Extreme care is necessary, not only to protect yourself but to avoid further damage to any injuries.

Superficial grazing may be accompanied by bleeding, but this is usually self-limiting because the blood clots easily. Try to control any severe bleeding by placing a pressure bandage over the wound. If an artery has been severed, blood will spurt from the site of the injury, and it is vital to staunch this until veterinary aid can be obtained. Tourniquets are dangerous if used for any length of time and should be avoided if possible, using a pressure bandage instead.

Many traffic casualties will suffer from shock, which can be fatal even if there are not serious injuries. Typical symptoms are weakness, and loss of colour from the extremities; the dog will appear cold, often shaking, and may be reluctant to stand. The heartbeat is noticeably raised, while the respiratory rate tends to be shallow and rapid. It is important to keep the dog warm until veterinary assistance is available, to minimize the effects of shock; if possible, wrap the animal loosely in a blanket. Do not give alcohol, which is likely to prove counterproductive.

Fractures and dislocations are common road accident injuries requiring veterinary treatment. Fractures may be simple, with a clean break in the bone, or compound, where the bone is forced through the skin, with a higher

RIGHT: *An improvized muzzle may be needed to prevent an injured dog from biting. A loop is placed over both jaws, with the knot at the top of the nasal region. The free ends of the bandage are brought round under the jaw and then crossed and tied behind the ears.*

LEFT: *A blanket may be used as a temporary stretcher.*

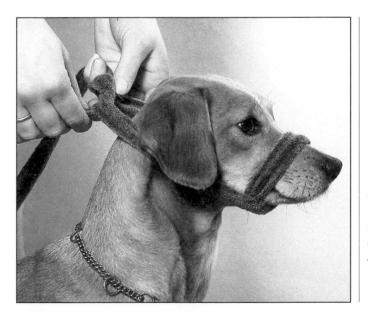

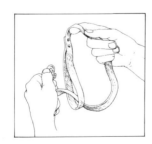

ABOVE: *An injured dog may need to be restrained. A simple noose can be made by looping the end of the lead through its handle and slipping it over the dog's neck.*

risk of infection developing at the site of the injury. X-rays will be needed to assess the damage before repair can be undertaken. Advances in veterinary orthopaedic surgery in recent years mean that many injuries that would once have been considered beyond repair can be treated with success. Fractured limbs can be splinted externally in less serious cases, but often require internal fixation, with pins, wires or plates or a combination of these to support the bone while it heals. Once the vet has set the break, such fractures normally heal well if the dog is strictly rested for a few weeks, but careful observation is needed in the early days to make sure that there are no associated internal injuries.

If a fracture or dislocation is suspected, the only appropriate first aid measure is to try to restrict the dog's movement, encouraging it to lie down and take the weight off the affected part of the body.

A dog which has been hit by a vehicle may seem relatively unhurt at first, but could have suffered severe internal injuries, so once it has been caught, take it to a veterinary surgeon. Such injuries are unlikely to be immediately evident to the layman but will be fatal if not treated.

A ruptured diaphragm is a relatively common internal injury after a road accident. The diaphragm is the sheet of muscle separating the chest from the abdomen, and if this is torn the dog will have difficulty in breathing and the internal organs may penetrate into the chest. Diaphragmatic tears can be repaired by surgery, although the anaesthetic risk is quite serious.

Another common road accident injury is a ruptured bladder, allowing urine to escape into the abdomen. If left untreated, the poisons from the urine will be absorbed into the dog's system and make it ill. It is important therefore to be sure that any dog which has been involved in a road accident is urinating normally afterwards. If there is a likelihood that the bladder has been damaged, your vet will need to take X-rays and possibly blood tests to establish whether surgery is needed.

BITE WOUNDS

If your dog is involved in a fight, it may receive bite wounds. These are rarely emergencies unless they penetrate a vital organ, but it is wise to have any deep bite treated with antibiotics to prevent infection developing. In summer in particular it is important to ensure that wounds are kept clean and dry to prevent attracting flies, which will lay their eggs on the broken skin, leading to 'fly strike' (maggot infestation). Dusting with an antiseptic powder combined with an insecticide, which your vet can supply, will prevent this problem.

Puncture wounds, with little bleeding, may be inconspicuous at first and may not be spotted until an abscess has developed. This should be treated by your vet, who will open and drain the abscess and prescribe antibiotics. If the abscess bursts before the dog can be taken to the vet, wipe away the discharged matter with cotton wool soaked in warm water and bathe the wound in a solution of one teaspoon of salt to a pint of warm water to encourage draining, or wash it out with a solution or hydrogen peroxide. The dog should then be treated by the vet to prevent a further abscess forming.

ARTIFICIAL RESPIRATION

Accidents such as drowning or electrocution may cause a dog to stop breathing. In such an emergency, artificial resuscitation may be necessary to save the dog's life while veterinary attention is being sought.

This is usually carried out with the dog lying on its right side, while gentle, even pressure is exerted over the rib cage by pressing down at about five-second intervals. Check that the airway is free, pulling the tongue forwards if necessary. Repeat the process until the heartbeat can be felt. It is worth continuing for several minutes if no response is evident, although, as time elapses, the chances of success will almost certainly be reduced.

An alternative method with a small dog is to hold the animal by its hindlegs, head downwards, and swing it gently back and forth to drain water from the lungs. The mouth must be kept open, and the tongue should be pulled forward to ensure that it is not blocking the airway.

If the dog's chest wall has been punctured, the normal pressure differential between the chest and the outside world will have been lost and you will have to adopt a different approach. Close the dog's jaws tightly and exhale up the nose for a few seconds, pausing briefly between each breath. This will maintain the oxygen supply to the lungs if the normal pressure differential between the chest and the outside world has been lost.

BURNS AND SCALDS

Dogs are sometimes at risk in a kitchen, where they may be splashed with hot liquids or cooking oils. They may also manage to singe themselves by lying too close to a fire. It is essential to cool down the burned skin as quickly as possible by immediately running cold water over the affected area or applying a pad soaked in cold water to it, to decrease the inflammation. Anything other than the most minor of burns will require veterinary attention. Healing is usually a very slow process, and the risk of infection is high. Hair may never regrow if the skin has been badly burned.

Occasionally a dog may be burnt by caustic chemicals such as turpentine. Treat as for burns, additionally washing the coat to remove the chemical.

Dogs, and especially puppies, may receive burns from chewing an electrical wire. You can reduce the risk of this

ARTIFICIAL RESPIRATION

It may be beneficial to give artificial respiration and heart massage to a dog in an emergency. First, check that the tongue is not blocking the air passage (1), and with the left side of the body

uppermost, exert firm but gentle pressure over the rib cage, at approximately five second intervals (2). The presence of a femoral pulse will confirm that the heart is beating (3).

by keeping electrical appliances unplugged. If it does happen, do not touch the dog until the current is turned off, or you could electrocute yourself. Sometimes the electric shock may kill the animal outright; it may be unconscious, requiring artificial respiration, but the commonest result will be severe burns to the mouth for which veterinary attention should be sought without delay.

FOREIGN BODIES

Foreign bodies sometimes penetrate the skin, and grass seeds rank amongst the most common, especially between the toes. The first sign is that the dog starts licking the area, which will be acutely painful. If the dog will allow you to investigate, it may be possible to remove the grass seed with tweezers, but often this will have worked its way deep into the flesh and will require veterinary attention. If the injury has festered, the dog will obtain some relief if the affected area is bathed in warm salt water, but the sooner veterinary aid is obtained the better, as the grass seed is likely to continue to work through the flesh and may set up a chain of abscesses.

Dogs living in fishing areas sometimes get fish hooks caught in their mouths. Never attempt to remove a hook yourself, as removal is likely to start the injury bleeding profusely, but seek veterinary aid.

Some dogs, and particularly puppies, will swallow all sorts of unsuitable items such as pebbles and stones, small balls or fragments of toys. Once again this is a matter for the veterinarian. If a foreign body is swallowed, there is a danger that it may lodge in the digestive tract and cause a total or partial blockage or, in the case of sharp objects such as pins or bones, perforate the gut. A blockage may be indicated by repeated vomiting, although symptoms will depend to some extent on the part of the gut where the object is stuck. In such cases the veterinarian will be able to locate the offending object by X-ray. It is not always necessary to operate to remove this kind of foreign body; some will pass through the gut if their passage is assisted.

Other dangerous objects, such as a needle and thread, may lodge in the throat, causing gagging and choking. Open the dog's mouth and investigate; the offending object may be accessible for removal, it is best to seek veterinary assistance as it is easy accidentally to push the object further down the airway or to cause bruising and tearing to the delicate tissues, quite apart from the risk that the dog may well be uncooperative and even bite. Fortunately, while the dog may be very distressed, it is unlikely to suffocate before veterinary treatment can be obtained. If it does lose consciousness, open the mouth and check that the airway is clear before attempting artificial respiration.

HEAT STROKE

If a dog is confined where it cannot escape from direct sunshine it can rapidly succumb to heat stroke. It is regrettably common for dogs to be left in a car parked in the direct sun, when heat stroke is very likely to occur; dogs in outdoor kennels or doghouses with poor ventilation are also at risk. The short-faced breeds are particularly vulnerable. Symptoms are excessive panting, drooling, vomiting and signs of shock, and eventually unconsciousness. The dog should be cooled down immediately with cold water; signs of recovery should be evident within five minutes or so, when the dog will need to be dried carefully and given water to drink; massaging the legs to improve the circulation is also recommended. As well as the obvious effects of heat stroke, the dog will be vulnerable to hypothermia if the cooling-down treatment is too effective. Following first aid measures, veterinary assistance is recommended.

POISONING

Dogs are susceptible to a wide variety of poisons, including many found in the home. Research has shown that one in every 2,500 dogs consumes a potentially toxic chemical, more often early in its life. Veterinary advice should be sought immediately if you believe your dog has eaten a poisonous substance, or even if it has picked up a harmful substance on its coat or paws, since it is likely to ingest this when grooming. The treatment will depend upon the nature of the poison, so it is important to find out as much about it as you can.

All chemicals should be kept out of the reach of dogs. Certain poisons actually attract dogs, including metaldehyde, which is used as slug bait. Antifreeze might seem unlikely to appeal to a dog, but it contains ethylene glycol, another chemical which is attractive to animals but which is converted in the body to toxic oxalic acid; as little as 1oz (30ml) can kill a 15lb (7kg) dog.

Rodent poisons are potentially lethal; dogs may swallow them directly or ingest them by eating poisoned rodents. Many rodent poisons, such as Warfarin, are anticoagulants, which interfere with blood clotting, causing internal bleeding over a period of time. Fortunately, the use of highly toxic poisons for killing rodents, such as strychnine, thallium and fluoracetate, is strictly controlled in the United Kingdom. Many drugs that are used are now colour-coded with dyes to aid in their identification, so inform your veterinarian of any unusual colour seen in a dog's vomit.

Insecticides are also dangerous. Slug bait pellets are sometimes eaten by dogs, although some modern brands contain substances to repel pet animals. Many insecticides contain organo-phosphorus compounds, with controlled amounts being present in flea collars, to which some animals may be sensitive.

RIGHT: *Heat stroke is dangerous, because the only way that dogs can control their body temperature is by panting – expiring internal heat through their breath – or through the pores between their toes and on the inside of their ears. It is vital for a dog to have access to a cool spot and plenty of water in hot weather.*

Insecticides used to control parasites on dogs should be applied with care. Always read the instructions thoroughly before using an insecticide, and do not apply more than one drug at a time – a particularly common error if you forget that the dog is wearing a flea collar. Ensure that you keep dosages correct and do not use drugs specifically approved for dogs. Remember that the dog may lick its coat; if you are directed to brush, for example, flea powder, out of the coat, make sure that you do so to avoid the dog ingesting the excess when it washes.

Other toxic substances which dogs may come into contact with include weed-killers, lead-based paints, which should never be used on kennels, and many wood preservatives. Toxic substances on the dog's coat may be licked off or may pass through the skin directly. Many common household agents which could be spilled on to the skin are poisonous to dogs, including bleach, petrol, shoe polish, some crayons and pencils, many detergents and cleaning agents, and wood preservatives such as creosote or tar. When bathing wounds, use only disinfectants recommended as safe for animals, as the dog will almost certainly lick the injury after treatment and many commonly used disinfectants are poisonous to dogs even in small amounts.

If the dog's coat becomes contaminated with any noxious substance, it is a good idea to muzzle the dog to prevent it from licking the coat. Seek veterinary advice before attempting to clean the coat, as incorrect treatment in some cases can have serious side-effects. Some substances can be removed with large amounts of water. Oil-based substances such as gloss paint should not be removed with turpentine or turpentine substitute, which is poisonous and

BELOW: *To prevent a dog from worrying a wound, an Elizabethan collar may be used (see p206).*
For large dogs, a bucket with the bottom cut out can be fitted around the head; this Pekingese has a home-made version of soft plastic attached to the ordinary buckle collar. Although the dog may find the appliance an imposition, it may be essential to protect a wound in the early stages of healing from damage by chewing or rubbing with a paw.

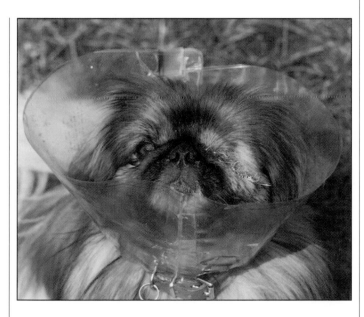

an irritant in itself, but with a waterless cleansing agent or butter or vegetable oil, which should then be washed off.

The incidence of poisoning is higher in young dogs, because of their natural curiosity and chewing instincts, and the risk is greatest for those which lack proper supervision. It is vital to keep household drugs prescribed for humans or pets in a secure place, and never to give medicines prescribed for one animal to another. Never keep medicines after the course of treatment for which they were prescribed has been completed.

If your dog suddenly becomes very ill, and could have had access to poison, telephone your veterinarian immediately. If you can identify the source of the poison this will assist treatment. It may be appropriate to administer an emetic (a pea-size lump of washing soda, or a strong salt solution will serve) to induce vomiting if the poison has been recently ingested – within half an hour – but this is not recommended for all poisons, so you must take veterinary advice. Do not attempt to administer an emetic if the dog is unconscious or if a corrosive or irritant substance has been swallowed; with irritant poisons, a demulcent mixture, such as milk and egg-white or olive oil, can be given to soothe the stomach.

SNAKE BITES

Britain has only one venomous snake, the adder, but in countries such as the United States or Australia snake bites are a more common hazard. Snake bites should be treated by applying a tourniquet, if possible, to prevent the poison from entering the general circulation, and placing an ice-pack over the swollen area, before seeking immediate veterinary aid. Whenever possible, the dog should be carried or transported in a car so that movement does not help the venom to spread through the body.

INSECT BITES

Insect bites are common, especially in the summer, usually occurring on the face or feet and resulting in pain and swelling. Bee stings should be bathed in a solution of bicarbonate of soda and the sting removed if found; wasp stings should be bathed in vinegar. Most stings are not serious and the dog will recover naturally, but if the sting is in the mouth breathing may be impaired and you may need to seek veterinary aid. Some dogs may show an allergic reaction, with alarming swelling and even collapse, and here again veterinary attention will be required.

HOME NURSING

Specialist treatment for a dog's illness or injury is the province of the veterinarian, but the owner can do much to assist the animal's recovery, and often this may be the most crucial factor. You may need to administer tablets, ear drops or eye drops, to coax a dog that has lost its appetite to take nourishment, to persuade a dog that has lost interest in life to keep up the fight, or conversely to restrain a convalescent from overdoing things.

In general, the sick dog needs to be kept warm and quiet. Warmth can be provided by an infra-red heater placed out of the dog's reach above the sleeping area, provided the dog also has access to a cooler place to avoid over-heating. A hot water bottle may be used, provided you make sure that the dog cannot accidentally burn itself – this applies especially in the case of a dog which is semi-comatose and unable to move easily. Avoid using boiling water, which could burn the skin, and wrap the hot water bottle in a thick towel as an additional precaution.

Unless the veterinarian has given specific instructions about fluid intake, it is a useful general rule to encourage the dog to drink. Although the dog can survive some time without eating, dehydration can kill, particularly if the animal is losing fluids through diarrhoea or vomiting. You can test for dehydration by gently pinching a fold of skin and releasing it: normally the skin is elastic and will drop back into place, but in a dehydrated animal the skin loses its elasticity and will remain pinched up for several seconds. Ensure that a drink is within easy reach of the dog and, if it does not take any, try dribbling a little water into its mouth with a teaspoon or a medicine dropper. If the dog cannot keep down sufficient quantities of water or cannot be persuaded to drink any, it may be necessary for the veterinarian to administer a saline drip into a vein or under the skin.

If your dog has to have an operation, it will not be released from the veterinary surgery until the vet is satisfied that it is in no immediate need of expert care, and you will be given information on nursing. Any animal that has undergone surgery should be kept warm and under observation for at least 48 hours afterwards. The veterinarian will advise you about diet: generally, after an anaesthetic, a light diet in small amounts will be recommended, but after some forms of surgery the dog may not be allowed to take food at all for some time. It is vital to follow the directions given in such cases.

RIGHT: *The femoral artery, running down each hind limb, is probably the easiest site to feel the pulse.*

BELOW: *Normal temperature, taken rectally, is about 38.5°C (101.5°F), but a slight rise after exercise is to be expected.*

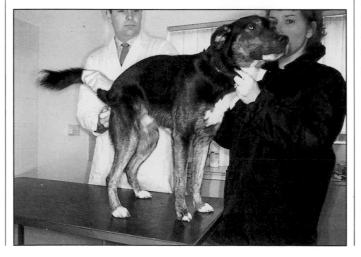

Any appointments for re-examination at the surgery should be strictly kept, and the operation site checked regularly for any sign of undue swelling, pain or discharge. If the dog shows no signs of recovering its spirits 24 hours after surgery, you should contact the vet for advice.

If the dog has had stitches inserted, these may be the dissolving kind which do not have to be removed, or the dog may need to visit the surgery about seven to ten days later to have them taken out. The dog's natural instinct to lick its wounds means that it may remove the stitches itself before the wound has closed if it is not prevented, and in some cases an Elizabethan collar (see p 205) will be fitted to prevent the dog from reaching the wound.

Your vet will normally give guidance on the administration of medicines. The easiest way to give a tablet is to conceal it in a suitable piece of meat: never mix it in with a bowl of food, as you cannot be certain that the dog has swallowed it. It may be necessary to administer the tablet directly.

This is not difficult with a dog that is used to being handled, but it can prove difficult in other cases. The key to success is to place the pill at the very back of the mouth so that the dog will swallow it almost automatically rather than attempting to spit it out. Grasp the upper jaw on either side with one hand, and raise it, holding the lower jaw with the other hand and using your first finger and thumb to pop the pill on to the base of the tongue. Hold the mouth closed, keeping the head slightly raised and tickling the throat so as to encourage the dog to swallow. For a right-handed person, the pill should be inserted with this hand. If you dislike placing your hand in the dog's mouth, use a pair of forceps for the purpose. There are also automatic dispensers that can be used. Try to give the pill on the first attempt. The dog is likely to become increasingly restless if the process proves protracted.

The medication may have a sugar or similar coating; it is vital that you do not break pills of this type because they may then have an extremely bitter and unpleasant taste and may also cause the dog to salivate profusely. The dog will probably resent any future attempts to give it pills. If you need help to restrain the dog, get someone else to restrain the neck with an arm so that the dog cannot slip away from you.

Initial dosing may lead to a noticeable improvement in the dog's condition, and it may appear as healthy as ever before the course of pills is completed. Nevertheless, always be sure to give all the pills prescribed by your veterinarian following the directions on the packaging implicitly. Failure to give a full course of antibiotics may not only cause the condition to reappear but can also lead to bacterial resistance to further treatment by the drug concerned. Antibiotics have altered the face of veterinary medicine, but they are not of value in every instance.

PILLS AND MEDICINES

LEFT: *Giving a pill. Hold your dog's muzzle with one hand, tilting the nose up; put your thumb in the space behind the canine tooth and press it against the roof of the mouth, forcing the dog to keep its mouth open. With your other hand, drop the pill as far back in the dog's mouth as you can, ensuring that it is on top of the tongue. Then hold the mouth closed and gently massage the throat until you feel the dog swallow.*

RIGHT: *Giving medicine. Measure the precise amount of medication into a syringe. Hold your dog's snout and place the syringe at the back of the dog's mouth, in the gap behind the canine teeth. Empty the contents of the syringe with steady pressure. If the dog chokes, let the head down without relinquishing your grip. Do not tilt the head too far back – this will lead to coughing as the fluid enters the larynx.*

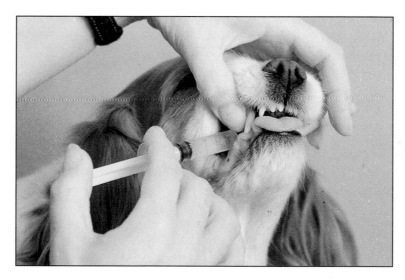

Liquid medicines are most easily administered with a syringe. The required quantity can be measured precisely, and then the syringe can be placed at the back of the dog's mouth from the right side, and its contents emptied with steady pressure from the right hand. The left hand is used to open the mouth sufficiently to allow the syringe to be placed within the dog's mouth while restraining both jaws. The situation is reversed for a left-handed person. In both cases, it is helpful to have someone else available to restrain the dog for you. If you run the medicine in slowly, the dog should not choke. If it does, let the head down without relinquishing your grip. The head needs to be at an angle of about 45° from the horizontal. Do not tilt it too far back as this will lead to coughing as fluid enters the larynx.

It is much harder to administer liquid medicine to a dog by means of a spoon, especially if you must give a specific amount. Avoid filling a spoon full because it will spill much more easily. Dosing will be easier to carry out if the dog is at a reasonable height off the ground – stand it on a table, for example, but protect the surface, both from the dog's claws and any spilled medicine.

Afterwards, wash the syringe or spoon thoroughly. Do not forget to show affection to the dog and give it a titbit if it has been well-behaved. It is a useful idea to open a puppy's mouth regularly, so that in later life it will let you administer treatments via the mouth when required.

With any medicine, it is important to follow the veterinarian's directions as closely as possible. Certainly, if the

Dogs with short legs and a long body such as Corgis are prone to suffering occasional back problems which will need careful nursing. Treatment tends to be supportive. The dog is kept as quiet as possible and confined to a small area so that it cannot injure itself further. Medical treatment may be given to decrease inflammation and ease the pain, and the owner will need to ensure that an immobile dog does not develop pressure sores.

directions say to administer medicine before a meal, this is important. Some drugs, such as tetracyclines, are not absorbed well from the intestinal tract in the presence of food; calcium combines with this group of antibiotics leaving lower quantities to be absorbed. Its effectiveness in fighting infection is correspondingly reduced. With regard to times of dosage, it is also important to adhere to these as far as possible. This will ensure that a therapeutically active level of the drug is retained within the body at all times during the course of treatment. For drugs such as tetracycline and ampicillin, the dose for a 25-pound dog should be 250 milligrams per day. If the pills need to be given twice daily, give them at, say, 8.00 am in the morning, and at the same time at night. The precise time is not as important as the time interval during which the level of the drug in the body is declining. It does no good to give the dog one or two pills then stop. In order to be effective, they must be administered regularly for at least five days. In certain circumstances, as with eye infections where the tear fluid is constantly washing the medication away, more treatments will be needed during the course of a day.

Other medications that may need to be administered at home include eye drops or ointment and ear drops. These are most easily administered if the dog is already used to regular grooming which includes checking the eyes and ears – another reason for daily grooming sessions. With eye drops, check that the dog's head is adequately restrained then cautiously apply the fluid as close as possible to the eye without actually touching the surface. If necessary, pull the lids apart gently, bearing in mind that the dog will probably blink when the medication makes contact with

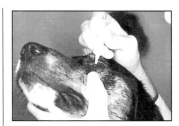

GIVING EYE DROPS

Hold your dog's head steady and carefully drop the medication into the eyes; try to avoid splashing drops out of the eye as the dog blinks. Treatment may well need to be applied several times daily.

the eye itself. Ointment is perhaps easier to apply since there is no risk of it being washed away with a blink, but restrain the dog for a few moments following application so that it does not wipe off the medication. To administer ear drops, turn the dog's head to one side before applying the medication, and afterwards massage behind the ears to ensure that the dog does not shake the medication out.

The only circumstances in which you are likely to have to administer injections to your dog is if it becomes diabetic. Your veterinarian will show you how to carry out the necessary injections of insulin, and if you are concerned you can practise using an orange as a substitute for the skin. The insulin will have to be administered subcutaneously (under the skin) rather than into a vein, which makes the process easier. Having filled the syringe, hold the scruff, the loose skin on the back of the dog's neck, and insert the needle through the skin. Draw back slightly to ensure that no blood appears in the syringe (this would indicate that you had struck a blood vessel) and if all is well, push the plunger firmly and then withdraw the needle. It is important to use a new needle each time. not only on grounds of hygiene but also because they blunt rapidly. Dogs' skin is surprisingly tough, and a blunt needle makes the process more difficult. Dispose of your old needles carefully by placing the protective covers back on them and returning them to your veterinarian. These injections will probably have to be administered on a daily basis.

Occasionally it may be necessary to nurse a dog which is unable to walk. Spinal injuries which have this effect are not uncommon, especially in the long-bodied breeds such as Dachshunds. Severe cases may not recover and may require euthanasia, but often the condition will respond to careful nursing. A dog which is unable to walk requires special care to prevent it from developing pressure sores from lying too long in the same position. These sores are most likely to develop on bony parts of the body, and bigger, heavier dogs run the greatest risk. Pressure sores should not be confused with the thickening skin commonly seen on the elbows of healthy dogs of the large breeds although the case is similar. These come from lying on hard surfaces for any length of time.

Caring for a paraplegic dog is a considerable undertaking. It can be made easier by making a foam bed with removable covers, or by encouraging the dog to lie on a bean bag. Do not allow the dog to remain in the same position for more than a couple of hours, and if any sores appear and form ulcers, contact your veterinarian. An additional problem is that such dogs are likely to be incontinent so their surroundings must be easy to clean thoroughly.

PARASITES

Parasites, whether external such as fleas or internal such as roundworms, are an unfortunate fact of life which most dogs will come into contact with from time to time. Although some may have a very minor effect upon the dog – wild animals are generally riddled with parasites of one kind or another, and carry on their lives nevertheless – the problem should never be ignored. Some parasites are intrinsically dangerous to the dog's health; others, less immediately dangerous in themselves, can build up their numbers into a severe infestation; and quite a few carry a degree of risk or unpleasantness to the dog's human companions.

EXTERNAL PARASITES

■ **FLEAS** Fleas are the commonest external parasites found on dogs, and most dogs will be exposed to these at some stage. It is important to act at the first sign of infestation to prevent a build-up.

Persistent scratching and biting is the most obvious sign of the presence of fleas, especially along the back and at the base of the tail. Grooming gives the opportunity to keep a regular check; although the fleas themselves may escape detection by their tiny size and agility, their presence will be betrayed by flea dirt in the dog's coat and in combings

EXTERNAL PARASITES

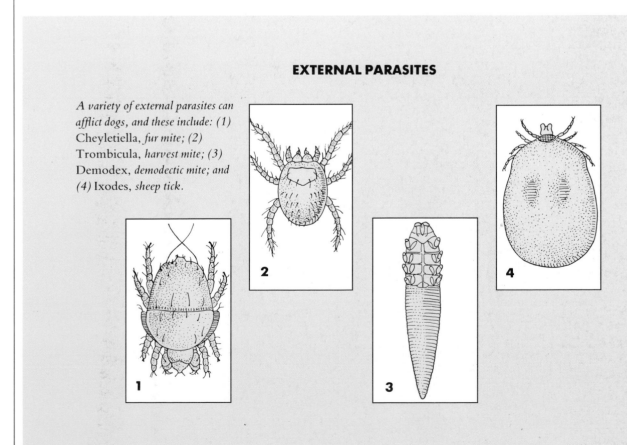

A variety of external parasites can afflict dogs, and these include: (1) Cheyletiella, *fur mite; (2)* Trombicula, *harvest mite; (3)* Demodex, *demodectic mite; and (4)* Ixodes, *sheep tick.*

LIFE CYCLE OF A FLEA

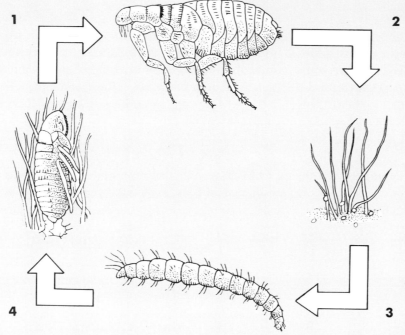

The female dog flea (1) lays her eggs on the floor (2) or on bedding, and in about a week they hatch to larvae (3) which spin cocoons, inside which the pupae (4) develop into adults within two or three weeks. The dog flea acts as an intermediate host for the larvae of the common tapeworm, Dipylidum caninum, *which makes it even more important that flea infestations should be controlled. Dog fleas can also bite the owner, and in fact the human flea,* Pulex irritans, *often lives on dogs and vice versa.*

caught in the comb – tiny blackish-red droppings.

Fleas are an apparently minor nuisance which must be dealt with promptly to prevent worse problems arising. A flea-bite itself is slight – a flea consumes less than one drop of blood, once or twice a day – but the nuisance value of fleas lies in the fact that they will breed in vast numbers throughout the dog's surroundings. Even in mild cases, their presence can cause not only scratching but also severe irritation leading the dog to damage its own skin, and some individuals show an allergic reaction to the flea saliva which is injected in minute quantities when the flea bites. Fleas can also spread various diseases and canine parasites, including tapeworms, and puppies bitten by fleas may suffer from anaemia, so control of fleas will help to protect your dog from unpleasant consequences. In addition, fleas are likely to move on to the human members of the family!

The dog can be treated with proprietary aerosol sprays or powders, taking care to follow instructions and remembering that not all preparations are safe for puppies or nursing bitches. Insecticidal shampoos and soaps are valuable in severe cases. Flea collars, impregnated with insecticidal compounds, are obtainable and long-acting, but are not completely reliable, and some animals may show an allergic reaction to them.

It is vital to treat the dog's surroundings as well as the animal itself, as fleas typically lay their eggs away from their host – and a single female flea may lay up to 800 eggs in her lifetime! The dog's bed and bedding should be washed about every three weeks. Regular vacuuming around the home will do much to remove flea eggs except for those close to the walls; it may be necessary to spray such areas, and your veterinarian will be able to provide a spray for use on carpets and furniture. In a really severe outbreak, a pest control agency or, in some areas, the local authority pest control office can be contacted to treat the house.

Other pets in the household should not be neglected. Fleas can be transferred between dogs and cats, so any cats sharing the same household will need simultaneous treatment, bearing in mind the fact that certain preparations used for dogs are unsafe for cats. When spraying the house against fleas, ensure that other pets such as fish are removed or adequately covered before and after treatment to avoid inadvertent poisoning.

■ TICKS Ticks are blood-sucking, wingless insects easily picked up in long grass. They are common in rural areas, especially where sheep are prevalent, but animals such as hedgehogs may carry them into urban gardens. Ticks bury their heads into the dog's skin and, since they are immobile, may be mistaken for small cysts, although on close examination the legs can be seen close to the skin.

Great care should be taken when removing ticks, as it is easy to pull off the body and leave the head embedded in the skin, where a sore is likely to develop. You can loosen their grip by dabbing them with alcohol, or with grease such as petroleum jelly or butter, and after a few moments remove them with tweezers. However, it is probably safer to kill them first by spraying them directly with a veterinary flea spray – they will shrivel up and drop off, or can be pulled off easily, complete with head. Any retained mouthparts should be removed with a sterilized needle.

Ticks do cause a dog some irritation, but the major threat they pose to canine health stems from the fact that they can transmit serious protozoal diseases. They do not themselves usually affect humans.

■ MITES Various mites can affect dogs, with skin mites giving rise to the condition commonly referred to as mange. The mite *Sarcoptes scabei* lives and reproduces in the skin, causing considerable local irritation. The incidence of infection is highest in young dogs, and often starts as red patches around the inside of the thighs and the neighbouring regions. Loss of hair may also occur around the eyes, and scabs, with an odour reminiscent of mouse urine, appear on the body. This is a highly contagious disease which can cause scabies in children. Infection is normally confirmed by a skin scraping carried out by a veterinarian. Infected dogs should be isolated and prolonged treatment will be needed to eradicate these parasites.

Another form of mange, usually associated with short-haired dogs such as the Dachshund, is caused by *Demodex canis*. Infections of this sort are known as follicular mange, as the mites actually live in the hair follicles, causing hair loss and inflammation. Over a period of time the skin will thicken and pustules form as the follicles become infected with bacteria, and the bacterial infection may in turn lead to a generalized illness.

RIGHT: *Persistent scratching can be symptomatic of a variety of skin disorders. Fleas are a common source of irritation and their presence can be detected by a careful examination of the dog's coat. Treatment is essential to prevent the dog from injuring itself.*

Demodex mites are acquired early in life, transmitted from the dam to her puppies, but actual symptoms may not appear until much later. The infection can be confirmed by means of skin scrapings, but the mites are often harder to detect, since they invade deeper into the skin. Treatment is difficult and prolonged, and antibiotics are needed to overcome any bacterial infection. Bitches suffering from *Demodex* should never be used for breeding.

Another mite causing problems is *Cheyletiella parasitivorax*, which can be contracted from other animals such as rabbits. This mite lives on the surface of the skin, causing irritation and a build-up of scurf along the back. As with other mite infections, it can be detected by skin scrapings and requires veterinary treatment with an appropriate shampoo preparation.

Most mites remain in close proximity to their hosts throughout their life cycles, but the harvest mite, *Trombicula autumnalis*, is an exception. The adult form, resembling a small red spider, is free-living; it is the larval form which is parasitic and will attach itself to the dog's skin, typically between the toes, causing intense irritation and upon inspection minute clusters of orange-red dots may be seen. Treatment with an insecticidal shampoo will overcome the problem, although infestation may recur.

Mite infections of the ear are also extremely common. The ear mite, *Otodectes cynotis*, inhabits the ear canal, where it can cause severe irritation and long-standing infections. If a dog rubs its ears repeatedly, they should be examined with a torch; the irritation may arise from a grass seed lodged in the ear, but ear mites are usually betrayed by an accumulation of dark brown wax in the ear canal, with a characteristic acrid smell. Ear mites should be taken seriously and veterinary advice sought. The veterinarian will prescribe ear drops to kill off the mites; if prompt action is not taken, infection may spread from the ear canal into the tympanic cavity, causing not only deafness but also damage to the vestibular apparatus, affecting the sense of balance. There is also a risk that the dog's persistent scratching can rupture blood vessels in the ear, causing a painful blood-filled swelling called a haematoma, which will probably need surgical treatment.

▌ LICE Lice are occasionally seen, most commonly on puppies. The adult louse, another wingless insect, lays its eggs and attaches them to the hairs – the small white eggs are often visible and are called nits. Infection can occur by direct contact from dog to dog, or via shared grooming implements. Lice are very fussy about the species of host they choose and those found on the dog cannot infest human hair. The whole of the life cycle is spent on the host, so that regular treatment of the dog should clear the problem.

LEFT: *Insecticidal shampoos developed especially for dogs are a valuable means of controlling external parasites such as fleas and lice. They may also have a residual effect, preventing reinfection for several days. All such shampoos must be used as directed; subsequent rinsing may not be advised in some cases.*

LEFT: *Regular inspection of your dog's coat for parasites is recommended, and as a preventative measure, it is a good idea to dust your dog at least twice a year with a reputable anti-parasitic dusting powder obtained from your veterinarian. It is important to treat the animal's bed and bedding at the same time.*

RIGHT: *Mange can be very difficult to treat successfully, especially if, as in the case of Demodex, the mites are located deep within the hair follicles. This particular mite is typically associated with Dachshunds.*

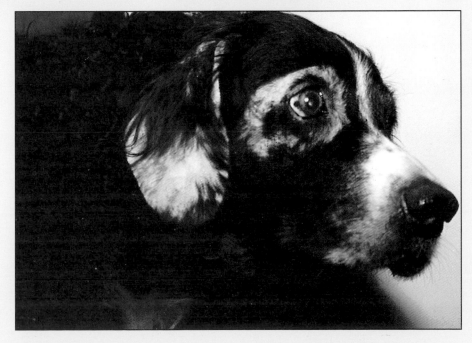

LIFE CYCLE OF THE ROUNDWORM

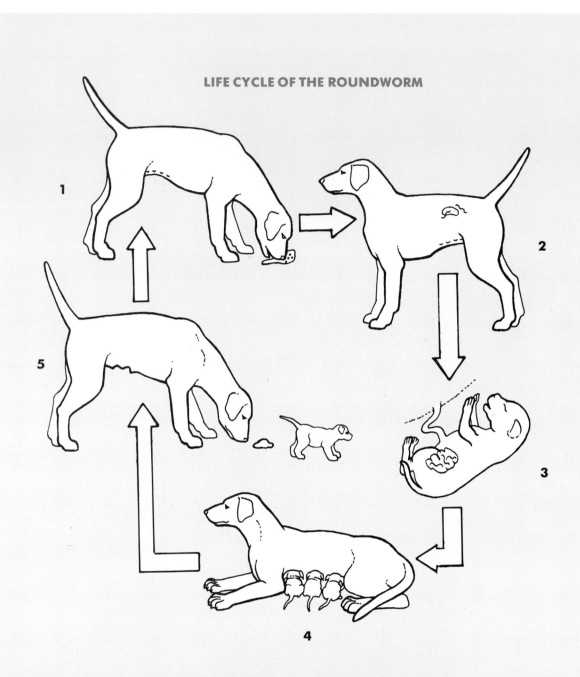

The embryonated infective eggs or larvae of the dog roundworm, Toxocara canis, *are ingested by the dog (1), and migrate to the body tissues (2) such as the kidneys. Unfortunately, the larvae unusually enter the tissues of developing foetuses (3) and localize in their intestines, being activated by pregnancy. After the birth of the puppies the larvae can also migrate into the puppies' systems and infect them through their mother's milk (4). The worms mature, passing eggs in the puppies' faeces which are consumed by the mother and can reinfect her (5). Alternatively, larvae which fail to establish themselves and are passed out in the faeces may find another host and begin producing eggs. The eggs are not immediately infective, but need a short period outside the body to mature.*

INTERNAL PARASITES

Dogs may be infested by a number of internal parasites. Some of these are a serious health hazard, while others have only minor debilitating effects upon the dog, although even the latter need to be tackled to prevent a heavy infestation or increased vulnerability to other problems. Worming treatments, therefore, should be a regular part of your dog's life from the age of about four weeks and throughout its lifespan, not only to safeguard the dog's health but to protect humans from the risk of infestation, especially vital in a home with young children.

Check with your veterinarian on the recommended working routine for your pet. You can obtain deworming preparations from a pet shop without prescription, but because worming is so important it makes sense to utilize your vet's specialist knowledge. For most adult dogs half-yearly dosing will suffice, although your vet may recommend more frequent treatment in some circumstances, for example if you have young children in your home or if your dog is particularly likely to be exposed to infection. Puppies and young dogs will also require more frequent dosing.

■ **ROUNDWORMS** Roundworms are very common in dogs, especially puppies. They may be vomited or passed in the stools, and look like lengths of white thread. The eggs are shed in the stool, but they are so small that they are not visible to the naked eye; your pet may well have roundworms without your knowing.

Roundworms can be passed on directly without the need for an intermediate host. The immature worms, called larvae, lie dormant in the tissues of the pregnant bitch and infect puppies by passing into the milk, ensuring that a large proportion of puppies become infected before they are weaned. The larvae develop into worms in the bowel, and the worms shed eggs into the stool, where these develop into larvae ready to infect a new host.

Since roundworms can cause such problems as potbelly, tummy upsets, intestinal obstruction and even lung damage, it is important to treat all puppies regularly against them. Your veterinarian will be able to supply you with a suitable drug. Breeding bitches should always be wormed approximately four weeks before the puppies are due to be born; this cannot destroy larvae dormant in the bitch's tissues, but will reduce the infestation. The pups themselves must be dosed regularly from the age of four weeks. Adult dogs are less likely to come to harm through harbouring roundworms, but an annual worming will do the dog no harm and prevent the build-up of serious infestation.

One species of roundworms, *Toxocara canis*, can employ humans as intermediate hosts and presents a slight but

RIGHT: *The dog tapeworm,* Dipylidium caninum, *uses the flea or louse as an intermediate host. It sheds eggs that pass out in faeces and are eaten by fleas or lice, and the dog infects or reinfects itself by eating these parasites.*

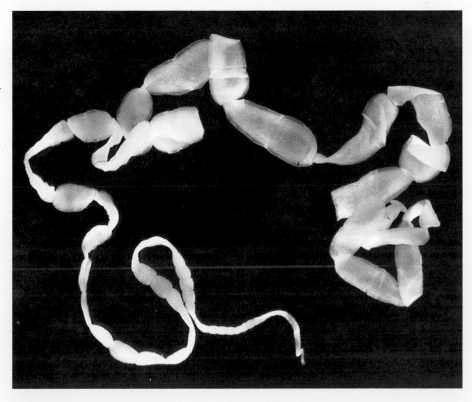

nevertheless real danger to human health if ingested. The larvae that hatch from the eggs migrate from the intestine to various organs such as the brain, liver and eyes. The life cycle cannot be completed in humans, but fits and blindness can result from this migration, known as 'visceral larval migrans'. Although such cases are rare, to neglect regular worming of your dog creates an unnecessary risk to humans.

■ **TAPEWORMS** A significant number of dogs are infested with tapeworms. These parasites take their name from their long flat ribbon-like appearance, although on examination it can be seen that the 'tape' is divided into segments. The adult tapeworm has hooks and suckers on its head to attach it to the wall of the bowel where it feeds on the food that the host is digesting. Mature segments break off from the end of the adult worm and are shed in the stool, sometimes adhering around the dog's anus. They resemble grains of rice and can sometimes be seen to move. These segments contain tapeworm eggs, which have to pass through an intermediate host, such as a flea, before they can infect another dog.

The most common tapeworm is *Dipylidium canium*, which uses fleas or lice as intermediate hosts; a dog contracts the infection if it ingests one of these parasites. Other tapeworms adopt vertebrates such as rabbits or sheep as intermediate hosts, and a dog can be infected by eating raw meat containing tapeworm cysts.

Tapeworms do not usually cause serious disease, but can lead to a noticeable loss of condition and may cause stomach pain, mild diarrhoea and possible anal irritation. Owners often notice an infestation because the segments are seen in the dog's faeces or around its anus. Tapeworm can be more resistant to treatment than roundworm, and it is best to obtain a suitable preparation from your veterinarian, together with an insecticidal spray to clear any fleas which could act as intermediate hosts to the parasite.

■ **OTHER WORMS** There are a number of other worms which can infect dogs, some of which are more likely to be encountered in kennelled animals such as racing greyhounds. Lungworms (*Filaroides osleri*) form nodules close to where the trachea divides to enter the lungs, causing a partial blockage of the airways; a dry cough during exercise is a common symptom. The tracheal worm (*Capillaria plica*) produces similar symptoms. Whipworms (*Trichuris vulpis*) affect a significant proportion of racing greyhounds; they localize in the appendix, causing intermittent diarrhoea.

Hookworms are potentially much more dangerous. Larvae can enter the body through the mouth or through the feet. The *Uncinaria* species localize in the feet, where they cause severe irritation, but the *Ancylostoma* hookworms migrate to the host's intestine where, feeding on blood, they can cause anaemia and severe debility which may prove fatal if left untreated. Affected dogs may require blood transfusions before they can be wormed safely. The effects of *Uncinaria* in the gut are less severe, but large numbers may cause diarrhoea.

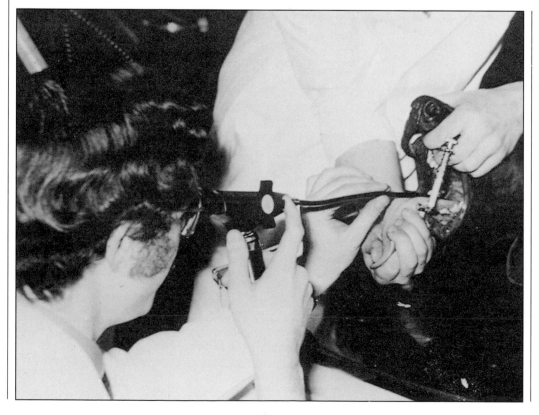

LEFT: *A fibre-optic endoscope can be used to examine a dog's throat and airways. This instrument is used to detect the presence of parasites such as lungworms, as well as to diagnose other disorders.*

LEFT: *Children are particularly vulnerable to some diseases, such as worms transmitted via the eggs of* Toxocara canis *in the dogs' faeces. However, the benefits of dog ownership far outweigh the small, but significant risk of infection, which can be considerably reduced by maintaining good measures of hygiene. Regular deworming treatements for the dog are strongly recommended, and children should be taught to wash their hands after touching the dog prior to a meal, and not to allow the dog to lick their faces.*

The heartworm (*Dirofilaria imminitis*) occurs in the warmer parts of the world, including Australia. It is transmitted by biting insects, typically mosquitoes; because it infests the host's blood vessels very close to the heart and pulmonary artery, treatment of heartworms *in situ* is dangerous, so regular preventative dosing of dogs in countries where this parasite occurs is recommended.

The most notorious worm affecting dogs is undoubtedly the giant kidney worm (*Dioctophyma renale*), which does not occur in Britain or Australia but is endemic in many other parts of the world, including parts of the United States. It is usually spread from raw fish. It is remarkable for its size – females may be 40in (100cm) long – and for its drastic effects upon its host. It localizes almost exclusively in the right kidney, which it gradually destroys over a period of time, and the only treatment is surgical removal of the affected organ.

▌ PROTOZOAL INFECTIONS Protozoa are microscopic organisms, some of which are parasitic upon the dog, causing various diseases. They are widely distributed, but cause disease more frequently in warmer areas of the world. Leishmaniasis, for example, is a disorder carried in the blood, like *babesiosis*, which occurs particularly in Mediterranean countries and may be transmitted from dogs to humans by insect bites. Other protozoa can affect the intestinal tract predominantly, causing diarrhoea, particularly in puppies. Such diseases are often referred to as coccidosis.

Another common protozoal illness, toxoplasmosis, can give rise to a much wider range of symptoms, and needs to be confirmed by laboratory tests. The dog only acts as intermediate host for this parasite, the final host being the cat; humans cannot acquire the infection from dogs, and cats only become infected if they consume an infected dog. The majority of cases of *Toxoplasma* in dogs can be traced back to the consumption of infected meat containing the toxoplasmosis cysts. A large number of dogs possess antibodies to *Toxoplasma*, which show that they have been infected, but have never exhibited clinical signs. There is a danger in pregnant bitches that this protozoan will cross the placenta, and cause defects in the puppies.

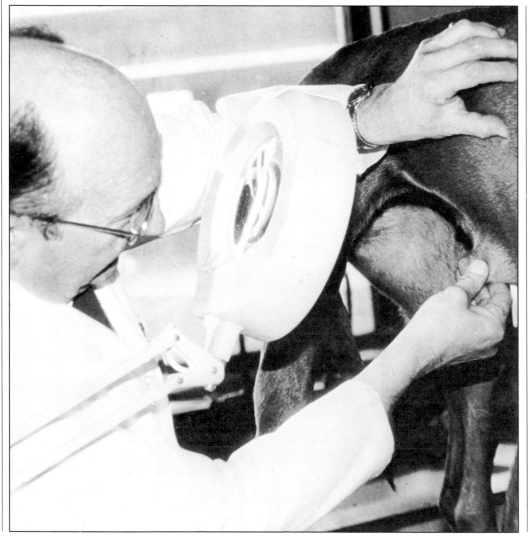

LEFT: *Here a veterinary dermatologist is examining a Great Dane, using an illuminated magnifying glass for a closer view of the skin and hair. Skin scrapings may also be taken for diagnostic purposes.*

SKIN DISORDERS

The condition of the dog's skin and fur is a good indicator of its health – poor health will be reflected in the coat. The regular grooming session provides the opportunity to check the coat over for parasites, balding patches or irritation of the skin. Such disorders are easily visible on short-coated dogs, but in long-haired breeds will usually, be covered by the coat in the early stages and only discovered by careful inspection. Many skin disorders found in the dog are caused by parasites, for example mange, while some are symptoms of other disorders, such as Cushing's Syndrome.

Some skin problems may be caused by an allergy, perhaps to a certain food, perhaps a sensitivity to flea bites, although it is not always easy to discover the predisposing agent; the condition may respond to treatment with anti-histamines. Eczema, creating severe irritation, is not uncommon and has a number of possible causes including dietary deficiencies, allergies and hormonal imbalance, which should be investigated by the veterinarian. Baldness, with the hair falling out in patches, may indicate a hormonal deficiency requiring treatment. Bald patches may also indicate the presence of ringworm, which is highly contagious and can be transmitted to humans.

RINGWORM

Ringworm, despite its name, is not caused by a worm but by a fungus which grows on the skin and hairs. Characteristically, it causes circular dry scaly or scabby patches on the skin, with hair breaking off around the circumference of the site. The dog's hairs become brittle and break off easily.

It is important to identify and treat cases of ringworm, as the condition is easily transmitted to humans either by handling an infected animal or from its environment. Diagnosis is confirmed by means of a special light known as a Wood's lamp, which shows the fungus up as fluorescent green in a darkened room. Specific antibiotic therapy, probably using the antibiotic *griseofulvin*, will be necessary, but this cannot be given safely to pregnant bitches for fear of causing foetal damage. A course of treatment will last at least a month.

The dog's environment will require treatment as well as the animal itself, as fungal spores will have contaminated its surroundings, where they may persist for a year or more. Particular care should be taken to disinfect its bed and grooming tools; alcohol or disinfectants of the iodoform type are effective against the spores. Any other animals, particularly cats, belonging to the household should be tested, as they may have been infected, although the symptoms are not generally as obvious in cats.

EYE DISORDERS

Disorders of the eye may be inherited conditions, such as progressive retinal atrophy (PRA), deformities of the eyelids, hereditary cataracts or narrow tear ducts; they may be the result of injury or infection; or they may arise from old age – old dogs may suffer from deteriorating sight, just as old people may.

Regrettably, inherited defects of the eye are associated with certain breeds. Reputable dog breeders are striving to rid their breeds of these problems by testing programmes and by withdrawing affected dogs from breeding programmes, but the complete eradication of any inherited trait is a long-term and far from easy task. Anyone purchasing a puppy of a breed known to carry such an inherited weakness should seek confirmation before purchase that

ABOVE: *An opthalmoscope enables a veterinarian to detect any eye problems early on, noting any changes in the retina at the back of the eye which may herald the onset of the condition known as progressive retinal atrophy (PRA).*

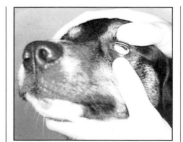

RIGHT: *The third eyelid can be seen at the corner of the eye, nearest the nose. It should not be confused with the white sclera, which forms part of the eyeball itself.*

RIGHT: *A seriously injured eye may need to be surgically removed by the veterinarian. The wound is closed with stitches, which are removed after a week to ten days.*

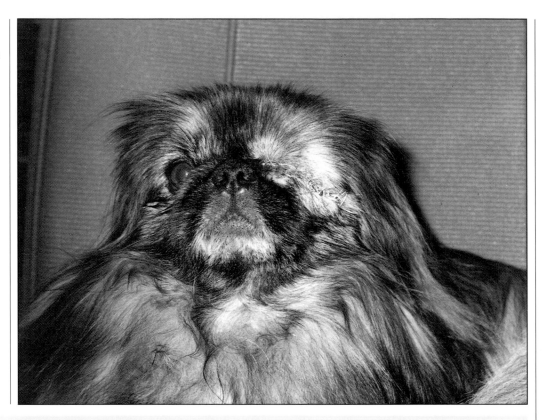

ANATOMY OF A DOG'S EYE

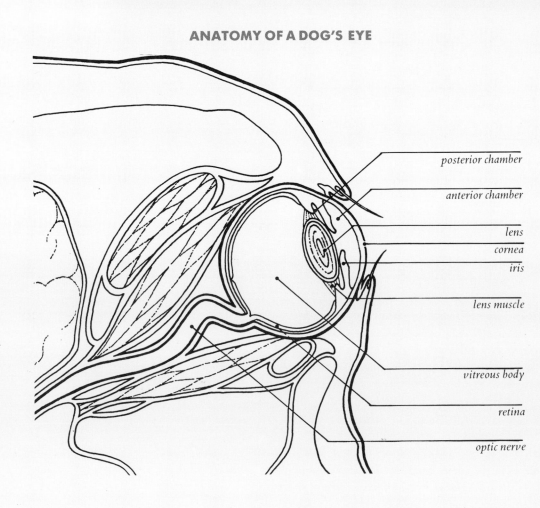

posterior chamber

anterior chamber

lens

cornea

iris

lens muscle

vitreous body

retina

optic nerve

220

the breeder is taking positive action to avoid perpetuating this in his or her kennels.

In addition to obvious defects, some breeds are predisposed by the requirements of the breed standard itself towards certain vulnerabilities of the eye. To name but a couple of examples, the Bloodhound's heavily wrinkled face, when over-emphasised, produces bad eyesight and deformity of the eyelids, and the very short face of the Pekingese makes the large round eyes vulnerable at the best of times; again, this feature can be exaggerated, with bulging eyes which are easily dislocated. Whilst there are very many sound, healthy pedigree dogs, it is important to be aware, when buying a puppy, that taking care to avoid strains with exaggerated show points can save a great deal of heartbreak and veterinary expense in the future.

Perhaps the most significant of inherited defects is progressive retinal atrophy. As its name implies, this is a progressive deterioration of the cells of the retina at the back of the eye where the image impinges. The condition can be generalized, affecting the whole retina, in breeds such as Poodles and Golden Retrievers, or confined to the central area as in Collies, Labradors and Briards. Affected dogs will usually show no signs of the problem in puppyhood but gradually develop symptoms beginning with poor night vision, the dog bumping into objects when light is poor; even in the daytime the pupils will be dilated widely. Deterioration of the sight continues, leading eventually to total blindness.

The characteristic changes in the eye can be detected by a veterinarian using an ophthalmoscope to view the retina directly. Sadly, there is no treatment possible. Breeds prone to PRA have eye testing schemes, and it is important to buy stock from a strain proved to be clear of this defect. If you suspect that your dog is having difficulty in seeing, consult your veterinarian.

Inherited deformities of the eyelids are entropion and ectropion. When the eyelids are turned in towards the eye, the condition is described as entropion. The inturned eyelashes irritate the surface of the eye, and can cause severe damage; the condition requires surgical correction. This is encountered most often in certain breeds including Chows, Golden and Labrador Retrievers, Setters and St Bernards.

The reverse condition, with the eyelids turned out away from the eye exposing the conjunctiva, is described as ectropion, and occurs most often in Spaniels and Bloodhounds. Again, surgery is required. Another problem that may be encountered in breeds such as the American Cocker Spaniel and Griffon Bruxellois is *distichiasis*, a double row of eyelashes, usually on the upper eyelid, which again irritate the surface of the eye and require surgical treatment.

In certain breeds such as Poodles, the tear ducts are too narrow to permit the tear fluids, which keep the surface of the eye moist, to drain away normally, and these run down the face, causing permanent weeping. This leaves a stain on the fur, especially obvious against a pale coat; if care is not taken to keep the face dry, sores may develop, especially in breeds such as the Pekingese where the face wrinkles retain the moisture. Mild cases merely require the use of preparations to remove the tear stains from the fur; these

*There are a large number of inherited problems which occur amongst dogs, often linked with particular breeds. For example, breeds which may suffer from the eyelid malformations termed entropion and ectropion which cause discomfort through to severe pain and requires surgical correction, include the Boston Terrier (**ABOVE LEFT**), the St Bernard (**ABOVE RIGHT**),*

*and the Bulldog (**RIGHT**). Other serious problems found in a number of breeds includes progressive retinal atrophy (PRA), causing blindness and hip dysplasia causing lameness. The existence of these problems is no reason to avoid buying a pedigree puppy but a very important reason for seeking out a responsible and knowledgeable breeder.*

can be purchased from pet stores. In severe cases, surgery may be necessary.

Another hereditary defect, found in Wire-haired Fox Terriers and Staffordshire Bull Terriers, is luxation, or displacement of the eye lens, requiring veterinary attention.

The colour merle, typically found in Collies, carries a genetic eye problem. Merle dogs often have white or blue irises to the eye, usually termed 'wall eyes'; they themselves have normal vision, but two merles should never be mated together as some of the offspring will be born with undeveloped eyes and will have to be put to sleep. This defect can be avoided by always mating merles to other colours.

Hereditary eye defects are fortunately restricted to a minority of dogs; however, dogs just as much as people are susceptible to eye infections such as conjunctivitis. Symptoms of eye disorders often include watering and reddening of the eyes, with frequent blinking. The dog may paw at the eye in an attempt to relieve irritation. Watering eyes may indicate an allergic reaction, an infection or a foreign body in the eye. Eye preparations prescribed for infections need to be applied frequently, several times daily, since the tear fluids will rapidly wash the treatment

out of the eye. Any discharge from the eyes should be taken seriously as it may be a symptom of a general infection.

If a foreign body such as a grass seed is lodged in the eye, it may be possible to wash it out with a solution of salt water (1 teaspoon of salt to 1 pint of cooled boiled water); if there is any difficulty in removing the object, or if it has penetrated the surface of the eye, seek veterinary aid rather than risk causing further damage. Injury to the eye can result when a dog scratches its eye on a twig or any sharp object. If there is any sign of blood, emergency treatment will be needed. Any injury to the eye should be treated by the veterinarian to prevent the risk of permanent scarring

RIGHT: *Collies are prone to certain inherited eye defects, including progressive retinal atrophy and collie eye anomaly. Responsible breeders are attempting to eradicate these problems by careful vetting programmes.*

to the surface of the eye, or of infection which could cause loss of sight.

Damage to the cornea, the surface of the eye, can cause a painful condition known as *keratitis*. The damaged cornea appears opaque or bluish. An ulcer can form at the site if the infection is left untreated, and this will be difficult to heal successfully and is likely to leave a scar. Dogs with prominent eyes such as Pugs and Pekingese are most vulnerable to corneal injury.

These dogs can also suffer from prolapse of the eyeball, in which the eye is forced out of its shallow socket by fighting or even by rough handling around the neck. Although this looks horrific, it can be corrected. The damaged eye should be protected with a damp, clean pad of cloth and the dog restrained while immediate veterinary assistance is sought. The veterinarian will replace the eye and normally stitch the eyelids together to hold it in place while it is healing; if action is taken fast enough the sight of the eye can often be saved. If, at worst, the eye needs to be surgically removed, the injury will normally heal well; although it is distressing for the owner, the dog will recover with remarkable speed and adapt well to the loss of an eye.

An abnormally bulging eyeball, often with a clouding of the surface, indicates the onset of *glaucoma*, a condition in which fluid builds up in the eye. Immediate surgery to drain this fluid may save the eye, but in some cases the eye will have to be removed.

Other eye complaints can be encountered more often in older dogs, notably cataracts, which cause opacity of the lens, giving the eye a whitish appearance. Hereditary cataracts are associated with some breeds, including Golden Retrievers and German Shepherd Dogs. Increasing clumsiness is often the first sign of a deterioration in vision, and the eye will appear clouded. If there is any reason to suspect that a dog is losing its sight, a veterinarian should be consulted without delay. Cataracts may be caused by diabetes, in which case treatment of the disease may halt their progression. In some cases the veterinarian may recommend removal of the lens to give a partial return of vision.

Most dogs will adapt well to blindness, since the sense of sight is less important to them than it is to humans and they can rely to a greater extent upon the senses of hearing and smell. If otherwise healthy, a blind dog can continue to enjoy life. However, it will require special consideration from its owner, who needs to recognize that in familiar surroundings the dog will cope well, but in strange places it will tend to bump into furniture and other objects.

EAR DISORDERS

Disorders of the ear include deafness and infections. Deafness may be inherited or may result from infection or the deterioration process of old age. Deafness may not be immediately detected, since a deaf dog will respond to the stimulus of other senses; however, it may appear stupid or disobedient, since it will not respond to the commands it cannot hear, and may bark continually.

Hereditary deafness usually occurs in white animals, the lack of pigmentation being genetically associated in many cases with an abnormal formation of the cochlea in the inner ear, where sound waves are received. In dogs this is commonly associated with white Bull Terriers. No treatment is possible, and dogs suffering from this condition should not be bred from. Deaf dogs can lead a normal life, but require particular care in training as they cannot respond to spoken commands and must be taught to look for hand signals.

Acquired deafness may result from ear infections or accidents, including the ingestion of lead poisons. It may be total or partial, irreversible or temporary. Like elderly people, ageing dogs often become partially or totally deaf and will require special consideration from their owners. Most will adapt well, although some individuals may appear distressed by the loss of vocal contact with their owners.

Ear infections are not uncommon, especially in breeds such as Spaniels whose long, heavy ears close off the ear canals to create an ideal environment for bacteria and other micro-organisms. Regular gentle cleaning of the outer ear is recommended to reduce the risk of infection, although it is important never to probe further than you can see. Signs of infection include holding the head to one side, repeated head shaking and rubbing of the ears; infected ears often smell unpleasant as well, and there may be an accumulation of wax.

Ear infections should never be neglected, as irreversible damage to the hearing may result, and if infection spreads to the middle ear the sense of balance will also be affected. If the dog shows a loss of balance veterinary attention is urgently needed. Irritation in the ear may also cause the dog to injure the tissue of the ear flap, leading to a swelling called a *haematoma* which may require surgical correction to prevent permanent disfigurement.

The major problem in treating ear infections is that the cause is rarely straightforward; bacteria, fungi and ear mites may all be involved, and frequent use of medication tends to lead to antibiotic resistance. The veterinarian will need to examine the ears with an auroscope to decide on the best course of treatment, and this usually needs to be maintained over a relatively long period of time to prevent recurrence. In persistent, severe cases, surgery will probably be the only solution, with an operation called an *aural resection*, to open up the vertical part of the ear canal. This will not be noticeable when the ear flap is in its usual position.

Foreign bodies, such as grass seeds, sometimes enter the ear. If a dog suddenly appears to have great pain in its ear, shaking its head violently and holding the affected side downwards, this is more likely to be caused by a foreign body than by an infection. Probing inside the ear may force the object further in, so in most cases of this type veterinary advice should be sought.

DENTAL PROBLEMS

The teeth of some dogs rapidly accumulate a brownish deposit called tartar which builds up on the teeth, pushing on the gums and making them sore and inflamed (a condition termed *gingivitis*). If the condition is left untreated, bacteria gain access to the root of the tooth, causing a painful abscess and loosening the tooth, so that it will have to be removed. The first sign of dental problems is often bad breath, although this may be a symptom of other problems, notably kidney disease. The dog may dribble, and will have difficulty in eating. Removing the tartar by scaling the teeth (in severe cases, under anaesthetic) 'stops the rot' and allows the gums to heal. Any seriously damaged teeth will be pulled out at the same time. Subsequently further accumulations may be prevented by brushing the

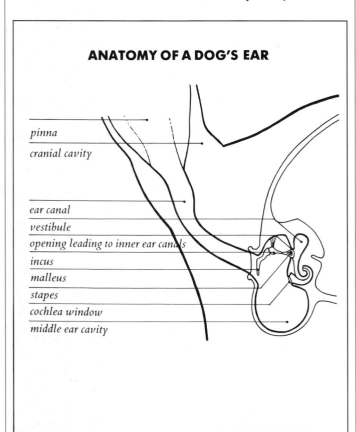

ANATOMY OF A DOG'S EAR

pinna

cranial cavity

ear canal

vestibule

opening leading to inner ear canals

incus

malleus

stapes

cochlea window

middle ear cavity

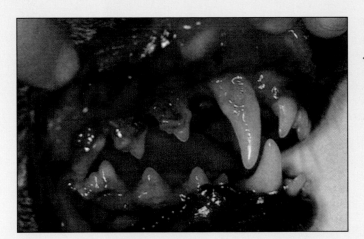

LEFT: *Dental problems such as the build-up of tartar which has led to gum disease tend to afflict dogs in the older age bracket. These teeth will have to be cleaned by a veterinarian, with the dog under anaesthetic.*

teeth weekly with a canine toothpaste, taking care to ensure that brushing does not make the gums bleed.

Cleaning a dog's teeth regularly will prevent the build-up of tartar, and puppies should be trained from the beginning to accept this treatment. A piece of dampened cottonwool, or a soft toothbrush, can be used to apply the toothpaste. Dental decay may be linked to diet; soft diets, based on home-prepared foods or on cans of dog food, tend to encourage the build-up of tartar on the teeth. A diet that exercises the teeth, including hard dog biscuits, can also delay the rate of build-up.

DIGESTIVE DISORDERS

Digestive disorders may be caused by the dog's diet, but may be a sign that something is wrong in the animal's system.

Diarrhoea and vomiting are symptoms associated with a variety of diseases rather than conditions in themselves, and may simply be a reaction to something the dog has eaten – dogs are scavengers by nature and not uncommonly will help themselves to something unsuited to their digestive systems.

Dogs vomit not infrequently, sometimes losing a meal, sometimes merely coughing up froth and bile. This is rarely real cause for concern. Vomiting may arise simply from bolting the meal too fast, from eating grass, or from having scavenged something unsuitable. Persistent vomiting, however, requires veterinary attention; possible causes include infection and even poisoning.

Similarly, diarrhoea may be a short-term reaction to a minor upset. Some dogs are sensitive to certain foodstuffs such as cows' milk. However, bacterial and viral diseases may give rise to diarrhoea, as may the presence of certain parasites, such as the protozoa *Coccidia*. Diarrhoea is often self-limiting if food is withheld for twenty-four hours and then small bland meals given for the next two or three days. However, if it persists it may indicate serious illness and veterinary advice should be sought. In the case of young puppies, veterinary aid should be obtained sooner because they can rapidly become seriously dehydrated.

Any trace of blood in the dog's stools suggests a digestive disorder in the lower part of the digestive tract, calling for veterinary treatment. Inflammation of the large bowel, known as *colitis*, will lead to faeces containing blood and with a jelly-like consistency because of their high mucous content. If the source of the bleeding is the small intestine, the blood will have been partially digested as it moved through the gut and will take on a reddish-brown appearance in the faeces.

Inflammation of the stomach itself, known as *gastritis*, is likely to be signalled by both vomiting and diarrhoea, as well as increased thirst. Food should be withheld, and veterinary attention obtained.

A serious problem, usually encountered in big, deep-chested dogs, is acute gastric dilatation, often linked with torsion. It can be caused by feeding the dog a heavy meal immediately before prolonged exercise. Gas builds up in the stomach, causing it to dilate, and then the organ can twist, leading to torsion. The dog becomes restless and tries to vomit. Its abdomen rapidly swells and signs of shock, such as profuse salivation and difficulty in breathing, are apparent. Immediate veterinary assistance is required for this condition, which otherwise will rapidly be fatal.

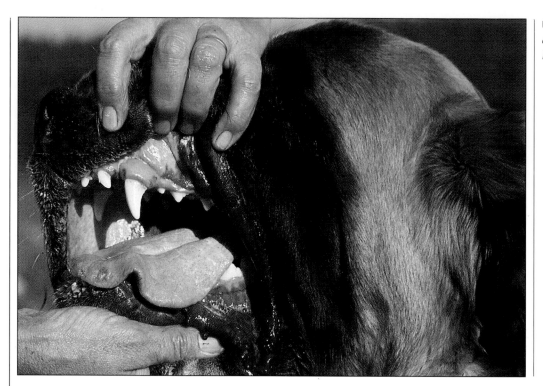

LEFT: *The bluish tinge on this dog's tongue is an indication of a kidney failure.*

URINARY DISORDERS

Some apparent problems of the urinary system are often behavioural in origin, such as a failure of house-training, the urge to territory marking, or submissive urination. These should be distinguished from genuine incontinence, the involuntary passing of urine, arising from a physical disorder.

Developmental defects may occasionally be responsible. The ureters normally run from each kidney, conveying urine for storage in the bladder. If one or both ureters link directly with the urethra, which leads from the bladder, or with the vagina, then urine cannot enter the bladder for storage but will be voided as soon as it is produced. Such 'ectopic' ureters can be corrected by surgery. The condition is most common in bitches, and usually becomes evident from the age of three months on.

Incontinence may sometimes occur as a sequel to spaying, and is a distinct risk if the operation is carried out when the bitch is too young. Such cases may respond to hormone treatment from the veterinarian.

Ascending infections result in *cystitis*, inflammation of the bladder, which causes frequent urination and requires antibiotic treatment.

In turn, an infection can be a predisposing factor in the development of bladder stones or *calculi*. The symptoms will depend on the part of the urinary tract where the blockage occurred. The dog will have difficulty in urinating and will show signs of pain; there may be blood in the urine. The veterinarian will probably need to examine the dog using a special contrast media X-ray technique to find the site of the problem. There are various options for treatment available, depending on the individual case. Some calculi may be washed through the tract or dislodged by means of a cannula, but occurrences in susceptible individuals are relatively common. A course of antibiotics may help to cure an underlying infection, but there can be a genetic susceptibility to urinary calculi, particularly in the case of Dalmatians, Dachshunds, Corgis and Basset Hounds.

Increased frequency of urination coupled with increased thirst is likely to indicate some degree of kidney failure, which will affect all dogs to a greater or lesser extent in old age, and may also arise in younger individuals as a result of infections such as infectious canine *hepatitis* and *leptospirosis*. Damage from these diseases at an early age will become more noticeable later in life.

Kidney failure is a progressive condition, and one of the first signs is foul-smelling breath; the dog may also show intermittent vomiting, decreased appetite and weight loss in the later stages. The body has a high reserve of functioning kidney tissue, but once the level falls to only 30 per cent of the total available, kidney or renal failure follows and the waste products of body metabolism that are normally filtered out of the body remain in the blood.

In order to diagnose the condition and assess its severity, your veterinarian is likely to want a urine sample for testing. This is most easily collected in a broad, flat saucer, and should then be transferred to a clean, dry screw-top container. Never use jars which have previously held jam, as traces of sugar are likely to remain in them and will interfere with the diagnosis.

In cases of chronic kidney failure, there is no effective curative treatment, but modification of the diet will improve the dog's state of health. The protein level of the diet needs to be reduced overall, while the protein itself must be of higher biological value in terms of its amino acid content. Eggs, for example, are a useful source of such protein.

Special canned foods are available from your veterinarian for dogs suffering from kidney failure, and their use is recommended. Water must be constantly available, and Vitamin B supplementation may also be required since these water-soluble compounds will be lost in increasing quantities via the kidneys. A deficiency of nicotinic acid will cause the tongue to turn blackish in colour, and this is a typical symptom of long-standing renal degeneration. Other changes, especially in the skeletal system, may occur in cases of chronic renal failure because a form of Vitamin D is synthesized in the kidneys and acts upon the intestines to regulate calcium absorption there, as well as exerting an influence on calcium stores within the body itself. A similar compound which stimulates the bone marrow also originates in the kidneys, and thus anaemia and resulting complications can also arise from kidney failure.

HEART DISEASE

Various congenital heart diseases can occur in puppies. In severe cases, puppies die shortly after birth. A puppy born with an incompetent heart valve will be low on energy and easily tired. It may be possible to correct the defect successfully by surgery, although the more elaborate equipment of a veterinary hospital may be necessary.

Heart disease may occur in older dogs. The four chambers of the heart are separated by valves, which may thicken in older dogs, causing blood to leak back into the previous chamber instead of being pushed forward. Several types of cardiac failure are recognized, and the symptoms depend upon which part of the heart is affected. If the left side is failing, the dog will be reluctant to take exercise, will tire rapidly and will have difficulty in breathing. Other typical symptoms are restlessness and prolonged bouts of coughing, especially at night. If it is the right side of the heart that is affected, this will lead to *oedema*, or build-up of fluid in the tissues, with an accumulation in the abdomen as well, known as *ascites*. Closer examination by a veterinarian will also reveal a swollen liver and spleen. In generalized heart failure, a combination of signs will be observed.

Once the condition has been diagnosed, it can be stabilized with drugs, and you should see an improvement in your dog's condition. The cardiac glycosides, of which digitalis is best-known, control the heart rate; by slowing its pace and improving its contractability, they increase cardiac output. Diuretic drugs remove excessive fluid and sodium salt from the blood via the kidneys and thus decrease the pressure on the heart itself. The initial dose of drugs will be higher than the maintenance dose, which will then be administered throughout the dog's life, especially if the dog is seriously ill. This may result in symptoms of toxicity such as vomiting. If you are concerned, contact your veterinarian.

Treatment will also entail modification of the dog's diet and lifestyle. It will need more rest to decrease the burden on the heart, and a diet low in salt is also recommended.

Occasionally dogs may suffer from *coronary thrombosis*, a blood clot forming in one of the main heart vessels. This may be fatal, but the dog may show the same symptoms as for valvular degeneration, perhaps crying out and losing consciousness. Treatment consists of the prescription of drugs to prevent the blood clotting and to slow down the circulation to decrease the strain on the heart.

RESPIRATORY DISEASES

There are several causes of respiratory disease. A common ailment affecting the trachea and bronchii of the lungs is *infectious tracheobronchitis*, commonly known as kennel cough from the fact that it is most likely to spread where large numbers of dogs congregate, as in boarding kennels, especially when ventilation is inadequate. It can be caused by a range of infectious organisms, commonly canine adenovirus type 2 (CAV-2), parainfluenza virus and the bacterium, *Bordetella bronchoseptica*.

The incubation period for kennel cough can be as long as 10 days, and the commonest symptom is a dry cough which can become paroxysmal. The cough occurs whenever the throat region over the trachea is touched. There may also be an accompanying thick nasal discharge. The illness is not life-threatening, and normally resolves itself in three to five weeks, but if it is left untreated secondary infections may develop which may leave the dog with permanently impaired breathing; antibiotics to prevent such infections are therefore recommended. An effective vaccine against the main causes of kennel cough is now available, and is recommended if a dog is being kennelled or attending shows. This vaccine may be given intra-nasally (sprayed up the nostrils) in some cases, rather than injected.

Coughing may arise from a number of causes, including tonsillitis, bronchitis, tuberculosis, asthma or even a foreign body lodged in the throat. Any persistent cough should be considered a warning sign, and the coughing dog should be isolated from other dogs and taken to the veterinarian. Because many coughs are highly contagious, your veterinarian will probably advise you not to bring your animal into the waiting room where it could infect others but to make a special appointment.

ANAL GLANDS IMPACTION

The dog has a pair of scent sacs, commonly called the anal glands, located inside the anus which produce a secretion which is deposited on the faeces as a scent marker. When the anal glands fail to empty properly, the resulting blockage causes the dog considerable discomfort.

The first sign of a blockage is likely to be the dog dragging its hindquarters along the ground in an attempt to relieve the irritation, and biting at the anal region. Inspection of this region will show a painful swelling of one or both anal glands. If the glands are left untreated, defecation will become painful and local infections are likely to develop, causing abscesses; in severe cases open channels (fistulae) may develop around the anal ring, and these are very difficult to heal successfully.

The blocked glands need to be emptied by a veterinarian, who will probably be willing to show you how to do this yourself should the need arise. It may be necessary to wash the sacs out with a salt solution and to give antibiotic treatment to reduce the risk of infection. Blockage may well recur, although increasing the roughage content of the diet by adding bran may help to prevent this. A regular check of the anal glands when grooming will enable you to spot any swelling and soreness before the condition becomes chronic. Although emptying the glands manually is not difficult, if carried out too frequently it may cause permanent damage and, in severe cases, surgical removal of the sacs may be advisable.

HIP DYSPLASIA

In a normal hip joint, the head of the thigh bone, or femur, fits snugly into the socket of the pelvis. In the case of a dog with hip dysplasia, the head of the femur may be abnormal and fail to fit in place correctly, or the pelvic socket may be too shallow to hold it.

Hip dysplasia is an inherited condition to which certain breeds, including German Shepherd Dogs and English Setters, are prone. As with other hereditary faults, conscientious breeders are trying to eradicate it from their stock, and buyers of puppies from affected breeds should take care only to purchase from kennels where breeding stock has been screened.

The condition will not be apparent in the young puppy. The first signs, lameness and reluctance to rise from the sitting position, may be manifested from about four to six

HIP DYSPLASIA

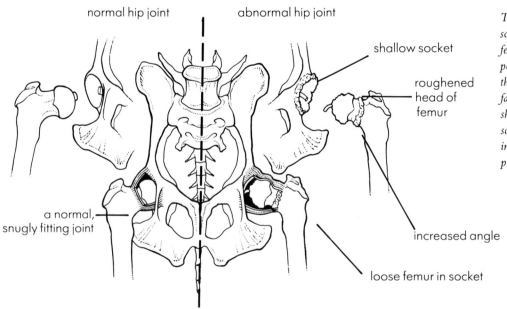

normal hip joint

abnormal hip joint

shallow socket

roughened head of femur

a normal, snugly fitting joint

increased angle

loose femur in socket

The hip joint is of the ball and socket type, with the head of the femur fitting into the socket of the pelvis. Hip dysplasia occurs when the development of the joint is faulty, or the socket is abnormally shallow. Breeding stock should be screened by radiography for this inherited problem to avoid its perpetuation.

months and tend to worsen progressively as the dog's increasing weight puts more strain upon the joint. The degree of dysplasia varies. Mild cases may merely manifest some lameness after exercise; other types can be surgically treated by operating upon the head of the femur or upon the thigh muscles. Severe cases, however, cannot be treated with any degree of success.

Another hereditary defect causing lameness is dislocation of the kneecap (luxation of the patella), associated with certain breeds and giving rise to lameness of the hind legs, typically appearing at about five months of age. Again, the degree to which the dog may be affected varies, but surgery may be necessary.

No dog or bitch with any degree of hip dysplasia, patella luxation or indeed any other inherited defect should ever be used for breeding, and in breeds where this problem is known to occur all breeding stock should be screened before any matings are planned.

METABOLIC DISORDERS

Metabolic disorders can sometimes be of acute onset, such as milk fever in a suckling bitch, although generally, these conditions tend to be more insidious and can be rather variable in their effects on the body.

DIABETES

Two forms of diabetes are recognized in the dog. The more common type is *diabetes mellitus*, or sugar diabetes, resulting from a deficiency of the hormone insulin, which is produced by the pancreas and stimulates cells to take up glucose present in the bloodstream. Insulin deficiency leaves the sugar to accumulate in the bloodstream, depriving the cells of this vital nutrient. Once a critical level is reached, glucose passes into the urine, giving it an unusually sweet and sickly smell, and increasing volumes are passed. Body tissues are broken down to meet the body's energy requirement, and this leads to weakness and weight loss over a period of time.

This disease is at least five times more common in bitches than dogs, and usually occurs after the age of five years. One of the more unexpected symptoms may be the formation of cataracts in the eyes. Blood-tests will confirm the disorder. In very mild cases, manipulation of the diet by eliminating carbohydrate (which will be converted to glucose) as much as possible, and feeding a relatively high level of protein, may be adequate. Otherwise insulin will probably have to be injected on a daily basis, and the dog's condition will have to be closely monitored through regular urine samples.

The other form of diabetes, *diabetes inspidus*, is much rarer. In this condition, there is a deficiency of the hormone known as ADH (anti-diuretic hormone), which acts on the kidney to control urine output. This deficiency leads to a greatly increased output of urine as water normally reabsorbed during its passage through the kidney is lost; consequently the dog will show greatly increased thirst. The most likely cause of this disease is a brain tumour. As with diabetes mellitus, the condition cannot be cured, but can be controlled by administering a synthetic form of the hormone to alleviate symptoms.

PANCREATIC INSUFFICIENCY

The pancreas is a vital organ, producing both hormones, such as insulin, and enzymes to help digest the food in the small intestine. In a case of pancreatic insufficiency, there is an inadequate output of enzymes, leading to an incomplete breakdown of food for absorption into the body. As a result, the food is excreted in a relatively undigested state in pale-coloured, loose faeces with a highly unpleasant odour. Since the dog is not obtaining adequate nourishment from its food, it loses weight over a period of time. Pancreatic insufficiency can be confirmed by laboratory tests.

Treatment consists of providing sufficient enzymes via the food itself, usually in the form of capsules or powders, to compensate for the deficiency. It may also help to add ox sweetbread (pancreas) to the diet, and some formulated rations are of particular value for dogs suffering from this complaint. Alternatively, increase the level of protein relative to that of carbohydrate and fat.

Pancreatic insufficiency seems to occur more commonly in certain breeds, such as the German Shepherd. Although treatment can improve the digestive process, and it is not difficult to cope with a dog suffering from this condition compared to one suffering from diabetes mellitus, many cases will not recover the lost weight and will remain thin.

ADRENAL DISORDERS

The adrenal glands lie close to the kidneys. The outer layer, known as the adrenal cortex, produces two major hormones, aldosterone and cortisol. Although the adrenal glands are small, they have widespread effects, and under- or over-production of these hormones cause significant disorders.

An abnormally low level of hormone production gives rise to Addison's Disease. This is more often seen in bitches than in male dogs, and the symptoms are particularly apparent after exercise. Vomiting and a loss of appetite result from a deficiency of cortisol, while a shortage of aldosterone leads to dehydration. Confirmation of the disease is by blood test. Once the condition has been diagnosed and stabilized, it is possible to provide synthetic forms of the hormones concerned, which will have to be administered throughout the rest of the dog's life to keep it in good health.

The reverse situation, an abnormally high level of

hormone production, results in Cushing's Syndrome. This may be caused by a disease of the glands themselves, or by a brain tumour. Under certain circumstances, the actual zone in the glands responsible for the production of the hormones may increase in size, and this will lead to an increase in synthesis. Symptoms are likely to include an increase in appetite and thirst, with a corresponding increase in urine production. In addition, there will be hair loss on both sides of the body. The abdomen will swell into a pot belly and the underlying muscles will weaken. Tests will be necessary to establish the precise cause of the condition. The prognosis is very poor if a brain tumour is responsible, but if it is the gland itself that is over-producing, some degree of treatment may be possible.

THYROID IMBALANCE

The thyroid glands, located in the neck, produce the hormones thyroxine and triidothyronine, which are important in controlling the level of body activity. If output

is depressed, dogs become sluggish, obese and very sensitive to cold surroundings. Other signs may include hair loss and a greasy skin. Supplementation of hormones will reverse these effects, but has to be given over a long period of time, although tablets are not expensive. A deficiency of dietary iodine can also lead to *hypothyroidism*; for this reason, some breeders use kelp (seaweed) powder as a general tonic. The Basenji appears to need relatively high levels of this mineral. Over-activity of the thyroid is a rarer condition in dogs, and generally results from a tumour of the thyroid glands.

DISORDERS OF THE NERVOUS SYSTEM

Fits occur occasionally, and are very alarming for the spectator. Without warning or previous symptoms, a dog will suddenly collapse on its side and its legs will start to move, as if it were running. Involuntary defecation and urination may occur, and the animal may froth at the mouth. After a minute or so, the dog will regain its feet, albeit often unsteadily, and will appear to be unharmed.

The cause of fits is variable and in some cases may never be established, although possible causes include poisoning, brain tumours and infections which affect the brain. They may also be caused by shock or by injury, either directly following a knock on the head, or as a delayed response days or weeks later. Puppies occasionally have fits as a result of dietary deficiency or a heavy infestation of worms, or even through teething problems.

In many cases the dog may be suffering from epilepsy, a condition which has been shown to be inheritable, and is sometimes described as *idiopathic epilepsy*. It is most common in the Cocker Spaniel, with seizures often beginning during the second year of life, although they can also occur earlier. Various drugs are available to control seizures, and it is important to follow the veterinarian's instructions. Because of the hereditary factor, a dog which suffers from epilepsy should not be used for breeding.

If your dog has a fit remove him to a quiet darkened room. During a fit, even the gentlest of dogs will not be in control of its actions and may bite, so it is best to throw a blanket over the animal before attempting to move it. Leave the dog quietly until the fit subsides and then seek veterinary advice. Normally the dog will recover from the fit quite quickly; if a fit lasts for more than ten minutes and shows no sign of subsiding, however, immediate veterinary attention should be sought.

RABIES

Rabies is the most serious disease affecting the nervous system, and the rabies virus can affect all warm-blooded species, including man. It has been eradicated in Great

LEFT: *Cushing's Syndrome is characterized by the dog losing hair evenly on both sides of the body, and gaining a pot-bellied appearance. It results from an abnormality of the adrenal glands, positioned close to the kidneys. Glandular disorders can have other widespread effects.*

ABOVE: *Rabies is caused by a virus and is usually transmitted in saliva. It is not necessary to be bitten to be infected by the virus, which can enter the body via a cut. In dogs, aggressive behaviour and a change in the voice are often the first signs of the disease.*

depending partly on the site on the body where the virus was introduced. From a leg, it enters the peripheral nervous system and moves to the central nervous system, giving rise to clinical symptoms. At first the dog's bark may sound different, and personality changes occur; the animal will not in every instance become aggressive immediately. Paralysis of the throat muscles follows, causing difficulty in swallowing. Infectious saliva drools from the mouth. Dogs do not exhibit the intense fear of water (hydrophobia) shown by human sufferers in the terminal stages of rabies. Instead, convulsions and finally a coma usually precede death.

Rabies can be transmitted not only by a bite but by the saliva of the infected animal, just before clinical symptoms appear, and this is clearly the most dangerous period for the owner. Any cuts on the hand, if contaminated by saliva, can provide access to the body for the virus. If you have the misfortune to be bitten by a dog that could have rabies, wash the cut immediately using alcohol, if available, or wash under running water and treat the wound with iodine. Contact your doctor immediately so that appropriate medical treatment can be arranged immediately to prevent the disease from developing; once symptoms are apparent, the likelihood of recovery is virtually zero. In areas where the disease is endemic, children in particular should be closely supervised.

Rabies at present is unlikely to be encountered in this country, but an illness that can produce similar symptoms is Aujesky's Disease, also known as pseudo rabies. The infection is most common in pigs, and dogs kept on pig farms, or those which may have eaten contaminated uncooked pork, are most at risk. The virus produces nervous symptoms; an affected dog often scratches and paws repeatedly at its face, which has led to the disease being termed 'mad itch'. Aggression towards humans and other creatures is not a feature of this disease. There is no cure.

OTHER DISORDERS

A dog which has recovered from distemper (see below) may be left with permanent damage to the central nervous system, causing a condition known as *chorea* in which the animal twitches and jerks uncontrollably; in severe cases it may develop fits and paralysis. Chorea is incurable. Mild cases may be ameliorated by veterinary treatment coupled with a careful diet to build up the animal's strength, but in severe cases euthanasia is the kindest answer.

Occasionally a nerve may be paralyzed. Damage to the radial nerve in the shoulder is not uncommon, resulting in characteristic lameness with the foot dragging along the ground. The injured nerve may heal naturally, but the affected leg will probably need to be kept straight with splints or plaster to protect the foot from damage in the

Britain by a stringent quarantine programme; in most other countries rabies inoculations are compulsory for domestic dogs.

In areas where the disease is present in the wildlife, it is virtually impossible to eradicate it. The main host species varies in different parts of the world. In mainland Europe, the fox is the most significant carrier, in northern Asia, the wolf, and in the United States racoons and skunks.

Infection usually occurs from a bite wound from an infected animal. The virus initially multiplies in the wound and then travels up a nerve to the brain. The onset of clinical symptoms may take several weeks or months,

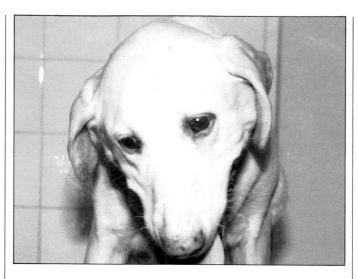

ABOVE: *A sudden stroke may well be indicated by a slight and subtle tilt of your dog's head, with the tongue possibly hanging out. This is a serious condition and you should contact your veterinarian immediately.*

meanwhile. Another vulnerable nerve is that which runs down the side of the face. If this is affected it causes paralysis of the side of the face, often with the tongue lolling; it is likely to heal naturally with time.

Older dogs may occasionally suffer from a 'stroke' or cerebral haemorrhage, caused by the rupture of a small blood vessel in the brain producing a blood clot there and resulting in partial or total paralysis. Recovery depends upon whether or not the clot breaks down naturally; the paralysis may continue for weeks and the dog will require dedicated nursing.

SERIOUS CONTAGIOUS DISEASES

Dogs are vulnerable to a number of diseases spread by viruses and bacteria, which may be transmitted not only by direct contact but indirectly by such routes as shared food bowls, insect bites or even carried on the wind, and can remain dangerous for up to a year after being shed by an infected dog.

Viral infections such as distemper, infectious hepatitis and parvovirus, as well as the bacterial infection leptospirosis, are serious and life-threatening diseases, and in many countries – though fortunately not, as yet, Great Britain – one has to add rabies to the list. Vaccinations are available to protect your dog against these diseases, and no responsible dog-owner should neglect this preventative care, since the unvaccinated dog is not only at risk itself but a source of danger to others. It is for this reason that repu-

table boarding kennels and dog training clubs will not accept dogs without proof of vaccination.

Puppies are especially vulnerable to infection, particularly during the period when maternal antibodies against disease, received from their mother's milk, have begun to wane at around six weeks, and before they are old enough for vaccination at around eight weeks. They should therefore be kept isolated from other dogs until they are fully protected by vaccination.

DISTEMPER

Distemper is also known as 'hardpad' because it sometimes causes the pads on the feet to thicken. Its other effects are much more serious and, although it usually affects young unvaccinated dogs, it can also strike older individuals with little or no immunity, often with fatal consequences. Distemper is a virus transmitted by close contact with an infected dog, spreading from body secretions such as urine and saliva. The virus localizes first in the tonsils and neighbouring lymph nodes. At this stage, the body may produce defensive antibodies to overcome the infection and symptoms will be relatively mild – an affected dog may lose its appetite for a short time and then recover without further trouble.

In certain cases, however, the infection spreads to other parts of the body, and about a fortnight or three weeks later from the first attack, the dog will become very ill. Symptoms include vomiting, bouts of diarrhoea and a high temperature. More significantly, the eyes and nose will be runny and the dog may develop a painful cough. It will lose its appetite, although it may have an excessive thirst. In over 50 per cent of cases derangement of the nervous system (see chorea, above) will appear, although this may not develop until years later; in the meantime the virus remains within the spinal cord and brain. Under stress, serious neurological signs ranging from fits to paralysis will appear, often with continuous twitching of the facial muscles, and sometimes there may be a distressing change of temperament. While this can often be controlled, other symptoms may not respond to treatment, and the dog may have to be put to sleep on humanitarian grounds.

A characteristic sign of a dog which has had distemper and recovered is 'distemper teeth', teeth which are a brownish colour, with pitted surfaces, because of damage to their enamel covering. In some cases the dog may permanently retain a dry, cracked nose leather and thickened foot pads.

Distemper is a very unpleasant disease, for which there is no real treatment, although antibiotics can decrease the risk of secondary infections, which may otherwise lead to pneumonia. Euthanasia will almost certainly be required once nervous symptoms are evident.

The distemper virus is similar to the virus that causes

TRANSMISSION OF A VIRUS

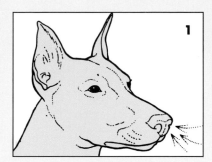

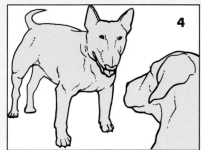

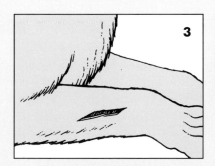

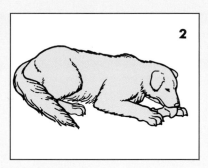

Diseases are more likely to spread where there is a high density of dogs, for example, at a show or in boarding kennels. Kennel cough is spread by airborne viruses (1). Some of the more resistant viruses may either simply be transmitted directly on contact (2) or, from contaminated items such as bedding, grooming implements and feeding bowls. Scavenging dogs are susceptible to disease by ingesting contaminated foods (3). Other kinds of virus can be spread by animal vectors – bites from insects such as ticks or, in the case of rabies, bites from other mammals (4). Open cuts or wounds are another danger as viruses are often carried in the bloodstream (5). A particular danger to developing puppies is that some viruses are small enough to pass across the placenta or contaminate the mother's milk and so infect puppies either before or soon after they are born (6).

IMMUNITY TO DISEASE

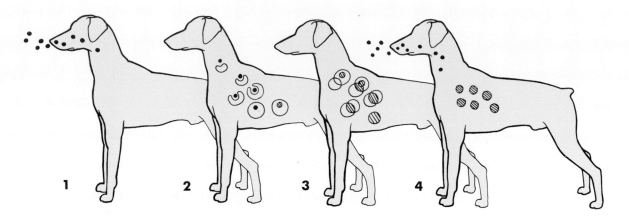

When foreign organisms such as bacteria or viruses enter the body, they stimulate the host to produce antibodies that attach to the organisms and neutralize them (1). These antibodies are produced both at the site of entry – the nose or intestines – and the bloodstream by white blood cells, the lymphocytes (2). Once neutralized the organisms can be engulfed by other white cells in the blood, the macrophages, and broken down (3). A vaccine stimulates the body to produce antibodies so that it can respond more quickly to future infection (4).

measles in humans, although it is not a zoonosis. Despite this, however, measles vaccine provides some protection against distemper, and is particularly useful in situations where young unvaccinated puppies may have been exposed to distemper. Administering distemper vaccine in these cases is unlikely to provide immunity, since any maternal antibody which the puppies receive from their mother's milk will neutralize it. The first distemper vaccination is normally given at the age of about eight weeks, when the level of maternal antibody is declining and the next vaccination is given about a month later, when there is no maternal protection left. Since the measles vaccine is not affected by maternal antibodies the puppy develops its own immunity to distemper earlier than usual. Measles vaccine should only be given to young puppies when recommended by a veterinarian.

INFECTIOUS CANINE HEPATITIS (RUBARTH'S DISEASE)

Infectious canine hepatitis (ICH) is another viral disease which, as its name suggests, affects the liver, causing severe inflammation. There are two forms of canine adenovirus, abbreviated to CAV-1 and CAV-2, and the former is responsible for this illness. The route of transmission is highly significant: if taken into the body via the mouth, its effects will be on the liver, but if inhaled, it is likely to cause a less severe disease affecting the respiratory tract.

When the infection involves the liver, causing hepatitis (inflammation of the liver), this is sometimes fatal. Some infected dogs may die suddenly without showing any symptoms beforehand. Others show the characteristic signs of abdominal pain and jaundice, which turns the mucous membranes, such as those on the inside of the mouth, a yellowish colour. There may be a raised temperature and occasional vomiting. The blood clotting system is also disturbed and haemorrhages may be evident. Infected dogs may show a bluish opacity of one or both eyes for a brief period, which will clear up in time.

The hepatitis may lead to convulsions and death; in other cases the dog will make a gradual recovery, although the weight loss typical of this illness will only be made up slowly. Because the virus itself is likely to localize in the kidneys, it will be excreted in the dog's urine for a considerable period of time, during which the animal is a potential danger to other dogs and should be isolated.

There is evidence to suggest that infection with CAV-1 can create permanent kidney damage, and that it may be a contributory cause of chronic renal failure in old age.

LEPTOSPIROSIS

Leptospirosis is caused by bacteria, normally either *Leptospira canicola* or *L. icterohaemorrhagiae*. Terriers and other 'ratters' are particularly at risk from the former strain, since this bacterium is commonly associated with rats and excreted in their urine. Infection can be spread by sniffing at urine, and male dogs, which make most use of urine as a scent marker, are therefore most vulnerable; it can also be passed on by contact with a dog which has recovered from the infection but is still excreting the bacteria in its urine. This group of bacteria can also survive for long periods in water, and may enter the body directly through the skin, particularly through a cut or wound. Vaccination will protect the dog against this potentially fatal disease, which can be transmitted to humans.

Early symptoms include vomiting, diarrhoea, lethargy and a high temperature; in the later stages the body temperature falls significantly, with increased thirst and laboured breathing. Cases of *L. icterohaemorrhagiae* infection are likely to develop jaundice, whereas permanent kidney damage may result from *L. canicola*, with ulcers often on the tongue and in the mouth.

Antibiotics can help to overcome this infection, but the earlier treatment begins the more likely the chance of success. It can be transmitted from dogs to people, so it is essential to handle affected dogs with care, preferably wearing gloves, and to disinfect wherever the sick dog urinates.

PARVOVIRUS

Parvovirus infection in dogs attracted great attention when it first appeared in the late 1970s; the disease assumed epidemic proportions. Early outbreaks occurred in Australia and the United States, and the virus soon spread to Europe. Its origins are still unknown, but it seems likely that it arose as a mutant form of the feline panleucopaenia virus. Indeed, in the early days of outbreaks, vaccines intended for cats were used to protect dogs from the disease. Now specific vaccines for dogs have been developed, and it makes sense to protect your dog against this serious illness. The recommended inoculation procedure depends to some extent on the breed concerned in the case of puppies. Check with your veterinarian.

The disease can take two forms, and the course of the illness depends largely on the age of the dog affected. In the case of puppies under five weeks of age, the virus affects the heart muscle and leads to sudden death from heart failure. Some puppies may survive, but they have a poor prognosis because the damage to their heart is irreversible; they can die suddenly and unexpectedly at a later time from the effects of the earlier *myocarditis* (inflammation of the heart muscle).

Older dogs usually develop the typical blood-stained diarrhoea as the virus attacks the intestinal lining. They may also vomit, and dehydration rapidly follows. Treatment is likely to necessitate the use of an intravenous drip, and a full recovery cannot be guaranteed. There is a good chance of permanent damage to the gut, and this in turn can restrict the absorption of foodstuffs. The weight loss is almost impossible to overcome after the acute stage of the illness has passed. In addition, intermittent outbreaks of diarrhoea throughout the remainder of the dog's life are not unusual.

The virus itself is very durable and can exist outside the body for at least a year, surviving exposure to most common disinfectants. As a result, infection is easily spread, especially where dogs congregate, at kennels and in shows. It can be transferred on clothes and shoes, as well as via feeding bowls. After an outbreak, the premises should be washed thoroughly with bleach (sodium hypochlorite). Protective footwear which can be immersed in a solution of bleach should be worn to reduce the risk of spreading the infection.

THE AGEING DOG

Old age comes to pets as to their owners, and the ageing dog needs special care.

The average lifespan of the domestic dog varies from breed to breed; in general, the larger breeds age earlier than the smaller ones, and giant breeds in particular tend to a short lifespan. Like their owners, individual dogs will show the effects of old age to a varying extent. Some dogs will be old at the age of seven or eight; at the other extreme, there are dogs in their late teens and early twenties which still enjoy an active life.

The effects of old age upon the dog are gradual and insidious. Coat colour fades, particularly around the muzzle, and the old dog becomes less active than before, moving more slowly and carefully. The teeth may begin to show signs of wear, and the dog may be reluctant to chew as it did when younger. The decrease in activity may predispose the dog towards obesity if the diet is not adjusted accordingly, although some breeds, such as Pekingese, may tend towards gauntness in old age. The senses of sight and hearing may begin to fail.

The ageing dog will need some special care if it is to live out its lifespan in comfort. As well as adjusting its diet to allow for reduced activity, the owner may find that, like a young puppy, the older dog may need to eat several small meals a day rather than one full-size one to make digestion easier. Some old dogs may become incontinent, particularly if there is some kidney failure; ensure that the elderly dog has frequent opportunities to empty its bladder, and contact the veterinarian if the animal is drinking greatly increased amounts. Although the old dog will no longer enjoy the long walks and runs of earlier days, moderate exercise should be encouraged to maintain condition. Regular grooming is important to maintain the ageing dog's pride in its appearance, to keep the fur and skin healthy and clean and to avoid the unpleasant 'old dog' smell.

As the dog's joints stiffen, so does its mind. Change of any sort is resented; the old dog will find it hard to adjust to major changes in routine, such as a move of home. Therefore, it is usually unkind to try to brighten up your elderly pet's life by introducing a new puppy.

It is important to keep an eye on the ageing dog's general condition, looking out for waning alertness, loss of muscular tone, dull eyes and a lacklustre coat. Warning signs include loss of weight, increased thirst, bad teeth and laboured breathing. Old dogs may become progressively deaf or suffer failing eyesight. Old age makes the animal more vulnerable to many diseases than in its youth, and there are a number of veterinary problems which are specifically associated with the elderly dog, including heart disease (see p 226) and chronic kidney failure (see p 225).

Inter-vertebral disc weakness is also seen more frequently. The discs between the vertebrae of the spinal column normally act as shock absorbers, but with time their outer casing may rupture, causing the softer, inner core to impinge on the spinal cord itself, giving rise to a degree of paralysis and considerable pain. Running upstairs or jumping on to a chair frequently precedes injuries of this type, and long-bodied breeds such as Dachshunds are particularly vulnerable. Veterinary attention followed by complete rest, keeping the dog confined in a small pen, may lead to some improvement. One form of paralysis,

AGEING

As with humans, ageing in the dog is an insidious process: the dog will become less active and hearing and sight may deteriorate gradually. The young dog is trim and alert-looking, with a good thick coat and dark pigmentation of the nose.

In middle age, there will be some signs of the ageing process. The dog will become less lively, and may tend to put on weight. The first white hairs will start to show on dark breeds, particularly around the muzzle.

The older dog is less active and the tendency to put on weight increases, particularly in a spayed bitch. The skin becomes looser and less elastic, and pigmentation is lost, the coat becoming paler and the nose pinker as the syntheses of melanin is reduced.

LEFT: *The large lump around the nipple of this ten-year-old Dachsund is a typical sign of a mammary tumour and the dog is having to undergo surgery to remove it.*

RIGHT: *Stitches show the site of the tumour along the same mammary chain, and the chances of survival for the dog increase the sooner the lump is removed.*

RIGHT: *With a little extra consideration from the owner, the elderly dog can continue to enjoy life. This ageing Beagle displays the tell-tale signs of old age in the loss of pigmentation, particularly on the face, but is otherwise healthy and continues to appreciate walks and play.*

however, is progressive by nature, and causes death within a week of the original signs, by preventing the muscles responsible for breathing from operating normally.

Osteoarthritis, a degenerative change in the cartilage lining the joints, typically affecting the hip and stifles, is more often encountered in larger breeds. It results in stiffness, which will be particularly evident when the dog gets up after a period of rest, yet disappears to some extent following movement. The condition will be made much worse if the dog is obese, since the joints have to bear more weight. Treatment is geared to relieving the pain associated with the condition, although if it occurs in a young dog, following a traumatic injury in particular, radical surgery may be necessary.

Old age may be associated with dental decay, and certain breeds, such as Yorkshire Terriers, are more prone to this problem than others. Caring for the dog's teeth throughout its life will help to minimize the problem by controlling tartar; however, in some cases decayed teeth will need to be removed by the veterinarian. An older dog that has lost most of its teeth will still be able to eat adequately if offered soft foods.

Neoplasms, or tumours, are also more commonly seen in middle-aged or old dogs. These uncontrolled growths are either benign or malignant (cancerous). Benign tumours do not spread through the body, but can cause problems if they are in certain sites, for example pressing on the respiratory system. They usually grow quite slowly compared with malignant growths and can be removed without fear of recurrence.

A high proportion of canine tumours affect the skin, and mammary tumours are extremely common in bitches, accounting for nearly half the total cases. The incidence of neoplasia in dogs has been estimated at four cases a year per 1,000 dogs. One third of these cases are malignant; nearly all bone tumours are in this category. Certain breeds are more susceptible to growths than others, including Boxers, Cocker Spaniels and Boston Terriers. The actual causes of tumours are not fully understood at present, although certain parasites and viruses can be involved.

Treatment depends very much on the individual case; a total recovery is sometimes possible if the tumour is affected early and affects the body surface. Surgery is often used to remove the tumour, and cryosurgery, using liquid nitrogen to kill the tumour cells, has been adopted increasingly to deal with tumours in specific sites, such as the anal region. Other methods of therapy include radiation treatment and chemotherapy.

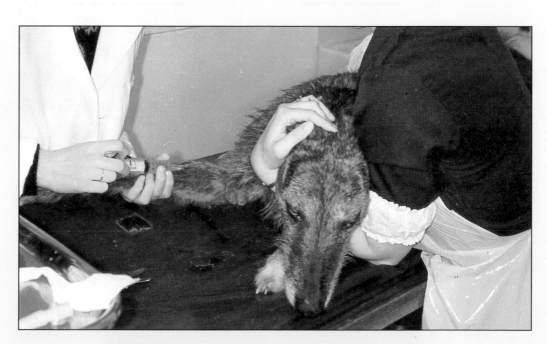

ABOVE: *The decision to have a dog put to sleep can be difficult and the advice of your veterinarian may be helpful at this time. The actual process is painless – an intravenous injection of barbiturate being administered by the veterinarian – and the dog loses consciousness within seconds.*

RIGHT: *The fading colour on the head of this Golden Retriever is one of the more obvious signs of ageing in a dog. Other more insidious and serious effects may be harder to detect in their initial stages.*

EUTHANASIA

Loving care, and veterinary treatment when appropriate, can prolong a dog's life and its enjoyment of life. Many a dog has lived for several contented years despite having an incurable condition, through the care of its owners and appropriate medication. However, there often comes a time when the responsible owner must decide whether life is becoming a burden to the animal and consider whether it is better to have it put to sleep. As the owner, you will be familiar with the normal behaviour pattern of your dog and will soon notice if there is a change. If your dog is eating and drinking normally, seems alert, and is going about life as usual, you can reasonably assume that it is still enjoying life. If you are in doubt, do not hesitate to discuss the matter with your veterinarian.

It is usually kinder to find the courage to make a decision and ensure that your dog is put quickly and painlessly to sleep than to risk the possibility of a drawn out and painful death. Euthanasia is quick and painless and need cause the dog no more pain or distress than having an anaesthetic. The most widely used method consists of injecting a measured overdose of barbiturate, usually into one of the leg veins. The dog then falls asleep and quietly passes away in a matter of seconds with no distress. The procedure is identical to that carried out for anaesthetic purposes except that the barbiturate solution used for euthanasia is much stronger.

While many owners prefer their pet to end its days in home surroundings, it may sometimes be less distressing for the animal to be left at the veterinary surgery. Dogs are highly sensitive to the mood of those around them, and if the owner is feeling very emotional his or her presence may serve only to upset the animal. However, in other cases the owner's presence may reassure the dog and also ease the owner's mind. You will know your dog and yourself best and can make the decision accordingly.

The veterinarian will deal with the body if requested, usually by incineration; owners may prefer to arrange for private cremation or burial in a pet cemetery. Local laws may prevent burial of your pet in your garden; if you do opt for this method, ensure that the grave is at least three feet (one metre) deep to deter scavengers such as foxes.

The loss of a dog can be a great emotional blow, especially for people living alone with no other companionship. Grieving for a pet is often underestimated by people but can be just as real as that for the loss of a relative. It is a common reaction to feel that one could never have another dog, but, if circumstances permit the acquisition of another, the demands of the new pet can help with the handling of grief. If you do decide to have another dog, recognize that it will not be a substitute but an individual in its own right. Do not rush into its acquisition, but choose it with care, and it will become a second companion.

Chapter Nine

BREEDING FROM YOUR DOG

TO BREED OR NOT TO BREED?

The decision to breed from your dog should not be taken lightly, for there are greater implications than the enjoyment of a litter of delightful puppies. Hundreds of thousands of dogs, pedigrees as well as mongrels, are destroyed each year because they are unwanted. To breed a litter irresponsibly, without thought for how the pups will be homed, is to add to a problem which is already serious enough.

The responsibility to find good homes for the puppies must be taken seriously. Pedigree puppies can usually be sold fairly easily; established breeders whose stock has a good reputation will often have a waiting list for puppies, but the beginner will have to work harder to place his or her youngsters. Mongrel puppies will be harder to home since there is always a superfluity of them; indeed, because of this fact and because the results of mating a mongrel are always unpredictable, it is generally inadvisable to breed from a mongrel bitch.

Remember that there are always many more people willing to buy puppies than there are people willing to care for them properly; hundreds of puppies sold to uncaring homes are turned out on the streets when their owners become bored with them, and are probably put to sleep after a miserable period as strays. It is the breeder's responsibility not only to find buyers for puppies but to try to ensure that the puppies are only sold to suitable homes. The possession of a pedigree, or the payment of a high price for the puppy, is no protection; animal sanctuaries find themselves receiving nearly as many expensive pedigree animals as mongrels.

Do try to ensure that puppies go directly from your home to their new owner and are not passed on for sale by a pet shop or puppy farm. It is stressful enough for a puppy to have to go to one new home without changing hands again, and passing through an intermediary ownership exposes it to an increased risk of infection as well as to feelings of insecurity.

Considerations to bear in mind before breeding a litter are whether you have the necessary time available to care for them properly, enough space and suitable accommodation for a growing litter, whether you can budget for the expenses involved and how you and your family will handle the inevitable disturbances to the household.

Time is an important factor. Whilst the bitch's pregnancy and birth will be straightforward in most cases, your watchful presence will be needed throughout just in case something goes wrong. Once the litter is born, the bitch will take care of them initially, but your supervision will still be required, and once they leave the nest you will be

ABOVE: *Puppies are delightful; they are also hard work, often expensive to rear, and a real responsibility.*

letting yourself in for a considerable amount of work – and also play, which is not only virtually irresistible with young puppies but also an important part in the socialization process, so that the puppies will grow up interacting happily with humans. If you are interested in breeding pedigree dogs, you will also need to spend considerable time learning the finer points of the breed standard and studying bloodlines in order to produce the best quality puppies possible.

The financial implications are greater than is sometimes imagined, and breeding dogs on a small scale is unlikely to

be profitable, especially if your time is taken into account. Expenses will certainly include the upkeep of the bitch, the stud fee, and the surprisingly high cost of rearing the puppies correctly. You must also budget for the possibility of something going wrong, perhaps the need for a caesarean delivery or simply failure to sell the puppies before they begin to eat you out of house and home.

It is a common belief that a bitch should be allowed to have one litter for her health's sake, this is not so. The bitch which has one or two litters is no less at risk of disorders of the reproductive system than the bitch which is never bred from. If you genuinely want and are prepared to take responsibility for puppies, all well and good, but it will make no difference whatsoever to the bitch's health whether she bears a litter or not.

Before setting out to breed a litter, you should ask your-self why you are doing so. If you are breeding pedigree puppies for the pet market, you should be thinking in terms of using stock which is reasonably well-bred and physically and temperamentally typical of the breed, even if not of show standard, to produce sound, healthy, attractive and good-tempered puppies. A customer who buys a pedigree puppy is entitled to expect an animal of correct physical type and character for its breed, so stock with serious faults should not be bred from. Temperament is vital in the pet dog, so nervous or vicious stock should also not be allowed to perpetuate their faults. If you envisage breeding for the show ring, it is vital to learn as much as possible about the appropriate show requirements. To begin with the best possible foundation stock and to undertake breeding intelligently and knowledgeably; it takes time, study and luck to breed show winners!

THE REPRODUCTIVE CYCLE OF THE MALE DOG

The onset of sexual maturity occurs from the age of six months onwards in male dogs, although this varies to some extent from breed to breed. As a general rule, males attain puberty at a slightly later age than bitches of the same breed, with certain exceptions such as the Beagle, where the situation is reversed. This delay is usually a matter of weeks, but can extend to months in a few breeds such as the Saluki and Chow Chow.

When introducing the young dog to stud work, always use an experienced brood bitch who will be familiar with the situation. An excited and frightened novice bitch may resent his attentions so much that she may put him off stud work for life.

Male dogs can mate all the year round, whenever there is a bitch in season, and will remain sexually fertile until well into old age, although their fertility will gradually decline. Stud dogs should not be mated too frequently, as this may cause a temporary decline in fertility.

THE REPRODUCTIVE CYCLE OF THE FEMALE DOG

Unlike the dog, the bitch has distinct sexual cycles, resulting in periods of oestrus. The age at which bitches begin their cycles varies; on average this is likely to be from the age of six months onwards, but slower-maturing breeds, such as German Shepherds, may not have their first heat until the age of 18 months, while individuals of some of the smaller and more rapidly maturing breeds, may be as early as four months.

It is inadvisable to permit a bitch to breed at her first season; the second or even third in the case of larger breeds that mature slowly is time enough. An immature bitch is not geared to produce strong healthy puppies, and her own development may be stunted by the demands of pregnancy and puppy-rearing.

On average, a bitch has two periods of oestrus each year, but in practice anywhere between two years and 18 months is not unknown. Some breeds such as Basenjis have only one period of oestrus annually. Climate may be significant;

MALE REPRODUCTIVE ORGANS

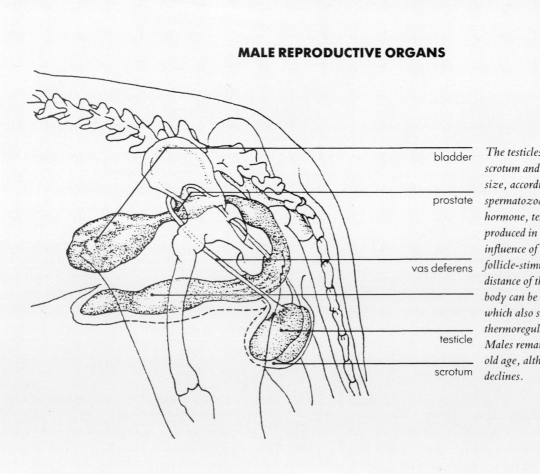

bladder

prostate

vas deferens

testicle

scrotum

The testicles are situated in the scrotum and they vary greatly in size, according to breed. The spermatozoa and the male sex hormone, testosterone, are produced in the testicles, under the influence of the pituitary gland and follicle-stimulating hormone. The distance of the testicles from the body can be muscularly regulated, which also serves as a thermoregulatory mechanism. Males remain sexually active into old age, although their fertility declines.

FEMALE REPRODUCTIVE ORGANS

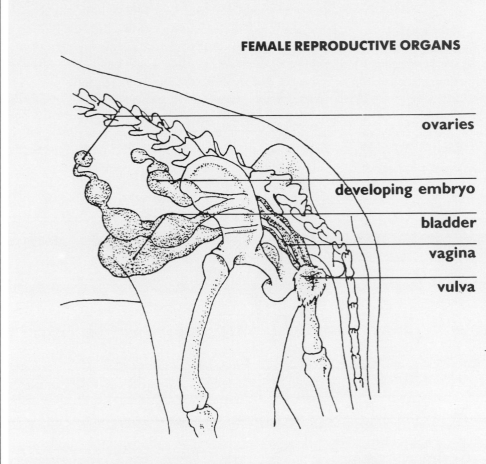

ovaries

developing embryo

bladder

vagina

vulva

The ovaries in the bitch are located in the dorsal part of the abdominal cavity, near to the kidneys, at about the third or fourth lumbar vertebra. The actual ovary is about one and a quarter centimetres (half an inch) long and the shape of a lima bean – its size increases during the pro-oestrous phase, reaching its maximum at about the time of ovulation. The fallopian tube connects the ovary with the uterine horns which are long and elliptical and unite caudally, forming the uterine body.

for example, German Shepherd Dogs come on heat every six months in Britain, but this figure falls to an average of 21 weeks in the United States. Some individual bitches have irregular heats; Greyhounds from racing strains are particularly unpredictable, perhaps because the fact that bitches cannot be raced when in season has led to selective breeding for infrequency of oestrus. The size of the dog has no significant effect on the length of oestrus cycles, nor does the time of year appear very significant, although Basenjis generally come into heat during the autumn.

There are four recognized stages of the oestrus cycle. The first is pro-oestrus, when the vulva enlarges and moistens and a bloody discharge is seen from the vagina. This occurs before ovulation and is in no way equivalent to the menstruation of female humans and primates. Menstruation does not take place in female dogs. The beginning of pro-oestrus may be indicated by a tendency to more frequent urination. During pro-oestrus, dogs are likely to be attracted to the bitch, but their advances will not be reciprocated; although a pair may play together, any attempt at mounting by the male will be rebuffed by the

female. Restlessness often accompanies this stage, which lasts an average of nine days, although it can range from two to 27 days.

The next stage is oestrus, or sexual receptivity. The bloody discharge will become clear, and the bitch will allow mating to take place. Readiness for mating is likely to be indicated by the bitch making advances to other bitches or to her owner; if she is caressed along the back, just above the tail, she will turn her tail to one side in invitation. Again, the length of this period of the cycle is variable; it may be as short as three days or continue for three weeks. The release of ova from the ovaries, or ovulation, usually occurs approximately two days after the start of oestrus.

It is not always easy to tell the appropriate time for mating; on average, the bitch is likely to be ready around the twelfth day from the first signs of bloody discharge, but individuals vary considerably and you may need to learn the cycle of your particular bitch. Some bitches have what is known as a 'quiet' season, with no apparent discharge, and require careful study of their behaviour to establish the right time for mating.

In the two or three months following oestrus, the hormone progesterone controls the reproductive tract, whether the bitch is pregnant or not, and this period is known as dioestrus. During this phase a pseudo pregnancy may occur, with the bitch showing all the symptoms of pregnancy although conception has not taken place.

The longest stage of the cycle is anoestrus, when there is no sexual activity apparent, and this lasts until pro-oestrus next occurs. Bitches will normally continue to come on heat into old age and will remain fertile, although breeding is not recommended after the age of six years old, because of the increased risks.

THE BROOD BITCH

Whether you envisage breeding for exhibition or for the pet market, you should only consider breeding from a bitch which is physically and temperamentally sound. Before you consider mating your bitch, do consider whether she has qualities that are worth perpetuating. Do not imagine that the stud dog's virtues will automatically cancel out her faults in the ensuing litter. If you are satisfied that she is worth breeding from, make sure that she is screened for any hereditary defects affecting that particular breed, many of which will not be apparent at an early stage without veterinary inspection.

RIGHT: *The quality of the puppies will depend upon the quality of their parents, on how the bloodlines of sire and dam react with each other, and also upon the care the litter receives from the breeder.*

If you are choosing a bitch with a view to breeding puppies of exhibition standard, start out with the very best you can afford. Do not go to the first breeder you come across, but study pedigrees and bloodlines within the breed beforehand and visit shows to see what today's top winners look like. The bitch should not be chosen on looks alone, or even on the show winning record of her breeder, but on her ancestry, and it is not the number of champions that appears in her pedigree that counts but how intelligently they were bred to each other. If she is descended from a family line of good producing bitches this will make the surest foundation.

First class bitches are not readily sold, and you may have to wait for what you want. If you start out with a puppy, it will be impossible to predict with accuracy how she will turn out; after waiting for her to mature, you could be disappointed in her as an adult. Starting out with an adult bitch may be more satisfactory since you are buying the finished article; breeders are unlikely to be willing to part with brood bitches of high potential, but sometimes older bitches with only a few more litters ahead may be available, or overcrowding may lead a breeder to part with good stock. However, many small-scale breeders prefer to start out with a puppy which will grow up as part of the family; even if she is disappointing from the show point of view as an adult, if she is well bred she may still be a serviceable brood bitch.

It is possible to obtain a bitch on breeding terms, which means that the breeder will part with her on reduced terms in exchange for the return of an agreed number of puppies. If you buy a bitch on breeding terms, it will pay to register the agreement with the Kennel Club to ensure that there can be no misunderstandings over arrangements. This can be a way of obtaining a better foundation bitch than you could otherwise afford, but it can be heartbreaking to have to part with the puppy you would have wanted to keep.

Before mating, the bitch needs to be in as good physical condition as possible to help her through the stresses of pregnancy and raising her family. She may need a booster vaccination beforehand to ensure that a high level of immunity will be passed to the puppies. Once pregnant, the bitch must not receive live vaccines, since these are extremely dangerous to the puppies.

CHOOSING A STUD DOG

The choice of a mate for the bitch will be influenced by the purpose for which the puppies are required. Bloodlines are important for those who wish to exhibit but the pet breeder is unlikely to worry about the finer points of a pedigree, so long as the stud dog is essentially sound and of good temperament. However, it makes sense to seek a dog which excels in the qualities you wish to produce in the puppies.

When choosing a stud dog, look at your bitch as honestly as possible and assess her faults as well as her strengths. You want a male dog that will complement her qualities; he should excel where she is weakest in the hope that her faults will be corrected in the litter, but he should also be at least reasonably strong in those areas where she is good so that you do not risk losing her virtues. If possible, it is advisable to see some of the stock he has already sired, to form some idea of the qualities he is likely to pass on.

You can use any old male of the same breed, and the puppies will be 'pedigree' in that you can register and sell them as such, but this is not the way to produce quality stock. If you want to produce the best puppies possible and to build up a reputation as a breeder, you will want the best and most suitable stud dog you can find. As a novice, do not hesitate to seek advice from experienced breeders and judges; the breeder who supplied your bitch will be an obvious source of guidance.

Stud dogs are advertised in the dog press, and may be seen in the flesh at dog shows. If you are breeding for the show ring, a study of pedigrees will be vital to help you make the most of your bitch by choosing a stud dog to bring out the best in her bloodlines. For the novice, however, familiarity with pedigrees will take some time to acquire, and it is recommended that you seek guidance from the breeder from whom you obtained your bitch, who will probably be able to recommend a suitable stud.

Avoid any stud dog which appears to have a doubtful temperament, for this could be inherited by his offspring. Nervousness or viciousness are undesirable traits in both pet and exhibition stock.

Once the stud dog has been chosen, the owner of the dog should be approached well in advance of the anticipated date of mating, to make sure the stud will be available. Do not leave this until the end of pro-oestrus, when it will probably be too late. You should also ascertain the stud fee, which will be influenced by the status of the dog, with championship winners commanding correspondingly higher fees. As an alternative to payment, some owners will accept the first choice of a puppy from the litter, the 'pick of the litter', especially if the bitch has a good pedigree. Before mating, check what happens if the mating is unsuccessful; some breeders will offer a free repeat mating in these circumstances. The owner of the stud will probably want proof that your bitch is fully inoculated so ensure that you have this to hand.

Do make sure that your chosen stud dog has been screened for any inherited condition that may affect that particular breed, such as progressive retinal atrophy (PRA) or hip dysplasia. You should already have had your bitch tested for these before considering breeding from her, and in many cases the owner of the stud dog will ask for confirmation of this.

MATING

The bitch is almost always taken to the stud dog, rather than vice versa. This is because, being highly territorial and needing to take a dominant role during courtship and mating, the male performs much better on his home territory than in strange surroundings. The female, as the less dominant and less active partner, is less affected by her surroundings.

Mating under these conditions is usually closely supervised to prevent the risk of injury to either animal. It follows the normal pattern described on pages 176/177, but because of the control exercised by the owners the courtship ritual will be circumscribed. The bitch, especially if she is inexperienced, is likely to be excitable and nervous, and the owner of the stud dog does not want to risk injury to his animal. Whilst some breeders favour as 'natural' a mating as possible, many prefer to exercise the maximum supervision. The bitch may be muzzled to ensure that she cannot bite – not always an unnecessary precaution, as not only stud dogs but the human handlers themselves may be bitten quite severely by a reluctant bitch. If there is some disparity of size between the partners – as may happen in, for example, toy breeds, where a very small dog may be mated to a larger brood bitch – human assistance will be required, and the experienced stud dog will expect this.

During the often protracted tie, when the two dogs are physically unable to separate, it is usual to hold them both firmly to prevent any sudden movement which could damage the genitals of both animals. After the mating is completed, the animals should be separated and allowed to rest. Some breeders recommend that the bitch be discouraged from urinating for an hour after mating.

After one supervised mating, many breeders will arrange for a second and possibly a third during the same heat period to maximize the chances of reproductive success.

ARTIFICIAL INSEMINATION

It is possible to have a bitch artificially inseminated, using semen from a dog in another part of the country or even further afield, if permission is granted by the governing canine authority. As rabies can be transmitted by semen, its movement from country to country is often controlled strictly by licence. Fresh canine semen can be kept viable for nearly a week, or it can be frozen indefinitely, to be thawed when required. Tests will be required to ensure that the bitch is in the oestrus phase, and ready to mate. The semen is carefully introduced, using a pipette, and the bitch's hindquarters are kept raised, so that none flows back from the cervical region where it was deposited and out of the vagina. A gloved finger is then inserted for about five minutes into the vagina, to mimic the effect of the tie: this is supposed to improve fertility.

MATING

Mating in dogs is usually supervised, certainly at a stud. Some ailments can be transmitted by sexual contacts between dogs, notably the canine venereal tumour and brucellosis. Any signs of abnormal swelling, possibly indicative of a tumour, should be reported to a veterinarian without delay, and the dog should not be mated. Screening for brucellosis is possible. As a prelude, the dogs sniff each other's genital region and after a variable length of courting, the bitch will allow the male to mount, standing with her tail aside. A tie is usually formed which lasts several minutes. Finally, the dogs swivel round and remain standing quietly facing away from each other, joined in the genital lock.

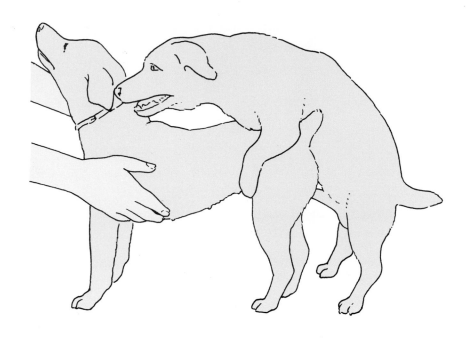

LEFT: *During her pregnancy, the bitch may act strangely at times, adopting a toy or an old slipper which she will tend as if it were a puppy. Normally this behaviour will cease when she has real puppies to care for. A false pregnancy is likely to produce similar behaviour.*

FALSE PREGNANCY

Not every mating is successful, and occasionally an unsuccessful mating may stimulate the bitch to undergo a false pregnancy, showing the symptoms of pregnancy such as putting on weight, but without having conceived. This will probably culminate with all the symptoms of the first stage of labour, nest-making, loss of appetite and even the production of milk for the non-existent puppies: it may be difficult to believe that she is not actually pregnant. Some bitches will undergo a false pregnancy after oestrus even without the stimulus of mating.

A bitch undergoing a false pregnancy will probably show changes of temperament as well as physical symptoms. She may become fretful, seeking out a suitable place to nurture her phantom puppies, and adopting an object such as a toy or a shoe which she will care for as if it were a puppy. Most cases of false pregnancy will sort themselves out if left alone. But if there is a lot of milk, it may be necessary for your veterinarian to prescribe drugs to dry it up. Recurring false pregnancies may cause a bitch considerable distress, and spaying should be considered in such cases.

PREGNANCY

The normal period of gestation is about 63 days although breed variations of a week more or less are not uncommon. The unborn puppies begin to develop some 19 days after fertilization. The major phase of growth takes place from about the thirty-third day, and by about five weeks the head and limbs are formed and the external sex organs can be differentiated.

In the first month after mating it is virtually impossible to detect any visual signs of pregnancy. At about four and a half weeks a veterinarian may be able to confirm that a bitch is pregnant, by careful palpation, although if the bitch is obese or very muscular, or if she tenses her abdomen, it may be difficult to feel the puppies. The time of examination is quite vital; at a later stage, it can be very difficult to distinguish puppies from abdominal contents. Never poke or prod the bitch's abdomen yourself to try to discover whether she is pregnant, as the developing embryos are easily injured.

Ultrasonic scans can be given by a veterinarian, and these can detect a pregnancy by the four-and-a-half-week stage. From the seventh week the puppies' developing

EMBRYOLOGY

Signs of pregnancy will not be apparent until about the fifth week. After fertilization the egg becomes a zygote – a mass of dividing cells (1). The zygote implants into the uterine wall, and here the puppies develop, forming a placental connecton with the mother. The bitch becomes progressively heavier and by the fifth or sixth week her nipples and abdomen begin to swell. The embryo continues to develop, with the body organs being formed first. By the 35th day the head, and limbs are formed and the external sex organs can be differentiated (2). As parturition approaches, the nipples become swollen and

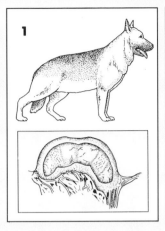 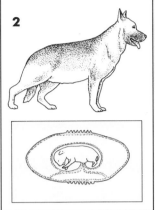 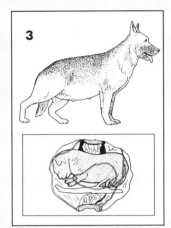

turgid, sometimes secreting milk and the abdominal swelling is typically pear-shaped. By the 55th day (3), foetal movements become

visible in the flank of the bitch. The embryo is fully developed, complete with body hair, colour markings and digital pads.

skeletal systems can be seen on X-rays, although unnecessary exposure to such radiation should be avoided if at all possible, since it can cause malformations in the foetuses.

From the fifth or sixth week, it may be possible to see signs of pregnancy as the foetuses begin to grow in size. The bitch's abdomen may start to appear distended, especially if she has not had a litter before. Simultaneously,

her teats will begin to swell and appear bright pink, reflecting the increase in blood flow to the region. However, some bitches show little or no sign of pregnancy.

By the 55th day, the embryos are fully developed, with body hair, colour markings and digital pads, and it may be possible to see foetal movements in the flank of the bitch.

RIGHT: *The final stages of pregnancy are most demanding for the bitch, as is apparent by this heavily pregnant Basset Hound – 95 per cent of the embryo puppies' growth takes place during this period. This is so that the bitch is not forced to carry the puppies any longer than necessary when they are approaching their maximum weight.*

CARE OF THE PREGNANT BITCH

For most of her pregnancy, the bitch will not need much extra care, although it is important to ensure that she is kept in top condition with sensible exercise and good food. She will not need significantly increased amounts of food until the unborn puppies have begun to increase rapidly in size, from about six weeks onwards.

Normal exercise is needed to keep her muscles healthy, although she should not be encouraged to jump at all. The embryos are protected by the fluid-filled sac in which each is contained, but, especially in the later stages, the bitch should be discouraged from mad galloping and play with other dogs to avoid the risk of serious bumps. During the last fortnight her increased bulk will probably make her reluctant to walk as far or as fast as usual, and she should be allowed to choose her own pace and distance. Avoid the temptation to feel her belly for signs of the developing puppies, and, when handling her, take care never to exert any pressure on the abdomen.

For the first six weeks she should be fed as usual; only in the latter third of the pregnancy does she need extra feeding to answer the needs of the growing embryos. As a general guide, you should increase the amount of food offered by about 10 per cent per week from about six weeks after mating. During the later stages of pregnancy, because her expanding uterus will be restricting the space for her stomach, she may not be able to swallow her daily food requirements in the usual one or two meals and she will need to eat smaller meals more frequently than usual.

About four weeks before her litter is due, the bitch should be wormed to reduce the infection being transferred to her puppies. This is important, as she will almost certainly be carrying larval worms which will be triggered from their dormant stage by her pregnancy and can be passed on to the puppies before they are born. Your veterinarian will provide guidance and the appropriate worming tablets.

Another reason for visiting the veterinarian is to establish whether the bitch needs a booster vaccination to ensure that she passes on the maximum immunity to her puppies through her milk. This will be given in the form of dead (killed) vaccines, for living vaccine given to the pregnant bitch is likely to cause serious defects in the unborn puppies.

The veterinarian will also advise on the need for dietary supplements. It is important to give such products only as advised. On a balanced diet, little if any supplementation is

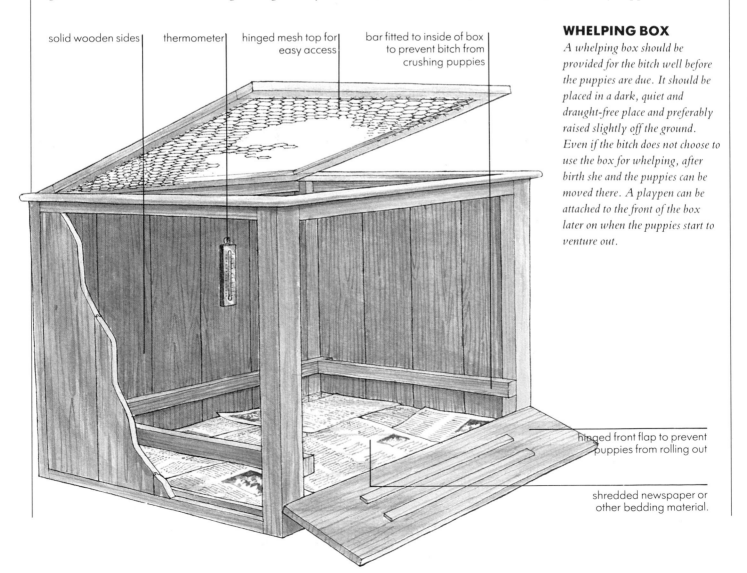

solid wooden sides   thermometer   hinged mesh top for easy access   bar fitted to inside of box to prevent bitch from crushing puppies

hinged front flap to prevent puppies from rolling out

shredded newspaper or other bedding material.

WHELPING BOX

A whelping box should be provided for the bitch well before the puppies are due. It should be placed in a dark, quiet and draught-free place and preferably raised slightly off the ground. Even if the bitch does not choose to use the box for whelping, after birth she and the puppies can be moved there. A playpen can be attached to the front of the box later on when the puppies start to venture out.

BASIC WHELPING BOX

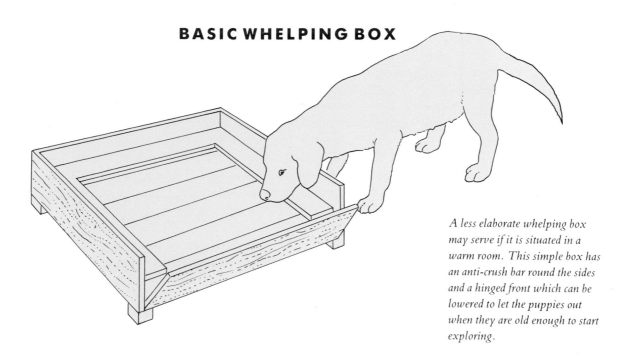

A less elaborate whelping box may serve if it is situated in a warm room. This simple box has an anti-crush bar round the sides and a hinged front which can be lowered to let the puppies out when they are old enough to start exploring.

strictly necessary, and overdosing can have serious side-effects. Sterilized bone flour, for example, is a valuable source of calcium and phosphorus, but excessive amounts will lead to skeletal and joint defects. In the last few days of pregnancy, pressure from the uterus can result in constipation and, if required, up to three teaspoonsful of medicinal liquid paraffin can be added to the food.

It is a sensible precaution to notify the veterinarian of the expected date for the arrival of the puppies, in case any problems arise during the birth requiring his assistance.

At least ten days before the puppies are due, decide where they are to be born and start familiarizing the bitch with this place to avoid the risk of her deciding to give birth on your bed or somewhere equally unsuitable. A quiet, warm part of the home, such as the spare room, is needed. A suitable box in which the bitch can give birth and rear the puppies should be provided well beforehand, and the bitch should be encouraged to sleep in the whelping box for the last 10 to 14 days of pregnancy to accustom her to it. Carpets and furnishings in the rest of the room should be protected with a layer of plastic sheeting covered by newspapers.

The whelping box needs to be large enough for the bitch to lie full length without difficulty, so that she can feed her puppies. Whelping boxes are often made of wood, but a cardboard box will be quite adequate. Three sides need to be high to prevent draughts, and the fourth low enough to give the bitch easy access, though still high enough to keep the bedding in place and to prevent the puppies from being pushed out. It is useful to fit a bar, known as a 'pig-rail', inside the box around the sides to prevent the bitch from

accidentally crushing the puppies against the sides. The box should be lined with newspapers rather than blankets, as these can be easily replaced and are less likely to hide any puppies.

With a long-coated bitch, the hair around the vulva and around the teats should be trimmed before she is due to whelp.

ABOVE: *Encourage your bitch to use the whelping box before giving birth so that she readily accepts it. The box needs to be positioned in a quiet spot, such as a spare room, and lined with newspaper so that it can easily be cleaned.*

255

BIRTH

Although the majority of bitches will not need human help in whelping, it is essential that the breeder be on hand just in case any difficulty arises. Many bitches will also find comfort in the breeder's presence.

Early signs of birth being imminent are apparent discomfort, loss of interest in food, and occasional vomiting. The most reliable indicator is a fall in body temperature, from about 38.5°C (101.5°F) to 37.5°C (99.5°F). The vulva also expands in size, and the two uppermost points of the pelvis above the legs appear more prominent, as the ligaments slacken in preparation for the birth.

The first stage of labour is characterized by restlessness. The bitch may cry out occasionally because of uterine contractions, and is likely to tear up her bedding. A clear discharge will be apparent from the vulva, and the bitch will spend considerable time licking and cleaning this area. This stage can last for a day, or possibly slightly longer in the case of a first litter, but usually abdominal contractions heralding the second stage will be apparent within 12 hours.

It is important that the bitch is kept quiet, with the minimum of disturbance, although food and water should be at hand if she wants them.

The onset of the second stage of labour will be characterized by noticeable abdominal contractions, panting and straining. The vulval discharge will become more noticeable, and about an hour into the second stage the first puppy should emerge. The water bag or *chorio-allantoic sac* in which each puppy is enclosed may rupture during labour, or the puppy may be born still wrapped in it. The bitch will normally break the sac by licking at the newborn puppy. This vigorous licking stimulates the puppy to start breathing, and the bitch will normally also bite through the umbilical cord connecting the puppy to its placenta.

The final stage of labour consists of the passing of the placenta or afterbirth, which should follow within a quarter of an hour of the birth of the puppy. The bitch may eat the afterbirth, but if not it should be removed and thrown away. It is important to check that the number of afterbirths passed corresponds to the number of puppies since if any is retained this will cause an infection in the

THE BIRTH PROCESS

1

2

3

4

A puppy in the process of being born is seen in the normal delivery position (1) emerging head first. A few minutes later the puppy is still emerging (2). The third and final stage of labour is the passing of the placenta which should follow within a quarter of an hour after the birth of each puppy (3). The umbilical cord is still connecting the mother and puppy and its greenish tinge is perfectly normal. The bitch may eat the afterbirth and will hopefully sever the umbilical cord herself. There is approximately a half hour interval between the birth of each puppy and they begin suckling almost immediately. In (4), one of the puppies is being licked and cleaned by the mother.

Do not handle the newborn puppies more than is absolutely unavoidable as this is likely to distress the bitch. If the bitch is very restless it may be necessary to remove the firstborn pups until labour is over to save them from being crushed, but normally each puppy will find its way to a teat soon after birth and will begin to suckle while the bitch washes it. This is beneficial to the bitch, as suckling stimulates the uterus and helps to speed up the labour.

After giving birth to all her puppies, the bitch should be taken outside to relieve herself. She may be reluctant to leave her family, but she should be encouraged to do so. The opportunity should be taken to remove the soiled newspaper from the whelping box and replace it with clean.

During the bitch's absence the breeder can quickly check over the litter to look for any abnormalities such as cleft palate (see below). When the bitch returns, encourage her to settle down and concentrate on washing and feeding her youngsters. Watch the puppies carefully and make sure that each has access to a teat. Normally all the puppies should be suckling within 30 minutes of birth.

FEMALE GENITALIA

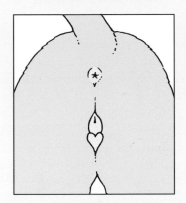

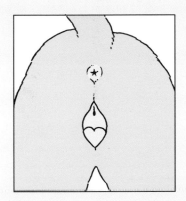

*The vulva is normally dark pink and constricted (**TOP**). Just prior to whelping the vulva dilates and swells and changes significantly in colour to a bright dark pink (**ABOVE**). The mammary glands may also swell.*

uterus. They are normally green in colour and this is not a sign of infection as a general rule.

Puppies are born one at a time, normally at intervals of 15 to 30 minutes. In small litters, the gap between puppies may be longer, extending up to an hour or so. The whole litter should be born within about six hours from the onset of the second stage of labour, but in a few instances, a longer period of time may elapse. A few bitches actually pause to rest during labour, which can be distinguished from a physical difficulty in giving birth by the lack of contractions. During labour the bitch may welcome a drink of milk and glucose from time to time.

The normal birth position for a puppy is head first, but occasionally the hindquarters may emerge first; usually this will not create problems unless the bitch tires.

BIRTH POSITIONS

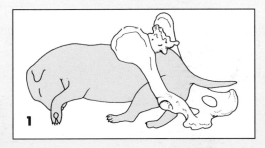

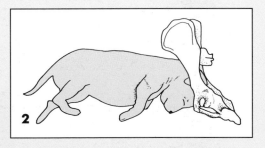

The position of the puppy immediately prior to birth may vary. Under normal circumstances, puppies are born head first (1), but in a proportion of cases, they emerge tail first (2). This is described as a breech presentation, and may cause problems, although in most cases this will rectify itself. It is a serious matter, however, if the puppy becomes twisted and stuck in the birth canal, and requires rapid veterinary attention.

GENERAL ASSISTANCE

If all goes well, the breeder should intervene as little as possible. However, there are circumstances where action by the breeder is needed to save a puppy's life.

If the bitch is inexperienced, or very tired she may fail to bite the cord or break the water bag of a puppy. Short-faced breeds such as Pugs may also have difficulty in achieving this task. The puppy cannot breathe until it is released from the water bag, so human intervention is essential. Make sure that the hands are clear, then break through the membranes with the fingers and lift the puppy out. Hold its head slightly downwards to drain fluid forward, wipe clear the nose and mouth of any debris, and insert a finger in its mouth to open the jaws and stimulate breathing. Gentle rubbing of the puppy with a towel will also encourage it to breathe. Once it is breathing satisfactorily, it should be placed back with the bitch.

If the umbilical cord has not been cut by the bitch, this will also have to be done by hand. The cord can be either torn or cut. Tearing simulates the biting action of the bitch, which makes the muscle tissue of the cord contract to seal off the blood capillaries. Hold the end of the cord nearest the puppy about 2in (5cm) from its body and then, with your right hand, tear the cord, exerting pressure towards the attached placenta, with your left hand remaining stationary. Never pull the cord overall, since this may result in an umbilical hernia.

Cutting the cord reduces the risk of causing an umbilical hernia through excessive force, although blood loss is more likely than with tearing. If the cord is to be cut, tie it off with a piece of clean thread about 2in (5cm) from the puppy's body and snip through it on the side of the ligature closest to the placenta, leaving the tie in place to prevent bleeding. The remaining stump soon shrivels up and ultimately sloughs off naturally. It can be dabbed with iodine to minimize the risk of infection. Once the cord is cut the puppy should be returned to its mother.

MORE SERIOUS PROBLEMS

Although birth is usually straightforward, occasionally problems may occur. Certain breeds are more prone to whelping difficulties than others, and it is sensible to ask the breeder of your bitch what problems may be anticipated.

You will need to call in veterinary assistance if the bitch is in second-stage labour for more than two hours without producing puppies. Delays of more than an hour between births are also likely to be a cause for concern. In some

LEFT: *A bitch with a newborn litter, like this Cocker Spaniel, should be left alone to recover from the ordeal of giving birth. She will lick her pups while they suckle, establishing the maternal bond.*

cases, a puppy may become stuck, half-way out of the birth canal. This is a serious condition, because oxygen starvation may damage its brain irreversibly within five minutes or so, and veterinary advice will be needed on the best course of action in such an emergency.

Failure to give birth after straining probably means that the first puppy is in an awkward position or even too large to pass through the birth canal normally. Difficulties can occur in breeds with large heads, such as the Bulldog, when the puppy's head may jam in the birth canal, and with breeds with a relatively small pelvic canal, such as Scottish and Sealyham Terriers. Deformed or dead puppies are also likely to form blockages, while the birth position of a puppy may be a source of problems, with breech (hindquarters first) presentations being more likely to become stuck.

In some cases where a puppy is jammed it may be possible to ease it out manually. Generally, assuming that the puppy is lying in a central position, you should gently and carefully pull it downwards with the bitch either standing or more usually lying on her side. Do not pull between contractions, but manipulate the puppy at this stage. If you are not making progress, contact your veterinarian

ABOVE: *Having been born, outside the whelping box, the first pup is shown to the mother, and then taken to the specially prepared and cosy box for its first experiences in a new world.*

immediately. He may be able to ease the puppy out, but sometimes a Caesarean section will be required, whereby puppies are removed via incisions made in the abdominal wall and uterus. Such surgery is likely to be necessary in the case of bitches which have fractured a pelvis previously, or are overdue by several days, if other methods have not stimulated birth.

If a bitch strains firmly at first, but does not produce a puppy, and then gradually strains infrequently and half-heartedly, she may be going into *uterine inertia*, where the uterus becomes tired and unable to contract properly. Most such cases respond well to drugs which your veterinarian can give to stimulate the contractions. If you are in doubt, seek advice too soon rather than too late.

POST NATAL CARE

Normally the bitch will recover quickly from the stresses of pregnancy and labour and will rear her litter without complications, but for the first three days she will need particular care and the breeder should keep a watchful eye out for complications. If she seems weak and unwell and displays little or no interest in her puppies, veterinary guidance should be sought. She may have lost too much blood during the birth or may have retained an afterbirth.

Most bitches have plenty of milk, but others may take up to twenty-four hours to come into milk after the birth; it is important to keep an eye on the situation to ensure that the puppies are being fed. The first feed is vital, since the

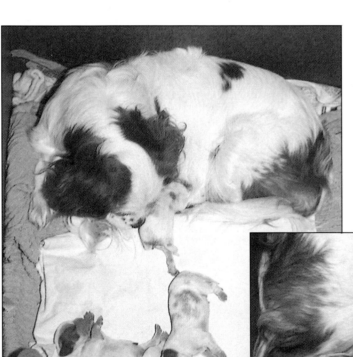

*Newborn pups, 24 hours old, are unable to see, hear or smell and rely on their sense of touch (**LEFT**), feeding every two hours and sleeping in between feeds. By the time they are one week old (**BELOW**), they will be able to crawl around their nest and will burrow into anything soft and warm, even a human hand.*

RIGHT: *A Dachshund suckles her young. Unlike many species, such as cats, the pups do not show teat preferences from one meal to the next.*

first milk, known as colostrum, contains protective antibodies (immunoglobulins) which will help to give immunity against illness until the puppies' own defence system is fully operational.

Even after the first feed has been taken successfully, continue to check that all puppies are feeding. Occasionally a weakling may be pushed away from the bitch's nipples by stronger siblings, and you may need to intervene by helping it to a feeding place. If the whole litter appears distressed and is not thriving it may be that the milk supply is inadequate. Check to see if the milk is flowing properly; if the bitch has insufficient milk of her own you may need to provide supplementary feeds.

Occasionally a bitch may reject a weakling puppy. However, sometimes it is possible to save a rejected puppy by keeping it warm and assisting it to reach a nipple, perhaps also giving it some supplementary feeding. However, often such puppies have some congenital defect and may die even with human care.

The right environment is very important during the early part of the puppies' lives. They are dependent at first on the temperature of their surroundings, since they are not yet able to regulate their body temperatures in the

same way as adult dogs. The room in which they are housed should therefore be at least 70°F (21°C). If additional heat is required, an infra-red lamp can be obtained. It is vital that this is positioned in such a way that there is no risk of accidentally burning the puppies or their dam. Lights of this type are produced exclusively for use with livestock; some emit heat with a minimum light output. They must not be covered, because the heat generated can present a fire risk. An alternative is to use a low wattage heating pad, positioned in the basket under a sheet of newspaper. These low wattage pads give off a gentle heat on their surface when the puppies are in contact with it. Always choose one of the metal designs rather than the similar greenhouse pads made of plastic, which can be broken by the bitch, leaving the electrical cord exposed.

Whilst the puppies are still blind and helpless, they should be handled as little as possible to avoid agitating the mother. If you do need to disturb them, make sure first that your hands are warm. The bitch will probably trust you in the presence of her youngsters, but her instinct for privacy at this time should be respected and she should not be exposed to visits from strangers or other household pets, which will stress her unfairly.

LITTER SIZE ACCORDING TO BREED

The great variation in the litter size of dogs of different breeds is apparent from the figures in this chart.
The biggest litter reported consisted of 23 puppies.

Breed	Mean litter size	Breed	Mean litter size	Breed	Mean litter size
Airedale Terrier	7.6	Dobermann	7.6	Norwegian Elkhound, black	4.8
Australian Terrier	5.0	English Foxhound	7.3	Papillon	5.0
Basenji	5.5	English Setter	6.3	Pekingese	10.0
Beagle	5.6	English Springer Spaniel	6.0	Pinscher, miniature	3.4
Bedlington Terrier	5.6	Fox Terrier, smoothhair	4.1	Pointer	6.7
Bernese Mountain Dog	5.8	Fox Terrier, wirehair	3.9	Pomeranian	2.0
Bloodhound	10.1	French Bulldog	5.8	Poodle, miniature	4.3
Boston Terrier	3.6	German Shepherd Dog	8.0	Poodle, standard	6.4
Boxer	6.4	Golden Retriever	8.1	Retriever	5.2
Griffon Bruxellois	4.0	Gordon Setter	7.5	Rottweiler	7.5
Bulldog	5.9	Greyhound	6.8	Samoyed	6.0
Bull Terrier	3.6	Irish Setter	7.2	St Bernard	8.5
Cairn Terrier	3.6	Kerry Blue Terrier	4.7	Schnauzer, giant	8.7
Chow	4.6	King Charles Spaniel	3.0	Schnauzer, standard	5.1
Cocker Spaniel	4.8	Labrador Retriever	7.8	Scottish Terrier	4.9
Collie	7.9	Lakeland Terrier	3.3	Shetland Sheepdog	4.0
Dachshund, smoothhair	4.8	Lapland Dog	4.8	Shih Tzu	3.4
Dachshund, longhair	3.1	Manchester Terrier	4.7	Siberian Husky	5.9
Dachshund, wirehair	4.5	Mastiff	7.7	Welsh Corgi (Pembroke)	5.5
Dalmatian	5.8	Newfoundland	6.3	West Highland White Terrier	3.7
Dandie Dinmont Terrier	5.3	Norwegian Elkhound, grey	6.0	Whippet	4.4

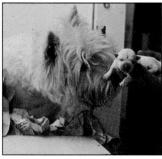

Most bitches do not object to careful handling of their puppies by their trusted owner, but disturbances should be kept to the minimum in the first days.

The safest way to hold a puppy is to use both hands to support both the forequarters and the rear.

You should however, with minimal disturbance to mother and babies, inspect the litter for any congenital abnormalities. Occasionally a puppy may be born with a cleft palate, a condition in which the roof of the mouth has failed to fuse together properly so that a hole is present from the mouth up into the nose. This prevents the puppy from suckling properly, and milk may actually be seen to run down the nose. It is not possible to treat this condition successfully, and affected puppies are best painlessly detroyed by the veterinarian.

The healthy lactating bitch will need extra food while she is supplying her puppies' needs as well as her own, and her food intake will increase as the litter grows. As a rough guide, she should be receiving 50 per cent more food than usual in the first week, 100 per cent more during the second week and then at least three times her normal ration from this point on as the puppies grow rapidly. Offer this in several meals throughout the day. It is also vital that the bitch receives an adequate intake of fluid to sustain her milk output. Water should be constantly available to her as always, but she can also be offered one of the special milk replacement foods used for rearing orphaned puppies, which are less likely to precipitate diarrhoea as may quantities of cow's milk.

POST-NATAL PROBLEMS

During the rearing period, inspect the bitch's breasts from time to time to be sure that none of the nipples are sore and swollen, indicating mastitis, a painful local infection which will make the bitch reluctant to allow the puppies to nurse. This condition requires treatment with antibiotics, and in addition some protection must be given to the nipples themselves to minimize discomfort.

The production of milk for the puppies calls for a considerable output of calcium from the bitch, and occasionally this may lead to calcium deficiency in her blood, causing a dangerous condition known as milk fever or eclampsia. This can occur at any stage, but it is most likely to develop from two weeks to a month after whelping, when milk production peaks. Bitches with large litters to feed are most at risk, although it has been suggested that a predisposition to eclampsia may be inherited.

In the initial stages, the bitch appears distressed and may start to ignore her puppies and lose her appetite. One of the functions of calcium is to assist in muscular contraction, and the bitch will begin to stagger as her muscles are affected. Her temperature will rise, and, without treatment, coma leading to death is inevitable. The veterinarian should be contacted immediately, and is likely to give an injection of a calcium-containing compound which normally brings about a speedy recovery. However, the bitch will not be able to continue to meet her family's demands in full and all or some of the puppies will need to be fostered or hand-reared.

HAND REARING PUPPIES

If puppies are orphaned or if the mother for some reason is unable to provide milk, it will be necessary either to find a foster-mother or to hand-rear them. Hand-rearing is a demanding and time-consuming task, not to be undertaken lightly, and if a foster-mother can be obtained, perhaps through your veterinarian, this will be preferable. Bitches will readily foster other puppies alongside their own without difficulties, provided their litter is relatively small, and bitches producing milk as the result of a pseudo-pregnancy will also be suitable.

If a foster-mother cannot be found, the necessary milk substitute powder can be obtained from a veterinarian.

Cow's milk is unsuitable, as it contains insufficient protein for the growing puppies. Special bottles and teats are available to facilitate feeding; it is worth obtaining a stock of such items before a bitch whelps, so that they are on hand for any emergency.

Hygiene is very important when rearing any young creature, and especially so if the orphans have not received any colostrum from the bitch. Food should never be left standing, but preferably mixed fresh before each food. Any stored in a refrigerator should be used within a day. After each feed, the utensils used shoud be sterilized, using a proprietary product used for cleaning babies' bottles, and then rinsed.

Puppies need to be fed very frequently during the early weeks of their lives – every two hours from about 6.00 am to midnight with a further couple of feeds during the night. Before feeding, milk should be warmed to about 100°F (39.8°C). Feeding must be carried out at the puppy's own

Special feeders are available for hand-rearing puppies. Care must be taken not to rush feeding, so as not to choke the puppy, and after each feed the stomach and ano-genital region must be gently massaged in imitation of the action of the bitch's tongue, to stimulate evacuation.

pace to avoid the risk of choking; any fluid which accidentally passes into the lungs may cause inhalation pneumonia.

Once the puppy appears to have had enough, wipe around its mouth with a cottonwool swab moistened with warm water. It is also important to wipe the abdominal and anal regions with a clean swab to mimic the dam's licking which stimulates the puppy to urinate and defecate after feeding.

Warmth is essential; a heating pad or infra-red lamp can be augmented with a warm but securely wrapped hot water bottle to substitute for the heat and comfort of the mother's body. If the puppy is too cold or too hot it will show signs of distress and start whining.

With loving care and the devotion of considerable time, the puppies can be reared without their mother, but it should be borne in mind that the breeder cannot provide the vital early socialization with their own species without which they may never interact comfortably with other dogs. A hand-reared puppy may grow up to be a particularly affectionate pet in response to the extra human contact in infancy; regrettably, in some cases it may never make up for the lack of early familiarization with its own kind and may prove nervous and neurotic.

A COMPARISON OF THE MAJOR NUTRIENTS IN COW'S AND BITCH'S MILK

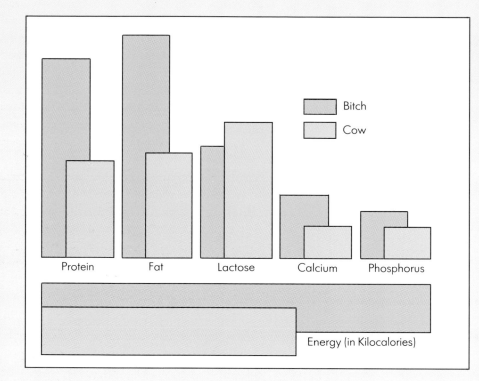

In terms of the major nutrients, milk from the puppies' mother contains approximately twice as much energy as cow's milk, as is apparent from the graph (DIRECT). A puppy would have to consume twice as much cow's milk as bitch milk to meet its needs, and cow's milk would also be detrimental to its growth and development, as well as being likely to cause severe diarrhoea. If puppies require supplementary feeding, they should be given a specially formulated bitch-milk substitute.

THE NEWBORN PUPPY

The puppy is born at a very early stage in its development, a helpless creature dependent on its mother for survival. Its eyes and ears are sealed shut, and it is thought that the sense of smell is also as yet undeveloped. It does have a primitive sense of taste, but at this stage it depends for survival almost entirely upon the sense of touch, which aids in finding the mother's nipple and in cuddling up to her and its littermates for warmth. Its limbs will not support it, but it can worm its way toward the vital sources of nourishment and warmth. It can cry weakly if distressed by hunger or cold.

The newborn puppy's behaviour is highly functional. As long as the conditions are suitable, it spends 90 per cent of its time sleeping and the rest feeding. It will go straight from a period of wakefulness to being asleep with no apparent signs of drowsiness in between.

During its wakeful periods the young puppy spends its time either searching for a teat to feed from, or simply suckling. Pups normally move about by sliding along on their stomachs making swimming-type movements with their front legs, and swinging their heads from side to side in the search for a warm object. If a pup fails to make contact with its mother after travelling a short distance, it will set off in the same manner in a new direction. Once it touches the mother's body, it will move along parallel with it until it contacts a suitable area, where it will burrow in and come to rest once its head and shoulders are covered.

After a few minutes, the puppy will make further exploratory movements in order to find a teat; when it finds one, it may not begin to suckle for some time, although there soon ceases to be any delay as the pup becomes practised. Unlike kittens, puppies do not appear to become attached to any particular nipple. Although the sense of taste is poorly developed, puppies will turn away from any bitter substance, while milk, on the other hand, does seem to have a positive attraction.

Newborn pups have a reflex which makes them withdraw any limb which encounters something painful. If a puppy finds itself away from its mother in a cold place, it becomes restless and more alert than usual and its breathing becomes more rapid. It will also make a mewing distress cry. Some studies have revealed the strange fact that a mother will often ignore this mewing, and may even squash a puppy that is crying in distress. However, she will respond to the sight of a puppy moving around some distance away and bring it back to the nest.

EARLY SURGERY

Docking and the removal of dew claws, if carried out at all, needs to be carried out in the first few days after birth when they are still minor operations.

The removal of dew claws, if present, is generally recommended to prevent problems in later life, although in a few breeds such as the Pyrenean Mountain Dog they must be retained if the puppy is destined to be exhibited in adult life. These vestigial toes, positioned about the foot where they will not touch the ground, serve no useful purpose in the dog and are likely to be disadvantageous, being particularly prone to injury. In addition, because they are not in contact with the ground they are not worn down naturally, and if the owner neglects to cut them regularly they will grow right round into the flesh, causing acute pain. If they are removed in infancy, these problems cannot arise; removal in adult life is a much more serious and painful operation, which may have to be carried out if one is torn accidentally.

Docking, the removal of all or a specified part of the tail, is a less clear-cut issue. Originally carried out to prevent injury to the tails of hunting dogs in undergrowth, today it is largely a cosmetic matter and increasingly the subject of argument. Approximately 45 breeds are required to be docked for show purposes, with breed standards specifying the amount of tail to be left on, ranging from the long dock of the Airedale Terrier to the stump of the Boxer.

Most dogs are bred as pets and there can be little justification for this unnecessary mutilation. However, the breeder who elects not to dock a litter should be aware that it may be harder to sell the puppies as typical specimens of their breed to a public accustomed to seeing docked specimens.

The removal of dew claws and docking can be carried out either by the breeder or by a veterinarian. Carried out at around three to five days, it causes minimal pain and bleeding. It does require skill and knowledge, so the novice breeder is advised not to carry out the operation but to seek expert help. It is probably best to ask your veterin-

DEW CLAWS

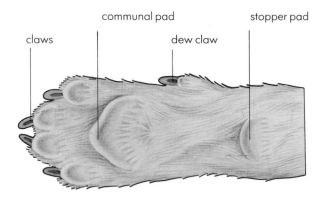

claws — communal pad — dew claw — stopper pad

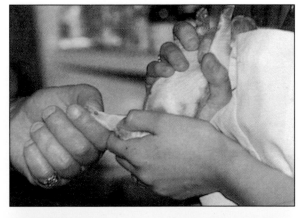

The dew claws are vestigial digits which generally serve little practica purpose. It is usual to remove them when the puppies are three or four days old, to prevent them from becoming a problem later on. If left on, these claws will not wear down like the other claws and will need regular trimming to prevent them from growing into the flesh: they are also vulnerable to injury from snagging on obstacles.

Removing the dew claws is a simple operation. In the first few days of life the puppies' nervous system is not sufficiently developed for this to cause much pain, and it can be performed humanely without distress to the pups or their dam. If dew claws need to be removed on an adult dog, this is a much more troublesome operation which needs to be performed under anaesthetic and will require stitches.

ABOVE: *With five puppies to two bowls and the mother considering joining in, the breeder's intervention may be needed to ensure that all the puppies obtain a fair share.*

RIGHT: *The young puppy needs some encouragement at first to take solids. Licking food from a finger is more inviting initially than the plate.*

BELOW: *A separate bowl for each pup ensures that individual intake is monitored.*

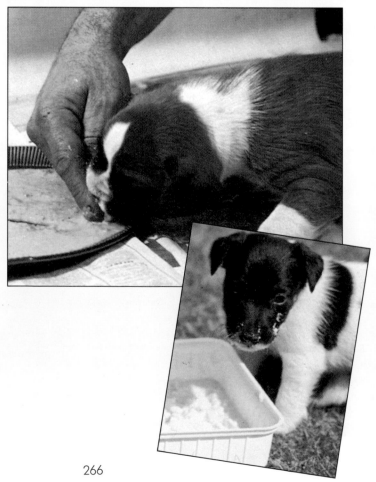

arian to undertake such surgery; however, if you have decided to have the puppies docked, it is advisable to seek guidance from an experienced breeder since your veterinarian is unlikely to be familiar with the exact requirements of all breed standards, and a tail docked too long or too short will spoil the puppy's appearance for exhibition.

ABOVE: *Tail docking was originally intended to prevent hunting dogs' tails from injury when they were working in thick cover but in most breeds today it is no more than a custom,* *perpetuated by breed standards. Breeds which are customarily docked, such as the Boxer, can be very attractive with the tail left intact as in the specimen shown here.*

WEANING

Weaning is a gradual process, and attempts to hurry the change-over from mother's milk to solid foods are likely to cause stomach upsets. In the wild, the bitch will initiate weaning by regurgitating food for the puppies. Some domestic bitches will do this, but in the domestic situation it is the breeder's responsibility to supply suitable food for the puppies. The canned foods manufactured specially for puppies are ideal for the purpose, or a little lean mince may be provided.

The age at which puppies should be weaned will be on average around three weeks; one factor is the size of litter. Weaning of a large litter should not be delayed, as they will be making heavy demands upon their dam, but a small litter may not need to be introduced to solid food until perhaps four weeks.

Until now the puppies' only source of nourishment has been their mother's nipples, and they have to learn a completely new technique of feeding in order to cope with solid food. Offer this on a flat saucer so that it is readily accessible, and be prepared to assist the puppies. They should be allowed to sniff the meat initially to arouse their interest. It may be necessary to offer a little food on the end of a finger to encourage them. Gradually they will take more.

All food should be easy to swallow, avoiding any large hard chunks on which a puppy could choke to death.

The bitch's attitude to her puppies will gradually change as they begin taking solid food. She will leave them for longer periods and will be less keen to suckle them, resulting in a lower output of milk and encouraging the puppies to seek alternative food elsewhere.

The first teeth will have started to emerge by the time they are six weeks old, as they begin to become independent. Once weaning is complete, they should be receiving four meals a day, with the first and last feeds of the day comprising a milk feed, either goat's milk or a milk-replacement food in the form of a powder mixed with water, being preferable to cow's milk, and perhaps mixed with some soaked biscuit meal or cereal. The other two meals, perhaps at midday and six o'clock in the evening, should consist of solid foods. Offer increasing quantities of the chosen balanced puppy food and augment the meat content of the diet with a little freshly cooked food. The precise amount will depend on the size and number of puppies.

Feed the puppies separately from the bitch to prevent her taking their food, or supervise their feeding. A separate dish for each puppy, rather than a large communal trough, will ensure that each has a fair chance at the food.

When the puppies are completely weaned from their mother's milk they can be separated from her, but they still need the security of siblings and of the familiar home before the litter is split up for sale. Plenty of human company and handling is important to encourage properly social development. The age at which puppies are split up and sold varies, some breeders preferring to retain the slower-maturing breeds longer, but it has been established that the best age for a dog to begin to interact with people seems to be between six and eight weeks, and this is therefore the most suitable age for a puppy to go to its new home.

The frequency of feeding is reduced gradually; the milk-based feeds are eliminated when the puppy is about four months old, and by the age of six months, two meals daily will suffice. As a general guide, puppies require about twice as much food as an adult dog of the same weight.

NORMAL DEVELOPMENT

Puppies grow and gain control of their senses extremely rapidly, especially during the first four weeks of life. By the time the puppy is a week old it will be able to crawl more effectively around the nest in search of food and

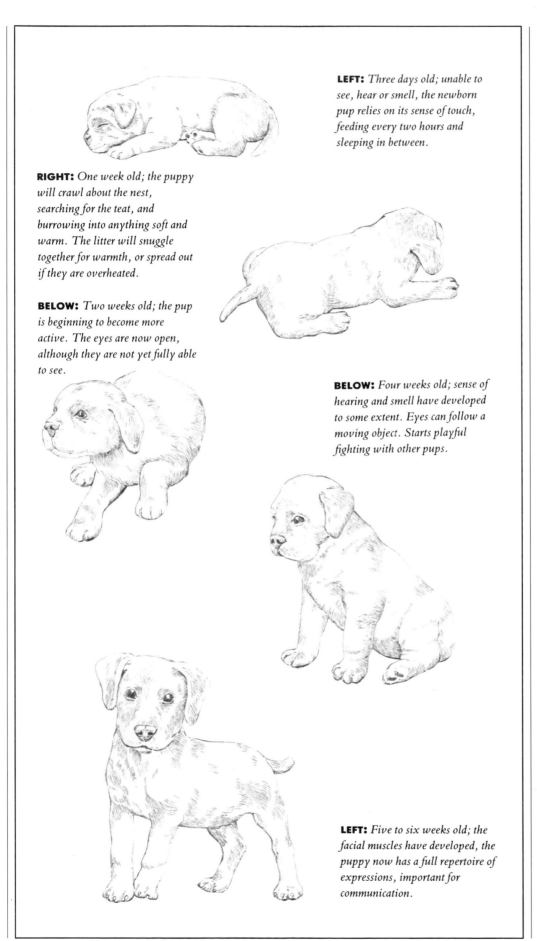

LEFT: *Three days old; unable to see, hear or smell, the newborn pup relies on its sense of touch, feeding every two hours and sleeping in between.*

RIGHT: *One week old; the puppy will crawl about the nest, searching for the teat, and burrowing into anything soft and warm. The litter will snuggle together for warmth, or spread out if they are overheated.*

BELOW: *Two weeks old; the pup is beginning to become more active. The eyes are now open, although they are not yet fully able to see.*

BELOW: *Four weeks old; sense of hearing and smell have developed to some extent. Eyes can follow a moving object. Starts playful fighting with other pups.*

LEFT: *Five to six weeks old; the facial muscles have developed, the puppy now has a full repertoire of expressions, important for communication.*

ABOVE RIGHT: *As these puppies grow, they will nurse standing up.*

BELOW RIGHT: *These Australian Cattle Dog puppies are nearly ready for full weaning. Soon their mother will begin to discourage suckling and her milk supply will dry up.*

warmth. The puppies sleep together to conserve body heat; they space themselves out gradually as they develop the ability to thermoregulate.

The puppy's eyes begin to open when it is approaching two weeks of age, but it still cannot see well and responds inconsistently to lights or moving objects. By the time it is four weeks old, the puppy's eyesight is almost as good as that of an adult dog and it will follow a moving object with its eyes in the same way as an adult. However, the brain is still not fully developed; for example, the puppy seems unable to recognize its mother until about a week later.

Hearing also begins to develop at about two weeks, when the ear canal opens, but takes a further week to develop effectively, with full hearing at around four or five weeks. General development of the brain, such skills as co-ordination of limb and head movements, walking and responses to touch, occur at the same time, so by the time the puppy is five weeks old it is ready to learn all the other abilities needed for adult life.

While the puppy is developing all these skills and capabilities, its range of experience remains fairly limited. It continues to spend most of its time sleeping or feeding, and when sleeping the litter huddles into a pile for warmth. When one wakes up, its movements will wake the others and all will tend to feed together.

At first puppies are not able to defecate or urinate without the stimulus of the mother's tongue. She attends to this for the first two or three weeks, and also ingests the waste matter, keeping the nest clean. After this time, the puppies will eliminate of their own accord, and will usually leave the immediate area of the nest to do so.

At four or five weeks the puppies are ready to start exploring, playing and interacting fully with each other. It is interesting that by this time the facial muscles have developed fully to give the puppy its full repertoire of expressions for social communications.

This period is critical for the puppy's social development. From about three and a half weeks to about twelve weeks it is learning social attutides both towards its own species and towards humans. At this stage, therefore, it is important to handle the puppies regularly and to ensure that they are used to people. It is also helpful to begin accustoming the litter to a certain amount of normal household noise and activity going on around them, in preparation for the world outside the nest. When they are ready to start exploring, a ramp should be provided to ensure that they can climb in and out of the nestbox without difficulty; a playpen around the box will be helpful to prevent them from wandering too far and getting into trouble.

Between six and eight weeks is the generally recommended age for a puppy to be sold. If it is taken from its mother and litter-mates earlier than this, it will not have completed its vital early socialization period with its own kind, and may never acquire the ability to interact normally with other dogs. However, if it is kept with its canine family too long, the converse problem may arise, with the puppy growing up too strongly orientated towards dogs at the expense of close relationships with humans. Puppies which are retained by the breeder past the age of eight weeks, will require plenty of individual attention to ensure that orientation towards humans is properly established.

VACCINATION, WORMING AND REGISTRATION

The puppies are protected from many infections at first by maternal antibodies which they received from their

ABOVE: *Puppies establish social attitudes through play. Here, a well-grown litter of Foxhounds competes for a plaything. They will be kennelled communally all their adult lives, and need to socialize to the world of the pack.*

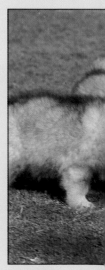

ABOVE: *These Spaniel puppies are having to compete for food with a single bowl between them. Any weaklings are likely to lose out.*

LEFT: *A row of individual bowls gives these Keeshond puppies a better chance of sharing out their meal equally.*

ABOVE: *All puppies need plenty of socialization with humans from an early age.*

mother's milk. This is termed 'passive immunity' and is one reason why hand-reared puppies, lacking that protection, are more vulnerable to disease. Until this protection wears off, as it does when the puppies reach an age to begin manufacturing their own antibodies, it is not possible to vaccinate them against infection. However, they will soon be ready for the first vaccination.

Also passed on from the mother is likely to be an infestation of internal worms, so it is important to worm the puppies regularly from the age of three weeks until they are weaned. Ensure that purchasers appreciate the importance of regular worming and know when the next dose should be administered.

Pedigree puppies should be registered with the appropriate association, which in Great Britain is the Kennel Club. Unregistered puppies are not eligible for exhibition at any but exemption shows, so this is essential in the case of a potential show dog. If a puppy is being bought as a pet there is no need for registration, although some owners prefer to know that the pup is registered, but if there is any likelihood that it will be used for breeding in the future registration is essential in order for the offspring to be eligible for registration.

The pedigree puppy when sold should be accompanied by a copy of its pedigree and by its registration papers. All puppies should be accompanied by a diet sheet so that their digestion will not be upset by an abrupt change of food and by advice on working and vaccination. No puppy should be sold until it is fully independent of its mother and able to cope well with solid foods; a puppy which is taken away from its mother too early, at four or five weeks, may never be able to retrieve the lost socialization period with other dogs.

GLOSSARY

Abscess   A collection of pus below the skin, surrounded by inflammation.

Achondroplasia   The form of dwarfing which affects the long bones of the limbs before birth – responsible for the short legs of such breeds as the Dachshund.

AKC   American Kennel Club.

Almond eye   A long narrow almond-shaped eye slanting at the outer edge, seen in the Poodle.

Alopecia   Baldness, often localized.

Alter   To neuter.

Anaemia   A reduction in the number of blood cells which may be due to a number of causes.

Angulation   The angle formed by the bones of a particular joint such as the hock.

Antibody   A substance produced by white blood cells to neutralize foreign proteins such as bacteria and viruses.

Apple-headed   Having a high domed or irregularly rounded skull, as seen in the Chihuahua.

Apron   In a long-haired breed, the longer hair on the chest, at the base of the neck, creating a frill, in breeds such as the Rough Collie.

Asthma   A respiratory disorder which appears to be hereditary in certain breeds such as the Maltese.

Back   Defined in various ways, depending on the breed concerned, but generally taken to be the region extending from the withers to the base of the tail, along the vertebrae.

Back-cross   Mating back of offspring to parent.

Bad-doer   A dog which fails to thrive; usually applied to a young individual.

Bad mouth   Faulty dentition, e.g. absent teeth or teeth which fail to meet correctly.

Balanced   Having all parts of the body in correct proportion to each other according to the breed standard.

Bandy legs   Legs which bow abnormally outwards.

Barbiturate   A type of drug used as a sedative, an anti-convulsant, or as an anaesthetic. It is also commonly used for painless euthanasia.

Barrel   The rounded body shape created by the ribs in some breeds.

Barrel hocks   Hock joints which are directed outwards, causing the feet to point inwards, sometimes termed 'spread hocks'.

Bat ears   Large broad erect ears as found in the French Bulldog.

Bay   The howling call of a hound in pursuit.

Beard   Long, thick hair on the lower jaw as seen in the Brussels Griffon.

Beefy   Over-developed or overweight.

Belton   A term used to describe a colour created by inter-mingling of white and coloured hairs in Setters; may be blue or orange.

Bench   The official resting area in which dogs are left in between classes at a benched show, comprising an open-fronted container in which the dog is secured by a bench chain.

Bile   A substance excreted by the liver to aid the absorption of fats from the bowel.

Bird dog   A dog trained for hunting birds.

BIS   'Best in Show', the best winner out of all the breed winners in a competition.

Bitch   Female dog.

Bite   The position of the lower and upper teeth relative to each other when the jaws are together.

Blanket   The colour of the saddle area in hounds.

Blaze   A white stripe running down the face between the eyes.

Blocky   Square-headed.

Bloodline   Relationship of dogs to each other, through several generations.

Bloom   The gloss on the coat of a healthy dog.

Blue merle   A colour created by a mix of blue and grey hair in a black coat, resembling marbling, typically associated with Cardigan Corgis, Rough Collies and Shetland Sheepdogs; less frequently, other merle colourings such as red merle also occur.

BOB   'Best of Breed' award.

Bobtail   A dog without a tail; a popular nickname for the Old English Sheepdog.

Bone   The appearance of the legs; a well-boned dog will have a sound and powerful gait.

Bossy   Having excessively developed shoulder muscles such as are typical of the French Bulldog.

Brace   Two individuals of the same kind.

Bracelets   Rings of hair remaining on the clipped legs of Lowchens and Poodles in show trim.

Breechings   Tan-coloured hair on the inside of the thighs.

Breed   A class of dogs with similar defined physical characteristics and related ancestry.

Brindle   A colour created by intermingled dark and light hairs, e.g. black and brown.

Brisket   The underpart of the chest, beneath the forelimbs.

Broken   Having an irregularly patterned coat colour.

Broken-coated   Wire-haired or rough-coated.

Brood bitch   A female used for breeding.

Brush   Thick tail, resembling that of a fox.

Burr   Visible inner surface of the ear.

Butterfly nose   Nose showing partial loss of pigment.

Button ears   Ears with the edge folded over to cover the opening.

Canid   Member of the genus *Canis*, which includes wolves, jackals and foxes as well as dogs.

Cancer   An abnormal, uncontrolled growth of a group of body cells.

Canine teeth   The four long, sharp teeth near the front of the mouth next to the incisors.

Carnassial teeth   The specialized ridged and sharp-edged cheek teeth used by carnivores for gripping and tearing; developed from upper **premolars** and lower **molars**.

Carrier   An animal which is able to pass on infection, but is not showing any signs of that infection.

Castration   Neutering of a male by surgical removal of the testes.

Cat foot   Tight rounded foot, as seen in the Pekingese.

CC   Challenge certificate, awarded at KC Championship Show for best entries of each sex of a specific breed.

CD   Companion Dog – a suffix awarded by the AKC for a dog that has achieved the minimum points score in Novice Classes at a specific number of shows.

Ch   Champion – a prefix used to indicate a winner of three Challenge Certificates under separate judges in Britain, or the accumulation of a specific number of points in other countries.

Cheeky   Having rounded, thickish and protruding cheeks.

Chest   The part of the body encompassed by the ribs.

China eye   A clear blue wall eye.

Chiselled   Having a head with a clean-cut appearance, especially below the eyes.

Choke chain   A collar which, correctly applied, should tighten or loosen according to the handler's grip; sometimes termed a 'check chain'.

Chops   The folds of skin or jowls on the upper jaw, especially pronounced in some breeds such as the Bulldog.

Clinical infection   A state of infection in which the animal shows the symptoms of the disease (see **Subclinical infection**).

Clip   Trimming of the coat, particularly significant in Poodles.

Clipping   Action in which the front legs are hit by the hind when the dog moves.

Cloddy   Low, thickset and relatively heavy.

Close-coupled   Having a body which is short from withers to hip bones.

Coarse   Unrefined; of poor quality.

Cobby   Short-bodied, stocky and compact.

Collar   White markings around the neck in breeds such as the Rough Collie; also refers to the means used to control a dog.

Condition   General state of health, from the dog's overall appearance.

Conformation   The framework of the dog in relation to the requirements of the breed standard.

Congenital   Present at birth (usually said of a congenital disorder).

Corky   Keen, lively and alert.

Couple   Two dogs; term typically used of a pair of hounds.

Coupling   Double leash or collar-ring to take two dogs.

Couplings   The loins (area between the ribs and pelvis, which can be variable in length depending on the breed).

Coursing   The hunting of game by sighthounds; typically refers to organized competitive hare coursing.

Covering ground   Stride, involving fore and hindlimbs.

Cow-hocked   Having hocks turned in towards each other, sometimes touching.

Crabbing   Sideways movement.

Crank tail   Tail carried down like a pump-handle.

Crest   Uppermost arched part of the neck; also the hair present on the head of a Chinese Crested Dog.

Cropping   The surgical removal of part of the ear leather to create a permanently erect effect; banned in Great Britain but practised with certain breeds such as the Doberman in the United States and in Europe.

Cross-breeding   Mating of two different breeds together, sometimes done deliberately to create a new breed or variety, (as in the cross-breeding of a Collie to a Greyhound to produce a Lurcher).

Croup   The part of the back nearest the tail.

Crown   The top of the skull.

Cryptorchid   A male whose testicles have failed to descend into the scrotum; the condition may affect only one testicle (unilateral cryptorchidism, sometimes called monorchidism) or both (bilateral cryptorchidism).

Culotte   The longer hair on the back of thighs of breeds such as the Pomeranian.

Cur   Mongrel; in some areas the term refers to a working sheepdog.

Cushion   Thickness or fullness of the upper lips, seen in breeds such as Bulldogs, Pekingese and Boxers.

Cystitis   Infection and inflammation of the bladder.

Dam   Mother dog.

Dapple   Having a coat of mottled appearance, with no one colour predominating; seen in Dachshunds.

Deadgrass   A dull yellowish colour.

Dehydration A reduction in the water content of the body due to excessive loss or inadequate intake of water.

Dermatitis An inflammation of the skin, sometimes called eczema.

Dew claw The vestigial digit terminating in a claw, found on the inside of the legs, slightly off the ground; often surgically removed to prevent injury.

Dewlap Pendulous skin under the throat, seen in breeds such as the Bloodhound.

Dish-faced Having a concave profile, as in the Pointer.

Dock To amputate all or part of the tail.

Dog Specifically, a male dog.

Double coat A weather-resistant outer coat with a softer insulating undercoat.

Down-faced Having the nasal bone inclining towards the tip of the nose.

Down in pasterns Having a weakness of the metacarpus, causing the feet to be at an angle from the forelimbs, rather than in a relatively straight line.

Drag A scent trail laid by dragging a strong-smelling lure, later to be followed by hounds in lieu of live game.

Drop ear Pendulous, long ears lying close to the head.

Dry skin Taut skin.

Dual Champion A dog which is both a working and a show winner; sometimes termed 'Bench and Field Champion'.

Dudley nose Flesh-coloured or light brown nose.

Dyspnoea Laboured breathing.

Ectropion A hereditary abnormality in which the eyelids are turned outwards from the eye, leaving the conjunctiva exposed; found in some breeds such as Bloodhounds and St Bernards. Surgical correction is necessary.

Elbow Joint below the shoulder.

Entire Unneutered.

Enteritis Infection and inflammation of the small intestine.

Entropion A hereditary abnormality in which the eyelids are turned inwards towards the eye, causing irritation of the eye surface; found in several breeds. Surgical correction is necessary.

Euthanasia 'Putting to sleep'; the painless destruction by a veterinary surgeon of an animal which is suffering from an incurable condition, to prevent a painful death, or of an unwanted animal which cannot be found a home.

Even bite Jaws where both rows of incisor teeth meet directly.

Ewe-necked Having a thick neck with concave arch.

Expression The combined features of the head creating the facial appearance typical of a breed.

Eye teeth The upper canines.

Fall Hair overhanging the face, as in Yorkshire Terriers.

False pregnancy A condition in which the female shows the signs of pregnancy without having conceived.

Feathering Fringes of fine, long hair on the belly, ears, backs of legs or tail, especially apparent in Setters.

Feral Having reverted to the wild, after domestication.

Fiddle fronted Having the front feet turned in, while the elbows are turned out.

Flag Long or long-haired tail.

Flanks Sides of the body from the last ribs to the hips.

Flews Pendulous upper lips.

Floating rib Final (thirteenth) rib on each side which is not joined to the others.

Flush To drive game from cover.

Forearm The area extending from the elbow to the pastern.

Foreface Muzzle or front of the head.

Foul colour Untypical marking or colour.

Front The part of the body that is visible when the dog is viewed from the front.

Furnishings Long hair on the foreface.

Furrow Slightly indented line running from the centre of the skull to the top of the nose.

Gastritis Infection and inflammation of the gut.

Gastro-enteritis Infection and inflammation of the gut and intestines.

Gait Leg movement. Categorized into types, including the walk, trot and gallop.

Gay tail Tail carried high, above the topline.

Gazehound A hound which hunts by sight.

Gestation Period between conception and birth.

Grizzled Of a bluish-grey colour.

Guard hairs The longest hairs in an animal's fur, which form the outer layer of the coat.

Gun-barrel front Very straight forelimbs.

Gun-shy Nervous of the sound of guns; an obvious fault in gundogs.

Hackles Hair on the neck and back which is erected in fear or anger.

Hackney action Movement with forelegs raised abnormally high.

Hard-mouthed Over-rough with retrieved game, marking this with its teeth.

Hare foot Narrow elongated foot, as seen in the Tibetan Spaniel.

Hare lip A malformed upper lip; hereditary in some toy breeds and generally associated with cleft palate.

Harlequin Having black or blue patches on a white ground; a pattern associated with Great Danes.

Harsh coat Stiff wiry coat.

Haunch Region above the hips.

Haw Membrane at the inside corner of the eye.

Heat Female's period of oestrus, when she is receptive to the male.

Height Shoulder height, measured from the ground to the withers in a vertical line.

Hepatitis An inflammation of the liver.

Hindquarters Rear part of the body.

Hip dysplasia A hereditary abnormal condition of the hip joint occurring in some breeds, causing lameness in varying degrees.

Hock Hindleg ('heel') joint between stifle and pastern.

Hocks well let down Hocks close to the ground.

Host The animal upon which a parasite lives.

Hound marked Hound type colour pattern of tan, black and white, the latter predominating.

Immunity The ability of the body to protect itself against infectious disease.

Immunosuppression Suppression of an animal's immune system by a virus.

Inbreeding Breeding closely related animals (eg mother/son) together; over a number of generations this can lead to concentration of the weaknesses of the strain. See **Line-breeding**.

Incisors The small front teeth between the canines.

Incontinence An inability to control the passing of faeces or urine or both.

Incubation period Period between contact with an infection and appearance of symptoms.

Isabella Fawn colour.

Jowls The pronounced fleshy area of the lips associated with some breeds such as the Bulldog.

Jacobsen's organ A specialized sensory organ located in the roof of the mouth and not found in man, which receives scent molecules from the air via the tongue and makes connection with the hypothalamic region of the brain to trigger an appropriate response.

Jaundice A yellow coloration of the body tissues, most noticeable in the whites of the eyes, and caused by a failure to excrete bile pigments, due to one of several causes.

Kiss marks Small spotted areas on the face, usually brownish in colour.

Knuckling over Having a weak carpus, causing the joint to protrude forwards.

Lay back The position of the shoulderblade relative to a vertical plane.

Leather Ear flap.

Leukaemia Cancer of the white blood cells.

Level bite Upper and lower jaws meeting exactly so that the incisors meet.

Line-breeding A form of **inbreeding** pursued deliberately to fix a desired type, usually avoiding the closest relationships such as mother and son.

Lippy Having excessively developed or overhanging lips.

Litter The puppies resulting from one whelping.

Liver Reddish-brown colour.

Loaded shoulders Over-developed shoulder muscles, pushing the shoulderblades out of alignment and creating a heavy appearance.

Loins Area extending from the last rib to the hindquarters.

Long dog Crossbred between two sighthounds.

Lumber Excess fat or musculature.

Lurcher Crossbred between a sighthound and another breed to give greater stamina or tractability.

Mane Long hair on and around the neck, resembling that of a lion, in breeds such as the Pekingese.

Mask Dark coloured foreface.

Membrane A thin sheet of body tissue.

Merle See **Blue merle**.

Metritis An inflammation of the womb.

Milk teeth The first teeth, which are shed and replaced by the adult teeth.

Molars The large chewing teeth at the back of the mouth next to the **premolars**.

Molera Faulty ossification of the skull.

Mongrel Dog of no recognized breed and with no fixed pedigree.

Monorchidism See **Cryptorchidism**.

Muzzle Jaws, nose and foreface; also a means of restraining the dog so that it cannot bite.

Nick A particularly successful mating between two lines.

Nephritis Infection and inflammation of the kidneys.

Neuter Castrated male or spayed female.

Nose leather Skin of the nose.

Occiput Highest back part of the skull.

Oestrus Breeding cycle of the female.

Otitis externa An inflammation of the outer ear.

Otter tail A tail which is thick at its base, round and showing no feathering, with hair divided on the underside, as seen in the Labrador Retriever.

Out at elbow Having elbows pointing away from the body.

Out at shoulder Having weak shoulderblades which tend to deviate from the body.

Outcross Mating of a dog and bitch which are unrelated although of the same breed.

Overshot Having the upper jaw protruding beyond the lower jaw, so that the upper incisors extend past the lower ones.

Pace A gait in which the legs on one side of the body move before those on the other.

Pack A number of hounds kept specifically for hunting.

Pads The tough yet vascular hairless areas on the underside of the foot.

Pancreatitis An inflammation of the peritoneum, a membrane that lines the abdominal cavity.

Paper foot Thin-soled, flat foot.

Parent club National breed club.

Particolour Having two colours evenly distributed in the coat, usually in a prescribed pattern.

Passive immunity The immunity from disease which puppies receive from their mothers' milk and which protects them until their systems are able to build up their own active immunity.

Pastern The part of the foreleg extending from the carpus to the digits.

Patella Knee cap.

Patella luxation An inherited abnormality of the knee cap causing it to dislocate; occurring in a number of breeds.

Pedigree The ancestry of a purebred dog.

Pencilling The black line present on tan-coloured toes.

Pharyngitis Inflammation of the throat.

Pied Having comparatively large patches of colour.

Pig eye Abnormally small eye.

Pig jaw Overshot jaw.

Pigeon toed Having toes pointing inwards towards the midline.

Pile Thick undercoat.

Plume Fringe of hair on the tails of breeds such as Setters.

Pneumonia A lung infection.

Point The rigid posture adopted by certain breeds of hunting dogs, notably the Pointer, upon locating quarry.

Points Colour of the hair on the extremities of the body,

Poke Carriage of the neck at an abnormally low angle.

Pompom Rounded tuft of hair left on the end of the tail after clipping in several Poodle trims.

PRA Progressive retinal atrophy, an inherited defect of the eyes gradually leading to night-blindness and eventually resulting in total loss of sight; an inherited condition occurring in a number of breeds.

Prefix The name of the kennel where the dog was bred, which appears in front of the dog's individual name.

Premolars The large chewing teeth between the canines and the molars.

Pricked ears Ears carried erect and with pointed tips.

Puppy A dog under 12 months old.

Pyloric stenosis A rare inherited defect of the stomach causing projectile vomiting and requiring surgical correction.

Quality A reflection of the dog's conformation and character.

Quarters Hind-legs.

Racy Tall and light-boned.

Rangy Tall and long-bodied.

Rat tail A tail with hair absent from the tip; a nickname for the Irish Water Spaniel, which shows this characteristic.

Recessive characteristic One of a pair of contrasting characteristics (eg longhair/shorthair) which, when an individual inherits a gene for each of the two from each parent, will be over-ridden by the other and will not express itself in that individual's appearance. An animal shows a recessive characteristic (eg the colour blue) only if it does not carry the other **dominant** characteristic (in this case black).

Recognition Approval of a breed for exhibition purposes by a governing body or association.

Registration The recording of a puppy's birth, giving appropriate details such as its ancestry, with a governing body.

Ribbed up Having long, well-angled ribs.

Ring Area where dogs are judged in competition.

Ring tail Tail carried up and round to form a near-circle; in the Afghan Hound, the tip of the tail forms a closed ring.

Roached back Convexly curved back as seen in the Whippet.

Roan Intermingling of coloured and white hairs, typically associated with Cocker Spaniels.

Roman nose Nose whose bridge forms a convex curve.

Ruff Long, relatively thick hair around the neck, as seen in the Chow.

Sabre tail Tail in the shape of a semi-circle.

Sable Having black hairs laced in or over a lighter coloured, typically gold, ground colour.

Saddle Black marking over the back resembling a saddle.

Saddle back Excessively long back.

Scissor bite Upper incisors overlap their lower counterparts when the jaw is closed.

Screw tail Short twisted tail.

Season The reproductively active stage of the bitch's oestrus cycle.

Second thigh Lower thigh.

Self-coloured Of one colour only.

Semi-prick ears Ears carried erect, with tips pointing forwards.

Service Mating of the bitch by a dog.

Set-on Point where the tail joins the body.

Set-up To position the dog in approved stance in the show ring.

Shelly Lacking in bone and substance; narrow-bodied.

Slab-sided Having ribs directed too vertically, creating a thin appearance.

Sloping shoulders Shoulder-blades set obliquely and positioned well back.

Snipy Having a weak, thin, pointed muzzle.

Spaying Neutering of a female by surgical removal of ovaries and uterus.

Spectacles Dark markings around the eyes, seen in Pekingese, and extending to the ears in some breeds such as Keeshonds.

Splashed Having irregular patches of white contrasting with a solid colour.

Splay foot Foot with toes spread wide apart.

Spring of ribs Roundness of rib cage.

Squirrel tail Tail carried upright and falling quite flat over the back.

Standard The breed description specified by the governing canine authority, to which dogs are judged in exhibition.

Staring coat A coat in poor condition with dry, harsh hairs characteristically separated.

Stern Tail of a hound or other sporting breed.

Sternum Breastbone.

Stifle Joint located between thigh and second thigh.

Stilted gait Gait associated with a straight-hocked dog, seen in the Chow.

Stop The point between the eyes where the nasal bone and skull meet, usually marked by a slight indentation.

Straight-hocked Having little or no angulation at the hocks; a fault in most breeds, but desirable in Chows.

Stud (i) Male dog kept for breeding, (ii) breeding premises.

Substance Good development, with solid bone and muscles.

Tartar A hard mineral deposit that accumulates on the teeth.

Tattooing A method of marking a dog for identification purposes, usually on the inside of the ear. At present there is no central agency in the United Kingdom carrying records of identification codes for all pets, although there are several commercial registration schemes.

Team More than two working dogs.

Terrier front Straight profile at the front.

Thigh The area of the hindquarter from hip joint to stifle.

Throaty Having excessive skin below the throat.

Thumb marks Black spots close to the pasterns, typically associated with Manchester Terriers.

Timber Bone, especially of the limbs.

Tongue Call of hounds when in pursuit of quarry.

Top-knot The tuft of hair at the top of the skull in some breeds.

Topline Profile extending from the withers to the tail.

Trace Dark stripe along the back, characteristic of Pugs.

Trail To follow by means of scent.

Tricolour Having three colours – normally white, black and tan.

Trim To groom by clipping or plucking hairs.

Tuck up Sharp curvature in the stomach region, associated with Greyhounds and similar breeds.

Tulip ear Erect ear with slight forward curvature of the side edges.

Type The physical appearance of the dog (or breed) in relation to qualities specified by the official breed standard.

Undercoat Softer, insulating fur under the top hairs.

Undershot Having the lower jaw protruding beyond the upper jaw so that the lower incisors extend beyond the upper when the jaws are closed.

Upper arm Humerus; foreleg.

Virus The smallest of living organisms, which invades the cells of an animal to multiply there. A high proportion of the dog's illnesses are caused by viruses.

Wall eye Eye with a whitish or bluish iris.

Weaving Action in which the front legs cross as the dog moves.

Well let down Having short hocks.

Wheaten Yellowish fawn.

Whelping Giving birth.

Whelp Puppy still dependent on its dam.

Whip tail Straight, pointed tail carried stiffly outwards.

Whiskers Hairs on the sides of the muzzle and lower chin.

Wire-haired Having a rough, textured coat.

Withers Highest point of the shoulders.

Wrinkle Loose skin forming folds on the face, as seen in the Pekingese.

Wry mouth Jaws twisted (especially the lower) so that they are not parallel.

INDEX

ACKNOWLEDGEMENTS

l = left, r = right, c = centre, t = top, b = bottom

David Alderton: 239; **Ardea:** 114, 123t, 148, 154b, 159, 169t; **Australian News and Information Service:** 14c; **Barnaby's Picture Library:** 56–7; **Peter Clarke:** 181, 206, 208, 219, 230, 238t, 239; **Crown Copyright:** 14t, 15t; **Anne Cumbers:** 44l, 67t, 82–3; **Sandy Davidson:** 188; **Hazel Edington:** 91t, 117, 147, 180, 213t; **Jean Paul Ferrero:** frontispiece, 12t, 25b, 32l, 45, 53t, 154t&c, 193b; **The Fotomas Index:** 67b; **Glaxo:** 215; **Marc Henrie:** 85t, 92, 97, 116–7, 130, 131b, 138r:t, c&b, 142, 163, 169r, 177, 198, 207, 256, 259, 260, 265, 273t; **The Mansell Collection:** 10, 34; **Amanda O'Neill:** 63t, 78b, 94, 101, 133, 138b, 166, 195br, 205, 220, 221; **P. Ploquin:** 150–1, 152–3b, 196, 269t; **Roy Miles Fine Paintings:** 35, 64; **Royal Veterinary College:** 216, 218; **Spectrum Colour Library:** 9b, 11, 12b, 13t, 22, 24b, 25t, 26, 36–41, 42t, 44r, 46t, 47, 48, 49, 52bl&r, 53–5, 56t, 60, 61t, 63c&b, 65t, c&bl, 68, 70l, 72, 79t, 80, 81l, 82, 85b, 86–90, 91bl&r, 98, 99, 102l, 112, 115, 121, 123b, 124–5, 127, 131t, 134, 139–41, 144, 149, 155t, 162, 164, 172, 179, 193t, 195l: t&b, tr, 199t, 211, 212, 223, 244–5, 248, 261–3, 266, 270–1; **Sally Anne Thompson:** 13b, 21, 23, 24, 46b, 59, 61bl&r, 62, 65br, 73t, 74l, 78t, 95, 100, 102–3, 104, 110, 118, 122, 128, 129, 136, 155b, 168, 189, 194, 200b, 201b, 204–5, 222, 226, 240–1, 253, 258; **Bradley Viner:** 124, 199b, 200t, 201t, 213b, 225, 232; **R. Willbie:** 83; **Trevor Wood:** 6, 14b, 15b, 16–7, 30–1, 50–1, 73b, 74–5, 79b, 81r, 103t, 108–9, 152t, 157, 158, 161, 167, 186–7, 190, 217, 236–7, 242, 273b.